普通高等学校"十四五"规划旅游管理类精品教材
旅游管理双语系列教材
总主编◎史 达

TOURISM CONSUMER BEHAVIOR

旅游消费者行为
（双语版）

TOURISM CONSUMER BEHAVIOR (BILINGUAL EDITION)

主 编◎史 达
副主编◎石芳芳
参 编◎衣博文 王 洋 那梦帆 祁潇潇

华中科技大学出版社
http://press.hust.edu.cn
中国·武汉

内容提要

"旅游消费者行为"是教育部高校旅游管理类专业教学指导委员会指定的四门核心主干课程之一。作为该课程的配套教材,本书旨在融合经济学、心理学和社会学等多学科理论,对影响旅游消费者决策行为的内部因素和外部环境进行了分析。同时,为了贴合实践,本书还结合旅游消费者购买活动的全过程,对购买前的沟通、购买的决策过程和购买后的反馈环节等进行了分析。本书的设计坚持以学生为本,并采用数字化的方式,在教材体例、课程资源、课后习题等各方面均为学生的学习提供最大的支持。本书不仅有助于旅游管理类专业的学生掌握旅游者在消费过程中的心理及行为产生、发展的规律,也能帮助旅游业从业者提高经营活动的科学性和服务水平。

Introduction

"Tourism Consumer Behavior" is one of the four core courses required by the Advisory Committee of Higher Education at the Ministry of Education on the major of tourism management. As a supporting textbook for the course, this book aims to integrate theories of economics, psychology and sociology, aiming to analyze internal factors and external environment that affect behavior of consumers in tourism. Trying not to stay away from practice, this book takes a closer look at and analyzes the consumer buying process: communication before buying, decision‐making process, and feedback after buying. The design of this book is student‐centered, providing as much support as possible to students in learning with a digital textbook format, digital course materials and exercises. This book is expected not only to facilitate students majoring in tourism management to gain insights into the rules that how consumers think and behave in tourism consumption but also to help people from the industry improve their business performance and service.

图书在版编目(CIP)数据

旅游消费者行为:双语版/史达主编.—武汉:华中科技大学出版社,2023.6
ISBN 978-7-5680-8940-1

Ⅰ.①旅… Ⅱ.①史… Ⅲ.①旅游-消费者行为论-高等学校-教材-汉、英 Ⅳ.①F590

中国国家版本馆CIP数据核字(2023)第114688号

旅游消费者行为(双语版) 史 达 主编
Lüyou Xiaofeizhe Xingwei (Shuangyu Ban)

策划编辑:王 乾	
责任编辑:聂筱琴 王 乾	
封面设计:原色设计	
责任校对:刘小雨	
责任监印:周治超	
出版发行:华中科技大学出版社(中国·武汉)	电话:(027)81321913
武汉市东湖新技术开发区华工科技园	邮编:430223

录   排:孙雅丽
印   刷:武汉科源印刷设计有限公司
开   本:787mm×1092mm 1/16
印   张:21
字   数:675千字
版   次:2023年6月第1版第1次印刷
定   价:59.80元

本书若有印装质量问题,请向出版社营销中心调换
全国免费服务热线:400-6679-118   竭诚为您服务
版权所有   侵权必究

总序
Foreword

华中科技大学出版社出版的旅游管理类专业的双语教材，首套包含《旅游消费者行为》《旅游学概论》《旅游目的地管理》《中国旅游文化》《旅游资源学》五本教材，由分别来自东北财经大学、山东大学、云南大学、西安外国语大学、北京第二外国语学院等多所在旅游管理国际化办学方面有较多经验积累的高校的三十多名教师合作完成。

我们都知道，旅游业是中国1978年改革开放后，较早对外开放的一个行业。旅游业的特性也决定了它始终具有国际化发展的元素和内在动因。从行业发展和顾客服务的角度来看，这个行业与人，比如国际游客的直接接触频率很高；对英文信息，比如各境外旅游目的地或英文版的旅游网站的搜索量很大。从语言要求上来看，英语是为大多数国际游客所能听懂的语言。在国内的很多知名旅游景点，我们会经常看到用熟练的外语给外国游客介绍中国历史文化景点的导游；在很多城市的街头巷角，会有一些当地居民用外语为外国旅客指路或者推介家乡的风土人情。他们亲切友善的表达，不仅传递了信息，还展现了一个国家的包容度和自信。所以，与其他服务业业态和商业业态相比，旅游业的国际化程度相对较高，对国际化人才的需求也更多。要想做到准确地把握不同国家旅游者的行为，达意地传递旅游和文化信息，就需要旅游业的从业者能够掌握和使用专业外语。

高等教育机构作为人才的提供者，要想满足行业对于国际化人才的需求，就需要从教师国际化和课程国际化等方面提供支撑。从目前高校发展的情况看，在经过多年教育国际化发展后，越来越多的教师已经具备较强的国际化视野和国际化沟通能力。但是课程国际化的关键环节——教材国际化却成为木桶上的短板。在国际化教材的使用方面，高校主要通过中国图书进出口（集团）有限公司来引进教材，或者由教师自制课程讲义和幻灯片。引进的教材几乎都为国外学者所著，里面的案例多以国外企业为样本，中国学生甚至教师对很多国外企业并不了解。特别是在新的旅游业态方面，中国的旅游业有着其他一些国家所没有的运营形态，比如数字化等，在这个层面上，中国的旅游业与国外存在较大程度的差异性。

而教师自制的讲义对于学生而言，其在课后很难进行阅读和复习。此外，随着中国教育改革和对外开放的不断深入，越来越多的国际留学生选择来华学习。这个时候再拿着境外的教材讲中国企业的案例，就显得有点不合时宜了。因此，由中国教师编著一套讲述"中国故事"的双语教材，让境外的读者也能更便捷地了解中国旅游业的实践与发展，就成为一项非常紧迫且有意义的工作了。首套五本教材涵盖了旅游管理类专业的三门核心课程，同时还包括"中国旅游文化""旅游资源学"两门非常有特点的课程，希望能够满足大多数读者的需求。

华中科技大学出版社是国内在旅游管理类教材出版方面的佼佼者。因为工作的关系，编者与李欢社长、王乾编辑在多次交流中碰撞出火花，并很快确定出版书目，组建写作团队。从筹备到五本教材全部完稿用时一年半。经历了严肃的周例会讨论、外审等多个环节，克服了各种困难，该系列教材终于能够与读者见面了，编者在内心充满了喜悦的同时，也有担心不能如读者所愿的不安。

因此，也希望读者在阅读过程中，如发现其中的问题或不足之处，能及时与我们进行沟通。编者将不断吸取读者的意见和建议，不断完善本套教材，以便能为旅游管理教育提供更多、更好的教材。

史达

2023 年 3 月 19 日

Foreword

The first set of bilingual textbook on tourism management majors published by Huazhong University of Science and Technology Press includes five textbooks: *Tourism Consumer Behavior*, *Introduction to Tourism*, *Tourism Destination Management*, *Chinese Culture and Tourism*, and *Tourism Resources*, which were jointly written by over thirty teachers from such universities as Dongbei University of Finance and Economics, Shandong University, Yunnan University, Xi'an International Studies University, Beijing International Studies University as they have accumulated experiences of international education in the field of tourism management.

The tourism industry, as we know, was one of the earliest industries that opened up to the outside world after China put in place the policy of reform and opening up in 1978. The qualities of the industry determine that it always has attributes and dynamism from within to pick up an international characteristic in its development. From a perspective of industry development and customer service, this industry has a high frequency of direct contact with people, international tourists, for example; as for information in English on tourist destinations or travel websites, the search volume is large; when it comes to language accessibility, English is the language that most international tourists can understand. At many popular tourist attractions in China, it is common to see tour guides fluent in English or other foreign languages introducing historical and cultural sites to international tourists; locals give directions to international travelers or introduce local culture in the neighborhoods in English or other foreign languages. Their kind words convey more than information. They are showcasing openness and confidence of a nation. For all these reasons, the tourism industry has a higher degree of internationalization and demands more international talent than other service and business formats. It is required that industry employees be able to use a kind of foreign language for business purposes to effectively understand the behavior of tourists from different countries and precisely deliver tourism and cultural messages.

As talent suppliers, higher education institutions need to provide support by offering international faculty and courses to meet the industry's demand for international talent. Over the years of international practice, the current development of colleges and universities shows that an increasing number of teachers have gained global visions and international communication capabilities. Textbooks, however, turn out to be the short stave of the barrel, hindering international course development. The text materials in use were either imported from CNPIEC or handouts and slides produced by teachers themselves. Imported teaching materials were nearly all written by foreign scholars and packed with cases of foreign businesses, which Chinese students and sometimes even teachers have difficulty understanding very well. It is worth noting that the tourism industry in China has what is not common in other countries when it comes to a nascent business format, such as digitalization, where differences can be identified between China and other countries.

On the other hand, teachers' handouts make it hard for students to do extension reading and review after class. We also witness more international students coming to study with us when China's educational reform and opening up further advances. It is inconvenient to use foreign text materials while talking about cases of Chinese businesses. As a result, writing textbooks, telling Chinese stories and facilitating overseas readers to get insights into tourism practice and development in China has become an imperative and meaningful task for Chinese teachers. This initial five-volume set covers three core courses in the tourism management major and the two distinctive courses on "Chinese Culture and Tourism" and "Tourism Resources". We hope that these books can meet the needs of the majority of the readers.

Huazhong University of Science and Technology Press excels in publishing tourism management text materials. The inspiring work discussions between the authors, President Li Huan and editor Wang Qian kindled the spark to confirm the book list for publication and eventually have the writing team pulled together. It took one and a half years from preparation to completion of all five manuscripts. This textbook set finally made it to be put in print after we undertook discussions at weekly meetings, went through external reviews and overcame difficulties. While being full of joy, we are concerned about not being able to fulfil our readers' expectations.

We look forward to hearing from you if any mistakes or errors are spotted during your reading. Any of your opinions and suggestions will be welcome so that we will continue to improve and provide you with better textbooks.

Shi Da
March 19, 2023

序言
Preface

"旅游消费者行为"作为旅游管理类专业的核心课程,自开设以来,在教材建设方面已经取得了很大的成就。国内各层次各类型比较成熟和常用的教材已有十余种之多。与教材建设相配套的课程建设、师资队伍建设等均已有比较完善的体系。但当检索相关英文教材信息时可以发现,以"旅游消费者行为"为书名的教材比较少见。仅有的个别英文教材多成书于数年前,且动态更新不足。大多数英文教材只是将旅游消费者行为作为消费者行为的一个子集进行教学设计。尽管旅游消费者确为消费者中的一类群体,但由于旅游消费和旅游产品的特殊性,特别是我国有很多借助于数字化平台而形成的旅游新业态在以英语为母语的国家中并不多见,所以出版英文版的《旅游消费者行为》教材就显得很有必要了。借助双语版的教材,不仅可以补充此类教材在英文出版物中的不足,而且可以更好地让以英语为母语的国家的读者学习和了解中国不同于其他国家的旅游业态和消费者行为,从而鼓励这些读者转变为来华游客,来中国感受不同的旅游文化,获得不同的旅游体验。

史达

2023 年 3 月 19 日

Preface

"Tourism Consumer Behavior", a core course required for tourism management major, since its inception, has made significant improvements in textbook development. There have been dozens of well-developed and frequently adopted textbooks written to meet various needs available in the country. A better system for relevant course and faculty development has also taken shape in line with textbook development. Despite all these, it is rare to identify the book titled "Tourism Consumer Behavior" when searching textbooks. Only some were written in English years ago and have not been updated in a timely manner. Tourism Consumer Behavior was represented in most English textbooks only as a subordinate topic of consumer behavior. Therefore, it is necessary to publish the textbook *Tourism Consumer Behavior* in English, although tourism consumers belong to consumers in a general sense. It is, however, worth a try when we take stock of the uniqueness of tourism consumption and products, especially in China, where a nascent tourism industry fostered by digital platforms is gaining momentum, which is not yet common in English-speaking countries. In addition to bridging the gap in this publication field, this textbook will help readers from English-speaking countries learn and better understand the distinctive business situation and consumer behavior in tourism here in China. We expect that these readers could also be encouraged by this textbook to visit China, immerse themselves in a different culture and obtain different experiences as a tourist.

Shi Da
March 19, 2023

目 录
Contents

Chapter 1　Introduction　　/ 001

1.1 What is tourism consumer behavior?　　/ 002
   1.1.1 The Features of Tourism Consumption　　/ 003
   1.1.2 The Definition of Tourism Consumer Behavior　　/ 004
   1.1.3 The Elements of Tourism Consumer Behavior　　/ 005
   1.1.4 How Tourism Consumer Behavior Changed over the Time　　/ 007

1.2 How to learn tourism consumer behavior?　　/ 011
   1.2.1 The Theories Apply to Tourism Consumer Behavior　　/ 011
   1.2.2 The Approaches to Explore Tourism Consumer Behavior　　/ 017
   1.2.3 The Factors that Influence the Tourism Consumer Behavior　　/ 020

1.3 Why the understanding of tourism consumer behavior is important?　　/ 023
   1.3.1 Government Perspective　　/ 024
   1.3.2 Business Perspective　　/ 024
   1.3.3 Community Perspective　　/ 025

Chapter 2　Tourism Consumer Perception　　/ 027

2.1 Tourism Consumer Sensation　　/ 029
   2.1.1 The Meaning and Category of Tourism Consumer Sensation　　/ 029
   2.1.2 The Characteristics of Tourism Consumer Sensation　　/ 033

2.2 Tourism Consumer Perception　　/ 034
   2.2.1 The Meaning of Tourism Consumer Perception: Perception Versus Sensation　　/ 034

2.2.2 The Characteristics of Tourism Consumer Perception / 035

2.3 Impact Factors and Process of Tourism Consumer Perception / 039

2.3.1 Impact Factors of Tourism Consumer Perception / 039
2.3.2 Impact Process of Tourism Consumer Perception / 043

2.4 Tourism Consumer Destination Perception / 044

2.4.1 Tourism Consumer Perception of the Tourist Destination Image / 044
2.4.2 Tourism Consumer Perception of the Tourist Destination Elements / 046
2.4.3 Tourism Consumer Perception of the Travel Distance and Risk / 048

2.5 Marketing Strategy Based on Tourism Consumer Perception / 050

2.5.1 Brand Marketing / 051
2.5.2 Tourism Experience Marketing / 051
2.5.3 Embedded Advertising / 052

Chapter 3   Learning and Memory / 054

3.1 Learning / 055

3.1.1 The Nature of Tourism Consumer Learning / 055
3.1.2 Learning Theory and Application in Tourism / 057
3.1.3 The Content of Tourism Consumer Learning / 063

3.2 Tourism Memory / 065

3.2.1 The Role of Memory in Learning / 065
3.2.2 The Memory System / 065
3.2.3 The Formation and Characteristics of Tourism Memory / 067
3.2.4 Memory Interference and Distortion / 072

Chapter 4   Motivation / 074

4.1 Tourism Need / 075

4.1.1 Overview of Need / 076
4.1.2 Theoretical Views of Need Related to Tourism / 077
4.1.3 Definition and Characteristics of Tourism Need / 079
4.1.4 Models of Tourism Need / 080

4.2 Tourism Motivation / 082

4.2.1 Definition and Forming of Tourism Motivation / 082

4.2.2 Characteristics of Tourism Motivation / 084
4.2.3 Theoretical Views of Motivation / 087
4.2.4 Classic Theories of Tourism Motivation / 089

4.3 Influencing Factors of Tourism Motivation / 092

4.3.1 Psychological Factors / 092
4.3.2 Objective Factors / 093
4.3.3 External Factors / 095

4.4 Tourism Demand / 096

4.4.1 Definition of Tourism Demand / 097
4.4.2 Influencing Factors of Tourism Demand / 097
4.4.3 Objective Obstacles to Realizing Tourism Demand / 098

Chapter 5　Attitude and Emotion / 101

5.1 Chapter Introduction / 102

5.2 Attitude / 103

5.2.1 Tourist Attitude / 103
5.2.2 Tourist Attitude Components / 104
5.2.3 The Multiattribute Attitude Model / 105
5.2.4 The ABC Model of Attitudes / 106
5.2.5 Tourist Attitudes and the Theory of Planned Behavior (TPB) / 107
5.2.6 Types of Tourism and Tourist Attitudes / 109
5.2.7 Tourism and Changing Tourists' Attitudes / 114

5.3 Emotion and Tourism / 116

5.3.1 Tourists' Emotions / 116
5.3.2 Tourists' Emotions and Destination Marketing / 117
5.3.3 Types of Emotions / 118
5.3.4 The Cognitive Appraisal Theory in Tourism / 123

Chapter 6　Tourism Consumer Personality / 126

6.1 What is the tourist personality? / 127

6.1.1 The Definition of the Tourist Personality / 127
6.1.2 The Features of the Tourist Personality / 128

6.1.3 The Inter-structure of the Tourist Personality / 129
6.1.4 The Factors Influencing Personality Formation and Development / 131
6.1.5 Classification of Tourism Consumer Personality / 133

6.2 The Primary Theories of the Tourist Personality / 137

6.2.1 Freud's Theory of Psychoanalysis / 137
6.2.2 Jung's Theory of Personality Types / 138
6.2.3 The New Freudian Theory of Personality / 139
6.2.4 The Trait Theory / 140
6.2.5 The Big Five Personality Model / 141
6.2.6 Plog's Theory of Tourists' Typology / 142

6.3 The Self-concept of Tourists / 142

6.3.1 The Definition of Tourists' Self-concept / 142
6.3.2 The Factors that Influence Tourists' Self-concept / 143
6.3.3 The Composition of Self-concept / 144
6.3.4 Self-concept and the Symbolism of Tourism Consumption / 145

6.4 Self-consistency and Travel Destination Selection / 147

6.4.1 The Definition of Self-consistency / 147
6.4.2 Application of the Self-consistency Theory in Tourism / 149

Chapter 7 The Impacts of Technology on Tourism Consumer Behavior / 152

7.1 Technology Types and Their Applications in Tourism / 153

7.1.1 Portable Devices: Audio Guides, Heritage Interpreters, Translators / 153
7.1.2 Immersive Experience Equipment: Augmented Reality, Virtual Reality, Holographic Projection / 155
7.1.3 AI Robots / 159
7.1.4 Big Data / 161

7.2 Technology Impacts on the Tourism Industry / 162

7.2.1 The Tourism Industry Perspective / 162
7.2.2 The Tourism Products Perspective / 163
7.2.3 The Tourist Perspective / 165
7.2.4 The Tourism Practitioner Perspective / 166

7.3 Technological Impacts on Tourism Consumers' Behavior at
　　Different Stages of Tourism　　　　　　　　　　　　　　　／168

　7.3.1 Pre-tourism　　　　　　　　　　　　　　　　　　　／168
　7.3.2 During Tourism　　　　　　　　　　　　　　　　　／170
　7.3.3 Post-tourism　　　　　　　　　　　　　　　　　　／172

Chapter 8　Reference Groups　　　　　　　　　　　　　　／174

8.1 The Definitions of Reference Groups　　　　　　　　　　／177

8.2 Types of Reference Groups　　　　　　　　　　　　　　／177

　8.2.1 Primary Reference Groups and Secondary Reference Groups　／177
　8.2.2 Aspirational Groups, Associative Groups and Dissociative groups　／178

8.3 Social Influence Theories　　　　　　　　　　　　　　　／178

　8.3.1 Self-concept　　　　　　　　　　　　　　　　　　／178
　8.3.2 Self-psychology　　　　　　　　　　　　　　　　　／179
　8.3.3 Conformity　　　　　　　　　　　　　　　　　　／179
　8.3.4 Existential Phenomenology　　　　　　　　　　　　／181
　8.3.5 Social Comparison　　　　　　　　　　　　　　　／181
　8.3.6 Social Psychology　　　　　　　　　　　　　　　　／181
　8.3.7 Other Theories　　　　　　　　　　　　　　　　　／181

8.4 Reference Groups Influence　　　　　　　　　　　　　　／182

　8.4.1 Informational Influence　　　　　　　　　　　　　／182
　8.4.2 Utilitarian Influence　　　　　　　　　　　　　　　／183
　8.4.3 Value Expressive Influence　　　　　　　　　　　　／183
　8.4.4 Normative Influence　　　　　　　　　　　　　　　／183
　8.4.5 Comparative Influence　　　　　　　　　　　　　　／184

8.5 The Power of Reference Groups　　　　　　　　　　　　／184

　8.5.1 Referent Power　　　　　　　　　　　　　　　　　／184
　8.5.2 Legitimate Power　　　　　　　　　　　　　　　　／184
　8.5.3 Information Power　　　　　　　　　　　　　　　／184
　8.5.4 Expert Power　　　　　　　　　　　　　　　　　／185
　8.5.5 Reward Power　　　　　　　　　　　　　　　　　／185
　8.5.6 Coercive Power　　　　　　　　　　　　　　　　　／185

8.6 Factors Determining the Influence of the Reference Groups　／185

　8.6.1 The Characteristics of the Product　　　　　　　　　／185

8.6.2 Consumer Characteristics / 186
8.6.3 The Characteristics of the Reference Groups / 186

8.7 The Application of the Reference Groups in Tourism Marketing / 187

8.7.1 Celebrity Effect / 187
8.7.2 Expert Effect / 188
8.7.3 Word-of-mouth (WOM) Communication / 188
8.7.4 Key Opinion Leaders (KOLs) and Key Opinion Customers (KOCs) / 189

8.8 Family Influence / 190

8.8.1 The Family Life Cycle / 190
8.8.2 Roles and Decision-making in the Family / 192
8.8.3 Intergenerational Influence / 193

Chapter 9 Culture / 195

9.1 Culture and Tourism Consumer Behavior / 196

9.1.1 The Meaning of Culture / 196
9.1.2 The Characteristics of Culture / 197

9.2 Subculture and Tourism Consumer Behavior / 200

9.2.1 Overview of Subculture / 200
9.2.2 The Influence of Subculture on Tourism Consumer Behavior / 201

9.3 Cultural Differences and Tourism Consumer Behavior / 204

9.3.1 The Measurement of Cultural Differences / 204
9.3.2 The Influence of Cultural Differences on Tourism Consumer Behavior / 208

9.4 Traditional Chinese Culture and Tourism Consumer Behavior / 212

9.4.1 The Spirit of Traditional Chinese Culture / 212
9.4.2 Brand Strategies for Tourism Enterprises Based on Chinese Cultural Characteristics / 215

Chapter 10 Marketing and Tourism Consumer Behavior / 218

10.1 Tourism Products and Tourism Consumer Behavior / 220

10.1.1 Understanding Tourism Products / 220
10.1.2 Tourism Product Life Cycle / 223

10.1.3 Tourism Product Brand / 226

10.2 Tourism Price and Tourism Consumer Behavior / 229
10.2.1 Understanding Tourism Price / 229
10.2.2 Tourism Product Pricing / 232

10.3 Tourism Distribution Channels and Tourism Consumer Behavior / 234
10.3.1 The Definition of Tourism Distribution Channels / 234
10.3.2 Types of Tourism Distribution Channels and Tourism Consumer Behavior / 235
10.3.3 Tourism Intermediaries and Tourism Consumer Behavior / 239

10.4 Tourism Promotion and Tourism Consumer Behavior / 240
10.4.1 The Definition of Tourism Promotion / 240
10.4.2 The Role of Tourism Promotion / 240
10.4.3 Tourism Promotion Mix and Tourism Consumer Behavior / 241

10.5 Marketing Innovation and Tourism Consumer Behavior / 242
10.5.1 Internet Marketing and Tourism Consumer Behavior / 242
10.5.2 Green Marketing and Tourism Consumer Behavior / 243
10.5.3 Cultural Marketing and Tourism Consumer Behavior / 243
10.5.4 KOL Marketing and Tourism Consumer Behavior / 244

Chapter 11 Tourist Purchasing Decision, Tourism Pre-purchasing, and Communication / 246

11.1 Tourism Consumer Decision-Making Process / 247
11.1.1 Need or Problem Recognition Stage / 248
11.1.2 Information Search and Collection Stage / 250

11.2 Communication / 252
11.2.1 Designing Persuasive Messages / 254
11.2.2 The Impact of Technology on Tourism Consumer Communication / 254
11.2.3 Online Consumer Behavior / 258

Chapter 12 Tourism Experience / 265

12.1 The Meaning and Type of Tourism Experience / 266

12.1.1 The Meaning of Tourism Experience / 266
12.1.2 The Type of Tourism Experience / 267

12.2 The Quality of Tourism Experience / 271

12.2.1 The Connotation of Tourism Experience Quality / 271
12.2.2 The Influencing Factors of Tourism Experience Quality / 273

12.3 Authenticity, Embodiment and Risk Perception of Tourism Experience / 277

12.3.1 Tourism Authenticity / 277
12.3.2 Embodied Experience / 278
12.3.3 Risk Perception / 279

12.4 The Strategy of Tourism Experience Marketing / 280

12.4.1 Focus on Destination Placeness / 281
12.4.2 Highlight Local Symbols / 282
12.4.3 Strive for Themed Experiences / 283
12.4.4 Enhance the Interaction / 284
12.4.5 5G＋VR＋Tourism Experience / 287

Chapter 13　Post-purchase Behavior of Tourism Consumer / 289

13.1 Tourism Consumer Satisfaction / 290

13.1.1 The Concept of Tourism Consumer Satisfaction / 290
13.1.2 The Characteristics of Tourism Consumer Satisfaction / 291
13.1.3 The Measurement of Tourism Consumer Satisfaction / 292
13.1.4 Factors Influencing Tourism Consumer Satisfaction / 294

13.2 Tourism Consumer Loyalty / 296

13.2.1 The Concept of Tourism Consumer Loyalty / 296
13.2.2 The Measurement of Tourism Consumer Loyalty / 297
13.2.3 The Classification of Tourism Consumer Loyalty / 300
13.2.4 Factors Influencing Tourism Consumer Loyalty / 303
13.2.5 User Generated Content (UGC) / 308

13.3 Tourism Consumer Complaints / 309

13.3.1 The Concept of Tourism Consumer Complaints / 309
13.3.2 The Types of Tourism Consumer Complaints / 310
13.3.3 The Reasons of Tourism Consumer Complaints / 312

Chapter 1
Introduction

Learning Objectives

After reading this chapter, you should have a good understanding of the following points:

(1) have an overview of this book's purpose, structure and features;
(2) understand the concept of tourism consumer behavior and know its history;
(3) be able to describe the characteristic of tourism consumer behavior;
(4) be aware of the importance of tourism consumer behavior in tourism industry;
(5) know the approaches to explore tourism consumer behavior;
(6) apply the knowledge and understanding gained to analyze tourism consumer behavior;
(7) recognize the factors that influencing the tourism consumer behavior.

Technical Words

English Words	中文翻译
tourism consumption	旅游消费
tourism industry	旅游产业
tourism consumer behavior	旅游消费者行为
mass tourism	大众旅游
Travel Notes of Xu Xiake	《徐霞客游记》
The Theory of the Leisure Class	《有闲阶级论》
conspicuous consumption	炫耀性消费

Knowledge Graph

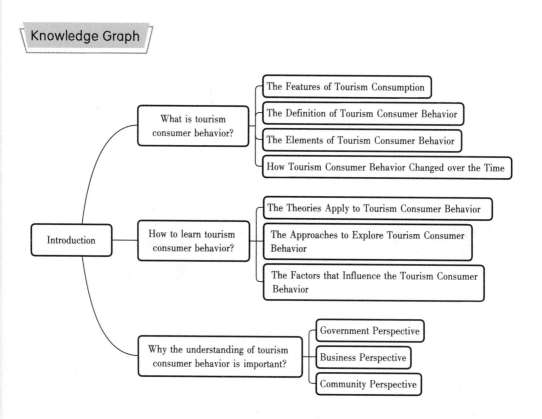

Consumption is an indispensable part of market activities, and consumer group is an important group in market economy. Consumer behavior is the embodiment of the internal psychological activities of consumers, which plays an important role in guiding the production of goods and services. Tourists are a special kind of consumers. In order to meet their own needs, tourists who have left their places of residence often purchase the products and services they need from local producers and sellers. Therefore, there are similarities and differences between tourism consumption and ordinary consumption. For example, tourists have allochthonous and temporary characteristics, and they do not necessarily consume. The characteristics of consumers are consumption, which does not require allochthonous or temporary. Therefore, from both theoretical and practical perspective, it is very necessary to learn the behavior of tourism consumers.

1.1 What is tourism consumer behavior?

To identify the tourism consumer behavior, we must understand how people perceive such things as destinations, accommodation and entertainment; how attitudes are formed and how tourists make travel decisions; how they rearrange on their trips; and how personalities and social network influence their decisions. We should also have an insight into what factors influence the individual's travel decisions.

1.1.1 The Features of Tourism Consumption

Why tourism consumption is different with daily consumption? Tourism consumption usually happens during the travellings and tourists have different expectations on the consumption. The expectation on a family holiday, for example, will be very different from the expectation of visiting a neighborhood open market. In general, the features of tourism consumption are as follows.

1)Tourism Consumption is an Integrated Consumption

Tourism consumption is viewed as engaging in tourism and travelling activities, including dining, accommodation, transportation, touring, shopping and entertainment. The tourism industry is usually defined as the range of businesses and organizations involved in delivering the services and products to travelers and tourists. It can be integrated with culture, sports, festivals, education, science and technology and other industries. Its influence thoroughly penetrates society, economy and culture.

The objects of tourism consumption include both tangible products and intangible services; there are both manufactured products and natural landscapes. Moreover, tourism consumption is usually accomplished by both economic and non-economic sectors. Economic sectors include transportation, communication, accommodation, etc., while non-economic sectors include government environmental protection departments, museums, customs, etc. That is the reason why tourism consumption is an integrated consumption.

2) Tourism Consumption Targets at Tourist Experience

As the final output of the tourism consumption, the tourist personal experience is dependent on the involvement of tourists themselves. Tourist experience is intangible but is viewed as the key element of tourism consumption. Tourist experience is highly valued which can lead to recreation and repeat visiting. Tourists themselves are increasingly involved in co-creating tourism experiences with the complex world-wide tourism infrastructure, which target at delighting the specific needs of tourists. As a result, the tourism products or services are affected not only by the tourism industry that offers the basic elements of the products and services, but also by the motional behavior of tourists.

The emotional relationship between tourism business employees and tourism consumers is also very important to the tourist experience. In the process of tourism consumption, because of the direct contact between tourism business employees and tourists, their personal attitude towards quality and service will have an impact on tourists' emotions, and even determine the success or failure of a tourism consumption activity.

3) Tourism Consumption is Vulnerable

The features of tourism sector increase its vulnerability to climate change, food, water, infrastructure, economy, personal security and health crises. For example, tourism industry is a highly weather-sensitive sector that is strongly influenced by the state of climate. The uncontrollable nature of service quality, the difficulties of offering the same experience offsite, the industry's seasonality and the need for physical embodiment render the industry especially vulnerable. Indeed, since 2000, tourism has been affected to some health crises resulting from disease outbreaks, including MERS and Ebola epidemics.

The vulnerability of tourism consumption is also due to the fact that tourism is a labor-intensive industry. During the off-season and special events, a large number of tourism employees may be laid off or be the low paid, which is easy to cause the loss of tourism employees. The decrease in the number of tourists and tourism income will also lead to the loss of employees and the inability of enterprises to maintain due to insufficient funds.

4) Tourism Consumption is Onsite

A basic feature of tourism is that the consumption is usually onsite. That is to say, whether within their own city or outside the province, tourists travel to the destination to go sightseeing or participate in some sort of activities. Besides, it is widely recognized that tourists are directly involved in the production and/or the delivery of most tourism products. Since the tangible tourist attractions and the intangible tourism services cannot be transported or transferred spatially, tourism consumers must go to the local place where tourism products are produced for consumption. And because tourism services cannot be stored, the production process of tourism services is also the consumption process.

Some people may argue that with the continuous development of Internet and VR technology, tourist can "virtual tourism", or "cloud tourism" at home. But this new mode of home-based tourism can still generate onsite consumption.

1.1.2 The Definition of Tourism Consumer Behavior

If the tourism related businesses are to optimize the effectiveness and efficiency of marketing, they must try to explore how tourists make their purchasing decisions or whether the tourists are delighted with the services or not. If the businesses understand the tourists' behavior, then they will know who to target at, when to intervene in the process and what kind of products to sell.

Consumer behavior in tourism is a difficult subject to explore, where the purchasing decision is usually of emotional elements like experience. Plan for a camping, for example, involves the tourists in budgets concerns, time availability and even weather forecasting. Tourists are affected in the decision-making processes by many determinants when they struggle with alternative choices. It is quite challenging to figure out how these factors influence the tourists when they are doing with the travelling plan. The process of planning or purchasing the camping will be very different from that of purchasing vegetable in the grocery. Tourists will definitely spend much more time in the consideration.

Before we get into more details of tourism consumer behavior, it is necessary to discuss its definition.

Consumer behavior is viewed as to the process of colleting and using information in making purchasing decisions and of using and evaluating products and services. The definition is general but cannot apply to tourism consumer directly. The tourism consumer behavior has some special aspects: it is an investment without tangible rate of return. For example, the tourist has no expectation of economic return on one's vacation plan. The process of tourism consumer behavior includes motivation, expectation, self-concept, personality, attitude, value perception, decision-making, satisfaction, trust and loyalty. As tourists are more sophisticated and multifaceted in their behavior, and there are many factors that affect tourism consumer behavior, researchers must do more sophisticated explanations to understand their consumer behavior.

Considering the broader nature of tourism consumer behavior, it requires an appraisal of the effect of social, economic and environmental changes, which will increase certain kinds of tourism activities. The rise in the worries of safety, the concerns on the food quality, the improvement of forms of communication, are examples of general and diverse factors that should to be taken into consideration for an assessment of the trend of tourism.

Based on the above researches and tourism industry practice, this book defines tourism consumer behavior as: the process which includes pre-purchasing, during the consumption and after purchasing, that the tourist pays for goods and services in order to satisfy their travelling experience.

In this book, tourism refers to an activity which incorporates a number of other sectors like hospitality, leisure and transport. Because the distinction between tourism consumer behavior and tourist consumer behavior is blurred, this book takes the above two terms as the same[①].

1.1.3 The Elements of Tourism Consumer Behavior

Tourism consumer behavior, thus, is largely affected by forces including internal influencers and outside environmental settings. As Figure 1.1 shows, internal influencers can be grouped into five major areas: perception, learning and memory, motivation, personality, attitude and emotion. Outside environmental settings can be categorized into three groups: social demographic, technology and culture. To understand the consumer behavior, one needs to explore the complex interaction of many elements, from the communication of pre-purchasing, decision making during the purchasing to post-

---

① If we look up on the Internet and journal databases, we will find that there are many Chinese researchers argue about the tiny differences between tourist consumer behavior, tourist behavior, tourism consumption and tourist consumption. But we seldom see that in English context. Foreign academia prefers the term like "tourist behavior" or "consumer behavior in tourism". To make it simple and to avoid unnecessary verbal argument, this book uses tourism consumer behavior and takes all the above as almost the same.

purchasing experiences. Figure 1.1 also shows the interaction of factors that are involved in tourism consumer behavior.

Part 1 sets the scene for the rest of this book, through Chapter 1. This introduction part includes key definitions, history, features and importance of tourism consumer behavior as a subject. After learning this part, the readers will have an understanding of the characteristics of tourism consumer behavior, and can tell the differences between tourism consumer behavior and daily consumer behavior. In addition, the readers will also learn and understand the theories and research methods related to tourism consumer behavior, so as to build a foundation for the learning of subsequent chapters.

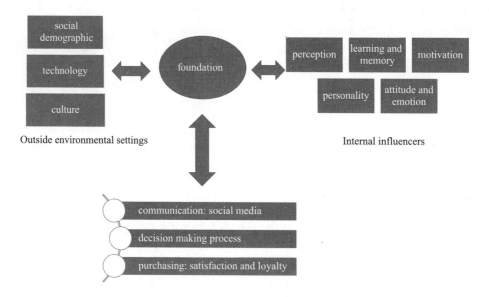

Figure 1.1 The framework of the book

Part 2 attempts to look at the tourists' internal factors in the process, through Chapters 2, 3, 4, 5, 6. The internal factors are related to the person and include psychological influences such as perception, learning and memory, motivation, personality, attitude and emotion. This part is more about psychology. Psychology is the basis of tourism consumer behavior. If we understand the tourists' psychological activities, we can understand tourism consumer behavior. The readers can further learn and understand psychology by reading the references and supplementary materials provided in this part.

Part 3 highlights the importance of environment to the tourism consumer behavior and suggests scenarios with which the tourists interact before making a final decision, through Chapters 7, 8, 9. This part focuses on the external factors that affect tourism consumer behavior. In fact, because tourism activities involve a wide range of elements, so there are many external factors affecting tourism consumer behavior. This part focuses on the above key external factors that have a significant impact on tourism consumer behavior. But the readers need to know that usually many external factors jointly affect the behavior of tourism consumer.

Through Chapters 10, 11, 12, 13, part 4 suggests that tourism consumer behavior is a sequence of problem-solving stages which include pre-purchasing communication on the information of the tourism products, the purchasing behavior itself, and post-purchasing behavior which may lead to either complain or customer loyalty. This framework recognizes the importance of communication before the tourists' decision-making process.

1.1.4 How Tourism Consumer Behavior Changed over the Time

We don't know who the first tourist was, nor do we know his/her first consuming behavior. But we do know that tourism has existed for centuries in sort of different forms and has given us a legacy of travel writing, dating back to Spring and Autumn Period and Warring States Period. It has also stimulated many Chinese greatest poems or artefacts. It is impossible to understand contemporary tourism consumer behavior without an appreciation of the history of tourism and how the behavior of tourists has evolved over time. Many of the main motivations for different types of tourist trips such as educational trip, luxury trip and culture trip have been around for centuries and even millennia.

The history of tourism consumer behavior is a complex subject. There is very little by the way of historical records from which we can derive a history or chronology of early tourism consumer behavior. The book must base the comments on existing knowledge rather than choose the stories that the authors prefer. This section will brief the history and development of tourism consumer behavior chronologically, which will help the readers to understand the current tourism industry much better.

1) Early Forms of Travel Behavior

Educational excursions and leisure travel already existed even before the Qing Dynasty. There is evidence that travel belongs to the recreational lifestyle and originates from the pursuit of entertainment and relaxation. The wealthy groups from the upper class cultivated their journeys for pleasure or educational purposes. Their writings tell us that they visited pastoral scenery, friends and relatives. They travelled to hunting grounds in order to participate in the hunting games. Confucius, who is considered the greatest of the ancient, travelled around all the states alone or with his students, pioneered the type of educational trip.

Leisure tour became more and more popular due to the development of road infrastructure and accommodations. These facilities were built for the transport of goods, government officers and soldiers, but also benefited wealthy families' travels.

From the Sui Dynasty, with the introduction of imperial examination system, the movement of students who were eager for an official status became increasingly important. Journeys to the county town, or the capital city of province or country became both a tradition and necessaries of education. Because of the fierce competition in the imperial examination, many students failed the exam or were disappointed with the government policies, since then, travelling has been viewed as a way of achieving self-realization and self-liberation.

Compare with the motivation of travelling in ancient China, the well-off Ancient Romans enjoyed relaxation or killed time in the seaside resorts or on the Greek and Egyptian beaches. The Ancient Romans have already had "bathing holiday", while many of them have been destroyed over the years, the remains of a few still stand. They also developed "summer health retreat" in swanky thermal baths and luxury locations.

2) Precursors of Mass Tourism

It is important to know that tourism also has existed in other continents for centuries. The readers can learn more by read other countries' historical records. An early type and precursor of mass tourism appeared in the Ming Dynasty and Qing Dynasty. It was like the grand tour attempted by young European nobles between the 16th and 18th centuries. The Chinese tourists at that time were usually government officers, dilettante artists or poets. The original goal was to widen one's field of vision, to be involved in nature and to learn from nature, or to express their love for nature. It was quite different with European nobles' purposes, like present the beginning of adult, expand one's knowledge and acquire social graces. At the same time, leisure and enjoyment became increasingly important as well. This created the differentiated pattern of travel.

As the free-spirited explorer, Xu Xiake, a famous traveler and geographer wrote the masterpiece *Travel Notes of Xu Xiake* to document details of his travels around the country in the late Ming Dynasty should be fondly remembered. He traveled throughout China for more than 30 years and spent most of his life visiting and noting about China's beauty spots. Xu's writing records the terrain, landform, folk customs and social life of many places. It is also acclaimed for its high literary quality.

Like the European grand tour usually lasted for one to three years, because of the transportation and road condition, the Chinese tourists also had to take months or even years in the trip. The European nobles travelled with companies of coachmen, equerries, tutors, and other staff. Many Chinese tourists at that time did almost the same. These staff provided safety, comfort and pleasure. So, the tourism was far away from mass tourism.

During the early phase of mass tourism, only a few of educated and rich elites traveled for pleasure. For these people, travelling was a symbol of their fortune and social level. For the majority of the population, travel for leisure was still rare. In European countries, the reasons of travelling were very different with Chinese scenarios. In European countries, some of the rich people of the middle classes learned and imitated the travelling behavior of the elites and the upper classes. As a result, nobles who wanted to avoid travelling together with the emerging middle classes tried to explore more exclusive destinations and entertainments, like they found renewed enthusiasm for bathing holidays and took up residence in luxurious spa towns with newly built casinos.

3) The Introduction of Mass Tourism

In this introductory phase, between the late of Qing Dynasty and the founding of the

People's Republic of China in 1949, we can see the original structures of modern tourism. In this period, the society changed from a handicraft economy to an industrial economy which was more dominated by machine-based manufacturing. The main feature involved in the industrial revolution was technological. The technological changes included the significant developments in communication and transportation, such as telegraph and radio, the steam locomotive and railway. It is obvious that the transportation was not created specially to facilitate tourists. However, since mid-19th century, the railway transportation had been greatly developed for its own purposes. The transport therefore is rightly considered to be the key of modern mass tourism.

The railways dramatically facilitated the mobility of tourists and made travel easier. Railways made day trips and excursions possible, and the improving transport technology made travel quicker and more convenient. Woosung Railroad which linked Shanghai and Woosung was the first railway built up in China. It began its service since 1876. Unfortunately, because it did not get the approval of the Qing Government, the Qing officials purchased and demolished the locomotive one year later in 1877. Though the lack of backup from the government, the railway construction has been lasted for a century with a steady growth since then. The introduction of new transport technology enabled not only an increase in passenger transport capacity, but also reduced the time spent on travelling. At the same time, steamship and rail travel enabled with steam locomotive broaden tourists' field of vision and stimulated their interest in travel writing. Guide books and travel brochures in the form of travel literature gained increasing attention. This kind of text created tourist destinations and related perceptions.

There were also many new developments in nonindustrial spheres which had given rise to the emergence of the middle-class. The most important factors include not only the rapid industrialization which had led to the huge improvements in labor rights and urbanization, but also changes in demographic, the increase in disposable income and changes in consumer demand. The demographic population of middle-class tourists was composed of the families of urban industrial workers, educated professionals working in the government and educational institutions, as well as the new professions, like artists, journalists and lawyers that had sort of freedom to spend their time and were able to pay for their journey out of the city.

This golden period saw the kick-off of a comprehensive process featured by a rapid development in a middle-class culture of travel and also its formation, popularization and diversification. It helped with the foundation for the coming mass tourism which was labeled with enjoying leisure time. But one must keep in mind that the leisure travel was still the privileges enjoyed by a small number of people. It was another century before the lower middle and working classes could go on holiday.

4) The Boom in Mass Tourism in the Modern Society

Thomas Cook, an outstanding businessman from England, is recognized as the pioneer of commercialized mass tourism. On July 5, 1841, Thomas Cook transported

Case Study 1-1

How does transportation change the tourism industry?

around 570 people, charging each person one shilling for the return train excursion from Leicester to Loughborough, and supplied them with meals and brass music. This is sometimes reported as the world's first railway excursion. Organized group tours and holidays with an all-inclusive service that reduced the travelling costs were an innovation of the 1840s.

Cook used Sunday excursions to attract workers out of the busy cities into the green countryside. It was a significant breakthrough. His business model affected the travel agencies later opened in Europe and then spread throughout the world in a short period. Over this period, the travel agency was built up as a specialized organization and was accepted by the public. In the early 1860s, Cook conducted business in personal tours and acted as a travel agent for the sale of domestic and overseas travel tickets. During this period, these inexpensive all-inclusive holidays were very successful and became very popular. The tourism then increased rapidly and the tourism industry and services, like bread and breakfast, hotels, guesthouses, tour guides had been extended. In tourism history, the opening of the Alps Mountains to tourists was viewed as another important event of the 19th century. In the time roughly between 1750 and 1850, mountains were not yet being climbed sequentially as sport. This was because of the mediaeval fear of the mountains. The build-up of mountain passes and the provision of coach services made the mountains accessible to the public. This created a group of people who were soon be called tourists, consisting of mountaineers, writers and artists, searching for natural beauty. Therefore, this opening marks the real breakthrough in humans' interactions with the mountains.

Finally, at the beginning of the 19th century, tourism became a kind of popular activity that spread across the world, throughout European countries and then to China. The history of Chinese travel agencies was not so far behind. It could be dated back to 1923, when a travel agency was set up under Shanghai Commercial and Savings Bank by its CEO Chen Guangfu, providing train and ship tickets booking services. The interesting thing is at that time, the main purpose of the establishment of travel department was to promote the Bank of Shanghai widely. In 1927, this department turned into an independent company—Chinese Travel Agency and it was the hallmark of the establishment of China's first travel agency. From then on, small-scale travel agencies began to emerge.

5) The Globalization of Mass Tourism

The development of tourism in the 20th century was stagnated because of the war. But since the end of World War II, tourism has become an important part of the world's economy. It ranked the third-largest export category and accounted for 7% of global trade in 2019. The development was boomed by many reasons, including rising affluence which leading to more leisure time and less working hours, the unprecedented construction of transportation which shorten the time of travel, and the information and communication technologies which connect the whole world.

1.2 How to learn tourism consumer behavior?

1.2.1 The Theories Apply to Tourism Consumer Behavior

1) Overview of the Theories

Using scientific insights, businesses can continuously adjust their marketing strategies and understand the elements that affect the consumer decisions of both individuals and groups. Understanding consumer behavior isn't an easy job. However, through understanding the tourist emotions, attitudes, businesses can strategize effectively their marketing campaign.

Over the years, many theories have developed by academia to explain consumer behavior. Since the very beginning, efforts were made to explore the motivational processes when consumers made their buying decisions. All social scientists are interested in this phenomenon and have contributed diverse theories to find out answers. Some economists believed that consumers are rational individuals and as a result they make rational decisions and behave in a well-planned and logical way.

Some other researchers believe that consumers are also social creatures that interact with different people and groups that from different cultures or subcultures. In order to explain the more uncertain and complex consumer behavior, the academia from the disciplines of sociology, anthropology, psychology, social psychology and other social science, developed some other theories. We will have a brief introduction of them.

2) Economic Theories

The economic theory can be traced back to Adam Smith. In traditional economics, people are regarded as rational individuals who have perfect information about the commodity and can get maximum value purely based on self-interest.

As per the economic theories, price is assumed to be the key motivation. Even though consumers are not economists or not aware of the economic principles when choosing between different commodities, they know that they should compare all the sellers' prices and will buy the one at the lowest price. It seems that they are born of rational.

There are many economic theories explain the above rational buyers from different aspects. Four major ones will be introduced here. They are marginal utility theory, income and savings theory, theory of reasoned action, Engel-Kollat-Blackwell model. Let us have a look of them in turn.

(1) Marginal utility theory.

Jeremy Bentham raised this theory. He viewed individuals as carefully calculating and comparing expected delights and pains of every considered action. His theory was applied in the 19th century to explain individual's behavior. As the consolidator of the classical and neo-classical tradition in economics, Alfred Marshall refined Bentham's theory. Marshall viewed individuals as the rational consumers who maximize their utility and do this by carefully weighing the felicific consequences of their purchase. As per this theory, an individual will continue to buy the product that will provide one with the maximum utility or satisfaction at a relatively lower price.

Both of these theories believe that individuals are definitely rational in all their daily movements and all the purchasing decisions are the result of assessments economically. Therefore, businesses need to plan their production and marketing based on this concept.

Though the theory offers a basic understanding of consumer behavior, businesses don't adopt the theory all the time, because it fails to explain why different consumers prefer different brands or products. It is not surprising to see some consumers or fans buy the product just because they love it.

(2) Income and savings theory.

The income of an individual or a family will determine the purchasing power. The theory is developed on the fact that the higher the purchasing intention is, the consumer behavior is more active. As the real determinant of buying behavior, purchasing power or purchasing intention is depend on family disposable income which is the income left after savings and deduction of taxation. It is unusually for a low-income family fly aboard for a long journey to enjoy the sea fishing.

This is not a comprehensive theory. It cannot influence consumer behavior along. It usually works with many other economic factors, like the availability and prices of substitutes, Engel Coefficient, price elasticity and so on.

(3) Theory of reasoned action.

The theory of reasoned action was originally conceived by Martin Fishbein and Icek Ajzen. Though the theory is based on the assumption of consumption rationality as that of marginal utility theory, this theory believes individuals will only take an action when they believe they can obtain some specific desired or extra result, rather than just maximum utility. During the action period, the consumer can also change their plan or go for an alternative action.

Businesses can learn some insights from this theory. The first implication is how businesses can associate consumers' purchasing behavior with some specific desired or encouraging results. For example, the travel agencies promote their luxury holiday products in such a way that make all those who purchase them will believe they have priorities over other tourists. The second implication that businesses can learn from the theory is that they need to understand the importance of moving consumers through the whole sales pipeline, keeping them busy in selection, where the consumers may not be attracted by other competing brands or change their action to purchase other products.

(4) Engel-Kollat-Blackwell model.

The Engel-Kollat-Blackwell(EKB) model is evaluated from the theory of reasoned action. EKB theory lays out a four-stage process which explains in more details on how individuals make purchasing decisions. These four stages are input, processing information, decision-making and variables in the decision-making process.

As the first stage, input refers to the input of information. In this phase, consumers obtain most of the details of the commodity either through mass marketing, online website advertisements, or word-of-mouth marketing. During the processing information stage, they integrate all the input with individual expectations or experience to make the best decision under their current conditions. The purchasing decision is rational because it is based on the information they collected. Rational insight leads consumers to the decision-making stage. In the last stage, the decision-making process has five variables or stages: recognition of need, information searching, evaluating alternatives, purchasing (or choosing), and post-purchasing outcomes.

What businesses can learn from this EKB model is that consumers obtain enough information about the products during the initial information stage. The input of information is very valuable that can help consumers to purchase repeatedly in the future. One tourism business that has a good understanding of this implication is the study trip, where businesses know how to target their products at K-12 students and their families, usually trigger consumer desires or offer a unique experience than purchasing different tourism products.

(5) Comments on economics theories.

Based on the assumption that market information is transparent and open to all the consumers, economics theories assume that consumers are rational in every purchasing decision. Therefore, the economics theories come to several useful conclusions for the understanding of consumer behavior. The first conclusion is that the lower the price of a tourism product or service, the greater the sales will be for that. The second conclusion is that the lower the price of a substitute tourism product or service, the greater the sales of this substitute tourism product will be. The third conclusion states that when promotional budget is higher, the greater volumes of sales will follow.

These above conclusions implicate that consumer behavior is purely based on self-interest. In reality, tourism consumer behavior is simply willing to explain the average effect and do not try to categorize all individual actions during purchase decisions. It does not always happen so. Tourists' decisions are also influenced by other interpersonal relation. Let us see them in the following parts.

3) Psychological Theories

These theories are based on the understanding that consumers learn from their past experience, and the results of their past purchasing experience will alter their actions on future decisions. So, psychological theories are also called learning theories.

(1) The Pavlov learning model: learning or stimulus response theory.

Pavlov was a Russian experimental psychologist. He and other followers did some laboratory experiments which aimed to explain questions like how and why people learn, remember and forget. The result of the psychological experiments helped academia to find out a so called stimulus-response model which could be applied to consumer behavior, based on four central concepts, namely drive, cue, response and reinforcement.

The response is the resultant reaction of different stimuli. Comparing with drives or motives which are strong stimuli, a cue is weaker. For example, if the stimulus is weak, say there is no novel experience in the destination, the response of tourists will be shifting from one place to a competing destination. In brief, different stimulus will lead to different degrees of responses under different scenarios. Then as the rewarding mechanism and process, reinforcement should be strengthened. For example, tourists can accumulate enough miles for free flights and upgrades on airlines. The purpose of giving free flights to high frequent flyers is nothing but to activate this reinforcement. It is here that tourism products preferences are strengthened leading to product loyalty.

This theory concerns the repeating in promotion since a single promotion of the tourism product can possibly be a weak stimulus, and it will be very hard to sufficiently arouse the tourists' attention to inspire the motive. As the powerful approach of reinforcement, repetition can both combat forgetting and provide reinforcement after purchase. Therefore, marketers should clarify which product-related drives or motives are the strongest. For example, pleasant views of the countryside may be identified for city dwellers and expedition for mountain hikers.

Though, the Pavlov model cannot offer an ideal theory for understanding tourist behavior because of the omission of perception, interpersonal and the subconscious influences which are also the important factors.

(2) Cognitive theory.

Cognitive theory concerns about what and how people think cause the arousal of emotions and adaptive behavior. According to cognitive theory, stimulation of want is triggered by customers' perceptions, their knowledge, attitudes and beliefs. As per the theory, the tourists make decision through gathering external information, interpreting that information internally, and taking the decision according to the information processing. For example, during the decision-making process, tourists' perception is the physical stimulus. Certain stimuli are stronger than others; for example, the quality of the local food, the convenience of the transportation or the accommodation. Both attitudes and beliefs play key roles in the cognitive process. The theory found that since strong attitudes and beliefs are formed, they are very difficult to be changed. In order to overcome this type of resistance by tourists, purposely designed marketing mix is required.

(3) Gestalt and field theory.

Gestalt is a German word which represents configuration or pattern. So, Gestalt theory that appeared in the early 20th century in Austria and Germany is also called as gestaltism or configurationism. The theory argues that behavior should be viewed in terms of all the elements that are working when an action happens. Therefore consumer behavior is not merely inspired by individual components, but also is the result of entire patterns or configurations.

Field theory is rooted from Gestalt psychology, and then developed by Kurt Lewin who was a Gestalt psychologist in the 1940s. This theory explains configurations of interaction between the individuals and the total field. In this theory, the field implies mutually interdependent facts or phenomena. So, consumer behavior is viewed as the result of individual psychological field existing when one makes purchasing decisions. Field theory implies that every consumer holds a different experience for an environment. This means that two consumers' experience of a product will be some difference, and no two experiences are the same for a consumer either.

(4) Motivation-need theory.

This theory was laid out by Abraham Maslow in 1943. So it is also called Maslow's hierarchy of needs theory. This theory focuses on the motivation which believes that five categories of human needs affect a person's behavior. Five elements are of increasing priorities, the basic element is physiological survival, then safety, love, esteem, and the most important is self-actualization. Only once a lower-hierarchy need is met, will a new higher-hierarchy need emerge, motivating the people to fulfill a higher-level need.

Since Maslow's hierarchy of needs theory offers an insight of individual motivations, primarily because products or services usually target at satisfying each hierarchy of the individual needs, it was broadly accepted by marketers to understand why customized marketing mix was so important to business success. A familiar current example comes in the form of luxury hotels which center on the leisure and comforts characteristics within their hotels during the holiday, convincing tourists that paying for an expensive luxury hotel is worthy because it fulfills some tourists' needs to offer esteem and self-actualization for oneself.

Though Maslow's theory is successful in explaining the tourists' needs, it cannot be tested empirically. It is hard for both academia and marketers to measure precisely how exactly satisfied one need must be before a next. Another problem of the theory may be culture-bound. Other cultures may question about the order of need levels. For example, Eastern cultures and societies that are more collectivism will regard the benefit of a group of people to be more valued than needs of a person. So, in some extent, this theory restricts itself to Western culture.

(5) Hawkins Stern' theory of impulse purchasing.

In our experiences, many consumers do impulse purchasing, rather than make decisions on rational action. That is the reason why Hawkins Stern put his emphasize on impulse behavior. In this theory, the individual's impulse purchasing decisions are mostly affected by sort of external stimuli like viewing a convincing elevator advertisement. Though external stimuli exert the greatest influence, the individual internal factor also plays a role.

According to Stern's theory, impulse purchasing can be divided into four levels. Level one represents the swift and pure impulse purchase, like buying a last-minute airline ticket on the way out of a supermarket. Level two is described as the reminded impulse purchase, which makes links between different products. For example, placing beers and wines in the close aisle. With the support of big data, marketers can find more associations between products and remind more. So, if an individual is going to get airline tickets online, one will be recommended with hotels or priority lounges and priority security services. Level three is called as the suggested impulse purchase, such as tacking on a pick-up offer as one books hotel room. Level four refers to the planned impulse decision, which considers that individuals know they want to buy a type of product or service, but just aren't sure of what exactly they want.

Marketers have already spent a long time to grasp the power of impulse purchases. From the color of package to the delivery speed of an order, it seems that everything has an influence on the customers' impulse control.

4) Social Psychological Theories

(1) Sociological theories.

Sociologists view behavior as the activities of a group or individual those are motivated by social pressures. Based on sociology, as social members, individuals are deeply affected and shaped in their consuming behavior by cultural and social contexts in which they live. The role theory is a typical one among many sociological theories.

Erving Goffman developed the role theory. The role theory views each individual as an actor. It conceptualizes everyday activity as the acting out of socially defined role, like leader, father or son. Each social role is a set of duties, expectations, rights and norms that an individual has to learn and fulfill. Since a person plays different roles at different times, one's roles vary. For example, while acting the role as a father, the role considers his position in the family and the expectations of his family members as well as.

(2) Veblen's theory.

Thorstein Veblen was both an orthodox economist and a sociologist. *The Theory of the Leisure Class* is one of his famous works. In this book, Veblen coined a new phrase conspicuous consumption, which was defined as spending more money on commodities than their real vale. This is because those individuals come from social groups and make purchases as per societal values. For example, because of environment protection concerns are becoming very prevalent, more and more consumers begin to choose vegetarian alternative on the menu. Or some tourists may be reluctant to accept the decisions of other fellow travelers; for example, to visit a popular museum that are not of their interests.

What the marketers can learn from the Veblen's theory is that, the marketers have to consider the influences of different social elements, which include family income, subculture class or educational background.

Although Veblen was not the first researcher to investigate the impact of social class on individual behavior, and his theory is criticized to be overstated, his observations inspired many other sociologists.

(3) Theory of achievement motivation.

Based on the work of Veblen, Mr. McClelland laid out the theory of achievement motivation. As per this theory, every individual is having a need for achievement, power, and affiliation and to make others be aware of one's achievement. Also, the aspire for achievement and other persons' awareness of this achievement varies in different degrees from individual to individual. Because a person has different degree of desire for achievement and others' awareness, so some people work around the clock to achieve their personal targets, and others are not as desperate as them.

(4) Cognitive dissonance theory.

Based on cognitive dissonance theory, when a customer makes a purchasing decision, even after a well-thought-out purchase, dissonance or discomfort will occur frequently. The consumers undergo some sort of post-decision discomfort. This anxiety is aroused by noise arising from comparing the merits and flaws of the product. In this scenario, some customers believe that there is nothing wrong with their own decisions, so they will ask for reassurances from producers or sellers. What marketers can learn from this theory is that they need to drop down consumers' cognitive dissonance with more transparent information. It is for this purpose that when a luxury cruise trip is sold, the cruise company sends an email of congratulation on the wise decision to the tourist.

5) Conclusions

Each of the above theories has a relatively fixed perspective in terms of their approaches of explanations. It usually focuses on one aspect of possible impacts on consumer behavior. Academia doesn't reach to the consensus as to which influencing factor is more important than others. The shortcomings of a single consumer behavior theory have led to the emergence of more complex consumer behavior models. The consumer behavior model can be viewed as a testable map of reality and as the sequence of factors that lead to complex decision-making processes. There are four famous models of consumer behavior, namely Bettman's information processing model, Nicosia model, Howard Sheth model and Howard model. The students who would like to pursue academic research can have more further readings.

Further Reading

Theory of Buyer Behavior

Further Reading

Psychoanalytic Theory

1.2.2 The Approaches to Explore Tourism Consumer Behavior

Because of the complexity, tourism is a multidisciplinary area that is theorized and explored by academia from different disciplines, like history, culturology, geography, business, sociology, psychology, economics and anthropology. A lot of research approaches have been used. But generally, most of the research methods applied in the tourism field can be categorized into quantitative and qualitative methods. Each method has its own specific research approach.

1) Quantitative Methods

Statistics and models have always been the basis of quantitative methods. In the last two decades the application of quantitative methods in the study of the tourism has gained popularity. The most important reason is that, as the development of information technology, more user-generated data can be collected, stored and analyzed. For example, regression analysis can be applied to predict the tourists' willingness to consume or tourism marketing planning. In recent years, the machine learning enables the big data analysis. This further encourages researchers to give quantitative methods higher priority to the tourism industry. Based on big data, OTA (online travel agency) categorizes tourists into different groups according to their purchasing behavior over a period of time, and recommends related tourist routes, destinations or hotels to tourists. By empirical, the results are observable as well as measurable. So, both local governments and tourism business managers keen to make more informed decisions, by devising better policies.

Because quantitative methods involve a lot of mathematical knowledge, you can learn these from the course of research methods. This part will introduce an increasingly popular method: experimental method.

Experimental method refers to the method of analyzing certain psychological phenomenon or behavior under the purposely controlled conditions. Through manipulating or changing one variable systematically, this method then observes the impact of this manipulation on another variable, finally explores the causal relationship between variables. Experimental methods can be divided into laboratory experiment method and natural experiment method.

(1) Laboratory experiment method.

Laboratory experiment method can help to strictly control the various factors, and can test and record experiment data through special instruments, which generally has high reliability. Usually, this method is mostly used to learn the psychological process and the physiological mechanism of some psychological activities.

(2) Natural experiment method.

Natural experiment method is a method which controls certain conditions in a purposeful and planned way to carry out research under daily and natural conditions. Natural experiment method is close to people's life, easy to implement, and has the advantages of both experiment method and observation method.

2) Qualitative Methods

Qualitative techniques are often misunderstood as a research method without using numbers or statistics knowledge. In fact, it involves theoretical research that together with methodological and philosophical knowledge to seek questions of meaning. These methods are highlighted as subjective, because qualitative methods are centered on amassing empirical materials (data) drawn from the empirical world. Its application in the fields of tourism researches is becoming more occurrent due to its ability of providing rich, in-depth knowledge and exploring the "how" and "why" of tourism related phenomena.

(1) Interview method.

Interview method refers to the method by which the researchers collect information directly from the respondent. Through face-to-face conversation, it can help interviewers to investigate the interviewees' attitudes and emotions. This method is used when the research of new problems or complex topics which initially lacked enough information or solutions. Usually, interviewers need to develop trust between themselves and interviewees to approach certain topics considered taboo. Interview method can be divided into structured interview, unstructured interview and semi-structured interview.

Generally, when doing structured interview, a well-designed questionnaire with a certain structure is used for interviews. The advantage of structured interviews is the quick response and the high response rate. But the attitude and experience of the interviewers have impacts on the final results.

Unstructured interview thinks that the interviewers talk free with the concerned issues by face-to-face direct contact. There is only one topic or a rough outline of the question. Sometimes the topic is not prepared before the interview but is discovered by interviewers during the free discussions. Researchers usually carry out unstructured interview in arranged meetings, which will take a long time.

Semi-structured interview assumes an interview guided with prepared questions. But the interview questions prepared beforehand is usually open, which allow the interviewer to deviate from the planned questions to introduce new issues. The semi-structured interview should only determine the main issues and framework, and the interviewer is eager to listen to the interviewees' opinion.

(2) Focus group method.

Focus group method refers to an interacting group assembled by interviewer to gain data about a specific issue. The advantages of this method are flexibility and fast results, which allows collecting valuable information and data about the intentions and aspirations of interest groups.

Focus group method is usually carried out with at least 4 to 6 discussion groups. In order to provide enough number of participants, and to achieve diversity of opinions, each focus group is suggested to consist 7 to 10 people who are not familiar with each other. It is recommended that the focus group questions should be well picked up and formulated. Considering the time limitation, the questions should be around 7 to 10. The typical focus group lasts 2 hours.

(3) Content analysis method.

Content analysis method refers to the research method that describe the content and communication process in an objective and systematic way. Content analysis tends to explore not only explicit data and information in the content text, but also implicit information. Explicit content is visible and superficial. On the contrary, implicit content is different from explicit one, which includes the important implications behind words or images.

(4) Observation method.

Observation method is considered as activity tracking and systematic description of ongoing issues and events. Observation can be either participatory or non-participatory. Participatory observation implies active involvement in the research. It makes the researcher possible to reach out to detailed and in-depth information about feelings, experience and behavior of those observed individuals. Non-participatory observation implies the researcher can observe the issue or event from outside without participating in it.

3) Mixed Methods Research

In the past years, qualitative and quantitative research methods were viewed in opposition. But more researches begin to combine and integrate qualitative and quantitative methods in the same study to gain a depth and breadth of understanding. Companies like Airbnb is using mixed methods to get in-depth user insights with actionable statistical results. This is because it offsets the weaknesses that are inherent when using either method alone. The disadvantages of mixed methods research may be very complex to carry out and execute. It can also be very labor-intensive and time consuming.

1.2.3 The Factors that Influence the Tourism Consumer Behavior

Individual's choice of a commodity sometimes is different with the choice of others. For example, one prefers a short trip to the countryside while other family members prefer a several-days visit to a historical city. This is because of many different determining factors that trigger consumer behavior actions. These factors can be categorized into three main groups as follows.

The first group consists of personal factors such as tourists' educational background, personality, aspiration, incoming, age or life style. The second group consists of social factors such as social class, culture or subculture, reference groups that can alter a person's decision. The third group consists of situational factors such as geographic location, time, physical ambiance. By understanding these factors, we can identify consumer behavior.

1) Personal Factors

Personal factors are also viewed as psychological factors. Personal factors are formed by personality and motivation which distinguish one from others. These factors are difficult to measure, but they indicate a consistent and robust response of the individual at the stimulus from the external environment.

(1) Attitude.

Attitude is an individual's stable psychological tendency towards specific objects, like people, ideas, emotions or events. People have certain attitudes that consciously or subconsciously inspire their purchasing decisions. The attitude of tourists to tourism products not only determines how they view tourism products, but also determines their decision-making and purchasing behavior. Attitude can effectively predict tourists' travel preference. The attitudes of tourists usually include yearning, expectation and curiosity.

(2) Perception.

Perception is a psychological process through which individuals receive sensory information about a certain product and interpret that into a relevant image. For example, whenever we browse a video advertisement, online review or promotion poster regarding a destination, our perception of that destination results from our interactions with the stimulus, like vision, sound, colour or story. Because different individual has different interpretation of the same stimulation, so the same tourism destination will be perceived differently by different tourists. As a result, individual's perception plays a definite role in regulating one's consumer behavior.

(3) Age.

Age is another primary factor that affects tourists' preferences. For instance, young generation have very different preferences as regard products or services, as compared to middle-aged tourists. The vibrant and flashy purchasing choices of a university student will be different from what a housewife will purchase. At the same time, there are late fifties people who are obviously more concerned on health or families. For example, as the generation of baby boomers come to retirement age, they are targeted by marketers with promotion regarding leisure tourism such as cruise tourism, medical tourism or pilgrim tourism, all of which are relevant issues with regard to their age.

(4) Occupation.

Occupation is related to the education background. The more educated the tourists are, the wider range of the knowledge of destinations they will have. Occupation largely drives the making of consumers' purchasing decisions. Individuals all prefer to buy the goods that are relevant for one's occupation. For example, a backpacker will have a different accommodation purchasing behavior in comparison to a family with two kids. Occupation usually determines the personal income or family income. The higher the personal income, the more purchasing power an individual will have and vice versa. Usually, higher income drives tourists to spend more on expensive products like customized tour to Maldives, while lower income makes tourists spend on normal products like a visit to the art gallery.

(5) Learning.

Learning means whenever individuals purchase commodities, they get a deep knowledge about it through experience. For instance, with the enrichment of tourism knowledge and experience, tourists have formed an attitude towards specific tourism products. They tend to buy tourism products that meet their own personality and needs, and are no longer satisfied with buying tourism products that are standardized by tourism agencies. The learning of tourism experience also makes tourists change the mode of group tourism. They are no longer willing to be a bystander, but tend to be an insider, hoping to visit and participate in some local activities of the destination.

2) Social Factors

Each society is known by some sort of social class. Individuals can identify themselves with different social class. Usually, social class rely on professional and family backgrounds, annual incoming, and sometimes postal code locations. Usually, people who belong to a high social layer spend more money and time to travel rather than to work. Specially, the people in the superior social layer prefer leisure or business travel. On the contrary, tourists who are in an inferior social layer spend less time in travelling. Or they travel in a group to get benefit from promotion discounts. So the social factors like culture background, social level or reference groups have a significant effect on their consume behavior.

(1) Cultural factors.

Cultural factors are usually basic requirements, traditions, taboos and values of the society in which people and families live. Culture is a scenario in which pepole and their life-styles form. Individuals all have their attitudes that are shaped by the values of the society or the community in which we belong to. One's behavior is steered by the culture consciously or subconsciously. So cultural value or norms can be viewed as rules of behavior. The interesting thing is that in a cultural society, we can see several different subcultures. Each subcultural society shares a common set of norms and attitudes.

(2) Family.

With its moral, ethical norms, family is the social elements with the highest influence on an individual. For example, the preferences of a person's behavior is affected by the stages of the family life cycle. Family can affect a kid's attitudes of the world, and this influence may last for a very long time. If the family members are the fans of a football club, the kids will usually keep this tradition when they grow up. In terms of travelling decisions, a family's attitudes regarding different types of destinations, transportation and accommodation etc. are very easily transmitted. When we were children, we learnt from our families when travelling together. And we have an inclination towards certain products and will keep in using those products even when we grow up.

(3) Reference groups.

Reference groups are viewed as groups of people that affect a person's value or attitude. Reference groups are changing with the time. Usually, reference groups include family members, close friends or even club teammates. Now, the reference groups include not only the direct interaction group, but also the film stars, sports stars, social celebrities, entrepreneurs and other public figures. With the development of the Internet economy, online celebrities and key opinion leaders will also have an impact on consumer behavior. Therefore, they also belong to the reference groups. Their abilities of characterizing the group, their rich knowledge and experience will affect the individuals. Tourism companies usually invite opinion leaders to help with the promotion because of these influencers have the ability to affect tourists.

3) Situational Factors

Except personal and social factors, individual's motives are also affected by the environment within which one recently lives. The concept of situation is different in different disciplines such as aesthetics, pedagogy, anthropology, sociology and psychology. The behavior of consumers will vary according to different situations. Faced with the same marketing stimulus, such as the same product and the same advertisement, the same consumer will respond differently in different situations. Usually, situational factors consist of physical surroundings, social surroundings and temporal perspective.

(1) Physical surroundings.

Physical surroundings mean the tangible material factors that constitute the consumer situation, such as smell, sound, light, and even weather and location. The material environment has a critical effect on individuals' emotions and feelings. For example, if the environment of the scenery is poor and noisy, it is difficult to attract tourists to stay for a long time. The journey environment will further influence the tourists' post-consuming reactions.

(2) Social surroundings.

Social surroundings usually involve the influence of others on consumers in consumption activities, such as whether others are with the consumer or how they interact with each other. There will be significant changes in the behavior of a person when traveling alone and with his family. For example, a person's accommodation and dining choices are very different from those of a family.

(3) Temporal perspective.

Temporal perspective refers to the abundance of time available to consumers when a situation occurs and can also refer to the time when an activity or event occurs, such as a day, a week or a certain time point in a month. As a situational variable, temporal perspective has influence on consumer behavior. For example, when there is no enough time for information searching, consumers will make a quick or even impulsive decision. Or the longer the tourist has not travelled since the last time, the easier the destination advertisement will attract the attention of the tourist.

Case Study 1-2

How does the scenic spot attract tourists?

1.3 Why the understanding of tourism consumer behavior is important?

With tourism industry becoming an important component of commercial activities, how tourism consume behavior is has become an important topic in the field of tourism research. How tourists receive the information of tourism destinations and tourism products and services, how they perceive and select that, and finally how they make decisions are all the main topics of tourism consumption behavior. Therefore, it is critical for the government, the business and the community to understand the mechanism of tourism consumption behavior.

1.3.1 Government Perspective

On shaping existing regulations to change consumer behavior, government needs to strengthen the applying of regulations. While some tourists followed local or national regulations, other tourists did not obey and that created confusion. For instance, there are many cases happened in safari parks, where there have regulations on how close tourists can get to wild animals to protect the wildlife and tourists themselves. But those rules were abused by some tourists.

On the topic of issuing a code of ethics for tourism, there should be more information of the government's progress in creating the code of ethics. Businesses sometimes hampered the environmental protection efforts on which sustainable tourism was based, so commitment from governments at all levels and collaborations with non‐profit organizations are needed. With the concerns of sustainability increasing, government which focused mainly on attracting more of tourists, should be changed to concern on environmental protection and sustainable developments. Tourists sometimes lack information about the environmental concerns of the destinations they will be visiting. Government must define itself as one of the stakeholders in sustainable tourism development, and put more its efforts in educating tourists, such as producing videos to promote public awareness about destinations. Meanwhile, government policies play the key role in transforming the entire model of tourism, since policies raised awareness, identified risks and impacted tourist behavior. Finally, in order to attract more tourists, the government needs to protect the rights of tourists, deal with tourists' complaints properly, and provide tourists with a satisfied tourism experience.

1.3.2 Business Perspective

Knowing tourist consumer behavior is not only an academic interest but will also offer deep knowledge to business for successful tourism planning and marketing mix. With the changing of generations and the increasing of income, tourists become more and more demanding and their preferences become more and more personalized. Only by finding and targeting at the niche market can business create added value for tourists.

Tourism consumer behavior is the critical factor in enhancing marketing campaigns which is carried out to promote and develop tourism products and services. In order to optimize the efficiency and effectiveness of marketing strategy, tourism business needs to understand the process of tourists making purchasing decisions to buy tourism products or services. If they understand the patterns of tourists' behavior well, then they will know when and how they need to intervene in the tourists' purchasing process. They will also know when and which tourists to target at with a customized tourism product and service. For example, the patterns of tourist traveling are highly influenced by social media. Therefore, an understanding of tourism consume behavior is the key to make marketing campaign more effective.

1.3.3 Community Perspective

The increasing number of tourists highlighted responsibilities for the community. Local community should work with governments and the tourism industry to initiate public awareness campaigns to govern the tourism consumer behavior morally.

As a comprehensive and coherent concept, sustainable tourism refers to an engagement in protecting cultural and natural heritages. Sometimes, tourists don't have understanding of the environmental concerns of the destinations they are going to visit. So, education campaigns and the social media should be applied as tools to educate tourists to be more respectful of local culture and natural environment when they are travelling.

Volunteers play a key role in orienting tourists and promoting appropriate tourism behavior, and building capacity for consumer advocacy. Usually, volunteers can offer both formal and informal education for sensitization of proper behavior. While volunteers can teach tourists and contribute to behavior improvements, their efforts will be limited without the full supports of the community. All stakeholders including indigenous groups need to take apart in it if the tourism industry is to become a sustainable undertaking.

Chapter Summary

This chapter has an overview of this book's purpose, structure and features. This chapter also introduces the concept of tourism consumer behavior and its history, describes the characteristic of tourism consumer behavior, highlights the importance of tourism consumer behavior in tourism industry. Finally, this chapter briefly introduces some approaches to explore tourism consumer behavior and analyzes the factors that influencing the tourism consumer behavior.

Issues for Review and Discussion

1. Conduct a small-scale survey among your friends to investigate one factor which you think is the most important when making decision of 5-day holiday.

2. The media can have a major influence on tourists' choice in tourism. Evaluate the ways in which OTA can use this feature to boost sales.

3. Design a small-scale tourist panel which can be used to evaluate the reasons for tourists choosing a particular tourism product.

4. Tourists sometimes are locked down in destinations due to force majeure such as natural disasters. Please analyze the psychological activities of tourists in these scenarios and propose proper solutions.

China Story

Music Festival in the Desert

Exercises

Recommended Reading

5. Uncivilized behavior of tourists occur from sometimes. Please analyze the causes of these uncivilized behavior from the perspective of tourism consumer behavior.

6. Discuss what changes will happen to business tourists with the development of Internet technology. What will be their novel demands and how do tourism businesses cope with these changes?

Chapter 2
Tourism Consumer Perception

Learning Objectives

After reading this chapter, you should have a good understanding of:
(1) the meaning of sensation;
(2) the meaning of perception;
(3) the influencing factors of tourism consumer perception and the influencing process of tourism consumer behavior;
(4) the theory of tourism consumer destination perception;
(5) the marketing strategies based on tourism consumer perception.

Technical Words

English Words	中文翻译
sensation	感觉
perception	知觉
neighboring principle	邻近原则
similarity principle	相似原则
closed principle	封闭原则
continuation principle	连续原则
ambiguous figure	双关图形
embedded advertising	嵌入式广告

Knowledge Graph

- **Tourism Consumer Perception**
  - Tourism Consumer Sensation
    - The Meaning and Category of Tourism Consumer Sensation
    - The Characteristics of Tourism Consumer Sensation
  - Tourism Consumer Perception
    - The Meaning of Tourism Consumer Perception: Perception Versus Sensation
    - The Characteristics of Tourism Consumer Perception
  - Impact Factors and Process of Tourism Consumer Perception
    - Impact Factors of Tourism Consumer Perception
    - Impact Process of Tourism Consumer Perception
  - Tourism Consumer Destination Perception
    - Tourism Consumer Perception of the Tourist Destination Image
    - Tourism Consumer Perception of the Tourist Destination Elements
    - Tourism Consumer Perception of the Travel Distance and Risk
  - Marketing Strategy Based on Tourism Consumer Perception
    - Brand Marketing
    - Tourism Experience Marketing
    - Embedded Advertising

Psychological research divides human perception into two different stages of psychological activity: feeling and perception. To have perception, we first need sensation, the awareness of stimuli. Once we have sensation, we can perceive, that is, we can grasp the meaning of stimuli with the participation of our stored knowledge and experience. Perception is actually a dynamic information processing activity that continuously receives stimulus information through human receptors and selectively processes it. Some scholars define tourism perception according to psychology. For example, in the study of Li Jie and Zhao Xiping on American tourists' perception of Xi'an, the definition of tourism perception is "a psychological process in which, through their sensory organs, people obtain information about tourism objects and the tourism environment". Alan Diklop defines tourist perception as "a process of transforming tourism information from the outside world into an internal thinking world". However, these definitions are only concepts of psychological perception and do not consider the characteristics themselves of tourist behavior.

2.1 Tourism Consumer Sensation

2.1.1 The Meaning and Category of Tourism Consumer Sensation

1) The Meaning of Tourism Consumer Sensation

Every day, there are countless external stimuli hitting our bodies. When we get up in the morning, we pull open the curtain to let in the bright sunshine, we hear the sound of water coming from the bathroom, and we smell the aroma of delicious rice floating from the kitchen. When these stimuli act on our sensory organs, what they produce is sensation. Psychologists define feeling as the neural impulse process produced in the body's receptors—the eyes, ears, nose, and other organs—to express the experience inside and outside the body. Feeling is the human brain responding directly to the stimulation of external sensory organs that are reflecting objective individual properties. Every morning, for example, a beautiful sight, a peaceful sound such as the *hua-hua* of running water, or a delicious smell is acting on your eyes, ears, nose and other organs, reflecting the sun, water, and rice—all of which have objective properties that spark the feeling. In addition to reflecting the various attributes of objective things, feeling can also reflect internal changes in our own bodies and help us understand our own physical states. For example, a person with a high fever will often feel heat throughout the body, dryness in the mouth and tongue, soreness in the limbs, and so on. Therefore, the feeling of tourism consumers refers to the neural process that represents the experience of the body throughout the whole process of tourism consumption[①].

2) The Categories of Tourism Consumer Sensation

Depending on the source of stimulation, sensation can be divided into two categories: internal and external. Internal sensation receives internal stimuli, reflecting the position of the body, its movement, and different states of the internal organs. External sensation receives external stimuli, reflecting the attributes of external things. The famous German psychologist Wilhelm Wundt once proposed that feeling and emotion are responsible for the basic process of experience-building. In the process of tourism consumption and experience, feeling is an important basis for tourists to build a happy tourism experience. These foundational feelings mainly come from the stimulation of external things in the process of tourism. Thus, this section's exposition of sensation also focuses on external sensation.

---

① Sun J X, Chen G H. Tourism Consumer Behavior[M]. 2th edition. Dalian: Dongbei University of Finance & Economics Press, 2019.

According to the sensory organs, external senses are divided into five categories: visual, hearing, smell, touch and taste. Among them, when visual and other senses coexist, people tend to primarily notice visual stimulation. This phenomenon is called "visual capture". However, although the things perceived through vision are often the most impressive, smell can awaken powerful memories and emotions associated with it, and experiments have proven that fragrant smells can evoke pleasant memories. A British travel agent triggered tourists' memories of the seaside sun by piping the smell of coconut sunscreen into various shops. Of course, tourists always build a complete tourism experience through the combination of multiple feelings.

(1)Visual.

The visual system gives human beings the ability to see, and its main objects are brightness, color, shape, and so on. People and animals perceive the size, light, shade, color, and movement of external objects, and obtain all kinds of information that is significant to the body's survival. Vision is the most important feeling for people and animals.

Related research by Chinese scholar Professor Zhu Rui and his collaborators shows that red is an easy color to use for inducing avoidance motivation, which can make people vigilant and careful. This helps them pay more attention to details so as to better complete detailed tasks. Blue can induce approach motivation, making people become calm and open, and helping them better accomplish creative tasks. While red tends to trigger excitement and attention, blue makes people calm. In a household layout, people often use a calming color such as blue to paint a study room, rather than using red or another exciting color. In product packaging, color leads consumers to make judgments about the content and characteristics of the product. For example, many cleaning products use blue or white to represent something clean and refreshing, and coffee-colored coffee packaging can reflect the rich aroma of coffee, with brown and yellow reflecting the light flavor. Color can be used in commodity packaging to let consumers have a specific feeling, without them using taste or their own experience to make judgments about the product.

In common speech, we often say that something is "a feast for your eyes", meaning it brings visual enjoyment. In the process of tourism, we are impressed by all kinds of strange, dangerous, beautiful, and secluded natural beauty, and marvel at a variety of magnificent, exquisite, and unique cultural landscapes. For example, Mount Danxia, a mountain with unique color, has gorgeous red sand and rock formations which are colorful and amazing to look at. The vegetation of nature brings the green smoke of spring, the boundless blue sea of summer, the full dye of autumn forest, and the silver of winter covered in snow, making people linger. The majesty of the Great Wall, the impressive array of the Terracotta Army, the quiet elegance of the classical gardens, these natural or human masterpieces all give people a visual and emotional feast.

(2)Hearing.

Hearing is the response of human beings to external sound stimulation via the auditory organs. This is an important sense, in humans second only to vision. The sounds we can hear generally fall into three categories: speech, music and noise. Auditory science identifies four attributes of a sound: tone, volume, timbre and persistence. The level of the sound's volume can affect consumers in various ways. When the volume of music is high, it can spark a lively atmosphere and make consumers feel excited; when the volume of music is low, it helps consumers and sales staff to better immerse themselves in understanding the products in front of them. Therefore, when shopping malls need to gather consumers (such as when they are holding promotional activities or trade fairs), they often increase the music volume; stores that require deeper communication between consumers and salespeople—such as antiques, calligraphy, furniture, and art stores—often lower the volume of their music. The different rhythm of the music gives people different feelings. When slow-paced music is played, people will slow down and feel relaxed, calm, and easily immersed; in contrast, fast-paced music is faster and more energetic, thus accelerating the speed of decision-making and increasing the amount of purchase. Therefore, some fast restaurants such as McDonald's play fast-paced music to speed up people's eating and improve the circulation rate of their restaurants, and some high-end shopping places use light, elegant music in the background to allow consumers to slow down and increase their length of stay.

Hearing and visual complement each other, thus providing the human brain with information from multiple aspects and making people form a more comprehensive understanding of objective things. Sound is caused by the vibration of the sound organ. According to whether or not the vibration is periodic, the sound can be divided into music and noise. Daily noise, from a psychological point of view, is a sound that we don't want to hear.

In the process of appreciating the beauty of the tourist landscape, we may not only receive visual enjoyment but also get an auditory impression. The rhythmic trend of the stormy waves, the powerful waterfall of the empty mountain, and the quiet trickle of different vocal fields are all pleasant to hear, giving people the enjoyment of musical beauty. For example, at the Mingxian Spring of Mount Huang in Anhui Province, the spring water runs with the sound of played strings, clear and melodious.

(3)Smell.

The olfactory system is what produces the sense of smell. Olfaction is caused by the engagement of the olfactory cells in the upper part of the nasal cavity. The types of smell include sweet smell, foul smell and strange smell produced by mixing. Fragrance types can be fruity, mellow, aromatic, or artificial.

Scientists have found that smells have a huge impact on human behavior, and marketers are increasingly applying olfactory features to marketing campaigns. A diffuse smell in the air is often a signal of specific brands or products. In hotel promotion, for example, the hotel's signature fragrance is regarded as an important symbol of its own company and other brands associated with it. The hotel's unique fragrance is introduced into the hotel's brand image recognition system, so that within the positioning of the hotel's own brand, the right fragrance can improve guest comfort and satisfaction. A signature scent can effectively improve the hotel space environment and promote the physical and mental health of hotel guests. So that guests subconsciously remember the fragrance and associate it with their experience of staying in the hotel, of course, a hotel will choose a scent that conveys its own brand, image, culture to give the finishing touch. Similarly, some fast-food restaurants release the aroma of hamburgers near gas stations, which can attract people to restaurants. Dunkin' Donuts from Korea has launched an interesting marketing experience: at bus stops, it plays theme music while releasing the smell of coffee. With the aroma of coffee floating past each passenger's nose, passengers will notice the Dunkin' Donuts advertisements, notice that the Dunkin' Donuts store itself is not far ahead, and then have the desire to buy coffee[①].

(4) Touch.

Tactile sensation has an important role in consumer behavior. Researchers have found that participants develop a high sense of dependence on a product just by touching the item for 30 seconds or less, which increases their willingness to buy the product. This is due to the tactile-induced endowment effect. The endowment effect is when an individual values an item more when he/she owns it. To take advantage of this, shopping malls often allow consumers to try on clothes: once consumers put on the clothes, they feel that the items are their own. In addition, their estimates of the value of clothes are higher than when they are not tried them on, thus greatly enhancing their willingness to buy. Apple retail stores make full use of endowment effect psychology by allowing people to play with Apple products in the store. By touching the product, consumers have an enhanced product experience and increase the likelihood of making a purchase. In addition, small goods are often placed next to the supermarket's checkout counter belt: consumers will touch these while checking out, thus increasing their motivation to buy them.

The impact of touch is also important in calming, relieving stress, or stimulating excitement. For example, massage stones inlaid on roads in scenic spots will massage tourists' feet, giving them a leisurely and healthy experience; if destinations let tourists get close to and touch some small animals or plants, this can bring excitement to the experience; and water-themed recreation activities can often bring tourists an immersive tactile experience.

(5) Taste.

The taste system refers to the receptors that perceive taste. For mammals, the taste system consists of the tongue and the nervous system that connects the tongue to the brain. There are four main categories of taste: sour, sweet, bitter and salty. All other tastes are produced based on these four categories. The primary role of the taste system is as a defense mechanism to reduce intake of problematic or poisonous food.

In marketing activities, sales terminals for food most often use taste marketing. This is very common in supermarkets and in shopping malls: by giving customers free samples and tasting activities, taste marketing can attract consumers and increase the sales

① Lin J, Ying D. Consumer Psychology and Behavior[M]. Beijing: China Renmin University Press, 2022.

opportunities for edibles goods.

Sour, sweet, bitter and salty flavors also represent different psychological feelings. A sweet taste represents goodness and happiness, often associated with love. For example, the advertising slogan "Love her, take her to eat Häagen-Dazs" is inspired by the sweet and beautiful feeling sweet tastes can bring people, especially the increase in happiness they can bring between lovers. In the same vein, a bitter taste represents bitterness, a sour taste represents sadness.

Taste plays a large part when people experience various objects. Professional companies known as "flavor houses" have been developing new condiments to cater to the changing tastes of consumers. Scientists have designed new flavor detection devices to test these flavored crystals. One flavor house family is called Alpha M. O. S., a company that sells a precision electronic tongue for tasting, and is currently developing an electronic mouth that can chew and smell food with artificial saliva. Both Coke and Pepsi use the electronic tongue to test the quality of their corn syrup. Bristol Myers Squibb and Roche also use the device to develop bitterness-free drugs.

2.1.2 The Characteristics of Tourism Consumer Sensation

1) Perceptibility

Animals are often more capable of foreseeing earthquakes than humans. This is because fish and birds can feel elements of the atmosphere (such as ground sound and ground light) that humans cannot perceive. This shows that humans and other animals have different sensitivities to external stimuli; this ability to sense stimuli is called perceptibility. Perceptibility is affected by the bodily state of the subject. Not all external stimuli can cause a response in the subject. Only stimulation within a certain range of intensity can produce sensation. This involves two concepts: the absolute value limit and the differential value limit of sensation. Absolute value limit refers to the minimum strength of a stimulus required for people to feel it. A stimulus that is below that absolute threshold cannot be felt. For example, we do not feel the infrasonic wave produced before an earthquake: lower than 20 Hz, it is below the human absolute valve threshold. The differential value limit, also known as the just-noticeable difference, is the smallest difference between the two stimulus intensities that an individual can perceive 50% of the time. The difference threshold increases with the amount of stimulation: although at 200 Hz we can notice a difference of just 20 Hz, at 2,000 Hz we may need a difference of 200 Hz to hear a change. In line with this, the voice intensity of service staff varies widely between premium western restaurants and noisy amusement parks.

2) Adaptation

Human sensory organs are more easily sensitive to new stimuli if they experience unchanged stimuli for a long time, but their sensitivity will gradually decrease. This is why when urban residents first come to rural areas as tourists, they often feel that the local air is particularly fresh, while the local residents do not have this awareness. Therefore, when pursuing a novel travel experience, tourists often choose destinations that are different from their environment of permanent residence. Such a destination can help tourists feel more excited and also make a deeper impression.

3) Interaction

The same thing does not only produce stimuli that act on a single sensory organ, but often acts on multiple sensory organs; in addition, the senses of different sensory organs are not mutually independent but are usually interactive. Scientists have confirmed that smell greatly increases taste, and that scented foods improve the taste experience for tasters. People with a poor sense of smell also like the sight of delicious food. Therefore, to attract more customers, the current catering industry pays more and more attention to the color, smell, and taste of food.

4) Group Variability

The feeling given by the same stimulus will vary due to individual differences, but in general, a feeling will show consistent similarities across a group, with sensory perception differences appearing across different ages, genders, and so on. For example, older people have good low-frequency hearing but suffer from poor high-frequency hearing, while women are more sensitive to smell than are men. Therefore, female tourists will prioritize a fresh and fragrant consumption environment more than male tourists will.

2.2 Tourism Consumer Perception

2.2.1 The Meaning of Tourism Consumer Perception: Perception Versus Sensation

Perception is a process of sensation and interpretation of the objective environment and the percipient's subjective state. Sensation is only the result of a certain operation of the human brain, while perception is the result of the synergy of various senses, such as vision, hearing, touch, and motion perception. Everything contains individual attributes, which are not isolated but a comprehensive whole. In the process of perception, the human brain transforms various sensory stimuli into an overall experience, thus forming a reflection of both the overall image of the objective things and the body's state. Perception is not the simple addition of various senses; rather, is the integration of sensations into a complete and meaningful image according to a certain relationship between them.

Perception is the human brain's reflection of a whole picture that acts directly on the sensory organs. Similarly, the perception of tourism consumers is the reflection in the tourist's brain of a whole picture directly acting on the sensory organs during the whole process of tourism consumption. The brain selects, organizes, and interprets stimuli to turn the otherwise messy sensations into a coherent, meaningful overall image in the brain. Perception and sensation both belong to the perceptual stage of the cognitive process and are a direct reflection of specific things. However, the difference is that sensation reflects the individual properties of things, while perception is a comprehensive reflection; sensation is determined by physiological factors in the body system's senses, while perception is largely influenced by individual expectations, knowledge, experience and motivation. It should be said that perception is an advanced cognitive process based on sensation.

In fact, in normal daily life, pure sensation does not exist: once sensory information is transmitted by the sensory system to the brain, perception occurs immediately (Huang Xiting, 2007). When we see an apple, we immediately recognize that "this is an apple" without perceiving it as anything else. It should be emphasized here that perception develops with the enrichment of human practical activities (which are closely related to people's knowledge and experience), is formed with the interaction of tangible stimuli and individual knowledge and experience, and has a more indirect nature than feeling. In addition, perception will be affected and restricted by many psychological characteristics, and people's emotions, interests, attitudes and values will affect their perception processes: when people are happy, they tend to feel that many things are better, and vice versa.

In short, sensation and perception are closely related and both belong to the primary stage of human cognition—that is, to the stage of perceptual cognition. Movement from feeling to perception is a continuous process. Feeling is the premise and basis of perception, and perception is the depth and development of feeling. Feeling is the basis of perception but may not produce perception; feeling is the individual obtaining the facts here and now, while perception is the individual organizing the sensory information and experience; the individual receives the stimulation by feeling, but determines its behavior via perceptual factors. Without feeling and perception, there can be no complex psychological activities such as memory, thinking, imagination and will. Because of these, feeling and perception are the basis of the formation and development of normal psychological activities, and also the beginning of understanding the world.

2.2.2 The Characteristics of Tourism Consumer Perception

1) Selectivity

The objective things that act on a perceptual person at the same time are numerous, but the perceptual person cannot perceive them all clearly in an instant. According to a person's own needs and interests, his/her consciousness will select a few things as clear perceptual objects, while the surrounding things are blurred into the background. This is the selectivity of perception. The key to perceptual selectivity is which things become perceptual objects and which remain as perceptual context. Figure 2.1 shows a common ambiguous figure. Whether the figure appears as two faces or a vase depends on the choice

Figure 2.1 Ambiguous figure

of perceptual objects.

On the one hand, the selectivity of perception is influenced by the objective characteristics of the perceived object: with distinct and prominent characteristics, complete images and relatively stable things can often attract the attention of the percipient first. For example, when tourists visit the Great Wall, they generally receive a deep impression of the magnificent Great Wall buildings, while the environmental factors such as the vegetation and the sky around the Great Wall automatically become the background of the perceived object. On the other hand, selectivity is also influenced by subjective factors such as personal interest, motivation, expectation, knowledge, experience, and so on. An obvious example is the perception of the strange rocks of Mount Huang: it is easier for Chinese tourists to perceive these natural stones as a strong image of oriental humanism than it is for western tourists. In tourism activities, different types of tourists always consciously and actively choose some tourist destinations or scenic spots as their perceptual objects, or unconsciously are attracted by a certain tourist scenery, which also shows why some people enjoy the mountains and others love rivers. Under the stimulation of the same tourist scenery, different people will have different perceptual experiences.

2) Integrity

When the perceptual object is only part of a whole, the perception will target the characteristics of the current perceptual object and transform it into a whole with a certain structure, which is a bottom-up perceptual processing process; this is also known as organizational integration.

In the process of organizational integration, perception generally follows several principles, given in the following sections.

(1) Neighboring principle.

The percipient tends to perceive spatio-temporally close stimuli as a group or perceptual whole. Looking at the parallel lines in figure 2.2, we generally perceive them as four groups divided by distance, rather than simply as eight parallel lines. This principle of proximity is also often reflected in tourists' perception of the sun. Tourists often tie into one whole their perception of tourist destinations that are similar in time and space. In small aspects, individual tourist attractions in the same city will be tied into a single group in a tourist's consciousness. For example, Beijing's traditional attractions, such as the Great Wall, the Summer Palace, are usually ranked as the most popular by tourists on the same Beijing tourist route. On a larger touring scale, some adjacent areas are perceived as destinations for a large tourist day. For example, when mentioning Malaysia, Thailand and Indonesia, people usually place them alongside Southeast Asia. The proximity principle emphasizes not only proximity in spatial distance but also in temporal distance. Therefore, the development of tourism transportation makes application of the proximity principle more common midway between tourists and their destinations. For example, the opening of the Wuhan-Guangzhou high-speed railway makes more tourists think of the "four-hour tourism circle" of Hubei, Hunan and Guangdong as a single unified tourism area.

Figure 2.2 Schematic diagram of the proximity principle of perception

(2) Similarity principle.

When faced with various stimuli, one's perception is more likely to combine stimuli that have similar properties in shape, color, performance, size, and so on to become the single object of perception. In figure 2.3, one prefers to perceive the two groups as a triangle and ellipse, respectively. In the process of tourism, consumers' perception of the destination also reflects similar principles. Tourists usually combine some destination perceptions that have similar characteristics into a single category. For example, the honeymoon tourism market has very popular romantic island resorts, such as the Maldives, Phuket Island and Bali Island, which fall into the same group in the minds of consumers. When consumers consider one area of tourism (such as honeymoon destinations), once they have chosen one of the corresponding destinations, they generally will not consider other similar tourism destinations. Under this principle of similar perception, destinations with similar tourism resources will form competing tourist destinations. Therefore, the destinations with higher homogeneity of tourism resources should pay more attention in tourism publicity to establishing their destination's uniqueness.

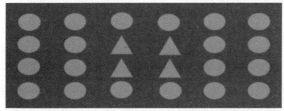

Figure 2.3 Schematic diagram of the similarity principle of perception

(3) Closed principle.

When multiple stimuli surround one space but make an incomplete form, the percipient tends to fill in the missing elements and build a uniform perceptual form. Figure 2.4, although incomplete, is still perceived as a rectangle. Under the closed principle, visitors have the desire to build a complete picture. Therefore, through advertising for tourist destinations, tourists can often build a complete destination impression by combining its vague elements.

Figure 2.4　Schematic diagram of the closed principle of perception

(4) Continuation principle.

The continuation principle of perception means that the perception is more likely to combine all stimuli with the leading stimulus to make one object of perception, often combining the stimuli into a whole by inserting continuity characteristics. Looking at figure 2.5, we will always see it as a curve and straight line that cross multiple times, but not as multiple discrete curves and straight lines. The continuation principle is often applied in the design of the tourist landscape, using the repetition of individual elements to create an interesting visual landscape for the sightseeing tourists. We see this especially in the urban landscape: in order to maintain the continuity of the street, the style of block buildings, heights, roofs, and even curtains are unified as far as possible. This is to help tourists see the whole block or city as a single object of perception, thus forming a distinct image for the tourist destination.

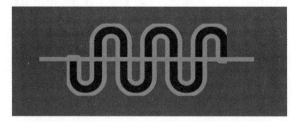

Figure 2.5　Schematic diagram of the continuation principle of perception

3) Constant

In reality, the state of the stimuli we feel is constantly changing, but for familiar things and environments, we can feel a relatively stable and constant world based on previous knowledge and experience. This is the constancy of perception pointed out by psychologists. Specifically, when the input stimulus information of external stimuli changes due to differences in angle, distance, movement, and other things, we can still recognize things by reference to what we already know of them. The permanence of perception includes the stability of perception in terms of stimulus size, shape, lightness, direction, and so on. A common example is that although a domestic white cat may look gray and black in the shadows, we can still recognize that it is a white cat. A tall building in the distance may appear to be only the height of one person, but we can perceive its actual height despite the change in perspective. The constancy of perception allows us to easily respond appropriately to a variety of external things in a familiar environment. However, when tourists come to a strange destination and into contact with unknown things, the permanence of perception cannot play a role, and it is easy to fall into a sense of tension and even panic when confronted with many strange things. Therefore, some tourism facilities (especially accommodation facilities) although they will emphasize their own uniqueness, will also try to decorate the interior into something that reminds tourists of a comfortable home. For example, some family hotels even in remote areas have begun to add bathrooms and install air conditioning.

4) Understanding

Percipients will always seek to understand and explain perceptual objects with the help of existing perceptual knowledge, which is the understanding aspect of perception. The more the percipient knows about the perceptual object, the richer the relevant knowledge and experience accumulated, and the more complete and profound the perception of the object. Because of the influence of understanding, tourists with different experiential backgrounds will have different understandings of the same scenery—for example, when visiting the Forbidden City, historical and cultural scholars will have a more profound understanding than ordinary tourists. More and more tourist attractions now pay attention to the improvement of tour words and exhibition halls, with the purpose of enriching tourists' awareness of scenic spots by improving their local knowledge and experience.

2.3 Impact Factors and Process of Tourism Consumer Perception

2.3.1 Impact Factors of Tourism Consumer Perception

1) The Characteristics of the Perceived Object

(1) The novelty of the perceived object.

People are psychologically driven to seek novelty. This is especially obvious in tourism: tourists travel to escape from their daily environments, hoping to have a new experience. Therefore, in the process of tourism and the psychology of "exploring new things and seeking different ones", the more new things there are to see, the more tourist attention will be attracted. For example, the strange landscape of Jiuzhaigou and the unique karst landscape of Huanglong have attracted more and more tourists.

(2) The stimulus intensity of the perceived object.

Because of perception selectivity, we know that there are many stimuli in the real world but not all are perceived. In the process of tourism, tourists are in an even more complex perception environment. What things can be more easily highlighted and successfully perceived by tourists? Studies have shown that the greater the stimulation intensity of a stimulus is, the more likely it is to arouse tourist perception. The stimulus intensity of external things is determined by two things. One is the prominence of the contrast between objects and their background. The greater the difference between objects and the background is—the more prominent it is in the overall environment—the easier it is to perceive. If a concrete building appears on an open and flat grassland, it will very easily attract attention. If the same building is placed in the background of a big city, it will be submerged between the buildings. The other is the novelty and uniqueness of the stimulus itself. Objects such as the Great Wall, the Egyptian Pyramids, the Eifel Tower, the Leaning Tower of Pisa, and other famous scenic spots have a unique appearance design and magnificent visual momentum. No matter their backgrounds, all are unique and particularly noteworthy.

(3) Frequency of occurrence.

The frequency of a perceived object's appearance will also affect tourists' perception of it. The higher the frequency of a stimulus, the more easily it will leave an impression in the minds of tourists and form a corresponding perception. Tourists who have been to Guilin and Yangshuo are most familiar with a signature dish: beer fish. The reason this dish leaves such a clear impression in the mind is its high frequency of appearance. Streets in Guilin and Yangshuo are hung with signs for beer fish and local tour guides constantly mention it to tourists, so it is natural that beer fish leave a strong impression on tourists. This is also why there are always so many tourism enterprises taking the trouble to distribute advertising leaflets to tourists.

(4) Variability.

In a relatively static background, things that change can increase tourists' perception. The water pouring among the rocks and the galloping horses on the grassland are more likely to become the object of a tourist's perception because of their movement characteristics. For example, "Impression•Liu Sanjie", directed by Zhang Yimou, puts a stage performance in a real landscape scene, using the waters of the Lijiang River as the stage and the mountain peaks and sky as the background. In the quiet night and the natural water and mountain scenery, the red blocking, the fishing fire, the white scarves, the fishermen's shouts, the changing stage, and so on all strongly attract the visual attention of tourists, leaving a deep impression on them.

2) Interest

Interest is the conscious tendency of people to actively explore something or engage in some activity. Tourists often make things they are interested in the objects of perception, and make the background those things that are unrelated to their interests (or simply exclude them from perception). A person who plans to travel to Guangzhou is particularly sensitive to news related to Guangzhou. People who plan to travel to China will also pay more attention to Chinese news than to the news from other countries. A frequent ski tourist pays more attention to changes in climate, snow conditions, and the price change of ski equipment than does the infrequent ski tourist. Tourists' interests are different, so their choices of perceived objects and perceived impressions will also vary.

3) Need and Motivation

Motivation is the internal driving force that directly drives people to engage in certain activities. In an experiment conducted by European and American scholars, the experimenters presented a vague picture to the subjects and asked them what it represented. It was easiest for subjects to imagine the picture as something related to food. Thus, the need and motivation have a clear impact on people's perception.

In general, only those things that can meet the needs and motivation of tourists can attract their attention and perception. A tourist area can accept various types of tourism at the same time, such as sightseeing, vacation, fitness, recuperation, business, and so on. Different tourists have different travel needs and travel motivations, and their perceived range, specific objects, and final overall perception and impression are also different.

In addition, some things are not perceptual objects, but when they are strong enough to interfere with the motivation's target, tourists will also shift their attention and include them in their perception. For example, the same tour buses are usually not noticeable, but when tourists are delayed because of a problem with tour buses, these will enter the scope of tourists' perception.

4) Emotion

Emotion reflects people's attitudes towards objective things. Emotional state refers to a person's subjective attitude and mental state when perceiving an objective thing. Emotional state largely affects how an individual perceives that object. As the saying goes, "a happy night is short, but a sad night is long", which reflects the impact of emotion on people's time perception.

There are both positive and negative emotions. Generally speaking, with positive emotions, people's perception of the object will be more profound and distinct; with negative emotions such as a depressed mood, the level of perception will be reduced, and it is difficult for objects of perception to become vivid and distinct. When tourists are depressed, their perception range is narrowed, their perception initiative drops, they may be blind to the beautiful landscape, and the explanations of a tour guide may be ignored; when tourists are happy, they may perceive various things as better than they actually are, will happily participate in tourism activities, and can actively perceive the beauties of the landscape. Therefore, tourism service personnel should pay attention to and try to mobilize the emotions of tourists to help them be in the best state to experience tourism.

5) Experience

Experience is the feeling gained from an activity. The more experience a person has of a particular activity, the more comprehensive his/her perception will be and the more he/she can be immersed in it. With prior experience, tourists are able to better understand and judge the meaning of the perceived object. This allows them to save perception time, expand their scope of perception, and obtain more and more profound perceptual experiences. Whether the mountain is steep, whether the transportation is convenient, whether the friendliness of service is sincere, and so on are all related to a tourist's experience. Tourism practice shows that tourists who revisit a tour are very different the second time around from the tourists who are visiting for the first time. Experienced tourists know which scenic spots should be toured, which should be avoided, what is interesting, what is more boring, and so on. At the same time, experienced tourists have more travel sophistication than inexperienced tourists.

6) Class Consciousness

In modern society, a person's income, educational level, and occupation are important indicators of his/her social class. People of the same class have similar values, lifestyles, attitudes towards people, and even (in the level of consciousness) things such as moral standards. Tourism, as a symbolic activity, also reflects to a certain extent the social status of tourists. There are certain differences among tourists of different classes: they choose different tourist destinations, arrangements of tourism activities, consumption levels, and so on. Generally speaking, tourists in the upper classes pay more attention to tourism experiences that symbolize social status, performance ability and economic strength; mid-level tourists pay attention to some status symbols, but are willing to accept cheaper tourism projects; lower-class tourists welcome good but inexpensive tourism products and are sensitive to travel distance—their ideal vacation locations are not far from home.

In addition to the above factors, demographic factors such as tourist income, age, gender, occupation, family structure, nationality and race also have a certain impact on tourism perception. For example, older tourists prefer relaxed and slow-paced travel, focusing on gaining more knowledge; archaeological tourists and medical tourists are different; and Buddhist believers treat temples as holy places of worship, while disbelievers have a completely different perception of religious tourism destinations and treat temples as general objects of interest.

7) Personality

Personality is the sum total of an individual's unique and stable psychological characteristics. Personality affects the breadth, depth, manner and speed of tourists' perceptions of surroundings. For example, tourists with neutral personalities spend little time in their choice of transportation vehicles and tourist destinations, and their personality affects their perception by narrowing the scope of the selected objects. Generally speaking, airplane travelers are very active, bold and confident, and train travelers are more sensitive to the perception of risk. In the work of tourism resources development, tourism area construction, reception service, and tourism marketing and publicity, the tourism industry should comprehensively consider all the subjective and objective factors affecting the tourist perception. In view of the above factors, tourism projects and tourism services are in line with the objective of tourists' perception.

2.3.2 Impact Process of Tourism Consumer Perception

1) Tourism Perception Value

The general value of tourism is more than the perspective of "achieving balance" and "obtaining". The former holds that consumers are rational consumers, and according to the professional definition and judgment that tourists form the perceived value of tourism based on the comparison of gains and losses in the tourism experience.

For the general tourist destination, the consumption object of tourists is the various products offered by the tourist destination. However, their tourism need is to obtain emotional value by experiencing the natural environment, cultural atmosphere and entertainment activities—which emotional value is ultimately the main product of the tourist destination. Therefore, the core tourism products of tourism destinations are the composition of the natural environment, culture and entertainment, which bring the value of physical and mental relaxation, physical activities and amusement to tourists and in turn create the products' functional and emotional value.

2) Degree of Satisfaction

Satisfaction is a psychological result of experience, an emotional feeling that can be divided into overall satisfaction and attribute satisfaction. Overall satisfaction is with the whole product and service; attribute satisfaction is with specific attributes of the product and service. A test (such as a survey) can directly measure specific results in these areas by comparing the actual results with initial expectations. When applied to tourism, overall satisfaction means the tourist's level of satisfaction after experiencing all the products or service attributes of the tourism destination.

3) Behavior Intention

Beyond perceived value and satisfaction, behavior intention is generally defined as a tourist's intention of re-visiting the tourist destination or recommending it to others. The tourism site development, tourism experiences available and tourists' overall experience of the tourist destination are all related to behavior intention.

2.4 Tourism Consumer Destination Perception

Tourism perception is one of the most important topics in tourism science. The series of cognitions and perceptions formed by tourists in the process of tourism can directly affect the quality and satisfaction of their tourism experience, and thus affect the sustainable development of tourism destinations. Timely and effective evaluation and measurement of tourists' perceptions are the fundamental ways to build the good reputation and healthy development of a destination.

A tourist destination is a complex set of facilities and services that can meet the needs of tourists, and it is a place where tourists choose to stay for a period of time to experience the attraction. Previously, the destination was thought of as a single, physical area. Whether it was big as a country or small as a park, so long as it could provide tourists with food, accommodation, travel, shopping and entertainment, it could be called a tourist destination. Now, people have come to realize that a destination can also be a perceptual concept. Tourism consumers can understand destinations subjectively, depending on their travel routes, their cultural backgrounds, the purpose of their tour, their education levels and their past experiences.

Tourism consumer perception of destination image, destination elements and tourism conditions (tourism distance, safety and risk) is of great significance to carrying out targeted and effective tourism marketing in tourism destinations. Therefore, it is necessary to briefly elaborate on established knowledge of the above three aspects.

2.4.1 Tourism Consumer Perception of the Tourist Destination Image

Tourist destination image refers to the sum of people's trust, opinions, impressions and expectations of a tourist destination. Tourists' perception of the destination is actually their perception of the destination's overall image, rather than of the destination itself. The tourist destination image is one of the important ways for consumers to evaluate the "gravity" of a tourist destination, which directly affects consumers' attitudes towards the destination and their final purchase decision behavior. Tourists' perception of the destination image is a dynamic change process. According to the different information stimuli perceived by consumers, generally speaking, tourism consumer perception of the tourist destination image can be divided into the following three subject stages.

1) Pre-stage of Generating Tourism Demand

Before they generate tourism needs, tourists' perception of the tourist destination image is mainly their original inner image of the tourist destination formed through personal life experience. The formation of this kind of perceptual image comes from the non-tourism information exchange and acquisition of non-tourism information in daily life: mainly through newspapers, radio, TV news and other media, as well as through the description of relatives and friends who have participated in tourism at the destination. This type of image is formed through years of accumulation. At this stage, a consumer's perception of a tourist destination image usually has two obvious characteristics. First, it has the characteristic of curing. Over time, the consumer gradually forms an opinion about a tourist destination via the most direct and simple subjective judgment, often based on mass media perspective or common views starting in childhood: our initial impression of Guilin comes from news media's statement that "Guilin landscape is the best". This solidified perception can help consumers establish a basic impression of a destination before making travel decisions, but it is also easy for consumers to have misperceptions brought on by stereotypes. Second, a consumer's perception of a tourist destination image is characteristically symbolic. Writer Lippman once said: "Before we observed the world, people told us what the world looked like. For most things, we imagine them first, and then we experience them." In fact, consumers with the most primitive perception of tourist destinations focus on destinations with the most prominent tourism resources. With the resources as the core, according to their own personality characteristics, consumers will extract simple cultural elements from the destination tourist attractions, imagine them in their minds, comprehensively evaluate them, and construct a composition with a certain symbolic significance. Paris, for example, in the eyes of most consumers is a symbol of fashion, while Shangri-La is a symbol of the sacred pure land.

2) Formulate the Tourism Decision-Making Stage

In this stage, tourists can actively collect the information related to the destination, select and process the information, and make their tourism decision after their demand for tourism is stimulated. This stage—consumer perception of destination image—is an image induced mainly through a series of advertising for tourism products (travel agency promotion, network media propaganda, postcards, travel magazine advertising, etc.), festival activities promotions, and tourist evaluation and formation of perception, all influenced by the marketing methods of the destination. Compared with the previous stage, the results of tourists' perceptions of the destination are more specific. However, influenced by their own demand motivation, consumers will be selective in the information they are interested in as they collect information, and the perceived results will have individual differences. The perceived outcome at this stage will also have an important impact on consumer purchasing behavior. The greater the difference between tourist destination image perception and tourist expectations and preferences, the less likely the tourist will be to choose that destination; if the conformity between expectation and reality is greater, the probability of selection will increase (Wang Jiajun, 1997).

3) Field Tourism Stage

After consumers leave their usual residences and arrive at the tourist destination, they officially enter the stage of field perception of the destination. As tourism resources are non-transferable and tourism products have the characteristics of both production and consumption, on-site perception becomes the decisive stage of the final destination image perceived by tourists. In this stage of activity, tourists will often compare the real entity with their image of the tourist area as perceived in the early stage. With this comparison, tourists constantly revise their impression, finally forming a more specific and comprehensive composite image of the destination. The positive and negative nature of this composite image will affect consumers' willingness to revisit. In the stage of field tourism, a consumer's perception of the destination image is also largely influenced by his/her manner of travel. Take independent travel and group travel as an example: group tourists are limited by travel agencies, often shown only one way of sightseeing, and the understanding of the destination's social culture is more watered-down; in contrast, independent tourists have more free time and space, can gain a more in-depth understanding of their interests, and have relatively more contact with local residents. As a result, their image perception of the destination will be more profound and comprehensive than the group tourists'.

2.4.2 Tourism Consumer Perception of the Tourist Destination Elements

Tourism consumer perception of the tourist destination image is their overall cognition formed through the perception of various elements of the tourist destination. Most tourist destination elements include tourism attractions, access channels (local transportation, transportation stations), reception facilities and services (accommodation, catering, entertainment, retail, and other facilities), ancillary services (various types of local organizations), and cultural factors.

1) Tourism Attractions

Tourism attractions are the most important activity resource for tourism destinations, providing tourists with the motivation to move from one place to another. Tourism cannot exist without attractions. They have two functions: one is to stimulate tourists' interests in traveling to the destination, and the other is to provide satisfactory services to tourists. Tourism attractions are divided into natural attractions, historical attractions, cultural attractions, and artificial attractions. In urban tourism, tourists tend to be more interested in historical and cultural attractions. In a recent study, some scholars have explored the perception of the Cantonese by domestic tourists (Lu et al., 2019). They found that when domestic tourists travel in Guangzhou, their perception of Cantonese people is mainly captured by the following four aspects: local characteristics, captivation, functionality and dialect understanding. Consumers' perceptions of tourism attractions are mainly reflected in the quality, price, and supporting services of the attractions. In perception of the naturally attractive qualities in any destination, take natural landscape resources as an example, the vast majority of tourists like landscapes to be unique, ornamental, complex, integral and vivid; the higher a landscape ranks in similar resources, the more easily it will be for tourists to perceive them and make a positive evaluation. In tourism resources, such as interaction with wildlife in zoos, consumers' perceptions can be more clear and profound. In the perception of the price related to the attraction, consumers often perceive not the exact price, but whether the attraction is worth it for the money (Lawson, Juergen, Kerry, 1995). In recent years, some scholars have also paid attention to tourists' perceptions of the attractiveness of the resort environment. For example, Chen Ganghua and other scholars found that Chinese tourists' perception of environmental recovery in the resort is mainly reflected in the following five aspects: compatibility, extent, mental away, physical away and fascination.

2) Access Channels

The access channels to the destination include the traffic that connects the source to the destination, as well as the traffic system that provides short-cycle services within the destination. Tourists' perception of traffic elements is mainly reflected in their perception of the safety, comfort, speed and flexibility of traffic. The safety of transportation is the primary point of tourists' perceptions of transportation. A safe and reliable transportation process can ensure the pleasure of the journey. Negative reports on traffic safety issues will often cause consumers to perceive risk in some kind of transportation. For example, after the September 11 attacks in the United States, many people were afraid to travel by plane. In addition, tourists' perceptions of the comfort and convenience of transportation also affect their evaluation of the destination. It is best to have a fast and direct means of transportation between tourists' accommodation points and other tourist points. Macau's special hospitality service has been praised by tourists in this respect. Finally, some flexible and innovative transportation modes within the destination (such as a scenic ropeway, shuttle buses in wildlife parks, and rides in amusement parks) are conducive to improving the quality of tourism as perceived by tourists.

3) Reception Facilities and Services

The reception facilities and services of the destination refer to a series of service facilities that meet the needs of tourists, including accommodation, catering, entertainment, shopping facilities, and so on. These reception facilities are usually invested in by the private sector because they can generate profits. Consumers' perceptions of tourist reception facilities and services are focused on their service quality, safety, characteristics and value-to-price ratio. Among them, the most important factor affecting consumers' perceptions is the quality of service. On the one hand, consumers will pay attention to appearance, service skill, service attitude and service quality (such as the appearance of the waiter, whether he/she can answer the consumers' questions, and whether his/her attitude is polite and sincere); on the other hand, they will also pay attention to the quality of the whole service process and whether destination hosts can quickly respond to the requirements of the consumers. Many consumers will have a quite high level of goodwill for the enterprises that can improve their personalized services. In addition, character is also an important aspect that affects consumers' perceptions of a destination. Take catering as an example, restaurants with local character and unique decoration styles can more easily become the object of consumer perception.

4) Ancillary Services

Ancillary services are services provided by various types of local organizations at a destination. In tourism activities, these services mainly refer to the ancillary services provided by the local tourism management agencies for consumers and the tourism industry, including marketing, development, information and booking services for consumers and the industry, and coordinating and supervising the operation of tourism enterprises. For tourists, although the auxiliary services provided by these government departments are not the focus of tourism activities, they can greatly affect consumers' perceptions of the overall image of the destination. For example, the improvement and high efficiency of ancillary services such as tourism identification systems, tourist complaint handling, and weather and traffic information provision in tourist cities will greatly improve the consumers' perceptions of a destination.

5) Cultural Factors

The cultural factors refer to the overall social and cultural environment of the destination, including the hospitality of the residents at the tourist destination, the manner of host and guest communication, the cultural literacy of the residents, the local customs, and so on. The cultural factors of a destination play a more and more prominent role in consumers' perceptions of the destination image. For consumers, a destination with a warm hospitality atmosphere, simple folk customs, and a unique local cultural atmosphere is often more noteworthy and attractive. The intensity of consumers' perceptions of cultural factors is influenced by their motivation, the cultural environment, their previous experiences and the destination itself. Taking ethnic minority tourism areas as an example, tourists who pursue different cultural experiences have a stronger and deeper perception of local culture than pure leisure tourists, and urban tourists who have never been exposed to traditional rural customs also have a stronger perception of rural cultural activities than do other tourists to rural areas.

2.4.3 Tourism Consumer Perception of the Travel Distance and Risk

Whether tourism consumers engage in tourism behavior is not only affected by their own perception of tourist destinations, but is also inseparable from their perception of relevant tourism conditions, mainly travel distance and risk.

1) Perception of the Travel Distance

Distance is an important limiting factor for tourist behavior. The distance measured under objective conditions is quite different from that perceived by the traveling individual. For example, most people feel that the journey home along a certain route is shorter than when they leave home along the same route. Several scholars have found that the impact of perceived distance on travel behavior is significantly higher than the impact of actual distance. This perceptual distance, also known as subjective distance, refers to how people estimate the actual distance between two places using their own information, knowledge, and experience. Their estimation of these distances is greater than the actual distance. People's perception of travel distance will affect their tourism attitude and behavior. The influence of perceived distance on tourism attitude and behavior is mainly manifested in the two aspects of obstructive effect and promoting effect.

(1) Obstructive effect.

Tourism is a consumption behavior that takes time, money, energy, and physical strength. The farther the distance of tourism, the greater the cost tourists have to pay, and the cost of tourism largely hinders tourism behavior. Tourism behavior cannot occur if the benefits derived from tourism are insufficient compensation for these costs. Therefore, we can understand the negative correlation between distance and tourism. The closer potential tourists are to a destination, the more tourists there are; the farther away from the tourist destination, the fewer tourists there are. It is clear that distance hinders tourism because international tourists are often fewer in numbers than domestic tourists, and long-distance domestic tourists are often fewer than close-distance tourists. For example, among Chinese inbound tourists, South Korea and Japan have more tourists than those in European and American countries, and distance is a factor in this that cannot be ignored. Distance is also an important factor in determining tourism behavior among domestic tourists.

(2) Promoting effect.

Long distance may also promote people's travel behavior. Because long distance means mystery and strangeness, and because human beings have the desire to explore the unknown world, mystery and strangeness can also constitute the unique attraction of a long-distance tourist destination. In addition, the idea that "distance produces beauty" expresses that long-distance tourist destinations are not only mysterious and strange, but also meet people's need for beauty. When the mysterious, strange, beautiful, and other subjective factors are part of the attraction, despite the obstruction of distance, people will still be drawn to long-distance travel destinations. For example, Tibet is far away for many tourists, but the mystery of Tibet itself makes these tourists travel thousands of miles to travel here.

From this, it is clear that perceptual distance both hinders and promotes tourism behavior. However, it is not always clear what role the perception of distance plays and how the degree of influence varies between tourists and the objective conditions of a tourism object. Members of the tourism industry, in order to attract tourists and continuously expand their tourism market share, should first develop, build and manage their tourist areas to provide high-quality tourism commodities for the market and create a good tourism image. Secondly, industry professionals should make full use of various marketing means to actively carry out tourism publicity, leave a deep impression on those potential tourists, and guide them to make tourism decisions.

From the above two aspects, it can be seen that distance perception can influence tourism decisions. Therefore, tourism operators should fully consider this factor and do a good job of targeted publicity, not only to attract nearby tourists, but also to try to attract distant visitors. This requires trying to change people's perceptions and attract tourists by promoting the unique characters of tourist destinations and products, so as to eliminate the effect of distance prevention on distant tourists①.

2) Perception of the Travel Risk

The perception of travel risk refers to a kind of uncertainty cognition caused by tourists who perceive unpredictable results along with the resulting beneficial consequences of tourism. Tourists' risk perception of the tourist destination directly affects the purchasing behavior of tourists as described in what follows. Tourism consumers perceive risk arising from different types of potential negative consequences. The main perceived risks include the factors enumerated below.

(1) Functional risk.

Functional risk refers to the poor quality of tourism products and services purchased by tourists, or products of good quality that nevertheless cannot meet the expectations of tourists.

(2) Economic risk.

Economic risk refers to the risk of money loss caused by the possibility that the price or value of the purchased product will not meet the payment cost.

(3) Social-psychological risk.

Social-psychological risk refers to the risk caused by the language barrier and cultural impact that tourists face, causing psychological problems or lack of self-perception when traveling in different places. This risk includes blows to self-esteem and self-confidence.

(4) Security risk.

Security risk refers to the damage caused by the political unrest, terrorism, natural disasters, and other unsafe factors that tourists perceive in their tourist destination②.

2.5 Marketing Strategy Based on Tourism Consumer Perception

Tourism consumer behavior is a dynamic process involving three stages: before, during and after travel. Therefore, the goal and effect of any marketing strategy will not

① Wei D. Tourism Consumer Behavior [M]. Tianjin: Nankai University Press, 2009.
② Shan M L. Travel Consumer Behavior [M]. Beijing: Enterprise Management Publishing House, 2021.

only be part of a certain stage or a certain behavior, but may also be interlinked through the whole process of consumption. For example, the development of an advertising strategy will first affect potential tourism consumers' perceptions of the destination, thus stimulating their travel motivations and affecting travel decisions. During travel, it can even affect their field experience, satisfaction, and loyalty to the destination. Tourism marketing strategy has a significant effect on the formation of tourists' tourism willingness, the establishment of tourism destination image, and the promotion of destination popularity. Because tourism marketing is a highly comprehensive and complex business, these marketing strategies are not completely separated, but are comprehensively cross-used by tourism enterprises and tourism destinations.

2.5.1 Brand Marketing

Brand marketing is an important way for enterprises to build a strong brand image and enhance brand awareness. Tourism itself is a fusion of food, lifestyle, travel, shopping and entertainment—an extraordinarily comprehensive industry. The narrow sense of tourism brand marketing refers to brand promotion of a tourist destination or a tourism product. The broader sense of tourism brand marketing is more structural, contains a single tourism product or enterprise brand, and emphasizes the overall characteristics of the tourism elements to make the tourism brand image deeply rooted in the hearts of the people.

Tourism brand marketing should deeply explore the nuances of each tourism brand, help tourists identify and remember the core values of tourism destinations, and improve tourists' perceptions of the tourism process. Therefore, tourism enterprises should delineate their own personality and characteristics, establish a clear brand image positioning, form their own brand core competitiveness, create differentiated advantages and maximize the transmission of "brand characteristics" to tourists. For example, Hunan Province clearly displays charm of personality and a characteristic image with the phrase "Beautiful Xiaoxiang, happy Hunan", and creates a unique competitive advantage for the Hunan tourism brand.

2.5.2 Tourism Experience Marketing

Tourism experience marketing refers to a new marketing method in which tourism enterprises plan marketing activities with a specific atmosphere according to the emotional needs of tourists and the attributes of tourism products and services, so that tourists can participate in and obtain a beautiful and profound experience. This produces emotional resonance and in turn expands the sales of tourism products and services.

The impact of the travel experience process on tourism consumer perception is very obvious. Whether before, during, or after tourism consumption, tourists are eager to enjoy sensory satisfaction and self-realization beyond product functions and benefits. These travel experiences will affect their travel decisions and subsequent behavior.

Now, more and more popular VR (virtual reality) technology has entered people's daily lives, and also have opened a new experience of travel destination marketing. In the first place, compared with traditional information methods such as text, pictures, audio and video, VR technology can provide more dimensions of sensory stimulation, allowing tourists to get an immersive experience. This immersive marketing method can greatly improve the depth and breadth of tourism consumers' perceptions, improve the expectations of tourists, and enable tourists to gain more emotional resonance after truly entering the tourism process. In the second place, VR technology also can let tourists perceive some distinctive features without traditional information avenues; it can give them access to more remote or not-regularly-open tourist destination resources, and at the same time ensure protection of vulnerable tourism resources; it also can give tourists a multi-angle, all-round understanding of tourist destination characteristics and improve their perception of tourist destination attractions. For example, in order to create the mysterious image of the city, Las Vegas has cooperated with Zero Latency VR (a world-famous multi-person interactive VR experience developer) to build an offline VR experience center at MGM Hotel to increase the memorability of its urban tourism offerings.

2.5.3 Embedded Advertising

Embedded advertising, also known as product placement advertising, refers to the strategic integration of products or brands and their representative visual symbols or even service content into movies, TV series, or TV programs, so that the product can leave an impression on consumers and achieve the purpose of marketing. Embedded advertising and media carriers are integrated to jointly construct an image of what may be the audience's real life or ideal situation, and give goods or service information to the audience without using advertising methods per se, so as to achieve a subtle publicity effect.

Embedded advertising takes full advantage of consumer unawareness. Casual attention in humans occurs naturally, without any effort of the will or conscious attention (which is the attention caused by stimulus or something else we are interested in). Embedded advertising makes consumers change from casual attention to unconscious memory, from unconscious memory to casual association, then from casual association to conscious observation. Finally, consumers move from the desire to the final action, which makes the audience produce consumption action imperceptibly.

In recent years, embedded advertising has developed rapidly and is widely used. The earliest embedded advertising appeared in the 1951 film *The African Queen*, featuring Gordon's Gin. This was followed by the appearance of "Reese's" chocolate in the film *The Alien*—the chocolate quickly sold out, and its total sales increased by 65%. As embedded advertising appears more and more frequently in movies and TV, businesses working through embedded advertising have gradually become more profitable, and

China Story

Image perception of tourism destination: How does the identity of "world heritage" affect Quanzhou?

embedded advertising has thus become an important form of advertising. In China, the typical example of the success of embedded advertising in films is Feng Xiaogang's film in 2004. Many scenes and plots in the film are designed to cleverly combine related brand advertisements with the movie, such as BMW automobiles, Sinopec Great Wall lubricating oil, and Canon printers, which frequently appear on the screen. The successful use of embedded advertising helped the film gain rich revenue.

Chapter Summary

After learning this chapter, we will have a understanding of the meaning of sensation, perception, the influencing factors of tourism perception, the influencing process of tourism consumption behavior and the theory of tourism consumer destination perception. Marketing strategies based on tourism consumer perception will help make some suitable business decisions.

Issues for Review and Discussion

1. Will there be deviations in tourism consumer perception? If so, how do these deviations or misunderstandings form?

2. Is the process of perceiving the tourist destinations image of tourism consumers only limited to the pre-stage of generating tourism demand, the stage of making tourism decisions and the stage of tourism implementation?

3. How to restore the safe image of tourist destinations in the eyes of potential tourism consumers?

Exercises

Recommended Reading

Chapter 3
Learning and Memory

Learning Objectives

After reading this chapter, you should have a good understanding of the following points:

(1) describe the concept of tourism consumer learning and the main learning theories;
(2) identify conceptual differences between theories;
(3) interpret the relationship between learning and memory;
(4) comprehend the formation and characteristics of tourism memory;
(5) understand how tourism companies use learning theories and the concept of memory when making marketing decisions.

Technical Words

English Words	中文翻译
behavioral learning theory	行为学习理论
operant conditioning theory	操作性条件反射理论
classical conditioning theory	经典性条件反射理论
cognitive learning theory	认知学习理论
sensory memory	感觉记忆
stimulus discrimination	刺激辨别
stimulus generalization	刺激泛化
analytical reasoning	分析性推理
analogical reasoning	类比性推理
memory interference	记忆干扰
episodic memory	情景记忆
semantic memory	语义记忆
iconic rote learning	图标式机械学习

Knowledge Graph

- Learning and Memory
  - Learning
    - The Nature of Tourism Consumer Learning
    - Learning Theory and Application in Tourism
    - The Content of Tourism Consumer Learning
  - Tourism Memory
    - The Role of Memory in Learning
    - The Memory System
    - The Formation and Characteristics of Tourism Memory
    - Memory Interference and Distortion

3.1 Learning

3.1.1 The Nature of Tourism Consumer Learning

Tourism consumer learning is an indispensable part of tourists' consumption. It is the process by which tourists acquire information that can be applied to their future consumption. Tourist behavior undergo relatively permanent changes during this process[1]. Therefore, tourism consumer learning is also referred to as the adaptive process in which the behavior of individuals is changed by experiences. The nature of tourism consumer learning includes the following three aspects.

1) Tourism Consumer Learning is Generally Obtained from Experience

Some scholars believe that tourism consumer learning involves the processing of empirical information; therefore, learning can also be considered to be the result of information processing[2][3]. The acquisition of experience may be conscious or subconscious. For example, when tourists reserve a room, they actively browse the hotel's website and room pages, and view other people's reviews to obtain information about the hotel. This is conscious learning. On the contrary, if one accidentally saw a promotional video of a destination, although they do not deliberately remember it, they

---

[1] 荣浩,张春燕. 旅游消费者行为学[M]. 北京:经济科学出版社, 2018.

[2] Mayer R E. Learning: Information Processing[M]// 21st Century Education: A Reference Handbook, Thousand Oaks: Sage Publication, c2008: 168-174.

[3] Hawkins D I, Mothersbaugh D L, Kleiser S B, et al. Consumer Behaviour: Building Marketing Strategy[M]. New York: McGraw-Hill Education, 2014.

could recall and recognize this destination in future. This is subconscious learning, with obvious contingency. Another example is this: people learn about a newly opened coffee shop from pictures shared by friends and travel notes when people browse Weibo—this is also subconscious learning. These two types of learning, conscious and subconscious, may run through the tourist consumption process.

2) Tourism Consumer Learning Is Accompanied by a Change of Behavior

Tourism consumer learning is accompanied by a change of behavior. Some of these changes can be overt. For example, tourists may learn to dive, swim and surf during their travels. These behavioral changes can directly reveal the process and result of learning. But some changes may be covert. Tourists who know more about landscape history tend to have deeper emotional experiences and have more fun than other tourists. The impact of learning on these tourists is imperceptible, but profound. Here is another example: tourists who have the experience of living in old industrial areas may pay more attention to detail than others when visiting the ruins of old industrial sites[①].

3) The Change of Behavior is Relatively Permanent

The process that leads to relatively permanent changes in tourist behavior is tourism consumer learning. The process and results of learning, such as the sport that tourists learn and the knowledge gained during traveling, may influence tourists' behavior for a long time. However, the behavior and behavior changes may not be permanent. Forgetting is inevitable. The sport or skills acquired during traveling will be forgotten if tourists do not practice them. The foreign language ability of tourists may be improved during trips abroad, but may fall back to the original level when they return to their own country because of lack of practice. The duration of behavioral changes due to tourism consumer learning may be influenced by a variety of reasons, such as motivation to learn, intensity of learning, emotions while learning, etc. Generally, the changes brought about by tourism consumer learning are still relatively permanent.

Tourism consumer learning is a process that continually changes to incorporate new knowledge. Tourists receive different stimuli and get different feedback before, during and after a trip. This feedback enables tourists to gradually have a better understanding of the elements related to a specific trip and constantly adjust their behavior in subsequent trips. Tourism consumer learning involves many concepts, from simple associations in advertising to complex cognitive activations. Psychologists have developed a variety of theories to explain learning. The following section will introduce the main theories of tourism consumer learning and their applications in tourism marketing.

---

① Caton K, Santos C A. Heritage Tourism on Route 66: Deconstructing Nostalgia[J]. Journal of Travel Research, 2007, 45(4): 371-386.

3.1.2 Learning Theory and Application in Tourism

Schools of learning theory can be divided into the behaviorism school and the cognitive school. Behavior learning theory focuses on the change of individuals when they encounter stimuli. Schools of cognitive psychology emphasize individual psychological changes.

1) Behavior Learning Theory

Behavior learning theory is regarded as stimulus-response learning. The theory holds that learning is the reaction to external stimuli. In tourism consumption, tourism learning is the result of optional and observable behaviors of tourists in the tourism environment. Classical conditioning theory and operant conditioning theory are two basic forms of behavior learning theories.

(1) The content and application of classical conditioning theory.

Classical conditioning theory refers to the behavioral theory of spontaneous responses to specific situations achieved through repeated exposure[1]. The theory has its inception in the famous psychological experiment by Ivan Pavlov. He found that when a dog saw food (unconditional stimuli, US), it would salivate (unconditional response, UR). Therefore, he connected the ringing of a bell, which did not cause the dog to salivate, to the food. He rang the bell every time before he feed the dog. After repeating this feeding process a few times, he found that even if he just rang the bell but did not feed the dog, the dog would salivate regardless because the it would have learned to associate the bell with the food at this point. In the process, the original bell becomes a conditioned stimulus with conditioned response ability. The dog's salivation in response to the bell becomes a conditioned response.

Classical conditioning theory has two basic features: repetition and condition stimulus. Individuals who learn the connection between two stimuli through the process of repetition produce the same response under the conditioned stimulus as previously only to the unconditional stimulus[2]. Many advertisers use classical conditioning in some way or another, such as the example of the slideshow and music we just mentioned, which brings about a certain response—tourists associate music with pictures, and generate positive emotional responses to the scenic spot (as shown in the figure 3.1).

Classical conditioning theory is usually applied in marketing through two phenomena: stimulus generalization and stimulus discrimination.

---

[1] Stuart E W, Shimp T A, Engle R W. Classical Conditioning of Consumer Attitudes: Four Experiments in an Advertising Context[J]. Journal of Consumer Research, 1987, 14(3): 334-349.

[2] Rescorla R A. Pavlovian Conditioning: It's Not What You Think It Is[J]. American Psychologist, 1988, 43(3): 151.

```
┌─────────────────────────┐                    ┌─────────────────────────┐
│ Unconditioned stimulus  │───────────────────▶│  Unconditioned reflex   │
│       (Music)           │             ▲      │   (Positive emotion)    │
└─────────────────────────┘           ╱        └─────────────────────────┘
                                    ╱
                                  ╱
┌─────────────────────────┐     ╱              ┌─────────────────────────┐
│  Conditioned stimulus   │── ─ ─ ─ ─ ─ ─ ─ ──▶│   Conditioned reflex    │
│     (Scence spot)       │                    │   (Positive emotion)    │
└─────────────────────────┘                    └─────────────────────────┘
```

Figure 3.1 Tourist leaning under classical conditioning theory

Stimulus generalization refers to the condition that once an individual learns to respond to a specific conditioned stimulus, other stimuli similar to the conditioned stimulus can also induce conditioned responses. Specifically, the reaction of tourists to a particular stimulus may expand to other similar stimuli. This phenomenon has been widely applied in tourism marketing. For example, promoters of certain scenic spots may connect their spots with other familiar and favourable tourist attractions when they advertise their locations, in order to increase tourists' familiarity and degree of favourability towards the scenic spots, so as to indirectly achieve a greater effect of marketing publicity.

Stimulus discrimination refers to the ability of tourists to distinguish between similar stimuli and respond differently when a conditional stimulus can elicit a condition reflex. This phenomenon always applies in differentiation strategy. Tourism managers prefer to present a different image for tourists to help them distinguish their products from other familiar products, and to build product loyalty. For example, Xi'an has successfully built the "Great Tang All Day Mall" based on its own historical and cultural foundations. Other cities have also built similar antique buildings, but the degree of tourists' love for "Great Tang All Day Mall" has not weakened.

(2) The content and application of operant conditioning theory.

Operant conditioning theory is also referred to as instrumental conditioning theory. It suggests that learning is a process of finding a particular stimulus that can yield the best results by trial and error[①②]. The theory was constructed by B. F. Skinner, an American psychologist. He carried out a systematic study on reinforcement, which led to the development of reinforcement theory. He found that learning is essentially a kind of change in the probability of responses, and reinforcement is a method to enhance the probability of responses. The connection between stimuli and responses is the result that has been learned. Therefore, individuals can learn by means of the trial-and-error method. Specifically, tourists learn which behavioral responses can result in a more favourable

---

① Iversen I H. Skinner's Early Research: From Reflexology to Operant Conditioning[J]. American Psychologist, 1992, 47(11): 1318-1328.

② Young H P. Learning by Trial and Error[J]. Games and Economic Behaviour, 2009, 65(2): 626-643.

outcome (reinforcement) in the process of repeating trial and error, and reduce the behaviors that bring harm by repeating the behaviors that produce favourable results. Classical conditioning theory emphasizes the reflexive behavior of tourists to stimuli without conscious control, while operant conditioning theory emphasizes the voluntary response of tourists influenced by outcomes[1][2].

Reinforcement plays a significant role in learning; it is regarded as an event that is applied to encourage a certain behavior to increase the chance of it happening again[3]. If marketers apply reinforcing stimuli after the travel consumer's consumption behavior occurs, the probability of such consumption behavior will increase. However, if the reinforcing stimulus is stopped, the probability of this consumption behavioral response will decrease and eventually disappear, which is called extinction. Therefore, when tourists are no longer satisfied with the services provided by the hotel or scenic spot, this reinforcement subsides, and the connection between the hotel or scenic spot and the tourists' satisfactory experience is no longer strengthened, tourists may not visit again.

Depending on the nature and purpose of reinforcement, it can be divided into positive and negative, and is widely applied in tourism marketing[4].

Positive reinforcement. This refers to giving tourism consumers a positive stimulus, thereby increasing the probability of their consumption behavior[5]; for example, the "member rewards" of an airline or hotel. Tourists can gain member points every time they use the service from the airline or hotel, and can then exchange the points for gifts or other perks.

Negative reinforcement. This refers to helping tourism consumers to eliminate aversive stimuli, thereby increasing the probability of their consumption behavior[6]. For example, in the advertisement of Liebao's online ticket purchasing system, an old man was going to his son's house for the Chinese New Year, but he had to wait at the station because he did not have a ticket. He looked very helpless and anxious. A girl used Liebao's online ticket purchasing system to help the old man buy a ticket to his son's house, and the old man was finally reunited with his son. The message conveyed by the advertisement is: as long as Liebao's online ticket purchasing system is used, the negative result of not being able to buy a ticket can be avoided.

Further Reading

Punishment in Operant Conditions Learning Theory

Further Reading

Reinforcement Strategies in Tourism Marketing

---

① Rescorla R A, Solomon R L. Two-process Learning Theory: Relationships between Pavlovian Conditioning and Instrumental Learning[J]. Psychological Review, 1967, 74(3): 151.

② Clark K R. Learning Theories: Behaviourism[J]. Radiologic Technology, 2018, 90(2): 172-175.

③ Baron A, Galizio M. The Distinction between Positive and Negative Reinforcement: Use with Care[J]. The Behaviour Analyst, 2006, 29(1): 141-151.

④ Ferster C B, Skinner B F. Schedules of Reinforcement[M]. New York: NY Appleton-Century-Crofts, 1957.

⑤ Shull R L, Lawrence P S. Reinforcement[M]// Lattal K A, Perone M. Handbook of Research Methods in Human Operant Behaviour. Boston: Springer, c1998: 95-129.

⑥ Sorce P, Perotti V, Widrick S. Online Shopping for Positive and Negative Reinforcement Products[M]// Khosrow-Pour M. The Social and Cognitive Impacts of E-commerce on Modern Organizations. Hershey: IGI Global, c2004: 1-14.

According to the above two behavioral learning theories, the connection between the stimuli and behavioral responses learned by tourism consumers will eventually form habits after repeated reinforcement, and these habits guide travel consumers to make corresponding behavioral responses when they encounter original or similar consumption situations. However, many complex consumers learning behaviors cannot be explained away as being simple habits. Travel consumers may not need to go through the process of trial and error, but can make behavioral plans through observation and imitation. These behaviors cannot be explained by simple behavior habits, but need to be explained through consumer cognitive learning process. Therefore, we will introduce cognitive learning theory in detail in the next section and look into its application in tourism consumption.

2) Cognitive Learning Theory

Cognitive learning theory refers to the process in which individuals complete learning through orderly cognitive processing of information when they encounter problems that need to be solved. This learning process involves the exchange of information about views, concepts and attitudes[①], unlike behavioral learning, which is an instinctive response to stimuli. Cognitive learning involves highly engaged mental processing of information and emphasizes the importance of such mental processing in problem solving. Indeed, the essential difference between cognitive learning and behavioral learning can be thought of as a difference in the understanding of behavioral responses. Behavioral learning explores the immediate response to a specific stimulus. Cognitive learning considers complex behavior to be compound responses based on conditioned connections. This conditional connection is generally expressed as an understanding of the relationship between elements in the situation. The following sections will introduce the representative cognitive learning theories.

(1) The content and application of insight learning theory.

Insight learning theory was proposed by cognitive psychologist Wolfgang Kohler. He believed that the learning achieved by individuals through observation, perception of relationships and understanding of the situation, rather than the accumulation of actions and blind attempts[②]. Learning refers to a person's interaction with situations. New ways of perception, imagination and thought are created as a result of this interaction, and these three elements collectively make up insight. Thus, insight learning is achieved by individuals reorganizing or reconstructing the form of things[③]; this is a complex cognitive learning process. Insight operates when an individual is trying to solve a problem, thereby avoiding a large number of random, blind actions unrelated to the problem. With this in mind, insight is also considered to be a type of learning that involves the use of rationality

---

① Hawkins D I, Mothersbaugh D L. Consumer Behaviour: Building Marketing Strategy[M].12th ed. New York: McGraw-Hill Education, 2014.

② Köhler W. Gestalt Psychology Today[J]. American Psychologist, 1959, 14(12): 727.

③ Simon H A. The Information Processing Explanation of Gestalt Phenomena[J]. Computers in Human Behaviour, 1986, 2(4): 241-255.

in light of the facts.

Insight allows individuals to solve problems through conclusions, inferences, or judgments. This kind of analytic reasoning is widely supported in tourists' consumption behavior. For example, we have seen various evaluations about tourism destinations in OTA platforms such as Ctrip and Qunar. Through positive and negative comment information, we will have made basic self-evaluation and inferences about the scenic spot, and decide whether to visit or not. Furthermore, insight also helps individuals apply what they have learned to other problem situations. This is analogical reasoning. For example, a tourist may have never driven a towed recreational vehicle (RV), but may associate the towed RV with their① own experience of driving a C-type RV to make an analogy inference, so as to have a basic understanding of the towed RV.

Furthermore, when an individual truly understands the relationship between things, the understanding gained through epiphany not only facilitates transfer, but is also not easy to forget. Therefore, when consumers understand the characteristics of the services provided by travel marketers, this information may remain in their memory, and they may continuously recall this information to make future consumption decisions.

(2) The content and application of sign learning theory.

Sign learning theory was proposed by the American psychologist E. C. Tolman. Tolman believed that learning is the cognition of "sign-gestalt". In the process of learning, individuals are not learning a series of stimuli and responses, but learn the sign for achieving the goal and the meaning it represents②. Therefore, learning is purposeful behavior rather than blind behavior. Furthermore, he also stated that individual behavior is not determined by reward or reinforcement with action results, but is guided by individual expectations of goals. In the absence of positive and negative reinforcement, learning can still occur in a latent manner. This latent learning has been supported by many consumer phenomena. For example, when travel consumers come into contact with various hotel or airline advertisements, they may subconsciously gather new knowledge and information from the advertisements and form opinions about products and services. Therefore, when choosing a hotel or buying air tickets, tourists may purchase products based on this information. At this time, latent learning will be manifested through explicit behavior. In other words, the results of learning may not necessarily manifest themselves. If the individual is stimulated (or reinforced) and has the motivation to operate (such as buying a ticket to travel, in the above example), the results of learning will be manifested through the operation.

Both insight learning theory and sign learning theory confirm that the relationship between stimuli and responses is indirect, and is mediated by consciousness. There is an intermediary variable (O) between stimuli (S) and behavioral responses (R), and it is advocated to extend the behaviorist S-R model to the S-O-R model, where O represents

---

① "Their" here denotes the neutral third-person pronoun.
② Tolman E C. Sign-gestalt or Conditioned Reflex[J]. Psychological Review, 1933, 40(3): 246.

the internal change of the individual. With the continuous development of e-commerce, the application of the SOR model in the tourism and hospitality industry has gradually increased to predict the behavior of tourism consumers. Many scholars hope to promote the development of tourism marketing by exploring the influence of user-generated content on social platforms such as Douyin and Weibo on tourism consumption intentions through the SOR model[1][2].

3) Social Learning Theory

(1) The content of social learning theory.

This theory, commonly referred to as observational learning theory, was proposed by A. Bandura, one of the leading figures of new behaviorism. As a significant development in learning theory, social learning theory incorporates cognitive learning theory and traditional behavioral learning theory. Social learning theory emphasizes the role of social conditions in the learning process[3]. Bandura believes that many human behaviors arise in social situations. Therefore, the main goal of social learning theory is to investigate how individual cognition, behavior, and environmental factors interact to affect individual behavior[4]. Social learning theory holds that individual learning is divided into two categories. One is the process in which individuals acquire behavioral response patterns through direct experience, which is often referred to as direct experience learning[5]. The second refers to indirect learning by observing and imitating how others behave and the consequences of their behavior (rewarding or punishing them), which is often referred to as learning through indirect experience and is also considered as observational learning[6]. In the process of observational learning, the objects that are observed and imitated are called models. Role models can be real people, or they can be people and things in the form of symbols[7]. For example, when buying outdoor sports equipment, reading the product's instruction manual or user guide is a process of observational learning.

Social learning theory states that learning does not necessarily require the process of reinforcement. Specifically, individuals can learn complex behaviors simply by observing others, without having to experience the reinforcement process first-hand. For instance,

---

①宋蒙蒙,乔琳,胡涛.基于SOR理论的社交网络互动对旅游行为的影响[J].企业经济,2019 (5): 72-79.

②Cheung M L, Leung W K, Cheah J H, et al. Exploring the Effectiveness of Emotional and Rational User-generated Contents in Digital Tourism Platforms[J]. Journal of Vacation Marketing, 2022, 28(2): 152-170.

③Bandura A. Social Learning Theory[M]. Englewood Cliffs, NJ: Prentice-Hall, 1977.

④James L R, Hater J J, Gent M J, et al. Psychological Climate: Implications from Cognitive Social Learning Theory and Interactional Psychology[J]. Personnel Psychology, 1978, 31(4): 783-813.

⑤Bandura A. Social Learning Theory[M]. Englewood Cliffs, NJ: Prentice-Hall, 1977.

⑥Chen A, Lu Y, Wang B. Customers' Purchase Decision-making Process in Social Commerce: A Social Learning Perspective[J]. International Journal of Information Management, 2017, 37(6): 627-638.

⑦Weaver G R, Treviño L K, Agle B. "Somebody I look up to": Ethical Role Models in Organizations[J]. Organizational Dynamics, 2005, 34(4): 313-330.

tourists staying in a smart hotel can learn how to use the service interface by watching the operation of the service platform by another customer, even if they are unfamiliar with how to use the interface. In this process, tourists were not reinforced, but they still learned how to operate the service interface of the smart hotel. In addition, Bandura believes that individuals can learn by observing the trial-and-error process in the behavior of others. Specifically, this is a process of vicarious reinforcement. It is not simply equivalent to copying other people's behaviors, but individuals guide their own behaviors by observing the results (i.e., rewards or negative feedback) of others' behaviors[1]. For example, two tourists go to an unfamiliar place together. Tourist A buys a local specialty food out of curiosity. After tourist A tastes it, they[2] find that the food tastes very bad, and tourist B infers that the food tastes very bad through the behavioral responses of their companion, so they do not buy this local specialty food. The behavior of tourist B is made by learning the possible taste of food through the behavioral response of tourist A. This process includes the individual's cognitive judgment on the behavior of others.

(2) The application of social learning theory in tourism marketing.

Tourist observational learning is very common in tourism consumption behavior. In order to reduce the possible economic losses and dangers caused by trial and error, tourism consumers pay more attention to observational learning. By listening to the introduction of friends and acquaintances, watching travel TV programs, reading travel diaries written by other tourists, etc., travel consumers can master travel knowledge and understand travel destination information. The information obtained through observational learning lays the foundation for tourists' high-quality travel experience. It also helps tourists avoid possible risks. Each traveller's experience can serve as a "model" for future tourists to follow and can either inspire or discourage other travellers. As a result, every customer is an advertisement for the travel industry, and every customer must receive consistently high-quality service.

Case Study 3-2

Celebrity Effect on Tourism Destination Development

3.1.3 The Content of Tourism Consumer Learning

Most individual behaviors are learned, and this is more so in the case of travel behaviors, compared with other behaviors, because tourism behavior is the behavior generated in order to meet higher-level needs after an individual's life has reached a certain level. Therefore, understanding the content of tourism consumer leaning can ensure that tourism business operators can better understand the behavior of tourists. In general, the content of tourism consumer leaning can be divided into three categories: travel motivation, travel attitude and travel consumption experience.

---

[1] Latham G P, Saari L M. Application of Social-Learning Theory to Training Supervisors through Behavioural Modeling[J]. Journal of Applied Psychology, 1979, 64(3): 239.

[2] "they" here denotes the neutral third-person pronoun.

1) The Leaning of Travel Motivation

Motivation is an important factor in tourists' behavior. Many tourists' motivations, including communication, success, and self-assurance, among others, are learned. For example, tourists and families may have a pleasant emotional experience on vacation. Tourists and their families become closer as a result of this emotional experience. Then the motivation to travel to promote family intimacy is generated and learned by tourists. Additionally, as tourists discover new information, their motivation will alter along with their cognition. Therefore, tourism marketers can influence their decision-making by encouraging tourists to learn new motivations.

2) The Learning of Travel Attitude

Tourists' attitudes towards tourism and their attitudes in the process of tourism also require a learning process. Attitudes of tourists are based on individual cognitions, such as beliefs, opinions, etc. The formation of these cognitions comes from the learning of information extracted by individuals in daily social life and social media. It can also come from the information transmitted to individuals by family members, relatives, friends, and their community. This information helps individuals form their attitudes. For example, social media, as well as relatives and friends, convey information to tourists about the importance of sustainable development and environmental protection. Tourists may learn the attitude of environmental protection from this information. The attitude of tourists may therefore change their travel behavior, such as the choice of hotels, the choice of transportation, and so on.

3) The Learning of Travel Consumption Experience

The learning of tourism experience means that tourists learn how to distinguish between different tourism products and how to deal with the risks that may arise from decision-making behaviors. In order to meet the needs of different groups of people, tourism companies launch a variety of tourism products and new incentives to attract tourists. Therefore, travellers not only need to learn and understand the characteristics of the product, but also need to learn how to change their behavior to adapt to new ways of travel, even though they may have some travel experience.

An important part of learning about travel experience is learning about risk. This risk comes from the uncertainty of consumption, including possible social risks (such as conflicts that may arise during travel), psychological risks (such as the possible gap between tourists' expectations and actual travel experience), and security risks (such as whether a tourist destination is safe). These are all things travellers need to consider and learn before traveling. Tourists can learn this information about risks through the travel experiences of others, social media reports, and the traveller's own travel experience. For example, when a volcano warning was raised in Bali, Indonesia in 2018, the Chinese Ministry of Foreign Affairs advised Chinese tourists on social media to make proper travel arrangements and to pay attention to their own safety. Some Chinese tourists who were planning to go to Bali cancelled their trips after seeing the foreign ministry's advice.

Case Study 3-3

The Brand Promotion of Zhangjiajie

3.2 Tourism Memory

3.2.1 The Role of Memory in Learning

The primary theories of learning were covered above. In both cognitive learning theory and social learning theory, we mentioned memory. What then is memory? What connection exists between learning and memory? The nature of memory and the significance of travel memory in marketing will be covered in more detail in this section.

Memory is the process of recalling information from the past, including experiences, impressions, abilities, and habits. Memory is also regarded as the capacity to recall prior experiences. Memory permits us to demonstrate what we have learnt and remembered through experiences or activities through structural or behavioral changes. Learning and memory work together in a symbiotic way. Learning is built on memory, which is also a prerequisite for learning. They are linked and indivisible from one another.

Memory plays an important role in the decision-making of tourism consumers. It enables tourism consumers to associate the knowledge and experience of certain products or services in the past with current purchase issues, so as to make judgments and choices quickly. By influencing the travel consumers' understanding of products, services and their value, memory prompts travel consumers to have reasonable expectations for the products or services they encounter, thereby affecting their satisfaction or loyalty to the products or services[1]. Therefore, it is very important for tourism managers to understand the formation of consumer memory and help consumers remember their brands and services.

3.2.2 The Memory System

Memory works in a complex way. The current understanding of memory mainly uses information processing methods and the belief is that people have three different memory systems: sensory memory, short-term memory, and long-term memory. These three memory systems play different roles when individuals process information.

1) Sensory Memory

Sensory memory stores information received by individuals from visual, auditory, tactile, and other sensory systems, and is a record of perception. Although the sensory information retained by sensory memory is very brief (measured in milliseconds or seconds), the information storage capacity is enormous. Sensory memory provides time

---

[1] Kim J H. The Impact of Memorable Tourism Experiences on Loyalty Behaviours: The Mediating Effects of Destination Image and Satisfaction[J]. Journal of Travel Research, 2018, 57(7): 856-870.

and possibility for further processing of information, and is of great significance to other advanced cognitive activities[①]. For example, when a tourist passes by a coffee shop full of flowers during their travels, they[②] smell the strong coffee aroma and the fragrance of flowers in the shop. Although this sensory information only lasts for a few seconds, it grabs the tourist's attention. This attention makes it possible for the tourist to decide whether to visit the coffee shop or not.

2) Short-term Memory

The memory system in which data is temporarily retained and manipulated is known as short‑term memory, also referred to as working memory. Compared with sensory memory, short-term memory has a relatively longer duration (5 to 20 seconds, no longer than 1 minute), but a more limited capacity. Short‑term memory is an active, dynamic memory system, which handles readily available information.

3) Long-term Memory

Long‑term memory refers to the memory system in which individuals retain information for a long time, including concepts, decisions, rules, event processes, emotional states, etc. Long‑term memory is also a relatively deep memory formed by individuals consciously processing and classifying short-term memory. Long-term memory contains different sub-memory systems. According to the nature of memory content, long-term memory can be divided into procedural memory and declarative memory. Procedural memory is the memory of how to perform things, and primarily includes cognitive skills and techniques, motor skills, and so forth[③]. This type of memory frequently needs to be learned gradually after making numerous efforts[④]. Declarative memory refers to memory about facts and events[⑤]. Declarative memory consists of episodic memory and semantic memory[⑥]. Semantic memory refers to the inherent knowledge stored in the brain, which contains information such as language, words, concepts, and principles[⑦]. It is an individual's most basic knowledge and feeling of a concept, representing the individual's understanding of things or events at the simplest level[⑧]. For example, consumers will classify Chanel as a luxury item and Hainan Province as a tropical island. In contrast, episodic memory refers to memory related to the experience of an event. Episodic memories are stored life events, either observed or self‑related, that often inspire

---

①林德荣,郭晓琳.旅游消费者行为[M].重庆:重庆大学出版社,2018.

②"They" here denotes the neutral third-person pronoun.

③Bauer P J, Dugan J A. Different Forms of Memory[M]// Chen B, Kwan K Y. Neural Circuit and Cognitive Development: Comprehensive Developmental Neuroscience. Amsterdam: Elsevier, c2020: 395-412.

④Galotti K M. Cognitive Psychology in and out of the Laboratory[M]. 5th ed. Beijing: China Machine Press, 1994.

⑤王甦,汪安圣.认知心理学(重排本)[M].2版.北京:北京大学出版社,2006.

⑥Galotti K M. Cognitive Psychology in and out of the Laboratory[M]. 5th ed. Beijing: China Machine Press, 1994.

⑦Schwartz B L. Memory: Foundations and Applications[M]. California: Sage Publications, 2020.

⑧Tulving E. Episodic and Semantic Memory[M]//TulvingE, DonaldsonW. Organization of Memory. California: Academic Press, c1972: 381-402.

imagination and emotion. Episodic memory enables individuals to reconstruct and re-experience past events[1]. Tourism companies usually tend to arouse consumers' episodic memory in marketing, because episodic memory can awaken consumers' emotions and stimulate consumers' purchase intention[2].

Events associated with the self in long-term memory are considered autobiographical memory. Autobiographical memory has the characteristics of episodic memory and semantic memory[3]. Specifically, autobiographical memory contains both the individual's experience of the event process and general information that focuses on the individual's facts[4]. For example, if you went to Hainan with your family during the summer vacation, the weather is hot, and your memory of the hot weather in Hainan is semantic memory. Some scholars believe that travel experience memory is an autobiographical memory because it is closely linked to tourists' participation and self-emotion[5][6]; therefore, they believe that travel memory is the memory related to the traveller's own travel experience extracted from autobiographical memory.

3.2.3 The Formation and Characteristics of Tourism Memory

In recent years, researchers have found that travel memory is more important than actual travel experience in predicting traveller behaviour. Therefore, understanding the formation and characteristics of tourism memory is crucial for the development and marketing of tourism destinations and tourism enterprises. Next, we will explain the formation of travel memory and the characteristics of travel memory in two parts.

1) The Formation of Tourism Memory

The formation of travel memory consists of three stages: encoding, consolidation, and retrieval.

(1) Encoding.

Encoding is when the traveller converts information into a form stored in memory. Such information refers to the collection of event-specific information (e.g., time and place

Further Reading

Factors that Affect Encoding

---

[1] Tulving E. Episodic and Semantic Memory[M]// Tulving E, Donaldson W. Organization of Memory. California: Academic Press, c1972: 381-402.

[2] Passer M W, Smith R E. Psychology: The Science of Mind and Behavior[M]. New York: McGraw-Hill Education, 2009.

[3] Kim Y, Ribeiro M A, Li G. Tourism Memory Characteristics Scale: Development and Validation[J]. Journal of Travel Research, 2021, 61(6): 1308-1326.

[4] McCarthy R A, Warrington E K. Autobiographical Memory[M]// McCarthy R A, Warrington E K. Cognitive Neuropsychology: A Clinical Introduction. Amsterdam: Elsevier, c1990: 296-328.

[5] Jalilvand M R, Samiei N, Dini B, et al. Examining the Structural Relationships of Electronic Word of Mouth, Destination Image, Tourist Attitude toward Destination and Travel Intention: An Integrated Approach[J]. Journal of Destination Marketing & Management, 2012, 1(1): 134-143.

[6] Yin C Y, Poon P, Su J L. Yesterday once more? Autobiographical Memory Evocation Effects on Tourists' Post-travel Purchase Intentions toward Destination Products[J]. Tourism Management, 2017, 61: 263-274.

of tourism activities) and vivid moments (e. g., sensory and perceptual information acquired through sensory systems) acquired by tourists during tourism activities. Encoding is the first process of tourists' memory operation. Meanwhile, it is also an active and selective process. In this process, it will be affected by many factors, such as the content of coding, the environment of coding, or subjective factors such as tourists' emotion, state, and motivation.

(2) Consolidation.

Information will be stored in the brain after encoding. According to theduration, capacity and type of information, it can be divided into the sensory memory, short-term memory and long-term memory, which we have mentioned above. However, memories are gradually forgotten over time. Moreover, the influence of the long-term memory of tourism consumers on their behavior and in tourism marketing may be far more significant than that of the other two types of memory. Therefore, how to consolidate the information in sensory memory and short-term memory is particularly important.

Consolidation reflects the process of tourists forming long-term tourism memory. In the process, the memory of tourists will become more stable. In the process of memory consolidation, the short-term memory stored by tourists during travel will gradually transform into long-term memory. Information in short-term memory decays rapidly. Tourist consumers need to ensure that information in short-term memory can be transferred to long-term memory through rehearsal, otherwise the information will be lost①. However, not all repetitions turn short-term memory into long-term memory.

Scholars divide rehearsal into two categories: maintenance rehearsal and integrated rehearsal. Simple rehearsal is another name for maintenance rehearsal. Specifically, simple, repetitive mental operations on short-term memory information can enhance memory traces. However, such maintenance rehearsal is often "use it and forget it". For example, although we read an unfamiliar number repeatedly before dialling it, we mightforgetit after the call. Marketers still prefer to use this method to consolidate consumer memory because it is simple, and easy to operate and promote②. Tourism businesses constantly strive to enhance the perception that consumers and potential consumers have of certain tourist sites or tourist-related goods by regularly exposing consumers to marketing activities and commercials. In this way, they can lessen the likelihood that consumers forget their destinations or brands.

Integrated rehearsal is the re-organization of information so that it is linked with other information that has been stored③. This method is usually used in tourism marketing to help consumers carry out deeper information processing. For example, a scenic spot can

---

①Atkinson R C, Shiffrin R M. Human Memory: A Proposed System and its Control Processes[M]// Spence K W, Spence J T. Psychology of Learning and Motivation. California: Academic Press, c1968: 89-195.

②Hawkins D I, Mothersbaugh D L, Kleiser S B, et al. Consumer Behaviour: Building Marketing Strategy[M]. New York: McGraw-Hill Education, 2014.

③林德荣,郭晓琳. 旅游消费者行为[M]. 重庆:重庆大学出版社,2018.

be built into cultural and creative products according to its own brand characteristics and integrated marketing with other clothing brands. In this way, the scenic spot deepens the consumer's memory of the brand by combining its own brand characteristics with other information.

Tourism companies also help tourists consolidate their travel memories through tangible goods such as souvenirs and postcards. For example, some intangible cultural heritage tourist attractions will carry out intangible cultural heritage experience courses. Tourists can make their own works of intangible cultural heritage under the guidance of professionals and take them back to their hometowns as souvenirs. The aim of this process is to help tourists consolidate their travel memory, because after this experience, whenever tourists see this souvenir, they will think of this experience activity, and repeated memories essentially lead to the consolidation of the memory of this travel experience. Of course, this also involves the last process of memory retrieval, which we will discuss next.

(3) Retrieval.

Retrieval is the traveller's recall of past information. If a piece of information can only be encoded and stored in memory, but cannot be retrieved, then this memory is useless and cannot provide a reference for tourists' future behavior. Therefore, a key link in the process of memory retrieval for tourists is recognition. Tourists need to identify the current situation or the correlation between the received information and the information in memory. The higher the correlation, the easier it is to retrieve the memory. Thomson and Tulving proposed the extraction of encode specificity in 1970. They found that memory retrieval was more favourable when encoding and retrieval environments were similar[1]. Bower's mood-dependent effect also demonstrates a similar effect[2]. Also, if an individual encodes information in a particular mood state, the memory is more easily retrieved in the same mood state than in a different mood state[3].

2) The Characteristics of Tourism Memory

Now think back to your past travels. What are some of your most memorable tourism memories? What are the characteristics of these memories? Researchers and marketers have found that tourism memories tend to incorporate various sensory and emotional elements, and are highly narrative[4][5]. Specifically, tourism memory has accessibility,

---

[1] Thomson D M, Tulving E. Associative Encoding and Retrieval: Weak and Strong Cues[J]. Journal of Experimental Psychology, 1970, 86(2): 255.

[2] Bower G H. Mood and Memory[J]. American Psychologist, 1981, 36(2): 129.

[3] Lewis P A, Critchley H D. Mood-dependent Memory[J]. Trends in Cognitive Sciences, 2003, 7(10): 431-433.

[4] Jorgenson J, Nickerson N, Dalenberg D, et al. Measuring Visitor Experiences: Creating and Testing the Tourism Autobiographical Memory Scale[J]. Journal of Travel Research, 2019, 58(4): 566-578.

[5] Rahmani K, Gnoth J, Mather D. A Psycholinguistic View of Tourists' Emotional Experiences[J]. Journal of Travel Research, 2019, 58(2): 192-206.

detail, vividness, sharing, valence and emotional intensity[1].

(1) Accessibility.

Accessibility refers to the ease of retrieval of travel memory. Tourists can retrieve past travel experiences by using things like photos, souvenirs, and advertisements. The accessibility of tourism memory can help tourists carry out cognitive rehearsal, which is the key for tourists to learn from past experiences and make decisions.

(2) Detail.

Travel and sensory aspects are both included in the details of travel memories. The time, location, companions, and other information are referred to as tour details. Try to recall: Can you remember all of your trips' dates and destinations? Researchers have found people are more likely to remember broad details about significant events[2], such as the year of a certain holiday, the day they went on their honeymoon, the first time they travelled alone, etc. When a tourist recalls an event, he or she is able to recall information linked to the tourist event through the senses of sight, touch, smell, and hearing in addition to the tourist details[3]. The vividness dimension takes into account vision individually[4]. The main source of sensory details is information that has been transferred from sensory memory into long-term memory that is relevant to the senses. These details will enhance tourism memories and have an impact on tourists' future behavior intention[5].

(3) Vividness.

Visual clarity and intensity of recall memory are referred to as vividness. It is specifically thought to be a mental reconstruction of previous tourist attractions by the tourist. Important and emotional events are often easier to reproduce. Vividness can be a key predictor of recall strength[6].

(4) Sharing.

Tourism memory has a social function[7]. Tourists share their tourism memories with

---

[1] Kim Y, Ribeiro M A, Li G. Tourism Memory Characteristics Scale: Development and Validation[J]. Journal of Travel Research, 2021, 61(6): 1308-1326.

[2] Tung V W S, Ritchie J R B. Investigating the Memorable Experiences of the Senior Travel Market: An Examination of the Reminiscence Bump[J]. Journal of Travel & Tourism Marketing, 2011, 28(3): 331-343.

[3] Boyacioglu I, Akfirat S. Development and Psychometric Properties of a New Measure for Memory Phenomenology: The Autobiographical Memory Characteristics Questionnaire[J]. Memory, 2015, 23(7): 1070-1092.

[4] Sutin A R, Robins R W. Phenomenology of Autobiographical Memories: The Memory Experiences Questionnaire[J]. Memory, 2007, 15(4): 390-411.

[5] Kim Y, Ribeiro M A, Li G. Tourism Memory, Mood Repair and Behavioral Intention[J]. Annals of Tourism Research, 2022, 93: 103369.

[6] Rubin D C, Schrauf R W, Greenberg D L. Belief and Recollection of Autobiographical Memories[J]. Memory & Cognition, 2003, 31(6): 887-901.

[7] Jorgenson J, et al. Measuring Visitor Experiences: Creating and Testing the Tourism Autobiographical Memory Scale[J]. Journal of Travel Research, 2019, 58(4): 566-578.

friends, family, or strangers through the form of stories[1]. The intimacy between people is increased when they recollect and share one another's memories in the form of stories[2]. Sharing travel recollections with one another also aids in the consolidation of travellers' memories. There are various ways to share tourism stories, such as online reviews, word-of-mouth, and so on. The researchers found that the evaluation and word-of-mouth of tourism consumers can influence the formation of brand image and the future behavioral intention of tourists[3]. Therefore, the sharing of tourism memory is very important for tourism marketing.

(5) Valence and Emotional Intensity.

The degree to which an experience is viewed as positive or negative in memory is referred to as its "valence". The valence of the event, the emotional experience at the time of the event, and the emotional experience at the time of retrieval are all included in this dimension[4]. The term "emotional intensity" describes the level of emotion felt both during encoding and retrieval[5]. Emotions embedded in travel memories not only interact with emotional content, but also influence travellers' future behavioral intentions. Emotions are the core of tourism memory. Recollections of emotional events are frequently more powerful than memories of non-emotional events because intense emotional experiences can cause the release of neurotransmitters and hormones that make memories stronger. Meanwhile, they also evoke emotions about past experiences in the process of retrieving their memories[6].

Through the discussion of memory formation and memory characteristics, it is not difficult to find that emotion plays a crucial role in memory encoding, consolidation, and retrieval. Moreover, the peak effect of memory also proves that we are more likely to remember the peak of an event because the peak of an event often contains a stronger emotional message. In order to boost the effect of memory on consumers, tourism businesses typically prefer to provide more emotional components in their marketing campaigns. For instance, tourism businesses may increase the involvement of tourism

Further Reading

Flashbulb Memory and Memorable Travel Experience

---

① Tung V W S, et al. A Famework of Memory Management and Tourism Experiences[J]. Journal of Travel & Tourism Marketing, 2017, 34(7): 853-866.

② Kim H, Chen J S. The Memorable Travel Experience and Its Reminiscence Functions[J]. Journal of Travel Research, 2019, 58(4): 637-649.

③ Prayogo R R, Kusumawardhani A. Examining Relationships of Destination Image, Service Quality, E-WOM, and Revisit Intention to Sabang Island, Indonesia[J]. APMBA (Asia Pacific Management and Business Application), 2017, 5(2): 89-102.

④ Sutin A R, Robins R W. Phenomenology of Autobiographical Memories: The Memory Experiences Questionnaire[J]. Memory, 2007, 15(4): 390-411.

⑤ Kim Y, Ribeiro M A, Li G. Tourism Memory Characteristics Scale: Development and Validation[J]. Journal of Travel Research, 2021, 61(6): 1308-1326.

⑥ Jalilvand M R, Samiei N, Dini B, et al. Examining the Structural Relationships of Electronic Word of Mouth, Destination Image, Tourist Attitude toward Destination and Travel Intention: An Integrated Approach[J]. Journal of Destination Marketing & Management, 2012, 1(1): 134-143.

activities, create highly engaging tourism projects, offer welcoming and considerate services, and more. Tourism businesses strive to give customers a satisfying emotional experience to improve their vacation memories.

3.2.4 Memory Interference and Distortion

When discussing memory formation, we mentioned that memories could be forgotten over time. But sometimes, the forgetting of memory may not be affected by time, but is interfered with other information. This kind of forgetting caused by the interference of old and new information is usually called memory interference.

Think about it: Can consumers remember the content of each advertisement clearly and accurately across similar advertisements? Therefore, creating unique advertising and marketing experiences is crucial for travel companies to help combat memory interference. Remember the tourism advertisement for "Deep Breath in Hainan" that we mentioned when discussing stimulus discrimination? It is difficult for tourists to have memory interference with regard to this advertisement because it has a short and clear slogan and the advertising content is clearly different from other similar advertisements for other regions. As a result, tourism businesses prefer creating differentiated advertising material while also creating catchy, succinct brand slogans as external cues to aid consumers in conjuring up memories of the brand. These slogans are usually very brief because consumers' memory capacity is limited. Advertising slogans that are too long may be rejected by consumers, which is not conducive to brand recognition and recall.

Furthermore, retrieved information can be subjectively distorted or false①. Advertisements, other people's stories, and online comments can distort individuals' memories of past travel experiences. Memory is malleable and the consolidation of memory is a dynamic process②. When a memory that has been consolidated is activated, the memory will enter an unstable state again③. In this state, this memory is like a newly encoded memory that is easily affected by new information. When the information is consistent, the memory has completed the process of reconsolidation④. However, when the new information is inconsistent with the information in the memory, the individual's consolidated memory is distorted. Some reasearcher found through bogus advertisements of Disney and Bugs Bunny that incorrect advertising information would distort the original

---

① Loftus E F, Bernstein D M. Rich False Memories: The Royal Road to Success[M]// Healy A F. Experimental Cognitive Psychology and Its Applications. Washington: American Psychological Association, c2005: 101-113.

② 王英英, 朱子建, 吴艳红. 记忆的动态变化:记忆的编码、巩固和遗忘[J]. 科学通报, 2016, 61(1): 12-19.

③ Nader K, Schafe G E, Doux J. Fear Memories Require Protein Synthesis in the Amygdala for Reconsolidation after Retrieval[J]. Nature, 2000, 406(6797): 722-726.

④ 王英英, 朱子建, 吴艳红. 记忆的动态变化:记忆的编码、巩固和遗忘[J]. 科学通报, 2016, 61(1): 12-19.

memory of individuals[1][2]. In the meantime, the more misleading information that was supplied, the falser memories were created, especially if people did not recognize that the recently acquired knowledge was incorrect.

Tourism memory interference and distortion prove the importance of post-experience management. It is necessary for tourism companies to change tourists' memory after the experience through advertising or other common methods. A strong positive distraction may make a tourist's bad experience better in retrospect[3]. Meanwhile, differentiating the brand or service from those of other enterprises is also an effective means to solve the memory distortion problem.

Chapter Summary

This chapter systematically introduces the nature of tourism consumer learning and related theories of learning, which provides a basic understanding of what tourism consumer learning is and what its specific content is. This chapter also provides an introduction of the relationship between learning and memory, the system, the formation and characteristics of memory, with a view to clarify the importance of tourism memory in tourism consumer behavior research and marketing.

Issues for Review and Discussion

1. Please explain what stimulus generalization is. When is it applied by tourism managers?

2. Please explain what memory interference is. How can tourism managers cope with it?

3. What is the relationship between tourism memory and emotion?

China Story

Study Travel: The "Roots-seeking Journey" of Ethnic Chinese Teenagers

Exercises

Recommended Reading

---

[1] Braun K A, Ellis R, Loftus E F. Make My Memory: How Advertising can Change Our Memories of the Past [J]. Psychology and Marketing, 2002, 19(1): 1-23.

[2] Braun-LaTour K A, Grinley M J, Loftus E F. Tourist Memory Distortion[J]. Journal of Travel Research, 2006, 44(4): 360-367.

[3] Braun K A. Postexperience Advertising Effects on Consumer Memory[J]. Journal of Consumer Research, 1999, 25(4): 319-334.

Chapter 4
Motivation

Learning Objectives

After reading this chapter, you should have a good understanding of:
(1) relationships between tourism need, motivation, and demand;
(2) several theories of tourism need;
(3) Plog's and Dann's tourism motivation theories;
(4) influencing factors of tourism motivation;
(5) the application of tourism motivation in tourism marketing industry.

Technical Words

English Words	中文翻译
need	需要
motivation	动机
demand	需求
Plog's tourism motivation theory	普洛格旅游动机理论
Dann's tourism motivation theory	丹恩旅游动机理论
travel career ladder theory	旅行生涯阶梯模型
psychoanalytic school	精神分析学派
humanistic school	人本主义学派

Knowledge Graph

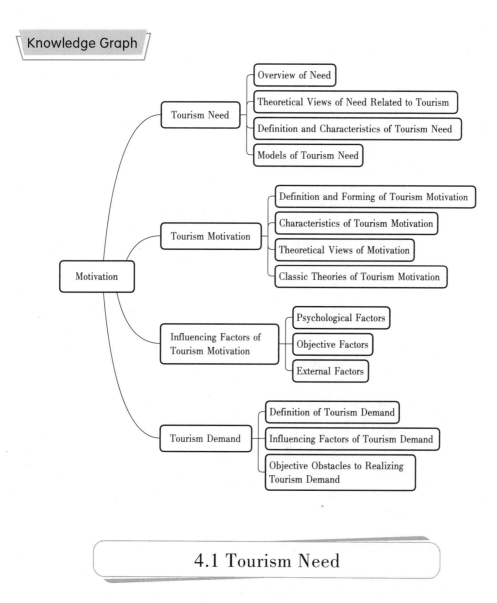

4.1 Tourism Need

Need is a state of psychological and physical deprivation, which refers to an inner state in which an individual feels a certain deprivation in their life and strives to rectify it (i. e., to satisfy their need). Although needs do not necessarily lead to follow-up actions, it cannot be denied that needs are the active source of organism activities and the basic driving force for human activities. Therefore, need is the concept most fundamental to the study of psychological motivations for why people act, and there are many classic academic theories of need. This section mainly introduces knowledge related to tourism need.

4.1.1 Overview of Need

1) Definition of Need

In the process of human development, in order to maintain the continuance of life and the human race, certain things are needed, such as food, water, air. Similarly, in social life, people also need to engage in social labor and interpersonal communication to maintain the existence and development of society. Need refers to a psychological state in which an individual feels a certain lack in their life and strives to obtain psychological satisfaction. It is manifested in an organism's requirements regarding its internal environment or external living conditions, and becomes the source of the organism's activities. This imbalance includes both physiological and psychological imbalances. For example, if there is a lack of water in a person's blood, they will need to drink water; if their blood sugar level drops, they will naturally feel hungry and then go to find food; if they lose their loved ones, they will have the need for love; if the social order is not stable, people will have the need for safety, etc. After needs are met, imbalances are temporarily eliminated, but when new imbalances arise, new needs arise. It is the generation of these needs that promotes individuals to engage in certain activities to meet their own needs, thereby making up for a certain lack or imbalance in individual physiology and psychology, and promoting the continuous development of human society.

2) Classification of Need

(1) Physiological need and social need.

Regarding the origin of need, need can be divided into physiological need and social need.

First, physiological need, also known as natural need, refers to need related to the preservation and maintenance of organisms to allow them to survive and reproduce. For example, the need for food, water, sleep, protection from cold, heat, sunlight, air, etc. Human physiological need is subjective, and with the development of social productivity, there is a tendency to continuously improve physiological quality of life.

Second, social need refers to high-level need caused by social life and subject to social constraints, such as the need for labor, communication, entertainment, respect, and other aspects of social life. Social need is expressed as social requirement of one kind or another, and when individuals recognize the necessity of the social requirement, the requirement may be transformed into social need of individuals. Social need is acquired, originates from human social life, belongs to the category of human social history, and varies with social living conditions. Social need is also necessary for individual life. If the need is not met, individuals will experience emotions such as anxiety and pain.

(2) Material need and spiritual need.

Regarding the content of need, need can be divided into material need and spiritual need.

First, material need refers to the need of individuals for substances and material products. Material need includes both natural need, such as air, water, rest, etc., and social need, such as physical aspects of working environments, cultural and recreational items, transportation. With the progress of society and the development of productive forces, people's material need will continue to develop, and the means to meet it will continually improve. Material need points to material products and is satisfied by possessing them. Examples include the need for certain work and labor conditions, for daily necessities, and for physical commodities that exist in certain forms, such as housing and modern means of transportation. Material need is the most basic and direct need of human beings, as well as the foundation of human society.

Second, spiritual need refers to the need of individuals for spiritual life and spiritual products, including the need for knowledge, aesthetics, art, religious belief, morality, communication, and achievement. Spiritual need points to the spiritual products of society. Examples include the need to watch a wonderful movie, to listen to a wonderful piece of music, to feel good about life, and to read newspapers and magazines, watch TV programs, and learn about current events and news. Consumers' spiritual desires are satisfied by possessing certain spiritual products. The satisfaction of spiritual and cultural needs is an indispensable condition for continuously improving the quality of human life and promoting the all-round development of human beings.

Material need and spiritual need are closely related. The possession of certain commodities can satisfy people's material need while satisfying certain spiritual need. For example, by having a spacious house, a person can not only have a place to live, but also meet needs regarding self-esteem and the respect of others. The satisfaction of spiritual need is inseparable from certain material products. If you want to listen to your favorite songs at any time, you must have a set of playback equipment. If you want to get the latest news reports, you must read relevant newspapers and magazines.

4.1.2 Theoretical Views of Need Related to Tourism

1) Developments in the Psychoanalytic School and the Humanistic School

Psychoanalysts from Freud to Adler and then to Jung have explained the fundamental drives of human behavior on the basis of compensatory deprivation. It is undeniable that potential tourists, even if they are not inherently deficient, are among those who have some degree of dissatisfaction with their environment in their personal life circles. Adler described traveling as an appropriate form of compensation for this dissatisfaction. Numerous empirical studies on tourism motivation support this view. For example, from a rather small sample, Crompton identified seven tourism motivations: escaping from perceived mundane environment, self-discovery and self-assessment, relaxation, showing personal prestige, returning, close family kinship, and enhancing social interaction[①].

---

①Crompton J L. Motivations for Pleasure Vacation[J]. Annals of Tourism Research, 1979, 6(4): 408-424.

However, the premise of the psychoanalytic school's need theory, that is, the proposition that the theory of deficiency compensation can suitably explain everyone's behavioral motivations, is increasingly under attack.

Humanistic psychologists believe that the psychoanalytic theory of mitigation motivation is wrong in trying to explain normal life phenomena with a law that describes pathological phenomena, and is therefore one-sided. Humanistic psychologists hold that maintaining the status quo is not the purpose of normal organisms, and that the inclination of normal life is towards action and progress. A very important concept in the need theory of humanistic psychology is that human actions are driven by a number of constant, hereditary, instinctual needs that are not just physiological, but also psychological[①]. This school of need theory is best known for Maslow's hierarchy of needs model. Maslow believed that human beings have at least five basic needs: physiological needs, safety needs, social needs, esteem needs, and self-actualization needs. Using Maslow's hierarchy of needs theory to examine the source of tourists' behavioral motivations, it is not difficult to judge that tourists' behavioral motivations generally exceed the fulfilment of basic physiological needs and safety needs. Through tourism, people acquire some kind of belonging and identity, such as when engaging in ethnic tourism or visiting relatives and friends. Through travel, people gain respect and recognition from others. This is reflected in the travel process through contact with the destination community and with others in the personal life environment after the travel process. Tourism is not only an opportunity and a way to gain aesthetic enjoyment and increase knowledge, but also a way to discover oneself, know oneself, express oneself, and realize oneself.

2) Alderfer's ERG Need Theory

Alderfer conducted research that was more in line with actual experience on the basis of Maslow's hierarchy of needs theory and offered a new humanistic need theory, according to which everyone has three basic needs: a need for existence, a need for relatedness, and a need for growth. Accordingly, this hypothesis is known as ERG theory[②].

First, the basic material needs of people, such as the physiological needs and safety needs put forth by Maslow, are tied to the desire for existence. The second need is the need for relatedness, which is involved with what people need to do in order to maintain crucial interpersonal ties. Such social needs and status needs are met through connections with others and map to Maslow's social needs and the extrinsic categories of esteem needs. Third, Alderfer divided the requirement for growth and development in his final point. It conveys a person's innate drive for growth, including Maslow's self-actualization needs and the internal categories of esteem needs.

---

① Schneider K J, Pierson J F, Bugental J F. The Handbook of Humanistic Psychology: Theory, Research, and Practice. California: Sage Publications, 2014.

② Alderfer C P. An Empirical Test of a New Theory of Human Needs[J]. Organizational Behavior and Human Performance, 1969, 4(2): 142-175.

The strict structure of Maslow's hierarchy of needs is based on the idea that higher-level needs can never be satisfied until lower-level needs have been fully met. The ERG theory disagrees with this notion that the different levels of need are set in stone. As an illustration, even if a person's needs for existence and relatedness are not entirely satisfied, they can still endeavor to fulfill their need for growth, and all three needs can simultaneously play a part. The "frustration-regression" concept, which states that when a person feels disappointed at a higher level of needs, their needs at a lower level may increase, is another idea put out by the ERG theory. For instance, if a person's need for social connection is not satisfied, their desire for more money or better working conditions will rise.

4.1.3 Definition and Characteristics of Tourism Need

1) Definition of Tourism Need

People's needs are diverse, and tourism need is a reflection of people's general need in the process of travel. Tourists are the main people who engage in tourism activities. The reason why tourists want to engage in tourism activities is to meet their own needs for tourism activities. Therefore, tourism need refers to a psychological state in which tourists or potential tourists feel a certain deficiency, namely, their desire and requirement for tourism. That is to say, tourism need is an individual's subjective wish and requirement, and this subjective attitude reflectsa person's requirements for objective conditions (including the individual's internal physiological conditions and external social conditions), and will be affected by social and economic conditions. For example, consider a person who wants to travel to Hainan in winter. This need is a subjective desire of their own, but this desire is not created out of thin air. It may be because the winter cold prompts them to find a warm place to take a vacation. The leisure time available during the winter vacation and economic conditions further prompt them to generate this need. Therefore, both intrinsic physiological conditions and external social conditions stimulate people, ultimately producing tourism need.

2) Tourism Need: Unity and Complexity

Human need is a complex phenomenon, and people want both to maintain unity and to pursue complexity and diversity. Therefore, tourism need has two contradictory characteristics, namely, unity and complexity.

Unity refers to people's tendency to seek balance, harmony, sameness, predictability, and lack of conflict in various activities. Any non-uniformity creates psychological tension. Therefore, in order to reduce psychological tension, individuals will seek to fulfill a single need at any one time. Due to the need for unity, tourists generally choose to visit very famous tourist attractions, choose hotels, restaurants, and transportation facilities that are well-known and can provide standardized services, and participate in familiar or traditional entertainment activities, because familiarity allows tourists to foresee the services they will receive and avoid unpleasant events and risks. Accordingly, in the process of tourism activities, tourists do not want to encounter unexpected things.

Complexity, on the other hand, refers to people's pursuit of and yearning for novelty, the unexpected, change, and unpredictable things. A life that is too monotonous cannot bring satisfaction to people, and will make people feel tired, nervous, and uneasy. Therefore, people not only pursue unity, but also long for complexity. They hope that their lives will be more colorful, and expect to bring more psychological satisfaction and pleasure to themselves through the complex things in life. Accordingly, tourists are willing to go to places they have never been to before, to choose a method of travel they have not used before, and to contact people and do things they have never contacted and done before.

The need for both unity and complexity can explain many phenomena that occur in tourism. Although these two viewpoints seem contradictory, combining the two can give a more comprehensive explanation for some tourism behavior phenomena. In real life, people need an organic combination of unity and complexity rather than only unity or complexity. The need for unity should be balanced by complexity to a certain extent, and the need for complexity should be balanced by unity to a certain extent. In a word, people always strive to maintain the best balance between their needs for unity and complexity, so that psychological tension is maintained at an acceptable level. Otherwise, too much unity will make people tired, and too much complexity will make people nervous and scared.

4.1.4 Models of Tourism Need

1) Gray's Wanderlust and Sunlust

In 1970, Gray proposed two driving forces for leisure travel (i. e., tourism): wanderlust and sunlust[①]. According to his explanation, wanderlust is an inherent and essential characteristic of human beings, which urges people to leave familiar environments and go to exotic places to appreciate foreign beauty. Sunlust refers to tourists chasing beautiful and exotic scenery. For example, people flock to the Caribbean and Mediterranean regions to "chase the sun". Gray interpreted wanderlust as an internal pushing factor and sunlust as a response to a pulling factor. The idea is valuable mainly in its explanation of the internal mechanism that leads to tourists' psychological imbalance, and which therefore forms the internal driving force of tourism behavior, rather than any clarification of the motivations of tourists. In addition, Gray's model also clearly reveals that tourism behavior is caused by the interaction of internal and external factors, especially by contradictions between the two.

---

①Gray H P. International Travel-international Trade[M]. Massachusetts: Health Lexington, 1970.

2) Travel Career Ladder Theory

Tourism need is described as having five different levels by travel career ladder (TCL) theory[①], a framework that describes tourism needs in relation to travel careers. The five levels of needs here include: relaxation needs, safety/security needs, relationship needs, self-esteem and development needs, and self-actualization/fulfillment needs.

In accordance with Maslow's hierarchy of needs, the needs of travelers are arranged in a hierarchy or ladder, with the lowest level being relaxation needs, followed by needs for safety/security, relationship, self-esteem and development, and lastly, needs for self-actualization/fulfillment. Although TCL theory holds that one level of needs in the ladder may be dominant, it does not hold that travelers simply have one degree of travel motivation. Only a small portion of the TCL's inception was influenced by Maslow's theories. The idea of a job in leisure or tourism played a similarly influential role in forming the TCL framework. This research's central thesis was that travel experiences affect people's motivation in different ways. According to this theory, a person can be considered to have a travel career, which is a pattern of travel motivations that alters over the course of their life and/or as they get more travel experience.

3) Ryan's Classification of Tourism Needs

Ryan's classification of tourism needs[②] is as follows:

First, intellectual need. This reflects the degree to which particular tourists are inspired to engage in different spiritual leisure activities, such as learning, exploring, discovering, thinking, or dreaming.

Second, social need. This desire may reflect how motivated each traveler is to engage in particular social leisure activities. The need for friendship and interpersonal connections as well as the need for one's own and other people's respect are both present in this component.

Third, the need for competency and mastery. This urge may reflect how driven each traveler is to engage in leisure activities that enhance their knowledge or abilities. These activities, which are typically physical in nature, can arouse feelings of accomplishment, mastery, challenge, and competition.

Fourth, the need for stimulus-avoidance. This desire may reflect how driven each traveler is to leave overstimulating situations in their various living locations. For some people, it stems from a need to avoid interacting with others and a desire for peace and quiet. Others might feel a need for relaxation and rest.

---

① Pearce P L, Lee U I. Developing the Travel Career Approach to Tourist Motivation[J]. Journal of Travel Research, 2005, 43(3): 226-237.

② Ryan C. The Tourist Experience: A New Introduction[M]. London: Cassell, 1997.

4.2 Tourism Motivation

This section introduces the concept and theory of tourism motivation. It starts with the connections and differences between tourism need and tourism motivation, aiming to clarify the concept of tourism motivation. Then, it elaborates on the driving forces of tourism motivation other than tourism need. Characteristics of tourism motivation are explained. Motivation theory refers to the explanation of "why people behave in this way". It next lists five kinds of classical theories of motivation. Finally, four commonly used motivation theories focusing on tourism are interpreted: Plog's tourism motivation theory, Dann's tourism motivation theory, Macintosh's tourism motivation theory, and Tanaka's tourism motivation theory.

4.2.1 Definition and Forming of Tourism Motivation

1) Relationship between Tourism Need and Motivation

Tourism motivation is the psychological driving force that induces and maintains individuals' tourist behavior and guides tourist behavior toward tourism goals. It is the internal psychological driving force that encourages people to carry out certain tourism activities. It has the functions of activating, guiding, maintaining, and adjusting tourism activities, and can also initially start them.

Tourism need refers to the tendency of individuals to automatically balance and choose to engage in pleasant leisure experiences when people are in a state of a lack of tourism. Humans in modern society have sufficient economic income, abundant free time, and an ever-expanding desire to understand the world, and consequently tourism need has gradually been internalized into the basic human needs system. If this need is not met, people will experience psychological discomfort.

Personal tourism needs are the inducing factors of tourism motivation. Without the need for tourism, the motivation for tourism will not be generated. For people in an environment where the pace of life is accelerating and work is highly stressful, their desire is to escape the hustle and bustle of the city, change their environment, enjoy a relaxed life, and allow their tired bodies and minds to recover. In addition, people also expect to go to the society and nature at appropriate times, and occasionally to experience the cultural customs and the beautiful natural scenery of a foreign country. This psychology of wanting to escape from the hustle and bustle of big cities and explore new and different places in foreign countries plays a decisive role in the generation of people's tourism motivation.

Compared with tourism need, tourism motivation is a category that affects tourist behavior more directly. It is the source of inner psychological power that is prompted by tourism need, is influenced by social beliefs and norms, and directly regulates specific tourist behaviors. To a large extent, tourism motivation is an instrumental realization of tourism need.

2) Driving Forces of Tourism Motivation

Tourism motivation is an important determinant of tourist behavior, and at the core of most tourism motivation theories is the concept of tourism need. Some scholars believe that in addition to tourism need, factors and conditions that promote or affect tourism motivation include tourism consumers' perceptions of tourism attractions, tourism attractions' ability to meet consumers' needs, and necessary economic conditions and leisure time. Tourism motivation is the internal driving force that makes people leave their places of residence to travel. People's social needs and curiosity form the intrinsic motivations for tourist behavior, which can also be said to be subjective conditions. However, if certain objective conditions are not met, people will ultimately not engage in tourism behavior. Generally speaking, the subjective and objective conditions that promote tourism motivation are encompassed by the following aspects.

First, personality traits. Different personal psychological characteristics make people's interests, hobbies, and attitudes to things different. People who have a wide range of interests and like new and exotic things are willing to make friends and are keen on traveling. People who like a quiet and stable life are happy to use their spare time to read, watch TV, and do housework at home, but are less willing to take part in travel activities that they think are time-consuming, labor-intensive, and expensive. The former always have a strong desire to travel, while the latter require certain factors to induce their desire to travel.

Second, economic factors. Tourism is a kind of consumption behavior. To engage in this kind of consumption, it is necessary to have sufficient ability to pay economically, that is, to have disposable income. Disposable income is the balance of personal income after deducting the cost of daily necessities and fixed expenses. The motivation to travel may arise only after a person or family's income exceeds their daily expenses. Today, the level of household income in our country is generally higher than previously, and the general quality of life is also constantly improving. The proportion of expenditure on daily consumption is slowly declining, and most households have more disposable income than previously. These factors have more or less promoted the generation of tourism motivation.

Third, time factors. Travel takes time. Whether potential tourists have leisure time determines whether they participate in tourism activities. Leisure time refers to the time people use to meet their spiritual needs, and is separate from time spent working, studying, and doing other necessary things, that is, the time people can freely use, including leisure time after a day of work, leisure time on weekends, and vacation time. Generally speaking, having leisure time after a day's work is not enough to motivate people to travel. Weekends and holiday periods, and especially work vacations, are the best times for people to travel, and are favorable factors for increasing people's travel motivation. Since May 1995, China has implemented a five-day work week. In September 1999, a new vacation system was introduced. The extension of public holidays gave birth to the first "National Day Golden Week". In recent years, the "three-day leave" granted for various statutory holidays has created more leisure time for people. In addition, tourist vacation systems in some departments have increased the time people can freely use and have created the conditions for people to travel abroad. At the beginning of 2013, *National Tourism and Leisure Outline (2013-2020)* promulgated by the state had the aim of "meeting the growing tourism and leisure needs of the people". The abundant leisure time all of this creates will be a favorable factor for the generation of people's travel motivation.

Fourth, social factors. Social factors refer to the economic development conditions, cultural factors, and social fashions of a country or region. As a part of modern life, tourism cannot exist without certain social and economic conditions. Therefore, people's living environment will have a certain influence on their travel motivation. Only when the economy of a whole country or region develops to a certain extent will there be sufficient economic conditions to build tourism facilities and develop tourism resources, thereby improving the comprehensive attractiveness of tourism and evoking people's interest and desire to travel. In order to have a sense of security and social identity, keep pace with their peers, and get social recognition, people will imitate each other, thus forming a fashion. When people regard tourism as being on the same level as other essential consumer goods, that is, when tourism becomes an indispensable good in people's lives, a fashion will form around it, like with other consumer goods. The report of the 19th National Congress of the Communist Party of China pointed out that Chinese-style socialism has entered a new era, and the main contradiction in our society is now the contradiction between the people's growing needs for a better life and unbalanced and insufficient development. In the new era of Chinese-style socialism, tourism has become the primary focus of people's needs for a better life. Tourism is a bridge for spreading civilization, exchanging culture, and enhancing friendship, and is important in improving people's living standards.

4.2.2 Characteristics of Tourism Motivation

In order to clearly understand the characteristics of tourism motivation, we first need to have a further understanding of the functions and types of motivation.

1) Functions of Motivation

Motivation is generated on the basis of needs, and has the following three functions as regards human behavior.

(1) Excitation function.

Motivation activates an organism to engage in a certain activity. An organism with a certain motivation is particularly sensitive to certain stimuli, which activate the organism to engage in a certain activity. For example, hungry people are particularly sensitive to food, and thirsty people are particularly sensitive to water, and both are thus prone to foraging activities.

(2) Pointing function.

Motivation is aimed at a certain goal or incentive, and is guided by the goal. That is, need becomes a motivation once guided by a goal. Due to the different types of motivation, the direction of people's actions and the goals they pursue are also different. For example, a student who has established a motivation to learn to engage in future practical activities has this image in their mind that can make them strive to pay attention to what they have learned and make unremitting efforts to accomplish the ambition they have established.

(3) Maintenance and adjustment functions.

When a certain activity of an individual is induced, motivation aims this activity at a certain goal and regulates the intensity and duration of the activity. If the goal is achieved, motivation prompts the organism to terminate the activity. If the goal is not achieved, motivation drives the organism to maintain and intensify this activity in order to achieve the goal.

2) Types of Motivation

Like needs, human motivations are diverse and can be classified differently from different perspectives.

(1) Physiological motivation and social motivation.

Regarding its nature, motivation can be divided into physiological motivation and social motivation. Physiological motivation is the inner driving force that prompts people to behave in order to meet their physiological needs, and is a lower-level motivation. For example, in order to maintain life and develop oneself, people need food. This physiological need will make people have the motivation to look for food. Social motivation is also known as psychological motivation or learned motivation. People grow and live in various social and cultural contexts, which determine their specific social needs. Various motivations are generated accordingly, such as work motivation, learning motivation, communication motivation, achievement motivation.

(2) Dominant motivation and auxiliary motivation.

Regarding its role in behavior, motivation can be divided into dominant motivation and auxiliary motivation. Dominant motivation refers to motivation that plays a relatively strong, stable, and dominant role in an activity. Auxiliary motivation refers to motivation that plays a weaker, less stable, and subordinate role in an activity. For example, a person may have many motivations for work, such as satisfying basic life needs, gaining social recognition, and reflecting self-worth. Among them, satisfying basic life needs is the dominant motivation, and the rest are auxiliary motivations.

(3) Intrinsic motivation and extrinsic motivation.

Regarding its cause, motivation can be divided into intrinsic motivation and extrinsic motivation. Intrinsic motivation refers to motivation that drives the behavior caused by an activity itself. Extrinsic motivation refers to the pursuit of some goal outside an activity caused by external factors. For example, some students' motivation for learning is in response to pressure from or expectations of parents or teachers, and some students only learn in order to obtain a certificate. Both types of motivation promote human behavior, and under certain conditions, extrinsic motivation can be transformed into intrinsic motivation. For example, praise or criticism and affirmation or denial by teachers and parents can stimulate students' learning activities, and gradually, students can also concentrate on learning in order to gain social recognition and appreciation, and come to regard learning as a pleasure.

3) Five Characteristics of Tourism Motivation

(1) Implicitness.

The implicitness of tourism motivation is reflected in two aspects. One is that tourists are often unwilling to disclose their tourism motivation. For example, the real motive of some outbound tourists is to show off their identity and status by traveling abroad, but when others ask about it, they say it is to broaden their horizons and appreciate exotic customs. The other is that tourists themselves often do not realize or cannot accurately express their real motives. For example, impulse buying behavior and some irrational consumption behaviors of tourism consumers, which cannot be fully explained by consumers themselves, are often external manifestations of consumers' subconscious.

(2) Multiplicity.

Tourists participating in tourism activities are not only motivated by one kind of motivation, but are driven by multiple motivations and want to meet various needs. For example, urban tourists participate in rural tourism to appreciate the natural scenery of the countryside, taste farm meals, or participate in agricultural activities to experience what cannot be experienced in cities. There are several motivations for such tourism activities, including escaping from the noisy environment of cities, feeling the tranquility of the countryside, escaping the tediousness and pressure of daily work, and experiencing rural life with family members. These travel motivations combine to form a motivation system, which drives people's travel behavior.

(3) Acquisitiveness.

The acquisitiveness of tourism motivation means that tourism motivation can be obtained along with the continuous accumulation of and change in tourists' learning and experiences. The original travel activity is not for entertainment, but an economic activity that people spontaneously carry out due to a need to go out to conduct business and barter. With the development of society, economy, and culture, people's access to information increases, the motivations for tourism activities become diversified, and tourists pay more and more attention to cultural and spiritual needs. It can be seen that with the enrichment of tourists' travel and life experiences, as well as the increase of tourists' learning and daily accumulation, their fear of unfamiliar environments will decrease, and their view of the external world will also change, which will lead to a higher level of tourism demand, and the formation of new tourism motivations will be stimulated.

(4) Complexity.

The complexity of tourism motivation is mainly manifested in the following two aspects. First, one tourism activity can be motivated by multiple tourism motivations, and one tourism motivation can induce engagement in multiple tourism activities. Similar tourism activities may not necessarily have similar tourism motivations, and similar tourism motivations may not necessarily lead to similar behaviors. For example, when inbound tourists come to China, some people are motivated to feel the charm of oriental culture, and some people are motivated to appreciate the beauty of natural landscapes. To understand the history and culture of China, some people may choose Beijing as their destination, while others may choose Shanghai, and some may choose Xi'an. Second is the conflict of tourist motivations. In some cases, tourists have multiple, similarly strong motivations in different directions, which causes motivational conflict. For example, tourists may want to go to natural tourist attractions to see natural scenery during their vacation, also think about shopping in Hong Kong. Both motives are strong, but the types are very different, and tourists can often only choose to indulge one of them.

(5) Sharing.

Tourists' motivations are inevitably affected by the motivations of their peers to travel. For example, most mass tourism involves participating in tour groups or traveling together with relatives and friends. This type of travel requires that all participants have reached a compromise, and tourists' travel motivation is shared. For example, for a married woman with children, her motivation to travel may vary with her companions. If she and her husband take their children on vacation, keeping them happy may be their shared motivation; if she travels with her best friends, shopping and entertainment may be their shared motivations.

4.2.3 Theoretical Views of Motivation

Building on our understanding of the concept and characteristics of tourism motivation, we will learn the classical theories of tourism motivation. Motivation is an important concept in psychology and other related disciplines, and many theoretical viewpoints have arisen regarding it. Considering that the relevant theories of tourism motivation are constructed based on the general theory of motivation, before introducing the theory of tourism motivation, it is necessary to explain several classical motivation theories.

1) Instinct Theory

Darwin's theory of evolution proved that humans and animals are part of a continuous system from the perspective of biological development. Some psychologists introduced Darwin's view of biological evolution into the study of psychology, thus placing the motives of human beings on the same level as the motives of animals in general, and proposed the theory of instinct to replace the theory of volition and intellectualism that had previously held sway[①]. It lists 18 human instincts. The basic claim is that instinct is an innate tendency to be extra sensitive to certain objects, and this sensitivity is subjectively accompanied by specific emotions. It believes that instinct is a purposeful behavior, and although the nature of external situations that cause instinctive behavior can be changed due to learning, and the pattern of certain behavioral responses can also be adjusted, the core emotions of instinct will not change. According to instinct theory, certain kinds of behavior correspond to certain kinds of instinct. For example, war is due to the aggressive instinct, and gathering is due to the saving instinct. However, such a statement obviously does not provide a good explanation for why certain behavioral patterns appear in certain species, but not others. Therefore, instinct theory has been widely criticized after a period of popularity.

2) Drive-reduction Approach

American physiologist Cannon put forward the concept of homeostasis, believing that organisms must maintain the balance of the internal environment of the body. Metabolic factors such as body temperature, blood-sugar, hormones levels, and nutrition need to be adjusted once they are out of balance. The autonomic nervous system is the mechanism for this type of adjustment, and its activity is involuntary. However, as biofeedback technology has demonstrated, these processes can also be brought under the control of the central nervous system and thus be controlled through conscious behavior. According to Hull, the needs of the body generate drives, which force the body to act, but which activities or responses are caused depends on objects in the environment. As long as the drive state exists, appropriate external stimuli will elicit certain responses. The connection between the response and the stimulus is strengthened just like in the conditioned reflex mechanism.

3) Arousal Theory

In 1995, when Berlein, the proponent of arousal theory, investigated human sensory experience, he found that a person's sense of novel stimuli develops with the repetition and duration of stimuli. The more a stimulus is repeated and the longer the duration of the stimulus, the novelty of the perceptual image will gradually decrease. The pleasure that people obtain from aesthetic activities is caused by two kinds of arousal. One is gradual awakening, in which the tension of aesthetic emotion is gradually increased in response to the process of perception and acceptance, and the critical point of final arrival yields a pleasurable experience. The other is so-called excitatory arousal, in which emotions quickly rise to a peak due to sudden shocks, yielding a tension-relieving drop-off pleasure as the arousal recedes.

---

①陈钢华,孙九霞. 现代旅游消费者行为学[M]. 广州:中山大学出版社,2019.

4) Incentive Theory

After the 1950s, many psychologists believed that all behaviors could not be explained by the motivational theory of reduced drive, and that external stimuli also played an important role in arousing behavior. Motivation should be explained in terms of the interaction between a stimulus and a particular physiological state of an organism. For example, a fed animal will re-eat when it sees another animal eating; the motivation is the stimulus itself. Humans often seek stimulation, rather than trying to relieve tension and bring the body back into balance. The incentive theory emphasizes the important role of external stimuli in eliciting motivation, and believes that incentives can evoke and guide behavior.

5) Cognition Theory

Based on experimental research on animals, American psychologist Tolman proposed that the motivation for behavior is an expectation of getting something, or an attempt to avoid unpleasant things. With experience, we also expect some way or means to achieve the purpose of our action. This is the starting point of expectancy theory. However, the theory of motivation has to explain not only how a person is motivated, but also why he acts one way and not another way. Activities to achieve an end can take many forms and many different paths, but why does one take one and not another? This requires investigating the cause-and-effect relationship inherent to how one views things, for people use means to achieve their goals according to their knowledge of cause-and-effect. This is where attribution theory comes in. Therefore, expectancy theory and attribution theory can be said to be the connecting branches of cognitive motivation theory. Cognitive theory of motivation makes a key distinction between intrinsic motivations and extrinsic motivations for human behavior. So-called internal motivation refers to the desire of human beings to perform a certain behavior from the heart, not due to an external reward. Extrinsic motivation refers to the desire to obtain an external reward when a person performs a certain behavior.

4.2.4 Classic Theories of Tourism Motivation

1) Plog's Tourism Motivation Theory

The tourism motivation model proposed by Plog is one of the most widely used models in the academic world[1]. In order to help some tourist destinations experiencing a downturn in tourist resources to reposition and successfully reverse the decline of tourism development, Plog classified tourists according to personality characteristics. According to Plog, tourist personalities form a continuum. At the two ends of the continuum are allocentric and psychocentric personalities, which correspond to adventurous to dependent

---

[1] Plog S C. Why Destination Areas Rise and Fall in Popularity[J]. Cornell Hotel and Restaurant Administration Quarterly, 1974, 14(4): 55-58.

tourist personalities. On this psychological continuum, the closer a person's psychological type is to the adventurous type, the more likely the person is to travel abroad, and the more adventurous and unfamiliar their tourism destinations. The direction of influence is always from left to right and is irreversible.

Allocentric personalities are adventurous, motivated to visit or discover new destinations, and rarely visit the same place twice. Psychocentric personalities focus their thoughts or attention on the trivialities of life, and they are therefore more conservative in their travel patterns, prefer safe tourism destinations, and often revisit. According to Plog's estimates, personality characteristics in the general population may have something close to a normal distribution, with allocentric and psychocentric personalities being held by a minority, and the vast majority of people falling in between. As figure 4.1 shows, among these people, those closer to the allocentric end are called near-allocentric, those closer to the psychocentric end are called near-psychocentric, and those in the middle are called mid-centric.

It must be noted that while Plog's theoretical model provides a useful way of understanding tourism motivation, the theory is difficult to apply because, as mentioned above, tourists may hold different motivations in different situations, and therefore show different personality types in terms of destination choice in different circumstance.

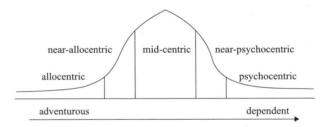

Figure 4.1 Plog's tourism motivation theory[1]

2) Dann's Tourism Motivation Theory

Dann divided tourism motivation into two forces: push factor and pull factor[2]. This is the push and pull model, which is widely cited in tourism motivation research. Specifically, push factor refers to desire from the heart, that is, what tourists want to do, while pull factor refers to the pull generated by the external environment, mainly referring to the attributes of tourism destinations, that is, what tourists can do. Push and pull motives represent the driving force for tourists inside and outside, respectively, and the model is an effective method for studying tourism motivation. Push-pull motivation theory truly combines tourism motivation with the attributes and characteristics of tourism

---

[1] Source: Plog S C. Why Destination Areas Rise and Fall in Popularity[J]. Cornell Hotel and Restaurant Administration Quarterly, 1974, 14(4): 55-58.

[2] Dann G M. Tourist Motivation an Appraisal[J]. Annals of Tourism Research, 1981, 8(2): 187-219.

destinations, and builds a bridge between product demand and product supply, enabling all activities in tourism destinations to be carried out around the needs of tourists. From the perspective of demand, studying the importance of various supply factors in the development of tourism destinations is of great significance for improving product quality, business performance, and tourist satisfaction.

Crompton's research supported the theoretical model of push-pull motivation and further divided push motivation into seven areas: escape, self-exploration, relaxation, prestige, return, relationship with close family and friends, and increased social interaction. He divided pull motivation into two categories: novelty and education. Later, Mannell and Iso-Ahola proposed two main push and pull factors: personal factor and interpersonal factor. They proposed that people's motivation for travel is to get rid of real personal or interpersonal conflicts, and to obtain personal or interpersonal compensation and rewards. The personal rewards brought by tourism mainly include independent decision-making, ability awareness, challenge, learning, adventure, and relaxation, while the interpersonal rewards stem from social interaction. Similar to Dann's tourism motivation theory, the tourism motivation model proposed by Iso-Ahola et al. includes two factors: escaping element and seeking element. Escaping element refers to the desire to leave the everyday environment, while seeking element refers to the desire to obtain an inner psychological reward by traveling to a contrasting environment.

3) Macintosh's Tourism Motivation Theory

American scholars McIntosh and Gupter, in their book *Tourism: Principles, Practices and Philosophies*, divided all people's tourism motivations into four categories: physical health motivation, cultural motivation, social motivation, and status and prestige motivation.

First, physical health motivation includes activities such as rest, exercise, play, therapy. This type of motivation is characterized by physical activity to relieve tension and restlessness. Second, cultural motivation comes from a desire to understand and appreciate foreign cultures, art, customs, languages, and religions. These motivations express a desire to know. Third, social motivation encompasses meeting new friends in different places, visiting relatives and friends, getting rid of daily work, family affairs. This motivation often manifests as boredom and aversion to the familiar, as well as a desire for escape and stress relief. Fourth, status and prestige motivation lead people to engage in study tours, exchanges, conferences, and research that is of personal interest. It is characterized by good interpersonal relationships in the communication of tourism activities in order to meet the needs of self-esteem, be recognized, be noticed, be able to display their talents, achieve goals, and contribute to humanity[①].

4) Tanaka's Tourism Motivation Theory

Japanese scholar Tanaka classified tourism motivations into four categories in *On*

---

①保继刚,楚义芳.旅游地理学[M].3版.北京:高等教育出版社,2012.

Tourism Business, published by the Japan Tourism Research Association in 1950.

First, motivation of mood. For example, homesickness, communication, and faith. Second, physical motivation. For example, treatment needs, maintenance needs, and exercise needs. Third, spiritual motivation. For example, the need for knowledge, informative need, and the need for joy. Fourth, economic motivation. For example, consumption and commercial needs.

4.3 Influencing Factors of Tourism Motivation

Influencing factors of tourism motivation include psychological factors, objective factors and external factors. Psychological factors include personality traits, cultural background, and learning. Objective factors include gender, age, occupation, education level, family structure, population, income, and health condition. Above two categories are both the factors related to the individual tourist, and are the primary and decisive factors that affect tourism motivation. In addition, the third category of influencing factors, i.e., external factors, refers to the various influencing factors outside tourists, including political environment, social culture, economic and technological level.

4.3.1 Psychological Factors

1) Personality Traits

Personality is an individual's inner self-reflection, which refers to the individual psychological characteristics that affect their personal behavior. Personality is usually characterized by the fact that a person's personality determines their personal preferences and thus affects their behavior. Both innate genetic factors and acquired social factors influence personality traits. Jung distinguished four types of personality: sensory thinking type, sensory emotional type, intuitive thinking type and intuitive emotional type. Different personality types show many differences in terms of rationality and sensibility, long-term and short-term, independence and conformity, etc. In the study of tourism motivation, scholars mostly use Plog's tourist personality classification to analyze personality, and tourists are divided into five types: adventurer, near-adventurer, intermediate, near-dependent and dependent. Different types of people show great differences in tourism motivation. The adventurer personality type belongs to allocentric tourists, whose characteristics are cheerful thinking and wide and changeable interests. At the other end of the spectrum are psychocentric dependent tourists, who are characteristically cautious, anxious and not adventurous; their strongest tourism motivation is rest and relaxation. Although Plog's model roughly divides people into these five main types according to personality and psychological characteristics, this division is not absolute. He also affirmed that there is some continuity in people's psychology, which is manifested in the obvious flexibility of people's behavior.

2) Cultural Background

Cultural background refers to a person's long-term cultural accumulation, namely, the sum of an individual's relatively stable value orientation, thinking mode and psychological structure. Culture encompasses enduring beliefs about which modes of conduct and what end-states of existence are preferred among people of a given social group. In cross-cultural studies, cultural background has a particularly strong influence on tourism motivation. Most Chinese tourists prefer destinations with cultural activities and show frugality in tourism consumption. Indian tourists are keen on religious tourism.

3) Learning

Learning is one of the intrinsic driving forces of tourist consumers' purchasing behavior. It refers to the ways that tourists obtain tourism experience. Tourists can learn from their own experiences of traveling in the past, and also from others' introduction of relevant tourism experience. In this learning process, tourists will establish their own views on relevant tourism destinations and tourism products, which will form basic acquisition standards for their future trips when choosing tourism destinations and tourism products.

4.3.2 Objective Factors

1) Gender and Age

In terms of gender, the differences between men and women are reflected in personality, behavior and brain power. Women generally have psychological and emotional characteristics of beauty, place more emphasis on external performance and emotional expression of tourism products, and are easily affected by external factors. Men, on the other hand, pay more attention to the overall experience of tourism services and are more independent in their consumption choices. Due to the different status and role of men and women in family and society, there is a certain degree of difference in their tourism motivation. For example, most men travel for business purposes, while most women travel to shop or to visit relatives. However, the motivation to travel is not static. In the past, men accounted for a larger proportion of tourists, and women accounted for a smaller proportion. With societal progress, women's increased employment, and the reduction of household chores, the proportion of female tourists will gradually increase.

Regarding age, children are naturally active and curious about things, and they tend to travel for entertainment. Young people are full of vitality, keen, and have a spirit of adventure. Because they often find studying and normal life and work to be monotonous and boring, they are an enthusiastic travel group. Middle-aged travelers comprise the main part of the tourism market. They have stable work, good income, and higher requirements regarding tourist facilities. The elderly, especially those who enjoy pensions, have more disposable time and discretionary income, prefer a slow pace of travel, and pay more attention to environmental health and transportation conditions of tourism facilities. It can be seen that people's different travel needs at different ages influence their travel motivation.

2) Occupation and Education Level

Occupation affects one's income and leisure time. Generally speaking, those with high income and relatively free work nature (such as financiers, business owners, senior staff, freelancers, doctors, lawyers, writers, photographers) are more likely to be motivated to travel. At the same time, choice of occupation is closely related to education level. Generally speaking, due to different occupations, there will be differences in income level, nature of work and working mode, etc., and people of different occupations also have great differences in demand for tourism. It can be seen from the occupation composition of foreigners traveling in China that businessmen, administrative personnel, workers, professionals and technical personnel account for a larger proportion of travelers, while farmers and service personnel account for a smaller proportion. The higher the occupational reputation, the greater the number and variety of outdoor recreation activities undertaken.

The improvement of cultural knowledge contributes to the understanding of things in the outside world, thus influencing people's needs and motivations. Level of personal education and accomplishment is obviously related to a person's education level. People with more education have more knowledge and information about the outside world, so they have more interest in the outside world and more enthusiasm to learn about it for themselves. Education also helps people to overcome anxiety and fear of unfamiliar environments. In addition, education level also has an impact on tourism activity preference and shopping consumption level. Generally speaking, the higher the level of education, the stronger the spending power.

3) Family Structure, Population, and Income

In terms of family structure and population, it is easier for elderly empty-nesters (those who leave behind only the elderly after their children become independent) and wealthy retirees to travel. Unmarried single people and "DINK families" tend to have a higher tourism demand. For people with a large family, the burden of life is heavy and their disposable income is relatively small. On the contrary, for people with no children, their disposable income is relatively large. This forms the main difference between different families regarding tourism need. In view of the trend of social development, the average number of families is gradually decreasing. With the decrease of the family-rearing population, the ability to pay for tourism is increasing correspondingly, thus promoting the emergence of tourism motivation. In the context of family tourism, it is necessary to explore the motivations for group travel, because the motivations of family tourists may be mixed, related to family structure and happiness rather than focusing on personal satisfaction. Their tourism motivation is based on the following four factors: family history and sense of belonging, cohesion of immediate relatives, family communication and family adaptability.

People's discretionary income is also closely related to tourism demand. When other factors remain unchanged, the greater people's discretionary income, the greater their demand for tourism products will be. The less discretionary income people have, the less demand there is for tourism products.

4) Health Condition

Whether people are healthy or not is the most basic reason for whether or not they travel. Tourism activities require a certain amount of energy and physical strength. The physical health of tourists is a factor directly affecting tourism motivation. It is difficult for someone who is seriously ill to travel, and people in poor health have to choose relatively short and less time-consuming trips. Due to differences in health status, the demand for tourism is correspondingly different. It is worth noting that with the improvement of people's living standards and the rapid development of medical care technology, people's average life expectancy is increasing and their physical health condition is also improving. In today's society, the proportion of the elderly traveling is much higher than previously, and the tourist group composed of the elderly will continue to grow and become one of the main sources of tourists in the future.

4.3.3 External Factors

1) Political Environment

Politics influences people's tourism motivation in various ways. A stable and orderly political environment is one of the important conditions for ensuring the rapid development of tourism. If the political situation is unstable in a country and there is social unrest and poor public security, both tourists from that country and foreign tourists will bear great psychological pressure, and tourism motivation will not develop, or at least will be difficult to produce. In addition, due to the different political environments of different countries, the motivations of tourists in different countries also have certain differences. For example, from the perspective of family culture and social background, the motivations and travel patterns of Israeli backpackers are characterized by a high degree of collective orientation①. Similar to Japanese backpackers, Israeli backpackers tend to support family and group values. Unlike Japanese backpackers, young Israelis travel to India and other more distant tourist destinations after completing their military service under the influence of state and military policy. They use this travel experience as a stage in the process of reaching a mature self, transitioning from obedience to social norms to an independent and free self. This special cultural background influences the motivation of Israeli backpackers to travel.

---

① Maoz D. Backpackers' Motivations the Role of Culture and Nationality[J]. Annals of Tourism Research, 2007, 34(1): 122-140.

2) Social Culture

With the increasing diversity of social culture, people with different social and cultural backgrounds have different values, attitudes, beliefs, and so on, and their tourism motivations are also bound to be influenced by social culture. Heavy workloads and long working hours are embedded in the Japanese cultural environment, making overseas travel difficult. As a result, Japanese tourists are especially eager for knowledge, enjoyment, and adventure when traveling abroad. As another example, changes in the social and cultural environment have had an important impact on the tourism motivation of the elderly in China. The improvement of Chinese elderly people's living standards has had a direct impact on their health and perception ability; changes in national policies have subtly promoted drastic changes in the social and cultural environment.

3) Economy and Technology Level

The level of economic development is a key factor determining the size of tourism demand. The higher the level of economic development, the stronger the degree of tourism demand. The development of information technology is an important factor in realizing tourism demand. The rapid development of information technology has driven the development of the media industry, providing tourists with comprehensive and well thought out information services and communication channels. At the same time, the development of transportation technology has also met people's long-suppressed travel needs and improved the convenience and comfort of travel.

4.4 Tourism Demand

Need or motivation is a category of psychology. As a kind of social behavior, it is deficient to examine the reasons behind tourist behavior on a purely psychological level. There are barriers between the need for tourism and the realization of tourism. Only by overcoming these obstacles can potential tourism need be turned into realistic tourism demand for both tourists and tourism commodity operators. Tourism demand is an economized concept, and it is a concept that manifests itself with fairly clear characteristics in the tourist purchasing decision-making system. There is a simple and easy to understand example that can help to explain the relationship between tourism demand and tourism need. When people are hungry, they will have a need to eat. If you confront them with two kinds of food that can satisfy their need—thick noodles and steamed bread—then experience will tell them that steamed bread is better than thick noodles. So they have a desire for steamed bread. However, unfortunately, it may be the case that they have no money and can only afford to buy thick noodles, so their demand can only be for thick noodles. In fact, even if people want to travel, they will inevitably face such economic constraints. Therefore, in order to better understand the full picture of the causes of tourism, this section presents the concept of tourism demand.

4.4.1 Definition of Tourism Demand

According to the point of view of general economics, demand refers to the relationship between the various possible prices of a commodity during a certain period of time and the quantity that consumers are willing and able to buy at these price levels. Obviously, the demand here is not equal to the demanded quantity, but refers to the relationship between the price and the demanded quantity. Demanded quantity refers to the quantity of a commodity that people are willing and able to buy at a given price. In the case of a certain demand, the demanded quantity can change with the change of the price. On the contrary, sometimes even if the price is fixed, as long as other factors change, the demand will change, and then the demanded quantity will change. Therefore, in general, the change in the demanded quantity due to the change in the price of a commodity itself (called the change in demanded quantity) is different from the change in the demanded quantity due to other factors (called the change in demand).

From this, a definition of tourism demand can be derived. Tourism demand refers to the relationship between the various possible prices of tourism products and the quantity that potential tourists are willing and able to purchase at these price levels during a certain period of time. The tourism demanded quantity refers to the quantity of a certain tourism product that people are willing to buy at a certain price during a certain period of time.

4.4.2 Influencing Factors of Tourism Demand

Tourism demand is the result of the interaction of many complex factors, which can be represented by the following functional relationship:

$$D_t = f(P_t, P_i, Y, T, L)$$

In this functional relationship, D_t is tourism demand, P_t is the price of tourism products, P_i is the price of other goods, Y is personal income, T is personal interest (preference), and L is leisure. The mathematical expression used to reflect the changes in tourism demanded quantity caused by changes in various factors is the tourism demand function.

Among the many factors that affect tourism demand, personal income and tourism product price are two very important factors. Generally speaking, with the growth of personal income, tourism demand is likely to increase accordingly, and with the increase in the price of tourism products, tourism demand is likely to decrease accordingly. However, in real life, the relationship between tourism demand and tourism product price and personal income is actually quite complex, and in-depth analysis is required to properly understand this relationship. For example, in terms of demand elasticity alone, price elasticity and income elasticity show different tendencies. A growing body of research seems to show that tourism demand is actually growing faster than national income. For example, tourism spending in Western countries was remarkably firm in the depression following the oil crisis of the 1970s. This seems to suggest that tourism demand is relatively income-elastic and price-rigid in the upward direction; that is, any proportional increase in income will result in a faster increase in tourism demand, and an increase in prices will not be matched by a proportional decrease in demand. In the direction of decline, tourism demand appears to be income-rigid and price-elastic; that is, if income is reduced, tourism demand is not correspondingly weak, and a slight drop in prices leads to more growth in tourism demand.

4.4.3 Objective Obstacles to Realizing Tourism Demand

When we talk about tourism demand, we generally refer to the actual effective demand, which is a realistic combination of sufficient tourism purchasing power and a clear purchasing tendency (tourism preference). If there are no other objective barriers, this combination can immediately lead to the purchase of tourism commodities. However, there are many people who have money and aspire to travel but fail to do so. Why? The obvious answer is that they do not possess the other conditions necessary to engage in the special activity of tourism: leisure, health, freedom, acceptance of what certain tourism experiences can offer, and so on. Although these conditions may not constitute the driving force of tourism when they are present, they may constitute resistance to tourism if they are not present.

1) Space Barrier

Tourism is an off-site behavior. Although the spatial distance from the place of residence to the tourist destination may fundamentally be the source of the value of the tourist attraction, it may also be a real obstacle faced by potential tourists. The larger the space span, the greater the natural and cultural differences between the two places, which will make tourists feel uneasy. A larger space span also means that tourists must achieve a larger scale of spatial movement, which will inevitably lead to longer travel times. In many cases, the time is too long and the travel costs are too high for many to bear. Although the development of modern transportation means provides new opportunities in this regard, the spatial barriers faced by tourists will never be completely eliminated.

2) Time Constraints

The occurrence of tourism depends on the time blocks that people can freely use, such as weekly leisure, public holidays, and paid holidays. In no society will the distribution of free time be equal. Therefore, for some people, lack of free time is a stumbling block for their travel. In addition, as humans are social individuals, the distribution pattern of the free time that each individual has is not determined autonomously. Thus, this free time is of little significance if the pattern appears to be different from the time required for some form of tourism. Therefore, only when there is more free time and it is evenly distributed throughout the year can tourism as a leisure method be effectively used to relieve people's sense of fatigue.

3) Cultural Differences

The famous British anthropologist B. J. Malinowski said: "Culture refers to that group of traditional artifacts, goods, techniques, ideas, habits and values." It is a phenomenon shared by a certain group or society, and often shows obvious differences with cultures of other groups or societies, thus forming the so-called cultural cluster, cultural group, or cultural circle. For tourists, to a large extent, traveling to a foreign country is motivated by a desire to experience certain cultural differences. However, if two cultures are irreconcilably opposed, or if communication barriers in terms of language, social norms, social systems, etc., exist between them, it will be difficult for the kind of tourism that tends towards culture to occur, and tourism demand will be curbed. In real life, this kind of cultural separation caused by people living in different cultural circles exists objectively, and constitutes a resistance to tourism under certain circumstances.

4) Physical and Mental Disabilities

Tourism can make people happy and facilitate the recovery and development of physical and psychological functions. Unfortunately, however, it often in turn requires that tourists are physically and mentally sound. People who are physically weak cannot go far, and those who are empty-minded cannot understand experiences deeply. It is difficult for these people to experience the real charm of travel. Many studies have shown that tourists' educational level directly affects their travel ability and orientation. The higher the education level, the higher the income level, the stronger the tourism ability, and the greater the interest in social and cultural tourism. This also means that the low level of understanding caused by insufficient education in turn becomes an obstacle to participating in social tourism. Even for natural sightseeing tourism, the level of aesthetic ability is a very key factor affecting tourism demand.

Chapter Summary

This chapter introduces an important factor of tourism consumer behavior, i.e., tourism motivation. The classification of need and three important theories of tourism need are discussed, such as Gray's wanderlust and sunlust, Travel career ladder theory, and Ryan's classification of tourism needs. Four commonly used motivation theories focusing on tourism are interpreted: Plog's tourism motivation theory, Dann's tourism motivation theory, Macintosh's tourism motivation theory, and Tanaka's tourism motivation theory. Influencing factors of tourism motivation have been discussed. Finally, the tourism demand is introduced. Several cases have been discussed about the application of tourism motivation knowledge in tourism marketing industry, such as backpacking tourism and senior tourism.

China Story

Development and Promotion of Educational Tourism Product

Exercises

Recommended Reading

Issues for Review and Discussion

1. For tourism, as a kind of psychological demand, luxury demand and prestige demand, the relationship between demand and price is different than with general consumer goods. There is a certain price threshold at which the relationship between the two changes direction. Below the critical point, the quantity demanded will increase as the price rises; above the critical point, the quantity demanded will decrease if the price continues to rise. If the price of a very famous tourist attraction, such as the Forbidden City, suddenly drops a lot compared to before, how will the demand change?

2. With reference to Plog's tourism motivation theory, discuss the personality characteristics and corresponding tourism behaviors of tourists with different personality types in the context of modern tourism.

3. Revisiting is a topic that is often discussed when people talk about travel. Please speak about one of your revisit experiences. It could be to a city or even a scenic spot. Considering the conditions of tourism motivation and Dann's theory of tourism motivation, analyze the possible patterns of tourists' revisit motivation.

Chapter 5
Attitude and Emotion

Learning Objectives

After reading this chapter, you should have a good understanding of:

(1) what attitudes are, how they are formed, and their role in tourists behavior;

(2) the multiattribute attitude model, the ABC attitude model, and the theory of plan behaviors, and their applications;

(3) the components of tourists' attitudes by perceiving the tourism products' features;

(4) the various types of tourists and tourism attitudes;

(5) what tourists' emotions are, and how they influence destination marketing;

(6) the various types of tourists' emotions;

(7) the cognitive appraisal theory in tourism and its applications.

Technical Words

English Words	中文翻译
multiattribute	多属性
theory of planned behavior	计划行为理论
cultural heritage	文化遗产
the emotion of awe	敬畏情绪
place attachment	地方依恋
World Tourism Organization	世界旅游组织
cognitive appraisal theory	认知评价理论

Knowledge Graph

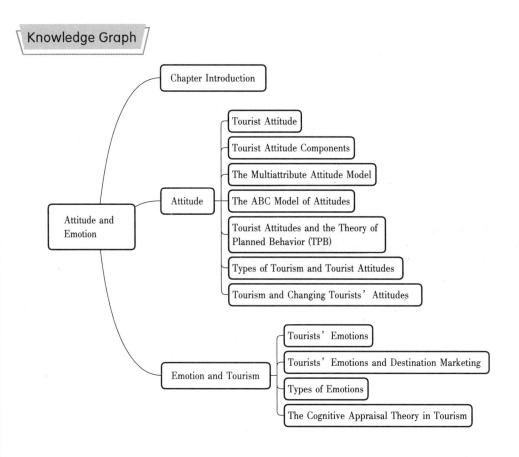

5.1 Chapter Introduction

People have opinions about virtually everything, including clothing, music and food, to name a few. A person's evaluation, feelings, and disposition toward a certain thing or idea are all components of his/her attitude toward that thing or notion. Individuals are put in the mental state of liking or disliking objects, and moving toward or away from them, depending on their attitudes. The study of consumer opinions toward a tourism product can be advantageous for businesses. Meanwhile, emotions are also an integral aspect of our daily lives and play a significant role in our personal and societal growth.

In the context of tourism, travelers are frequently exposed to novel experiences; as the stimuli change, so does the travelers' psychology, and they may experience positive or negative emotions such as happiness, excitement, sadness, regret, among others. These feelings are not only an integral element of the tourists' experience, but also have a substantial effect on their motivation, satisfaction, behavioral intentions and interpersonal interactions. Many of the individual qualities and forces that influence the behavior of travelers have now been identified. The decisions that travelers make are shaped by the interplay of a variety of elements, including those that are cultural, social, personal and psychological. Even though many of these elements are beyond the control of marketers, they can assist marketers in better comprehending client reactions and behavior.

5.2 Attitude

5.2.1 Tourist Attitude

Attitude is the most distinctive and indispensable concept in social psychology, with various definitions and theories of evolution. In the field of tourism, attitude usually determines a tourist's choices, which is one of the most important concepts in understanding tourist behavior.

Attitude is a psychological factor in tourism consumption behavior that is a large determinant of the direction of tourism behavior activities and has a guiding and motivating influence on tourism decisions. Attitude is the basis of tourism motivation and the source of tourism behavior, so it is essential to analyze tourists' attitudes. Attitude is the tendency to react to people, ideas, and concepts in a particular way, and it is expressed through words, expressions, and actions. The more certain a tourist's attitude is toward a tourism product, the greater the likelihood that the tourism consumption behavior will occur.

Attitude evolves as a result of wish fulfillment. When a person's affective and cognitive components are in equilibrium, his/her attitudes tend to be stable, but when they are more inconsistent than the individual's current tolerance of such inconsistency, the person's attitudes will be unstable and will undergo restructuring activities. A person's attitudes may also vary in terms of duration and intensity. Reciprocal reinforcement can occur within an attitude structure, which is a set of attitudes regarding a class of related objects, and reinforcement may lead to the awareness that others share the same attitudes. In addition, certain situations can enhance attitude stability.

A tourist's reaction to a destination may differ from another person's, due to inhibiting variables. Uncertainty, caution, or hesitancy can also be shown in holiday behavior. Some hurdles to positive attitudes include income dissonance and other limiting constraints, such as the influence of others on one's behavior. The advantages that people believe they will receive from traveling influence their preferences. When picking a vacation spot, vacationers carefully analyze the many combinations of perks that are available to them at each potential location, and their judgment can result in a desire to purchase a destination. Thus, one can influence a traveler's selection by emphasizing one or more unique advantages. The overall appeal of a destination will be determined by how interesting the person considering it believes the location to be.

5.2.2 Tourist Attitude Components

In the field of tourism, attitudes are tourists' feelings regarding a holiday destination or service that are based on numerous perceived product features. These feelings can be positive or negative. It is generally agreed that attitudes can be broken down into three categories: cognitive, affective and behavioral. The cognitive component, which may also be referred to as the belief or knowledge component, is made up of the evidence-based views and opinions that an individual has regarding a certain topic (a destination, an experience, or another person). The emotive component refers to a person's feelings and emotions in relation to a location or service, meaning that evaluations are made on the basis of those sentiments. The propensity to act, which can be either positive or negative, is known as the behavioral component.

1) The Cognitive Component

The cognitive component of a tourist's attitude consists of the visitor's knowledge and beliefs about the destination, it is an action guide, and it is the antecedent of the behavioral component. This element describes how and why a visitor's knowledge and emotions influence his/her choice of a tourism location. The cognitive component is created when the destination selection is finalized and a choice is made. The cognitive and behavioral components also convey the subjective associations that visitors have with a place, and the cognitive component describes the ideal future situation—return visits, recommendations and positive word-of-mouth. In addition to one's personal experience as a primary source, the opinions of other visitors conveyed by word-of-mouth are the most important secondary sources from which decisions can be made.

2) The Affective Component

The affective component of attitude is the evaluation of a location on an emotional level, which has a significant impact on tourist satisfaction, decision-making and behavior. Russell and Pratt constructed a spatial model of eight adjectives characterizing the components of the affective image, categorizing them as either positive (enthusiastic, aroused, pleasant and calm) or negative (sleepy, distressed, unpleasant and gloomy)[①]. The affective component is strongly tied to the notion of difference, which incorporates value-based responses about whether or not to conform to a preconceived image of a destination. This affective interpretation of a place is intimately tied to the conceptual component of the image and consequently affects tourist behavior and decision-making, destination selection, and visitor experience satisfaction.

---

① Russell J A, Pratt G. A Description of the Affective Quality Attributed to Environments[J]. Journal of Personality and Social Psychology, 1980, 38(2): 311.

3) The Behavioral Component

The behavioral component comprises anticipations of forms of behavior in particular contexts, and it can be operationalized as an action option. Behavioral intentions always refer to future behavior and are frequently linked to overall behavior. The behavioral component is described as a tourist's willingness or desire to revisit a destination or to recommend it to others. Therefore, the term "behavioral intention" refers to the tourist's future tendency/behavior after having visited a tourist destination. The attitude theory of Bagozzi posits that evaluations generate emotions that then impact an individual's behavior, and it portrays cognition, appraisal, emotional reaction, and behavior as occurring on a continuum[①].

5.2.3 The Multiattribute Attitude Model

Ajzen and Fishbein created a multiattribute attitude model that describes an individual's preference for an object as a consequence of the person's perception of the relevance and product features of that object[②]. A multiattribute destination is a set of traits that result in varying costs and advantages of desirability for different persons or market sectors. Individuals' perceptions (beliefs) regarding the extent to which certain items exhibit specific traits, weighted by the salience (importance) of each attribute to the individual, are believed to convey overall mood. The paradigm assumes that attitudes are determined by cognitive and affective elements—that is, by the relative importance of material and immaterial causes.

This multiattribute model is based on the individual's appraisal of available options. The choice behavior of a subject is determined by the subject's judgment of the expected benefit or loss from that behavior. Positive traits can compensate for negative ones, for example reinforcing the notion that buyers select a resort based on a combination of characteristics rather than a single one. In other words, a visitor may think that a resort has a particular characteristic, but if that feature is not significant to the visitor, it is irrelevant. The model is articulated as follows:

$$A_0 = \sum_{i=1}^{n} B_i a_i,$$

where A_0 = attitude towards the object;
B_i = the strength of the belief that the object has attribute i;
a_i = the evaluation of attribute i;
n = the number of attributes salient beliefs about the object

Further Reading

Application of Multiattribute Attitude Models

---

① Bagozzi R P. The Self-Regulation of Attitudes, Intentions, and Behavior[J]. Social Psychology Quarterly, 1992, 55(2): 178-204.

② Ajzen I, Fishbein M. Attitude-behavior Relations: A Theoretical Analysis and Review of Empirical Research[J]. Psychological Bulletin, 1977, 84(5): 888.

5.2.4 The ABC Model of Attitudes

The affect, behavior, and cognition (ABC) model of attitudes[①] was presented by Baron et al. This model states that attitudes are composed of three components: affect, behavior and cognition, and that attitudes are formed as a result of the interplay among these three components. In this model, a person's affective responses to an attitude object are referred to as the person's feelings or emotions; a person's behavioral responses to an attitude object are referred to as the person's mental readiness to respond to the attitude object, and they refer to his/her intention to act or react; and a person's cognitive responses to an attitude object are referred to as the person's thoughts, beliefs, or knowledge regarding the attitude object, which can include responses to both external stimuli and internal needs. A person's cognition relates to his/her thoughts and beliefs. For instance, a person may initially create a belief about the attitude object (cognition), and follow that by forming personal feelings regarding the attitude object (affect), and ultimately, by forming personal behavior in relation to the attitude object (behavior). The perceptions that the person holds determine his or her formation of beliefs. Perception is fundamentally a cognitive activity that seeks to make sense of the sensory data received.

The ABC model of Attitudes can be used to study the attitudes of tourists and the interrelationships between those attitudes, and thus to gain a better understanding of the mechanisms that shape tourists' attitudes. Because attitude subjects' degrees of motivation toward the attitude object vary, the three attitude components may be weighted differently during the attitude creation process. The process of developing an attitude involves three distinct tiers of influence: the standard learning level, which is predicated on the processing of cognitive information (the cognitive-affective-behavioral intention), the low-intervention level, which is predicated on the processes of behavioral learning (the behavioral-intentional-emotional behavioral intention), and the hegemonic experience level (the emotional-behavioral-cognitive intention).

On the basis of their feelings regarding the available choices, individuals then establish their behavioral intentions to choose, such as when purchasing a travel product. Individuals in the experience level have limited knowledge of the possibilities and only have a general comprehension of the options. They base their decisions on external factors (such as the advertising), and the experiences that they have after making a purchase decision tend to reinforce their preconceptions. The effects of the three levels of the ABC model of attitudes are caused primarily by the degree to which individuals are involved in the decision-making process, or, more specifically, those effects are caused by differences in the amount of time and effort individuals invest in collecting and processing relevant information for a decision. When relevant information is acquired during the process of tourists' decision-making, the order of interaction between the cognitive, affective, and

---

①Baron R A, Byrne D, Watson G. Exploring Social Psychology[M]. Boston: Allyn & Bacon, 2001.

behaviorally purposeful parts of the tourist attitude formation process shifts, because decision-making is an iterative process. A person's level of involvement is frequently proportional to the significance or impact of the decision-making behavior on the individual. When the decision-making behavior is vital to the tourism experience and travel cost, the individual is more invested in it.

5.2.5 Tourist Attitudes and the Theory of Planned Behavior (TPB)

The theory of planned behavior (TPB) considers humans to be rational and, as a result, it is frequently employed as a central framework for analyzing rational consumer behavior. According to this hypothesis, a person's attitudes, subjective norms, and perceived behavioral control determine that individual's intents. Ajzen defined subjective norms as "perceived social pressure to perform or not perform an act"[1]. Perceived behavioral control is defined as an individual's perception of the ease or difficulty of performing an act.

The theory of planned behavior states that behavioral intentions are shaped by those three conceptual factors. Individuals believe, first, that the behavior will lead to a useful purpose; second, that other people approve of the behavior and its value; and third, that they have the resources, ability, and plans to carry out the behavior. The belief that the behavior will lead to a useful purpose is the most important factor. The most important component that defines aim is one's attitude. A person's attitude toward an activity is the extent to which he or she perceives the performance of a certain behavior will be positive or negative. When the consequence of certain conduct is judged positively, individuals tend to have positive attitudes; in this situation, a person is likely to have a strong attitude toward performing the behavior.

Attitudes are positive or negative value dispositions that a person acquires via learning and experience, and that influence the individual to respond and behave consistently toward clearly defined goals, such as the purchase of a product or a visit to a specific location. In the context of tourism, attitudes refer to tourists' dispositions or feelings[2]. People's perceptions about an object typically shape their attitudes toward it. A person develops his/her own set of beliefs when coming to the realization that aspects of each belief in the belief set are linked to specific outcomes. As a result, the subjective value of the outcome influences the creation of attitudes to a degree that is directly proportional to the degree to which the belief is maintained. Attitudes are positive or negative value dispositions that a person acquires via learning and experience to react and behave consistently toward predefined goals, such as the purchase of a product or a visit to a specific location. In the field of tourism, an attitude is a disposition or feeling toward a

Further Reading

The Theory of Planned Behavior in Rural Tourism

---

①Ajzen I. The Theory of Planned Behavior[J]. Organizational Behavior and Human Decision Processes, 1991, 50(2): 179-211.

②Moutinho L. Consumer Behaviour in Tourism[J]. European Journal of Marketing, 1987, 21(10):1-44.

place or service, and it is based on the perception of many product features. Attitudes can be positive or negative. Specifically, tourists' attitudes are determined by the complete benefits that tourism provides to the tourist—the greater the benefits, the more positive the tourists' attitudes.

Individuals view subjective norms as social referents, and such norms are a second predictor of individuals' intentions. Subjective norms are a person's impression of a social referent, or a behavior that others believe he/she should or should not perform. These norms are based on the beliefs of those around the person. An individual's opinions, attitudes, and choices can be significantly influenced by anyone who serves as a reference group, because individuals always base their evaluations on those of a certain group. When a person is engaging in a certain behavior, the person may consider the opinions of others (such as friends, family members and coworkers) and adhere to those opinions. People always use groups as their standard of judgment, and anyone who acts as a reference group can have a significant impact on an individual's beliefs, attitudes and decisions. Thus, subjective norms are normative beliefs about what influential people think they should do, based on the rationale that people always use groups as their standard of judgment. In other words, in tourism, subjective norms are determined by others' subjective perceptions of visitors' behavior, and favorable evaluations assist tourists' tourism behavior.

The perception of behavioral control has a nonvolitional dimension and refers to a person's confidence in his/her capacity to accomplish a specific behavior. In general, whether an individual has sufficient resources and opportunity to conduct a certain behavior is the primary factor that determines the intensity of that individual's desire to engage in that behavior. It is believed that significant components in the formation of an individual's perceived behavioral control include the individual's judgments about the (un) availability of resources (also known as "control beliefs"), as well as his/her assessments of the results of those resources (also known as "perceived competence").

The chance of behavioral achievement can be influenced by several resources and opportunities, including facilitators, the context of the opportunity, available resources and control of action. Incorporating the actor's perceived level of behavioral control can provide information about the actor's perception of probable action restrictions. A traveler's degree of control over a tourism behavior is determined by the traveler's belief in the behavior's attainability; the greater the traveler's confidence is in the attainability of the behavior, the greater the person's control over the tourism behavior is and the greater the likelihood is that the traveler will engage in that tourism behavior.

Behavioral intention is an individual's expectation of a particular behavior in each situation, and it can be operationalized as a probability of action. Although behavioral intention can be described as an individual's attempt or purpose to perform a particular behavior, it signifies an individual's expectation of a particular behavior in each situation. The TPB paradigm states that an individual's behavioral intentions are a product of his/her attitudes, subjective norms and perceived behavioral control, and the planned behavior theory has been the basis for a significant amount of research on destination choice intentions. Indeed, the TPB is well-suited to explaining and forecasting the travel decisions of destination visitors. Therefore, an examination of tourists' attitudes enables a more precise identification of target markets and a more thorough examination of tourists' needs and ability to satisfy their needs. Tourism behavior intentions can be anticipated on the basis of tourists' attitudes and their subjective norms for behavior, which are highly connected to observable behavior. In general, visitors' attitudes, their subjective norms, and their perceived behavioral control are relatively important predictors of tourism intentions. Moreover, tourism intentions and perceived behavioral control are relatively important predictors of tourism behaviors—although the production of tourism behaviors can vary across populations. Thus, some studies have revealed that attitudes about tourism have a major impact on travel intentions, whereas others have found that attitudes and perceived behavioral control influence tourist intentions simultaneously. According to the TPB model (figure 5.1), people's behavioral intentions are the outcome of their attitudes, subjective norms, and perception of behavioral control.

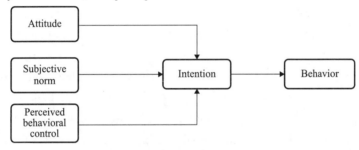

Figure 5.1　Theory of planned behavior (TPB)

5.2.6 Types of Tourism and Tourist Attitudes

1) Tourist Attitudes toward the Environment

Environmental attitudes are a collection of beliefs, feelings, and behavioral intentions related to a person's environmental behavior, and usually refer to the attitude that individuals hold toward the environment and environmental issues. Individuals' environmental knowledge can significantly influence their environmental awareness and environmental attitudes, and that increased environmental knowledge can stimulate positive environmental attitudes. Environmental attitudes influence an individual's behavioral tendencies toward the environment, and they play a role in predicting environmental behavior. Furthermore, one's attitudes toward nature and resource use will influence one's choice of tourist destinations, so environmental attitudes are increasingly being integrated into tourism research.

Environmental attitudes are an individual's evaluative position toward a particular object or environment and are a significant predictor of environmental behavior. Environmental attitudes are regarded as psychological dispositions that are characterized by cognitive and emotive judgments of environmental activities or issues. Dunlap and Van

Liere developed the New Environmental Paradigm scale by employing a three-structure scale in their research (i.e., the balance of nature, limits to growth and human domination of nature)①. Fairweather et al. expanded upon the New Environmental Paradigm to investigate the environmental perspectives held by travelers in general, and their endpoints consider both the biocentric point of view and the anthropocentric point of view, in order to gauge people's thoughts on striking a healthy balance between human endeavors and the preservation of the natural world②. Fairweather et al. identified three types of groups of visitors to New Zealand: those with biocentric values toward nature, those with ambiguous values toward nature, and those with anthropocentric values toward nature, each with very different attitudes toward the environment. For instance, the biocentric segment favored the use of ecolabels and was willing to pay more for environmentally friendly accommodations. The anthropocentric segment, on the other hand, viewed humans as the primary cause of environmental problems and viewed anthropocentrism as the solution. Therefore, general perceptions of resource management practices and ecologically responsible behavior are important indicators of whether visitors care about the environment—that is, whether they hold pro-environmental attitudes and support resource management techniques.

Another important indicator of whether visitors care about the environment is whether they engage in environmentally responsible behavior. The logical conclusion that can be drawn from this line of reasoning is that those tourists who are found to be environmentally aware tend to be committed to taking action to protect the environment, whereas those tourists who are found to be less environmentally aware are more likely to believe that environmental problems will solve themselves on their own. How tourists feel about the environment can have a significant influence on how they vacation. For instance, vacationers who have a favorable attitude toward the natural world are more likely to conduct ecologically friendly behaviors than those who have a neutral or negative attitude toward the natural environment. Interestingly, current research has also found that tourists' positive, proactive environmental attitudes significantly stimulate their preference for hotels that are ecologically responsible, and that such tourists are willing to pay more for green hotels.

Pro-environment views are essential in molding tourists' eco-friendly behavior. However, these views and behaviors are not carved in stone; they are impacted by specific environmental forces, such as the tourists' moral beliefs, their obedience to the law and their political engagement. These characteristics exert a greater effect in establishing eco-

---

① Dunlap R E, Van Liere K D. The "New Environmental Paradigm"[J]. The Journal of Environmental Education, 1978, 9(4): 10-19.

② Fairweather J R, Maslin C, Simmons D G. Environmental Values and Response to Ecolabels among International Visitors to New Zealand[J]. Journal of Sustainable Tourism, 2005, 13(1): 82-98.

friendly views among tourists who are female, and are relatively older, better educated, and have higher incomes. It has been found that visitors who exhibited eco-friendly behavior were also more satisfied with their behavior.

On the tourism sector side, marketing managers should first study the background characteristics of their targets for tourism (i.e., their moral standing, legal compliance, political activity) and should attempt to tailor their company's offerings to the tourists' eco-friendly attitude. It is also essential to segment visitors according to their sociodemographic features and to give special attention to women, the elderly and the educated, who are more sensitive to environmental concerns. Visitors of various nationalities must also be considered, thus necessitating the modification of marketing methods. Through appropriate education, communication, and other programs, government organizations should seek to promote the eco-friendliness of their country as tourism destinations. Efforts also need to be made to maintain the biophysical environment of tourism destinations, such as by tightening environmental regulations, setting green standards for enterprises associated with tourism, and applying strategies for sustainable development.

2) Tourist Attitudes toward Cultural Heritage Tourism

Cultural heritage tourism often includes a process of reconceptualization of the self, society and culture by the tourist, and therefore the tourist's attitude toward cultural heritage becomes a concern. Tourists' personal attitudes toward cultural heritage affect their actual experience of cultural heritage tourism and determine their specific behaviors in cultural heritage tourism.

Cultural heritage is often seen as a pull factor in attracting tourists, whereas tourists' positive attitudes toward cultural heritage are seen as a push factor. It has been suggested that tourists who are interested in cultural tourism hold more positive attitudes toward visiting cultural heritage destinations, and therefore, tourists' attitudes toward visiting cultural heritage sites are positively influenced by their cultural tourism involvement. Attitudes usually reflect an individual's perceived evaluation of an object and form the person's initial expected value before acting on it, so the perceived authenticity of cultural heritage can be influenced by a tourist's attitude toward visiting. Furthermore, travelers' attitudes are related to their travel experiences before, during and after the trip. Attitudes act as an important influence on individuals' behavioral intentions, and as attitudes increase positively, individuals' intentions toward their behavior become stronger. Therefore, tourists' attitudes toward visiting a World Heritage Site can influence their loyalty toward visiting a World Heritage Site. Attitudes play an important role in predicting individual loyalty[①].

The cultural heritage attitudes held by tourists and their cultural-heritage-

---

① Yoon Y, Uysal M. An Examination of the Effects of Motivation and Satisfaction on Destination Loyalty: A Structural Model[J]. Tourism Management, 2005, 26(1): 45-56.

conservation behaviors are crucial to the sustainability of cultural heritage tourism. As subjects of cultural heritage tourism activities, those tourists who see cultural heritage as their personal heritage generate tourism behaviors that clearly distinguish them from other tourists. According to the notion of component composition of attitudes—the cognitive components, affective components and behavioral intentions—all three are highly correlated and thus form a complex system of attitudes, which are related to behavior when the cognitive component is aligned with the affective component. For example, it has been suggested that tourists first recognize the importance of cultural heritage for social development and the cultural identity of future generations (the cognitive component), and at the same time they develop a strong identity and emotional identification with cultural heritage (the affective component), thus achieving a congruence between the cognitive and affective components, and that in turn leads to a behavioral tendency to preserve heritage. The process often ultimately manifests itself in concrete acts of heritage conservation.

3) Residents' Attitudes

The attitudes of individuals are a function of the numerous benefits and costs involved with tourism—that is, attitudes are a function of the outcomes related to tourism development. Thus, sustainable community tourism development has arisen as an alternate management strategy. Residents play a significant part in the paradigm of sustainable development, of course, making it is essential to comprehend and evaluate their thoughts and attitudes toward tourism development. Experiences strengthen people's attitudes, which are strongly tied to their values and personalities. Maintaining a degree of support and engagement necessitates monitoring the reactions of locals to tourists, as sentiments do not change rapidly. If locals dislike or fear tourism, their resistance and antagonism can impede the growth of the local economy. Understanding their perspectives on tourism policy is therefore an integral aspect of the process of planning for sustainability and is a crucial indication of the future success of local tourist development.

Tourism contributes to revenue generation, job creation and diversification of the local economy. Indeed, tourism has been a significant contributor to local economic growth and foreign exchange for decades. That said, there is also emerging evidence that mass tourism can have detrimental effects on host communities, including residents' daily life, notwithstanding the benefits that tourism provides. Cultural and ecological resources have been negatively impacted by unplanned, rapid development and a large tourist population. Tourism's actual contribution to development plans has been increasingly criticized due to its relatively few genuine benefits, unequal distribution of benefits and hefty social costs. Empirical data have revealed that the impacts of tourism development on host communities are varied, and analyses of social concerns linked with rapidly expanding communities, such as resort towns, now focus on residents' interpretations of situations and changes that may exist in the impacted communities. Some governments are coming to realize that the public good must be considered alongside the needs of tourists and investors.

Indeed, residents are the most important stakeholders in the tourism development process, regardless of their vocation, because they are immediately impacted by tourism. Local attitudes toward tourism and evaluations of tourism's impact on their communities must be continuously evaluated. For tourism-based economies in local communities to be sustainable, citizens must also be willing to engage in the process. In addition, ecotourism, green tourism and sustainable tourism have been utilized to make tourism more environmentally friendly and reduce dissatisfaction among residents. "Tourism that meets the expectations of present visitors and host communities while protecting and developing future prospects" is the definition of "sustainable tourism" (World Tourism Organization). Sustainable tourism is a unique kind of tourism that improves the quality of life of host communities, provides a high-quality experience for visitors, and protects the host communities and the quality of the environment on which tourists depend. In other words, sustainable tourism improves the quality of life of the communities that are hosting tourists, while it also provides a high-quality experience for visitors. The goal of sustainable tourism is to maximize the positive effects of tourism on the local culture and natural environment while minimizing its adverse effects on the local population. A detailed analysis of the impacts of tourism can assist government planners, local policymakers and tourism promoters in identifying real concerns and issues for the development and implementation of suitable policies and actions.

Because the perspectives of locals on tourism have a sizeable bearing on the expansion of the industry, the residents' general disposition is an important factor for helping predict how well the industry will do. By gaining an understanding of residents' feelings, decision-makers and those responsible for the development of destinations can more correctly evaluate how the community feels about tourism expansion. Therefore, it essential to have a technique that can measure residents' attitudes toward the development of tourism. Choi and Sirakaya developed a scale to measure locals' attitudes toward sustainable tourism (SUS-TAS)①, and they tweaked it so that it could also measure attitudes toward the notion of sustainable development. Seven factor domains were determined during the process of constructing the SUS-TAS:

① perceived social costs (minimization of negative sociocultural impacts);

② environmental sustainability (conservation of physical and man-made resources, ethics, policies, and standards as well as minimization of negative impacts);

③ long-term planning (integrated, long-term participation);

④ perceived economic benefits (optimization of economic benefits);

⑤ a community-centered economy (benefits for residents in terms of access to recreational facilities, community reinvestment fund, a locals-first policy, promotion of local businesses and local participation);

---

① Choi H S C, Sirakaya E. Measuring Residents' Attitude toward Sustainable Tourism: Development of Sustainable Tourism Attitude Scale[J]. Journal of Travel Research, 2005, 43(4): 380-394.

⑥ ensuring visitor satisfaction (visitor satisfaction, maintaining the attractiveness of the destination);

⑦ maximum community involvement (leadership role, active participation, involvement in decision-making, cooperation, information and communication).

This scale has contributed to gaining a better grasp of the perspectives held by locals on the expansion of tourism.

5.2.7 Tourism and Changing Tourists' Attitudes

Understanding people's attitudes is the initial step toward altering or enhancing them, and changing attitudes is challenging. The attitude of a person conforms to a pattern, and altering that pattern can involve numerous difficult modifications. It is easier for a corporation to design items that align with existing beliefs than it is to alter those opinions, although there are instances in which the great expense of attempting to alter attitudes can be worthwhile.

Although it is difficult to alter an individual's attitude, Allport asserted that in some instances prejudice might be lessened by establishing connections between groups[1]. It is likely to be extremely challenging to create in the tourism industry the conditions that Allport described, but even so, tourism effectively contributes to world peace by bringing people of all cultures and ethnicities together and reducing preconceptions and stereotypes. Furthermore, D'Amore developed the idea that tourism might bridge psychological and cultural divides between individuals and promote an appreciation for the diversity of the world[2]. The primary argument is that the millions of human contacts that occur every day between tourists and hosts can foster the sensitivity and understanding required to improve global relations among individuals, groups, and even governments. The time spent at destinations, the quantity of activities, the purpose of the visits, visitors' contentment with their vacations, the locations' attributes, the cultural distances, the languages, and the intensity of prevacation attitudes all can influence attitude change in the tourism industry. Tourism is not simply an industry with economic impacts, it is also a tool for fostering social connections. Tourism is an enlightening experience which teaches us all that the world is not composed of just a single way of living and that there are alternative ways of life.

Several studies have sought to explore the changes in attitude caused by interactions between tourists and hosts. When two cultures come into contact, equality between the host and the guest is one of the most important components for both parties to attain a pleasant outcome. The contact theory explains cross-cultural contact and interaction between visitors and hosts. This theory posits that intercultural contact creates a chance for mutual awareness, which can ultimately increase mutual understanding and acceptance

---

[1] Allport F H. The Structuring of Events: Outline of a General Theory with Applications to Psychology[J]. Psychological Review, 1954, 61(5): 281.

[2] D'Amore L J. Tourism—A Vital Force for Peace[J]. Tourism Management, 1988, 9(2): 151-154.

while also decreasing prejudice, conflict, and friction between groups. However, initial contact alone does not inevitably result in a favorable intercultural encounter, as other elements frequently influence the interaction's environment.

In‑depth tourism experiences have an undeniably favorable effect on visitors' perceptions of the host nation. Positive results of attitude change identified through intergroup social contact include the promotion of mutual understanding, an increase in empathy for the outgroup, improved intergroup relations through the elimination of prejudices and stereotypes, and a decrease in negative feelings toward the outgroup. Interestingly, solo visitors may be more effective at reducing bias, whereas the limited contact that groups of tourists have with the local populace on organized tours, the consequent attitude shifts may be minor. Furthermore, the frequency of contact with locals and the number of trips are effective factors for altering perceptions.

Once tourists' attitudes toward a location have been developed, they initially exhibit a certain consistency (in terms of the attractiveness of the destination) that first and foremost depends substantially on "innate information". The influence of innate knowledge on the views of tourists is therefore exceedingly ambiguous and unpredictable, because the combined effect of tourists' unconscious attention to pertinent information leads to both positive and negative attitudes toward the image of the place. Attitudes do not remain unchanged over time, however—they are both reasonably stable and prone to change. This variability depends to a large extent on the intervention of contingent changes in external stimuli or conditions, also known as "induced messages", which can strengthen or change tourists' attitudes toward a destination by turning an otherwise unconscious reception of information into a conscious and positive one, through several incentives. For example, tourists can receive information about a destination in a positive way because they are offered a number of incentives. The image of a destination as a "tourism resource" is also malleable, so the image planner can transform the destination's scenic spots, hotels, urban environment, cultural atmosphere, traffic conditions, service quality, and other environmental elements by physically processing the original information to highlight the advantages and characteristics of the destination. When the image of the destination is frequently and continuously stimulated in the form of "induced messages", visitors tend to acquire a positive attitude toward the image of the destination and, as a result, make a more favorable choice for that destination.

It is imperative that tourist destinations properly acknowledge, in terms of the significance of their image, the reality that tourists' attitudes play a role in determining whether the destinations will receive tourism dollars. Tourists' perceptions are influenced by appearance. The findings of an in-depth analysis of a destination's image can provide a potential solution to issues confronted by the location and should be given serious thought. The most effective ways to change a tourist's perspective on a destination are to induce the input of information into the tourist's decision-making system and to exert as much psychological pressure as possible in favor of the destination.

5.3 Emotion and Tourism

5.3.1 Tourists' Emotions

An emotion is not a straightforward, plainly observable thing, and it is frequently difficult to comprehend. Emotions are characterized by bursts of powerful feelings that are associated with a particular response. Emotions come from the appraisal or assessment of certain stimuli that can be related or unrelated to individual or group goals. The vast majority of academicians are of the opinion that emotions can be broken down into three components: the subjective experience, the expressive components and the physiological arousal. Basic-emotion theorists and causal-evaluation theorists are two groups of researchers who have contributed to the development of the classical school of emotionology. Fundamental emotion theorists[1] hold that there is a fixed number of discrete emotions, describe the emotional space as having a discrete nature, and name a precise number of discrete emotions. They also state that other feelings are variable. Because their theories are consistent with the evolutionary perspective, they believe that all people experience the same feelings, and the interaction of all of these factors define a person's emotional state (feelings, action tendencies, evaluations, motor performance and physiological activity). In somewhat different thinking, the argument posited by causal appraisal theorists[2] is that assessment comes before and ultimately results in emotion. They acknowledge that evolutionary factors impact the relationship between appraisal and other emotional components. According to them, assessment is the key to emotion, and in their opinion, emotion develops when an occurrence is viewed as being extremely relevant to the conclusion of the evaluation procedure. Thus, the emotional space consists of potential "evaluation dimensions" in which changes in emotional categories are observable.

There is no question that tourists may experience a wide range of feelings as a result of their tourism experiences. Emotions play a significant part in both the cognitive assessments and the behavioral reactions of tourists, so a more in-depth understanding of feelings and how they are connected to the activities that take place in tourism settings will benefit the field of travel design. Certain referents (e.g., people, events, and situations) can bring about particular feelings. For instance, a tourist may experience frustration if a scenic place is unclean and congested; on the other hand, if the inhabitants are hospitable and patient, the tourist may experience joy and a sense of being at peace.

Emotions are omnipresent in the tourist industry, they play an essential part in the

---

[1] Ekman P. An Argument for Basic Emotions[J]. Cognition & Emotion, 1992, 6(3): 169-200.
[2] Ellsworth P C, Scherer K R. Appraisal Processes in Emotion[M]. Oxford: Oxford University Press, 2003.

formation of unforgettable experiences[①], and they are the single most significant component of the travel experience, with research having shown that feelings can influence every stage of the travel experience. Both the pre-trip phase of tourist motivation and the process of choosing a destination are heavily influenced by tourists' emotional experiences. Throughout a trip, tourists experience a varied degree of emotional intensity from day to day. In the post-consumption phase, tourists' emotions have been shown to influence their satisfaction, destination attachment, and loyalty.

5.3.2 Tourists' Emotions and Destination Marketing

It is essential for destination marketers and tour operators to attempt to comprehend the emotions evoked by the tourism experience. The major incentive for purchasing and consuming things such as tourism is emotional stimulation. Tourists are provided with hedonic consumer experiences in which imaginations, emotions and pleasures are fundamental components, and pleasant and enjoyable emotions and sentiments are essential components of the tourism experience. Therefore, it is imperative that academicians and business leaders alike have a better understanding of the significance of emotions in the consumer travel experience. Indeed, numerous studies have explored the emotional experiences of visitors before, during and after planning a trip, and for decades, tourism experts have endeavored to examine the significance of emotions in the tourism experience. When planning a vacation, visitors are believed to experience a variety of positive emotions, including fantasy and immense pleasure, which have a significant part in their decision-making and choice of destination. The emotions felt during a vacation are a vital element of the destination experience, and their strength varies throughout the course of travel. After a vacation, it is well known that emotions have a substantial impact on tourists' contentment, referral intentions and overall positive behavioral intentions.

In addition, favorable emotional connections with a location are related to a happy experience and destination loyalty. Emotion is clearly fundamental to the visiting experience. The emotional experience of visitors influences their perceptions and beliefs at the site, and visitors' opinions of a destination's emotional experience influence their evaluation of the destination's image. When the destination evokes feelings that are aligned with the tourists' anticipated benefits, the tourists view the image of the destination favorably and the destination image comprises an emotive image that is tied to the psychological emotions that the location can inspire in a visitor. Consequently, visitors' emotional experience contributes directly to their feelings and their overall image of the destination.

Because tourists' feelings have a considerable impact on their overall impression and level of pleasure with a particular location, it is essential for marketers and tour operators to construct an all-encompassing and consistent picture of a destination location based on

---

① Aho S K. Towards a General Theory of Touristic Experiences: Modelling Experience Process in Tourism[J]. Tourism Review, 2001, 56 (3): 33-37.

the various feelings that are elicited by the destination. Marketing strategies should highlight the emotional sensations (such as happiness and love) that the destination can elicit. Tourism suppliers should attempt to ignite, arouse and create good feelings by their advertising throughout the pre-tourism period. For instance, destinations employ sophisticated pictures, visuals and music in their advertising to evoke emotional appeals, and advertising campaigns with emotional appeals can effectively influence visitor motivation. During the journey, tour operators should strive to provide guests with memorable experiences that exceed their expectations. Destinations should innovate their product offerings, such as by providing visitors with the opportunity to interact with the local community to co-create a living experience.

It is also crucial to consider aspects that can negatively impact a tourist's mood, such as a lack of restrooms, exaggerated souvenir pricing, child labor, and being coerced into purchasing trinkets. All of these problems contribute to an unfavorable view of the destination's image and a decrease in tourists' pleasure, which ultimately influences their future travel plans. Therefore, important stakeholders, such as marketers, local residents, tourism authorities and the government, should be included in the destination planning, in order to mitigate these issues and foster a sense of shared responsibility.

5.3.3 Types of Emotions

1) Positive Emotions

Positive emotions are the specific, intense feelings that are first in a person's thoughts and are naturally pleasurable and desirable.

People derive happy emotions from their leisure travel experiences, and several studies have demonstrated the connections between leisure tourism and positive emotions. Specific positive feelings experienced by travelers include curiosity, affection, amusement, elation, happiness, enthusiasm and pleasure. Clawson and Knetsch believed that leisure travel has five stages: anticipation, travel to the destination, experience specificity, travel away from the destination and reflection[①]. They contended that happy feelings rise throughout the anticipation and arrival phases, with positive feelings peaking during the destination encounter and then diminishing as the individual goes home and reflects on the trip. The happy feelings of visitors follow a "peak" model, in which the strength of positive emotions increases before the trip, peaks during the holiday, and declines afterward, before returning to baseline within a few days to a few weeks.

Not only do travelers experience an increase in the strength of pleasant emotions during their travels, but individuals who have traveled during a certain period of time feel happier than those who have not. Positive emotions are obviously elicited by leisure travel, and these feelings can also influence tourism business outcomes, such as travel satisfaction and intention to return. Emotion, as a significant psychological component of

---

① Clawson M, Knetsch J L. Economics of Outdoor Recreation[M]. Abingdon: RFF Press, 2013.

tourists' attitudes, is deemed essential for the research of tourist behavior, because people make purchases on the basis of their emotions. Therefore, depending on the peak change in travelers' disposition, promises of good times in tourism advertising can be effective, and tour operators can build programs to enhance the pre-trip experience, including by providing social events for participants in a trip. In a similar vein, travel agencies can collaborate with companies that provide services for creating memories, such as photography and book publishing, in order to heighten customers' sense of satisfaction following a trip.

2) Negative Emotions

Positive and negative emotions are typically viewed as opposites, and from that perspective, negative emotions are viewed to be undesirable and to result in poor outcomes. Positive emotions are typically more prevalent, while negative emotions are more potent than positive ones. In a tourist setting, positive emotions typically result in positive visitor behavior and favorable reports, whereas negative emotions tend to result in negative behaviors, such as visitor complaints or a termination of services. In general, the value of a negative sentiment about an event is dependent on the nature of the event or the consumer experience, as well as on the environment in which it occurs. In the context of hedonic tourism, unpleasant feelings frequently have bad outcomes. For instance, feelings such as regret, disappointment, and sadness may result in decreased satisfaction with a destination and a diminished propensity to advocate for and generate positive words about that destination. Individuals who have negative feelings (such as wrath, disgust, or disdain) toward an unethical incident are more likely to spread unfavorable verbal reviews and are less likely to return to the location in the future. Visitors' assessments of the value of an encounter and their subsequent level of pleasure are both negatively impacted when they are experiencing negative emotions. The evaluation of inconsistent motivations brought on by the environment, other people, or oneself (i.e., the inability to obtain the desired hedonic value) causes unfavorable emotions, and those emotions typically result in unfavorable outcomes in terms of the visitor's evaluation and planned behavior.

The effects of negative emotions may not be as straightforward as they appear at first look, however. At the same time, negative emotions can also have good cognitive and behavioral effects, such as improved relationships, greater motivation, higher memory performance and fewer judgment errors. Specifically, guilt in negative emotions prompts individuals to evaluate their own conduct. Memory stores the processes of self-evaluation and guilt together, and consequently, guilt encourages future prosocial behavior. A visitor who feels remorse following a tour of slums, for instance, may donate to better the living conditions of the inhabitants. It is the phenomenon known as "tourist guilt", which can be described as a self-conscious "moral" sensation brought on by a person's anxiety after realizing that he/she has violated moral, social, or ethical standards. In contrast to the widely held idea that negative emotions lessen pleasure and hedonic value, research has shown that feelings of guilt can enhance the pleasure that is gained from hedonic

Case Study 5-2

consumption. For instance, feelings of both excitement and guilt can coexist when one receives an unexpected upgrade on a plane. As a result, guilt may boost both the sensation of pleasure and the hedonic value of the experience. This, in turn, has positive implications for both the satisfaction and purposeful behavior of tourists.

Guilt and other unpleasant emotions can have beneficial effects for society and the environment in addition to the person. In particular, feelings of remorse and melancholy can encourage prosocial and sustainable behavior. For instance, tourists are prepared to pay more for social contributions and environmentally friendly practices. Therefore, the experience of unpleasant emotions also affords visitors possibilities for change and personal growth.

Negative emotions can result in both negative and beneficial results outside of a hedonic environment, as well. Oftentimes, such unfavorable results can be attributed to the fact that if some individuals are disappointed that their visit did not meet their expectations, those results may generate lower levels of satisfaction. Even while the presence of unpleasant feelings is to be anticipated during a visit to a gloomy tourist site, the actual experience of such feelings can result in a lower likelihood that the individual will return to the location. First, the realization by visitors that their trip is a morally meaningful experience from which they can learn a great deal about events that took place in the past is a beneficial outcome of the uncomfortable feelings that they encounter. Second, in relation to danger zone tours, the emotional experience that tourists have during danger zone tours enables them to constructively reconstruct their memories and identities by coming to terms with the experiences that they have had in the past. In addition, research conducted on volunteer tourism has revealed that in the post-trip phase, when reflecting on their experiences, the volunteers explained that they had discovered meaning in their lives, that the experience of volunteer tourism had changed their behavior, and that they now had a different perspective on material possessions. Those effects were discovered during the phase in which volunteers were asked to explain how they felt about their experiences after returning home from their trips. Thus, bad feelings in a non-hedonic situation can prompt individuals to think about their lives as a positive result of the non-hedonic experience. This shows that negative emotions can also lead to positive value thinking for individual in non-hedonic situations.

3) The Emotion of Awe

Awe is a complicated emotion, a human emotional response in the face of enormous external stimuli, comprising amazement, adoration, terror, humility and other complex emotions. As a pleasant emotion evident in people's everyday actions, awe is not just among the basic human emotions, but is also regarded to be an essential aspect of an individual's experience of universal culture. Awe is easily evoked in massive, unexpected and harsh natural situations. Key features of awe are a perception of vastness and a need to adapt.

Perceived vastness refers to the tremendous force of emotional impulses that make an

Case Study 5-3

Note

individual feel small, powerless, frightened and humble when encountering something that is staggeringly large in scale, breadth, complexity, capability, or number. The urge to adapt suggests that when an individual encounters anything outside his/her previous experience, it affects the person's perception of the universe and inspires new mental patterns.

Imagined immensity can arise from three triggers: social, physical and cognitive triggers. Social triggers are such things as culture and art, and other things relevant to the individual's social and psychological communication. Physical triggers are such things as natural phenomena and other things that individuals can detect intuitively through sight, hearing, touch and the other senses. Cognitive triggers are such things as relativity and other knowledge on the basis of which humans can develop deep cognitive processing and perception. These three triggers of awe can function concurrently or independently. Awe occurs as a process of cognitive evaluation of one or more of the three triggers, and the feature of perceived vastness may arise, with individuals building an implicit psychology of feeling small, helpless, and bewildered in light of their environment.

The sensation of awe rarely derives from ordinary chores and mundane tasks. Tourism experiences may be a good source of amazement, in that many tourist locations offer magnificent landscapes, significant heritage value and unique cultural experiences. Awe has been defined as the experiential award that visitors expect. Therefore, awe is especially applicable to tourism. Wonder-inspiring experiences have a beneficial effect on visitor satisfaction, with awe fostering a greater connection of visitors to the environment around them and a desire to extend memories and recreate experiences, which can lead to behavioral and attitudinal loyalty and a strong sense of place. In contexts such as nature tourism, cultural tourism and black tourism, awe induces significantly more ecstasy, love, and a sense of the significance or insignificance of the self, a sense of the presence of something greater than the self, a sense of connection to the world around oneself, and a desire to prolong the tourism experience as much as possible.

The experience of wonder serves as a crucial link between visitors' perceptions of their environment and their level of contentment, and destination marketers can promote awe and wonder through appropriate tourism techniques. An element of awe can be included in the design of the tourism product, for instance, while promoting the most stunning historical structures, landscapes, and temples, to increase the awe-inspiring experience of the visitor throughout the trip. To inspire awe and wonder, it is also essential to add to the cultural history of a site by providing competent interpretive services. In addition, striking a balance between authenticity and commercialization can substantially impact the inspiration of awe in tourists.

4) Place Attachment

Place attachment is the relationship between a person and a specific environment. The word attachment emphasizes emotions, while location emphasizes the environment to which people emotionally and culturally connect themselves. Individuals are integrated into or interact with the natural environment, prompting a variety of experiences, including lived experiences, use of space and interactions with locals. Therefore, place attachment is generated when people's subjective understandings, perceptions and descriptions of a location combine to form a feeling of place and a local identity. When visitors relate place attachment to action, they create a strong emotional attachment to the location, and that presents itself in actual supportive acts. A location includes both physical (i.e., environmental) and psychological components (e.g., identity and a sense of belonging). People form place attachments if the surrounding environment fits their needs.

Ramkissoon et al. identified a second-order reflectivity factor that consists of four dimensions that are defined as follows①. Firstly, place attachment, denoting the practical utility of a location, was defined as the functional attachment of visitors to a particular location, and their impressions of the one-of-a-kind qualities of the location's environment for the achievement of a given objective (e.g., qualities making a particular landscape ideal for hiking). Secondly, place identity refers to the symbolic dimension of place and the link between place and personal identity, including cognitive and affective elements. Thirdly, place effects represent a person's emotional connection to a place. Fourthly, place social relations reflect the role of the socially shared experiences that are associated with a location.

The usual components of a place attachment include relationships with significant persons (such as family and close friends) and the association of experiences with the place that occur while one is in the company of others. In essence, the concept of place attachment shows an individual's emotional connection to family and community, as well as the intricate link between humans and nature. Place attachment provides individuals with a sense of belonging and the perception of a significant life purpose. Consequently, tourism and leisure studies frequently conceptualize place attachment as the extent to which individuals perceive value and identify with certain natural areas.

Multiple interactions with one's surroundings often eventually result in the formation of a place attachment, and that can be characterized by the presence of emotional implications such as joy, love and even grief. Place attachment is a meaningful construct that only comes into play at the conclusion of a vacation, once all of the different tourism experiences have been completed. Place attachment can be thought of as the overall connection or relationship that exists between a person and a location, from the point of view of human-environment interaction. Individuals create a pattern of emotional experiences with a place through time, and that pattern of emotions eventually matures into place attachment. Indeed, emotions play a critical role in the development of place attachment because of this pattern of emotional experiences. The experiences that a traveler has in a particular location become stored in his/her memory, where they can

---

① Ramkissoon H, Smith L D G, Weiler B. Testing the Dimensionality of Place Attachment and Its Relationships with Place Satisfaction and Pro-environmental Behaviours: A Structural Equation Modelling Approach[J]. Tourism Management, 2013, 36: 552-566.

arouse powerful feelings and, as a result, shape the visitor's behavior. The feelings of love and joy, along with those of happiness, awe, attention and inspiration, are at the heart of meaningful travel experiences. These feelings contribute to the formation of a sense of local identity as well as an attachment to a place. Attachment, as applied in the context of a tourist destination, centers on numerous experiences that are evaluated collectively. Strong bonds can result from heightened positive feelings. Specifically, place attachment is viewed as a measure of tourist attitude loyalty, as well as a separate construct of destination loyalty and a positive vacation experience.

Positively rated destination pictures, emotional experiences at the destination, perceived authenticity of a place, perceived tourism impact, and familiar tourism behaviors are connected with place identity and place attachment. In addition, the combination of sensorial, emotional, social and intellectual components provides an experience that is both attractive and memorable and that in turn works to build visitors' attachment to the location. However, developing a sense of attachment to a destination requires first and foremost that tourists have positive feelings about that location, such as joy, love and happiness. Therefore, visitors who experience more positive emotions are more likely to engage in their travel experience (for example, to explore new things, to be more open-minded and to interact with more people), and actions of engagement and appreciation are essential for the development of place attachment.

5.3.4 The Cognitive Appraisal Theory in Tourism

Emotions, as defined by Roseman, Spindel, and Jose's cognitive appraisal theory[①], are mental states that result from the processing or evaluation of information that is personally relevant. Rather than the actual occurrence of an event, a person's analysis and perception of that experience are what determine whether an emotion will be felt and what the emotion will be. For instance, one can experience happiness when viewing an occurrence as being positive and within the person's control, whereas one can experience wrath when viewing an occurrence as being a barrier to the person's achievement of a goal. According to Zeelenberg and Pieters's research, the major mechanism for eliciting and differentiating emotions is evaluation[②]. And two people who have different evaluations of the same event will have different emotional responses[③]. For instance, the winners and losers of sporting events are likely to have contrasting interpretations of the identical stimulus event, as well as distinct emotional responses to that event.

---

①Roseman I J, Spindel M S, Jose P E. Appraisals of Emotion-eliciting Events: Testing a Theory of Discrete Emotions[J]. Journal of Personality and Social Psychology, 1990, 59(5): 899.

②Zeelenberg M, Pieters R. Beyond Valence in Customer Dissatisfaction: A Review and New Findings on Behavioral Responses to Regret and Disappointment in Failed Services[J]. Journal of Business Research, 2004, 57(4): 445-455.

③Roseman I J. Appraisal Determinants of Discrete Emotions[J]. Cognition & Emotion, 1991, 5(3): 161-200.

Understanding and interpreting emotional experiences is currently dominated by the paradigm of cognitive evaluation. The cognitive appraisal theory takes into consideration shifts in feelings and provides a solid foundation for comprehending the factors that contribute to and are affected by emotional states.

Specifically, cognitive appraisal is a process of information processing that functions as a causal factor in determining emotion. Emotions are therefore the mental state of a person, produced by the evaluation of pertinent information. The cognitive appraisal theory proposes a structural interrelationship of motivation, cognitive appraisal and emotion. This interrelationship is proposed in order to explain how emotions are generated and why different people experience different emotions in response to the same event. The interrelationship deals with different cognitive appraisals to capture the nuances of emotions by assessing stimuli related to people's goals, motivations, wants and needs. According to the cognitive appraisal hypothesis, emotions result from the individual's evaluation of events and situations in connection to his/her motives, goals and requirements.

In tourism research, the cognitive appraisal theory focuses on the mechanics that underlie how visitors respond to stimuli or evaluate the outcome of an experience[①]. According to the theory, feelings are the consequence of a person's evaluation of an experience, which the person makes using a combination of different appraisal characteristics incorporated into cognitive processing—an information processing activity that evaluates the influence of the experience on the person's desired benefits and goals. A particular emotional response is produced as a result of the distinctive quality of the evaluation in conjunction with the tourist's subjective judgment of the experience.

Chapter Summary

This chapter introduced what tourists' attitudes and emotions are, and how they influence tourists' behavior and destination marketing. The related models and theories of attitudes and emotions include the multiattribute attitude model, the ABC attitude model, the theory of plan behavior and the cognitive appraisal theory. Meanwhile, the components of tourists' attitudes are analyzed by perceiving the tourism products' features. The various types of tourists' attitudes and emotions are also explained.

China Story

The Tourism Experience of Pingjiang Road

Exercises

---

① Moyle B D, Moyle C, Bec A, et al. The Next Frontier in Tourism Emotion Research[J]. Current Issues in Tourism, 2019, 22(12): 1393-1399.

Issues for Review and Discussion

1. How attitudes influence the tourists' behavior? Please use the TPB model to explain it with an example.

2. Why tourists' emotions are important?

3. Please choose your own tourism experience to explain the place attachment.

Recommended Reading

Chapter 6
Tourism Consumer Personality

Learning Objectives

After reading this chapter, you should have a good understanding of the following points:

(1) comprehend the definition, features, inter-structure, classification, and the factors influencing personality;

(2) know the main theories of personality and relate them to tourist personality;

(3) understand the definition of self-concept, composition, and its influencing factors;

(4) understand the definition and application of self-consistency in the tourism marketing industry.

Technical Words

English Words	中文翻译
the choleric tourist	胆汁质旅游者
the sanguine tourist	多血质旅游者
the phlegmatic tourist	黏液质旅游者
the melancholic tourist	抑郁质旅游者
the Big Five personality model	大五人格模型
tourist self-concept	旅游者的自我概念
actual self-concept	真实的自我概念
ideal self-concept	理想的自我概念
social self-concept	社会的自我概念
ideal social self-concept	理想的社会自我概念
expected self-concept	期待的自我概念
self-image consistency	自我形象的一致性

Knowledge Graph

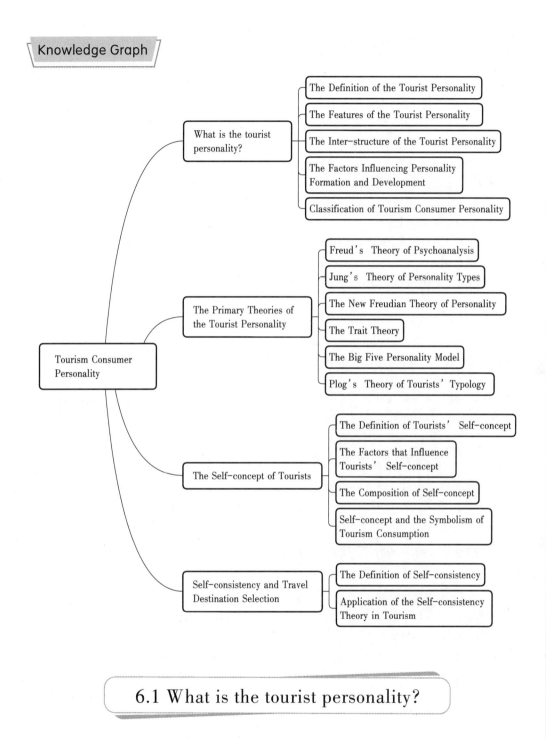

6.1 What is the tourist personality?

6.1.1 The Definition of the Tourist Personality

The English word personality, derived from the Latin noun persona, initially referred to the actor's mask. Psychologists have extended that to refer to the external behavior and psychological characteristics of the individual, although the definition of "personality" has not yet received a unified understanding. The more commonly accepted definition is that it is the sum of stable psychological signs with certain tendencies that an individual has created and developed through social interactions, based on innate qualities and under specific social and historical conditions. It includes traits, self-awareness, behavior patterns, and other aspects that distinguish one individual from others. Thus, personality affects tourists' tendencies, travel decisions, and preferences for different tourism products. Simply put, the travel tourist's personality is the tourist's overall mental outlook. The personality structure of the tourist is multilevel, multifaceted, and consists of a unique combination of complex psychological characteristics. These levels of characteristics are as follows.

First, the characteristics of the possibility of the tourist to complete a particular activity—in terms of the person's ability to do the activity.

Second, the dynamic characteristics of the tourist's psychological activities—that is, the person's temperament.

Third, the characteristics of the attitude and behavior mode of the tourist to complete the activity tasks—that is, the individual's personality.

Fourth, the characteristics of the tourist's activity tendencies, such as the tourist's interests, motivations, ideals, and beliefs.

These characteristics do not exist in isolation, but instead are organically combined to regulate and control the behavior of tourists.

6.1.2 The Features of the Tourist Personality

As the essential psychological characteristics that reflect the fundamental mental outlook of tourists, the personality characteristics of tourists have the crucial elements of complexity, differentiation, stability, and plasticity.

1) The Complexity of the Tourist Personality

Complexity refers to the tourist personality being composed of various psychological phenomena. Some psychological phenomena are apparent, in that other people can feel and perceive them—such as enthusiasm, impatience, directness—whereas other psychological phenomena are not easily detected and cannot be distinguished. The complexity of the personality characteristics of tourism tourists will affect their decision-making process and the formulations that marketers use in destination marketing strategies, making it important to pay attention to the interpretation and mining of hidden psychological phenomena.

2) The Differentiation of the Tourist Personality

Differentiation refers to the differences between specific types of tourists—distinctions that are composed of unique psychological personality tendencies and characteristics, and that are different from the spiritual outlook of other tourists, thus leading to special psychological activities and behavioral activities of the tourists. This is not to say that there is no similarity between tourists in terms of personality psychological tendencies and personality psychological characteristics, nor does it mean that there is no commonality at all. Indeed, in terms of specific personality and psychological aspects, many tourists share certain similarities. For example, extroverted tourists pursue novelty and stimulating tourism activities, while introverted tourists tend to enjoy quiet and casual activities.

3) The Stability of the Tourist Personality

Stability refers to the fact that tourists obtain different social experiences through various social activities, gradually form psychological trends with certain tendencies and relative strengths, and often show fairly predictable psychological characteristics and preferences in future actions. Still, the stability of personality does not mean that the tourists' psychological trends and preferences are immutable. For example, when we say someone is an extrovert in terms of the strength of their character, they tend to take adventurous tourism activities such as outdoor sports. Even so, they may also participate in leisure tourism activities such as beach vacations, under the influence of friends.

4) The Plasticity of the Tourist Personality

Plasticity means that the personality of the tourist is changeable. Personality is the product of psychological development, which in the process of formation is influenced by the individual's sociohistorical conditions and social interactions. Therefore, with changes in the environment, the growth age, the development of the mind, and the continuous enrichment of the tourism experience, the personality of tourism tourists will change to varying degrees. For example, adventure travelers who once paid less attention to enjoyment and quality will shift to valuing the quality and comfort of travel products as their age and income levels change.

6.1.3 The Inter-structure of the Tourist Personality

1) Temperament[①]

In the 5th century B.C., the famous ancient Greek physician Hippocrates observed that different people have different types of temperament. He believed that disposition is due to the proportion of specific fluids in the body, and according to this theory, there are four types of human temperament, named after those bodily fluids: choleric, sanguine, phlegmatic, and melancholic temperaments.

(1) Choleric tourist.

Choleric tourists like to be unconventional in shopping, by pursuing new, exotic, and exciting fashion items. Once they feel the need, they will quickly generate the motivation to buy and close the deal, but they are often not good at comparison and the lack

---

① Krivoshchekov S G, Balioz N V, Nekipelova N V, et al. Age, Gender, and Individually-typological Features of Reaction to Sharp Hypoxic Influence[J]. Human Physiology, 2014, 40(6): 613-622.

thoughtfulness. If the salesperson neglects them, that can arouse their irritability and even prompt violent reactions, reflecting the characteristics of impulsive shopping behavior.

(2) Sanguine tourist.

Sanguine tourists are good at sociability, have strong flexibility, and can obtain product information through many channels. Such tourists have strong adaptability to new people and new things, such as the shopping environment, so they are keen to observe and respond quickly when shopping and can easily communicate with the salesperson. However, sometimes their interests and goals are easily transferred, or they are unable to choose because of too many products. Their behavior often have vibrant solid characters, and their interests often change, reflecting the characteristics of imaginative and indeterminate shopping behavior.

(3) Phlegmatic tourist.

Phlegmatic tourists tend to be cautious, meticulous, and serious in shopping. Most are relatively calm, are not easily interfered with by advertisements, trademarks, packaging, and rarely influence by others. They like to make purchasing decisions through their observations and comparisons. They will actively buy products they are familiar with for a long period of time, and they tend to be cautious about new products, reflecting the characteristics of rational shopping behavior.

(4) Melancholic tourist.

Melancholic tourists tend to be more thoughtful when shopping, are sensitive to things around them, and can observe complicated details for others to follow. Their shopping behavior is prudent, sloppy, and persistent. They lack shopping initiative and are not interested in or are suspicious of others' introductions, thus reflecting the characteristics of cautious and sensitive shopping behavior.

The influence of temperament on tourist purchasing behavior is the main manifesto of the above temperament types. Of course, in real life, because environmental factors influence tourists, few people are exactly one typical temperament type, and most have mixed characteristics. However, as a marketing worker, one must learn to discover and identify the characteristics of tourists in terms of temperament and how it influences tourist behavior in purchasing activities. It is important for marketers to conduct targeted sales services, which can better meet the needs of tourists and ensure marketing effectiveness of work.

2) Ability

Ability refers to the personality and psychological characteristics that are necessary for a person to complete an activity, and it can influence the effects of the completed action. Tourists' ability is mainly composed of their capability for perception, analysis, and evaluation, for choice and decision-making, for memory, for imagination, and so on. Among tourists, their perceptual ability refers to their ability to respond directly to commodities' external characteristics and connections. The analytic and evaluative abilities of tourists refer to their power to organize, process, comprehensively analyze, compare, and evaluate varied commodity information, in order to make accurate judgments on the quality of specific commodities. Choice decision-making ability refers to the power of tourists to make timely and decisive purchasing decisions after thoroughly selecting and comparing things.

Abilities can usually be divided into two types: general skills and unique/special abilities. General skills refer to the essential competencies with standard features that must be possessed in many activities. Unique/special abilities are those needed to complete certain specialized activities. For example, appreciation, inspection, discrimination, evaluation, decision-making, and the like are collectively referred to as purchasing capacity. Tourists with solid purchasing ability make quick choices, make purchases decisively, and have noticeable effects. On the contrary, tourists with poor purchasing ability are often hesitant, and the salesperson should give them appropriate guidance.

3) Tendency, Interest, and Values

Personality tendency refers to people's attitude and tendency of consciousness that they hold toward things during interactions with objective reality. Personality determines people's attitude toward reality and the tendency and choice of the object of cognitive activities. Personality tendency is the dynamic structure of the personality system, and it is less affected by physiological, genetic, and other congenital factors than other aspects of personality are.

Interest is not innate, it is produced and developed in social practices. Need is the foundation for generating and developing interest, need is the source of personality tendency and even the whole enthusiasm within personality, and personality can form and develop only under the impetus of need.

However, values belong to the highest guiding level of personality. Values guide and restrict tendency in human thought, and the entire mental outlook, and they form the full power and real motivation of human words and deeds.

Personality disposition is a dynamic system based on people's needs and guided by their values. Personality tendency embodies the positive characteristics of people's attitudes and behavior toward their social environment. The influence of tendency on tourists' psychology is reflected mainly in their selectivity of psychological activities, the mood and experience of the public toward them, and consumer behavior patterns.

6.1.4 The Factors Influencing Personality Formation and Development

Personality formation is affected primarily by the interaction of three elements: genetic factors, environmental factors, and social practice factors.

1) Genetic Factors

Genetic factors refer to the physical characteristics that individuals are born with, such as the structure and morphology of the body, as well as the structural and functional aspects of the sensory organs, the motor organs, and the central nervous system, especially the brain. These physiological characteristics fundamentally affect the formation and development of personality and directly affect the appearance of different types of character. However, genetic factors do not play a decisive role in personality formation.

2) Environmental Factors

In all of the individual's work in terms of personality formation and development, the environmental factors associated with one's family, school, and social culture have the most direct and essential influence.

(1) The influence of family environment on personality.

The family is the center of children's lives. Personality is primarily influenced by the family, whose members (especially the parents) are the children's earliest teachers. The members' life experiences, values, behavior, educational attitudes, and educational methods can influence the formation of children's personalities through words and actions and in other subtle ways. The child's status in the family will also leave a deep imprint on his/her personality. For example, if children are spoiled by their families, they will develop flawed characters such as capriciousness, petulance, and obstinacy; children also can quickly form independent, strong, helpful, and creative characters. Furthermore, the parents' personality characteristics will also influence the children's personality through their words and deeds. The saying "Like father, like son" refers superficially to heredity, but the family environment and disciplinary practices also play a significant role in the influence of a child's personality.

(2) The influence of school and formal education on personality.

Education at school is a kind of education in which some educators exert a normative influence on the future members of the society in a purposeful, planned, and organized way to promote the socialization of their students and to form and facilitate the students' personality adaptations to their social environment. In particular, education can eliminate and control the influence of some harmful factors in the children's background, giving them more positive guidance so that their personality development helps them adapt to social norms and values in a positive direction of growth. Therefore, education plays a leading role in the formation and development of character. For example, no matter how good a person's vocal talent is, without music teacher training, the person will not learn verbal skills and will not know the melody of music, rendering it impossible for him or her to become an excellent singer.

(3) The influence of social culture on personality.

In the social lives of humans, the influence of culture is ubiquitous and constant. Sometimes it is evident, sometimes latent, but in any case, social culture always constrains individuals' words and deeds and imposes cultural requirements on their unique personalities. To survive in their social culture, the individuals must adapt while growing up, and they must respond to the requirements of society. That response leads to the individual personalities being highly consistent with the salient social culture.

3) Social Practice Factors

We have now established that family environment, school education, and social culture are the external influences on the formation and development of a student's personality. What kind of personality will be formed depends mainly on the process of social practices that the student experiences. Individuals play specific roles in social practices and assume certain social responsibilities, and children must adapt to the social environment in order to live and develop. The need to adapt to their social environment urges individuals to form and develop an attitude system, behavior pattern, and other personality characteristics that are in accord with the social cultural requirements.

6.1.5 Classification of Tourism Consumer Personality

1) Personality Classification of Personality Tendencies

The famous Swiss psychologist Carl Jung believed that the direction of vitality flow determines the person's personality type. Those individuals with inward-flowing vitality belong to the introverted type, and those with vitality outflow belong to the extroverted type. Introverts love quietness, tend to be shy in personality, do not quickly reveal their feelings, and pay attention to their own, subjective world. Extroverts are happy to engage in suitable activities, love social activities, express their emotions intensely, and pay more attention to the objective, external world of others. Nevertheless, this classification has major limitations and is too simplistic. Most people are appropriate introverted or extroverted, or two extreme balances. There will be internal and external differences, even in people of the same level of education, gender, or occupation.

In a study designed to investigate "the extent of the popularity of tourism destinations, there have been significant changes", researchers have found apparent differences in many essential aspects of the travel behavior of people with an introverted personality and those who are extroverted. The essence of an internal character strongly demands that one's life be predictable. Therefore, such a person's typical approach as a tourist will be to drive to a familiar destination. Because of one's relatively quiet personality, his/her travel motivation is mainly relaxation. His/her ideal holidays include the tourist destination and all activities, accommodations, equipment, restaurants, and entertainment, and those things should be fixed and booked or estimated in advance.

People with the extreme opposite personality, extroverts, are eager to have some things in life estimated rather than precisely determined. Because of his/her adventurous personality, the extrovert usually travels to places that are more remote and neither well known nor visited often. Such an individual is willing to take a plane to travel to the destination. Because such an individual is more active, he/she likes to travel abroad and be exposed to different cultural backgrounds. The ideal holiday, in his/her mind, is full of novelty, unpredictability, and complexity, and he/she seeks to experience new things and to avoid repetition.

Nevertheless, most people belong to an intermediate type between the two, in terms of their choices of actual tourism activities. Although people with middle-type personalities do not have a strong spirit of adventure, they do like to travel. In fact, they are the most active people in the tourism market and represent the mass tourism market. Because their personality is deeply affected by the environment, even the person with an introverted personality will change their personality after a long-term process. People who originally had middle-type personality may become closer to the external personality, and then change their choices of the location and content of tourism activities. Therefore, when a tourist at a tourist location has transformed from having a small number of extroverted characteristics to having a large number of introverted characteristics, it may indicate that this tourist's choice for a travel location will have become more commercial and ordinary.

Another similar classification method is to divide tourists into two categories: psychocentric tourists and allocentric tourists[1]. In English, the prefix "psycho" means soul, mind, or self; the prefix "allo" means different, other, non-self, or varied in form. Therefore, psychocentric people are good at all, and they tend to be worried, more depressed in mood, and less attracted to adventure; allocentric people, in contrast, are more confident, curious, and eager to contact the outside world, so they like to take risks and try new things in life. There are many similarities between introverted people and psychocentric types, and between extroverted people and allocentric types, and their similarities extend to their tourism behavior.

2) Personality Classification Using Lifestyle

The individual's lifestyle, simply speaking, even in the ways that he or she spends time and money, is also affected by culture, social class, reference groups, family members, and the like[2]. Lifestyle can be reflected in a person's daily work, activities, values, needs, and cognitive performance, and it can effectively reflect the person's personality characteristics. It can help us understand all types of tourists and their travel behavior.

(1) Calm and peaceful tourism consumers.

Those who seek a peaceful life have their own unique lifestyle. Wells in 1972 analyzed the lifestyles of such tourists, and the results showed that their cultural level and occupation gave these people enough money for tourism. Still, because they attached great importance to their homes, they tended to use their excess money to buy furniture, repair houses, stay at home with their family or watch TV without traveling. Even if such an individual does travel, he/she is willing to take a quiet vacation on the lake and enjoy relaxation. They also like outdoor activities and fresh air and love hunting, fishing, and camping. Such people like children and often regard them as essential to their lives. These

---

[1] Plog S. Why Destination Areas Rise and Fall in Popularity: An Update of a Cornell Quarterly Classic[J]. Cornell Hotel and Restaurant Administration Quarterly, 2001, 42(3): 13-24.

[2] Cassill N L, Drake M F. Apparel Selection Criteria Related to Female Consumers' Lifestyle[J]. Clothing and Textiles Research Journal, 1987, 6(1): 20-28.

people love to be neat, pay attention to their health, and do not want to take risks, so they have always been skeptical of advertising[1]. By understanding the complete picture of this kind of person, one knows which products and advertising methods meet their interests, needs, values, and attitudes, which is very beneficial to publicizing tourism products for them.

(2) Communicative tourism consumers.

Friendly, communicative tourists differ from the tourists who prefer a quiet and peaceful lifestyle. This type of person is active, outgoing, confident, receptive of new things, more willing to take the initiative to communicate with people during travel, likes to travel to exotic destinations, likes to travel around the world, and does not limit the meaning of holidays to rest or relaxation but instead sees a holiday as an excellent time to seek new knowledge and make new friends. They are relatively more interested in culture, visiting art galleries or museums, listening to classical music, or watching traditional theater, which are some of their reasons for overseas travel. These traits suggest that sociable travelers prefer to travel far away or abroad and that the travel industry should emphasize benefits other than rest or recuperation when promoting destinations to these types of travelers.

(3) Tourists who are interested in history.

Some people are motivated by an interest in history. History has therefore shaped the direction of tourism and the arts, and for decades tourists have been drawn to places of historical and cultural significance. The human desire is strong to remember the past, to understand it, and to remember it.

According to the relevant research, history-loving tourists are relatively tranquil and are very interested in the cultures of the past. Hence, most such tourists think that their holidays should have an educational significance and be able to increase their knowledge, and they are encouraged to turn their holidays into history lessons, visit museums and art galleries, visit historical sites, and learn about different cultures and customs. Entertainment becomes a secondary motivation for these travelers[2]. The tourists who are interested in history attach significant importance to their education and knowledge, generally speaking, in addition to having a strong sense of responsibility for their own country and human history, and a strong sense of responsibility for their children and family. Such tourists often think that holidays should be arranged for children and that happy families can spend their holidays together. Therefore, if tourism publicity and sales service personnel want to attract this type of tourist, they must focus on providing historical tourist sites. Promotions of a vacation or destination should highlight the educational and educational opportunities it offers and the family-friendly nature of the trip.

---

[1] King D A, Wells M G. Molecular Beam Investigation of Adsorption Kinetics on Bulk Metal Targets: Nitrogen on Tungsten[J]. Surface Science, 1972, 29(2): 454-482.

[2] Solomon G F, Schmidt K M. A Burning Issue: Phantom Limb Pain and Psychological Preparation of the Patient for Amputation[J]. Archives of Surgery, 1978, 113(2): 185-186.

(4) Tourism consumers who plan to drive.

An analysis of a series of unique personality traits of travelers who drive a station wagon found that those who are not interested in owning a station wagon and traveling in this kind of vehicle are generally not interested in outdoor activities[1]. Instead, they prefer to spend their time and money on the so-called elegant lifestyle, such as going to the theater, attending cocktail parties, and so on. In short, they prefer indoor leisure activities, and even when traveling, they like to go to big cities for holidays. The most striking feature of these people's lives is their high sense of responsibility for their work. They receive great satisfaction from their work and hope to advance in their careers. That said, these people tend to work long hours every day, and their work life is not easy, so they do not want to take long vacations.

On the other hand, people who own and like to drive station wagons tend to be less outgoing and friendly, and prefer to stay at home at night rather than attend cocktail parties and spend their money on luxuries. Still, they are willing to spend a few dollars on a station wagon. Because these people are more conservative and orthodox, their lifestyle is primarily family-centered, and their family-based purchase of a station wagon make it easy to enjoy a series of family activities. In addition, they believe that people should not be burdened by long work hours, and they adhere to the concept of having sufficient free time.

(5) Tourism consumers who travel first and then pay.

Most modern people have a credit card, so they adhere to the trend of "enjoy first, and then pay" as a new form of consumption. This consumption pattern is followed not only for buying clothes, furniture, cars, and other products, but also for purchasing tourism services. It is also valued because of the safety of traveling without much cash. Generally speaking, if a person thinks of travel as a luxury, he/she is more likely to be opposed to traveling first and then paying, whereas if people regard tourism as a necessity of life, they will consider a credit card to be easier to use. In the United States, people may not hesitate to purchase luxury goods such as jewelry, high-end race cars, and resort villas in installments or via loans. Still, they do not necessarily purchase invisible products such as travel in installments. According to one survey in 1988, up to 90% of Americans will be willing to use credit cards to purchase gasoline, pay for accommodations, or pay meal fees during vacation, but they are unwilling to buy airline tickets, entertainment tickets, or pay group fees in installments, especially if this kind of expenditure is "for the purpose of playing"[2].

Only those with extraordinary personalities can buy tourism services with peace of mind. In addition, travel abroad is usually more commonly done with credit cards,

---

[1] Melamed B G, Weinstein D, Hawes R, et al. Reduction of Fear-related Dental Management Problems with Use of Filmed Modeling[J]. The Journal of the American Dental Association, 1975, 90(4): 822-826.

[2] Hawes D K. Travel-related Lifestyle Profiles of Older Women[J]. Journal of Travel Research, 1988, 27(2): 22-32.

because of the increased risks of carrying cash and the danger of counterfeit banknotes of the local currency in foreign countries. Credit cards with travelers' checks and appropriately small amounts of cash are not only convenient, but also can make the journey safer, and avoid unnecessary risks. In addition, such travel is becoming a trend.

As mentioned earlier, communication-oriented overseas tourists are more outgoing, active, confident, and receptive to new things. They are not afraid of spending money. They are generally younger. They view the use of credit cards when traveling as a positive convenience. Whether they are an office worker, a housewife, or a young student with no formal income, applying for more than one credit card remains quite attractive—a situation that may be attributed to the advertisement of credit cards, and the influence of those in television and movies who have a considerable degree of social status and credit and who deliberately set out to appeal to people with credit cards. Notably, although the issuance and usage of credit card have increased significantly, the cost of using credit cards or installment payments, as well as travel clubs, may not have increased relatively. In the future, if tourism marketers wish to promote the benefits of using credit cards for travel, they should emphasize the convenience of using credit cards instead of the benefits of delayed payment.

6.2 The Primary Theories of the Tourist Personality

6.2.1 Freud's Theory of Psychoanalysis

Sigmund Freud's theory of psychoanalysis encompasses motivation as well as personality or individuality. In addition to Freud's notion of a personality system composed of the id, ego, and superego, introduced in his motivation theory, Freud also proposed his psychosexual theory of the stages of personality development. He believed that personality formation depends on how the individual copes with and deals with the crises that arise in different psychological periods during childhood. Freud proposed five psychosexual stages of development: the oral, anal, sexual/phallic, incubation/latency, and sexual stages, and at the end of each stage, the individual faces some crisis[①].

The oral stage (birth-1 year old). In the oral stage, the baby's primary desire is met by putting objects in his/her mouth, and he/she mainly relies on sucking, chewing, swallowing, and other activities to obtain satisfaction. Babies also get most of their pleasure from oral activities. If the child is restricted from its desired oral behaviors during this period of oral activity, that may have a negative impact. A crisis occurs when a baby is about to be weaned or no longer suckled with a bottle. If a baby's oral needs are not

---

[①] Ewen R B. An Introduction to Theories of Personality[M]. Hove: Psychology Press, 2014.

well met, the individual can become "fixated" orally as an adult, and will display behavioral tendencies such as dependence on excessive oral activity. Such adults have a so-called oral personality, presumably due to the oral period of development not being smooth. Behaviors such as gluttony, alcoholism, smoking, nail-biting, pessimism, dependence, and suffering from germaphobia are characteristics of an oral character.

The anal stage (1-3 years old). During the anal stage, the child's primary desire is met mainly by defecation and urination, which generate the stimulation of pleasure and obtain satisfaction. This is a crucial period in the training of young children in hygiene habits. If the toilet training and control are too early or too strict, it may leave a negative effect. Adults who have the so-called anal-retentive character tend to be tidy, stubborn, stingy with cash and possessions, and other characteristics.

The sexual/phallic stage (3-6 years old). In the sexual/phallic stage of development, the child's primitive desire is met primarily by focusing on the sexual organs to obtain satisfaction, and these young children like to touch their sexual organs. During this period, young children are able to distinguish the male and female genders and they focus on their parent of the opposite sex as exemplifying their object of sexual love. This has led to boys favoring their mothers over their fathers, a phenomenon known as the Oedipus Complex. Similarly, the Electra Complex is the phenomenon that girls love their fathers in competition with their mothers.

The incubation/latency stage (6 years old to adolescence). During the incubation/latency stage, the post 6-year-old children's interests have expanded beyond a primary interest in their own body and in their parents, to having a focal interest in the world around them. They have moved from the original desire to a latent state with no psychosexual focus. During this period, boys and girls become emotionally estranged from each other, and most group activities display the trend of separation between boys and girls.

The sexual stage (adolescence to adulthood). The onset of the sexual or genital stage (after the onset of adolescence) differs by gender, beginning with boys at about 13 years of age and girls at about 12. During this period, individual sex organs mature, and the differences in the physiological and psychological characteristics of the two genders begin to be significant. From this period on, the sexual attraction toward others of similar age and the opposite gender begins to be the ideal of sexual life, and a sense of marriage and family develops. At this point, the gradual development of sexual psychology reaches maturity. Freud's theory of personality is based on instinct, especially sexual instinct.

6.2.2 Jung's Theory of Personality Types

Carl Jung at one time supported Freud's psychoanalytic theory, but he later invented analytic psychology because of their differing views. Analytical psychology covers a wide range of content, and tourist behavior analyses should be most closely related to personality type[①]. According to Jung's theory of personality types, the personality structure is formed by many opposing internal forces, such as feelings/senses versus intuition, thinking versus emotion, extraversion versus introversion, and so on; in one person, these opposing personality tendencies can often be out of balance or biased. For example, some people make decisions more intuitively and emotionally, while others make decisions more rationally and logically. These two opposite personality tendencies can form many combinations, such as the sensory-thinking type, the sensory-emotional type, the intuitive-thinking type, and the intuitive-emotional type. An analysis of these personality types can help marketers understand the behavioral characteristics of each type of personality in order to formulate more effective marketing strategies to meet tourists' needs. Taking the decision-making of buying certain stocks as an example, both the thinking-type and the feeling-type will study the financial statements and financial performance of the listed companies to obtain relevant facts and data. However, feeling-type individuals are more likely to include recommendations from others in their decision-making, and they are more likely to use a broker who provides a complete service rather than a partial service. Intuitive-thinking and intuitive-emotional tourists make intuitive decisions and focus on their imagination. Still, intuitive-emotional tourists' decisions are more likely to reflect the opinions and comments of others.

6.2.3 The New Freudian Theory of Personality

Some of Freud's colleagues and disciples, known as "the new Freudians", disagreed with Freud's view that personality was primarily determined by instinct or sexual instinct, and they believed instead that the formation and development of personality and personal social relations are inseparable. Alfred Adler, for example, believed that man has considerable autonomy and is not subject to the whims of the id and the blind daze of the unconscious. Human beings are born with the innate drive to pursue excellence, and it is a common personality trait. As a result of the pursuit of real life and the resulting consequences, different people gradually form each other's unique style of life. According to Adler, the average person's lifestyle develops between ages four and five years. Once an individual's lifestyle is formed, it is not easy to change, and it will have a far-reaching influence later on the individual's behavior.

Harry Stack Sullivan, another representative of the new Freudian theory, argued that individuals constantly seek to establish mutually beneficial and valuable relationships with others. Sullivan was very concerned about the individual's efforts to relieve various kinds of tension, anxiety, and restlessness. Like Sullivan, Homy was interested in studying anxiety, and focused on the effects that a child's relationship with their parents has on behavior, especially the effects of an individual's desire to suppress anxiety. Khoni divided people into three types, according to their personalities: first, the submissive type

---

① Shelburne W A. Mythos and Logos in the Thought of Carl Jung: The Theory of the Collective Unconscious in Scientific Perspective[M]. Albany: Suny Press, 1988.

refers to individuals who tend to blend in with others, especially because of wanting to be loved and appreciated; second, the aggressive type of person is highly motivated and always wants to outdo and win the admiration and respect of others; third, the go-it-alone type tends to be independent, self-sufficient, and free of all constraints.

Based on Khoni's theory[①] of these types, some scholars in the 1960s began a personality test known as the compliance-aggression-detachment (CAD) test to understand the characteristics of the tourist behavior of these different types of personality. Initial CAD research identified several relationships between different personality types of tourists and their usage patterns of products and brands. For example, highly docile tourists prefer to buy branded products, aggressive tourists prefer products with a masculine image, and self-indulgent tourists prefer to relax and drink tea.

6.2.4 The Trait Theory

The personality theories introduced above use mainly qualitative methods such as personal observations, self-reporting, and projection techniques to measure people's personalities. In contrast, the trait theory measures people's personalities according to specific psychological characteristics and is an empirical and quantitative analytic theory of personality. The theory of idiosyncrasy holds that a person's personality is made up of many qualities. A trait is a quality possessed by a person that influences that person's behavior. As a neuropsychological structure, a personality trait enables the individual to respond to stimuli relatively consistently. Instead of categorizing personality as an absolute type, the theory of idiosyncrasies suggests that there are dimensions of idiosyncrasies and that each person behaves differently in these dimensions. For example, generosity, modesty, and the like are qualities that everyone may possess in varying degrees. Personality differences exist because different people have different performance levels in various characteristics. Cattell's theory of personality is typical of the theory of personality idiosyncrasy. According to Cattell, traits make up a personality—some are universal, some are unique to the individual, some are genetically determined, and the environment influences others. Personality traits can be divided into two main types: surface traits and root or source (or global) traits. Surface traits are the individual personality characteristics in each specific behavior, and the root or source traits reflect and underlie a person's overall personality and are the building blocks of human personality; they are based on the surface trait reasoning set.

In the field of tourist behavior research, some experts and scholars try to predict certain tourist personality traits and determine how they closely correlate to the marketing activities of enterprises, such as tourism innovation, people's sensitivity to interpersonal influence, and so on. Generally, such studies greatly help us undestand how tourists choose whether to consume a broad range of products, but they are not as helpful in

---

① Orakzai S B. Conflict in the Swat Valley of Pakistan: Pakhtun Culture and Peacebuilding Theory-practice Application[J]. Journal of Peacebuilding & Development, 2011, 6(1): 35-48.

predicting which brands tourists will choose. For example, a particular personality is a good predictor of whether a tourist will buy a car but not a precise predictor of which car a tourist will buy.

6.2.5 The Big Five Personality Model

Since the 1980s, personality researchers have reached a consensus on the model of personality description and put forward the Five-Factor model of personality, also known as "the Big Five model" or "the Big Five personalities". It is based on the assumption that there are five core personality traits selecting many words in the dictionary describing a person. The Big Five model divides personality into five dimensions, and each dimension represents a range between a pair of extremes[①].

1) Extroversion

People who are high in extroversion tend to be warm, social, decisive, active, adventurous, and optimistic. This trait is used to indicate whether a person is introverted or extroverted. People who are low in extroversion (i.e., are introverts) tend to be quiet, reserved, and think before they speak.

2) Agreeableness

People high in agreeableness tend to be trusting, direct, altruistic, compliant, humble, and empathetic. People with high agreeableness are friendly, cultured, and caring, while people with low agreeableness are self-centered, indifferent, and hostile to others.

3) Conscientiousness

People who are high in conscientiousness tend to be competent, organized, diligent, accomplished, self-disciplined, and cautious. Cautious strong people generally work seriously, with hard work and self-discipline, whereas those who are low in conscientiousness are sloppy and unreliable.

4) Neuroticism

People who are high in neuroticism tend to be anxious, hostile, depressed, self-aware, impulsive, and vulnerable. People who are low in emotional instability/neuroticism tend to be emotionally stable, cope well with stress, are rarely sad, and are relaxed.

5) Openness

People who are high in openness are imaginative, creative, aesthetic, emotionally rich, have diverse interests, and are insightful. Open-minded people are flexible and enjoy new experiences and new ideas. People who are low in openness dislike change and tend to avoid new ideas.

---

① McAdams D P. The Five-factor Model in Personality: A Critical Appraisal[J]. Journal of Personality, 1992, 60(2): 329-361.

The Big Five model was developed in the context of American culture; whether it can be applied to other cultures and whether it can accurately describe the personalities of our Chinese tourists is not conclusive. We also do not know how significant it is for studying the tourist behavior of our Chinese tourists. Some Chinese experts and scholars have found that the Chinese personality model includes competence and incompetence, other‐orientation and self‐centeredness, atmosphere, and stinginess, which are personality descriptions that are not found in the Big Five model of Western. Furthermore, the "Openness" dimension in the Big Five model has no counterpart in the Chinese personality model.

6.2.6 Plog's Theory of Tourists' Typology

According to Stanley Plog, tourists' personalities lie on a continuum, the two ends of the which are the "psychocentic" personality and the "allocentric" personality[①]. Psychocentric tourists tend to concentrate on trivial matters, they are more conservative in their travel patterns, they prefer "safe" tourist destinations, and they often revisit a destination multiple times. This type of tourist strongly demands predictability in life, their behavioral tendencies are passive, and relaxation is their main tourism motive. Their ideal vacation travel should be well-organized and pre-arranged, including all of the trip's activities, tourist facilities, restaurants, and hospitalities.

Allocentric personalities are adventurous and willing to visit or discover new destinations. Such tourists do not need prior anticipation and arrangement in their lives, and they yearn for the unforeseen. Their behavioral tendencies are active, proactive, and flexible. Their ideal vacation travel is complex, changeable, and cannot be estimated in advance. They like to visit lesser-known tourist destinations, go abroad, are happy to fly, and are eager to talk to people from different cultures and historical backgrounds. Their motivation is rarely to travel to the same place twice.

6.3 The Self-concept of Tourists

6.3.1 The Definition of Tourists' Self-concept

Self-concept is the total of what an individual perceives, understands, and feels about himself. Everyone gradually forms an opinion about themselves, such as considering themselves to be ugly or beautiful, fat or thin, having average or outstanding ability, and so on. One's self‐concept answers questions such as "Who I am" and "What kind of person am I", and it results from the combined effect of the individual's experience and

---

① Plog S C. A Carpenter's Tools: An Answer to Stephen L. J. Smith's Review of Psychocentrism/Allocentrism [J]. Journal of Travel Research, 1990, 28(4): 43-45.

the external environment. It is generally believed that tourists will choose the products and services that are consistent with their self-concept and will avoid choosing products and services that contradict their self-concept. It is in this sense that the study of tourists' self-concept is significant for enterprises, and especially for tourism enterprises whose main products are services. The self-concept of tourists can be classified into five dimensions. First, actual self-concept: how tourists see themselves. Second, ideal self-concept: how tourists want to see themselves. Third, social self-concept: how tourists feel about how others perceive them. Firth, ideal social self-concept: how tourists want others to see them. Fifth, expected self-concept: how tourists expect to see themselves in the future. This falls between their actual and ideal self-concepts.

The diversity of tourists' self-concepts means that tourists may choose different self-concepts to guide their attitudes and consumption behaviors in different situations. For example, when an individual interacts with family members at home, his behavior is generally dominated and guided by his actual self-concept; when he communicates with classmates and friends outside the family, his behavior is generally dominated and guided by his social self-concept; in cinemas or museums, his behavior is generally dominated by the ideal social self-concept.

Carl Rogers believed that the purpose of human behavior is to maintain the consistency of "self-concept" and behavior. If the ideal self, the actual self, and the self-image are inconsistent, a certain degree of tension and anxiety will arise. Many decisions of tourists are guided by their self-concept. For example, when people buy clothes, cars, and other products, they generally think their products or brands must suit their identity.

6.3.2 The Factors that Influence Tourists' Self-concept

Individuals in the socialization process form their self-concept through interacting with others and contacting the environment to reflect on their behavior. The process has three primary aspects.

1) Reflected Evaluations

Reflected evaluations comprise the evaluation information that an individual obtains from others about himself. A person will have an excellent self-concept if he had received positive reviews when he was young, whereas if a person received a negative evaluation, his self-concept may include a feeling of inadequacy. For example, if a student, especially a primary school student, is often praised by teachers in school, his academic performance is generally not bad. If teachers criticize him, however, his academic performance is generally not very good, and he may become negative, even if he studies hard.

2) Social Comparison

In social life and work, individuals often determine the relevant standards for measuring themselves by comparing themselves with others—that is, by social comparison. For example, many students are concerned not only about their own grades, but also about how their grades compare with the grades of other students in the class, especially the grades of their classmates and good friends. When a person goes out into society, he compares himself with his colleagues and judges whether they are more affluent than he is and live better than he does. When a person has children, he feels he is better than his children, or other people's children. No matter who, from comparisons within the family and in society, and from comparisons at study and at work, people develop and enrich their self-concept through social comparison.

3) Sense of Self

At a young age, most of an individual's knowledge of himself comes from the reflection of others on himself. However, with age and mental maturity, at a certain point people begin to see and evaluate themselves in a way that is called "self-feeling". In self-feeling, if a person gains confidence from successful experiences, he will feel better about himself, and his self-concept will improve.

As can be seen from the above influencing factors, the self-concept is formed and developed based on the synthesis of a sense of self that is gained through self-feeling, the reflected evaluations of others, and social evaluation. There are four essential components to this process: the actual self-concept, which is how one sees oneself; the ideal self-concept, which is how one wants to see oneself; the social self-concept, which is how others see one; and the ideal social self-concept, which is how one wants to be seen by others. There is a clear internal connection among the four elements. Usually, people have the will and inner impulse to transform from their actual self-concept to their ideal self-concept, and this impulse becomes the fundamental driving force for people to modify their behavior constantly as they continue to seek self-improvement. Furthermore, people also strive to make their image conform to the ideal requirements of others or of society, and ultimately, they strive to conduct behaviors that follow society's ideal standards. It is precisely under the impetus of that will and motivation that the self-concept impacts people's behavior more deeply, restricting and regulating their way, direction, and degree of behavior.

6.3.3 The Composition of Self-concept

Scholars have discussed the composition of self-concept from different perspectives and formed numerous viewpoints. Two viewpoints are presented here.

1) William James's View of the Composition of Self-concept

The famous American psychologist William James was regarded as a pioneer in the study of the psychology of the self. James believed that an individual's self-concept consists of material, social, and spiritual components. All three components are accompanied by feelings of self-evaluation and behaviors of self-seeking.

First, the material self comprises one's pride or feelings of inferiority in one's body, clothes, and family possessions—for example, the pride of being a well-dressed person. This self pursues an attractive physical appearance, the satisfaction of desires, such as decoration, dressing up, caring about things in the family, and so on.

Second, the social self estimates one's reputation, status, relatives, and property in society. This self evaluates primarily one's own social status, social circle, and the like, and therefore the social self reflects people's desire to socialize. Under this ego, people seek attention, fame, competition, and ambition.

Third, the spiritual self is one's sense of superiority or inferiority in one's intellectual ability and morality. This evaluation focuses on people's minds and morality. This ego seeks the accumulation of wisdom, peace of mind, and moral conscience.

2) Charles Glenn Walters's Four-part Composition of Self-concept

Charles Glenn Walters, the American author of *Consumer Behavior Research*, believed that the self-concept consists of four components[①].

First, the true self is the true essence of a person. Consumers' buying behavior often does not happen until after they have a thorough, objective, and comprehensive understanding of themselves. Many, however, are unknowing and unaware of themselves, and therefore are dominated by their subconscious. This is the true reflection of the consumer and belongs to the true self.

Second, the ideal self is what kind of person the consumer wants to be, not what kind of person he/she is in reality. This self is related to the objects of worship, belief, and goals that a person pursues and desires. It is difficult to fully realize the ideal self because people's pursuits and expectations are endless. Consumers can attempt to realize their ideal self when they buy "prestige" products, such as high-end clothing, jewelry, luxury cars, and private yachts.

Third, self-image is the consumer's view and understanding of himself/herself, and is a mixture of the faithful and ideal self. The consumption process is a vital way to express one's self-image, and consumers make consumption choices according to their self-image. However, there are also a small number of cases in which consumers adopt consumption activities that are inconsistent with their self-image.

Fourth, the self in the mirror is what consumers believe others think of them. This kind of self is related to one's view of others, such as other people's knowledge, age, status, and the like, so it is an interactive relationship.

There is a clear internal connection between these four selves. People have the will and inner impulse to transform from actual self-concept to ideal self-concept, and this impulse will continuously modify their behavior as consumers. At the same time, people will also try their best to pursue the image that meets the requirements of others or of society, which means their self-concept affects their behavior at a deeper level, restricting and regulating the way, direction, and degree of their behavior.

6.3.4 Self-concept and the Symbolism of Tourism Consumption

People buy a product or service not only because of its use value, but also because of

---

[①] Walters C G. Consumer Behavior: Theory and Practice[M]. New York: McGraw-Hill Education, 1974.

the identity of the self-concept it gives the consumers. Especially in modern society, where quality is increasingly essential, products and services convey essential information about the self to the outside world. For example, Ferraris and Rolls-Royces are not just a means of transportation; they convey a higher symbolic value. Today's rich and diverse tourism products and services, such as adventure tours, self-driving tours, and overseas tours, reflect the self-concept of different groups of people and are symbolic products. Consumer behavior and marketing scholar Russell W. Belk uses the extended self to illustrate the relationship between such products and self-concept and believes that the extended self consists of two parts, the self and the possession. To a certain extent, people tend to define their identities in terms of external possessions. Therefore, possessions are not only external manifestations of one's self-concept, but also are an integral part of self-concept.

Products or services that are easily regarded as symbols by consumers usually have three characteristics in common. The first is visibility of the item's purpose—that is, the product's purchase and the consumer's disposition are easily felt or seen by others. Secondly, differences exist—some consumers can buy while others cannot, due to differences in purchasing power. Products or services used as symbols are not available to everyone. Finally, there should be personality, in terms of the degree to which the product or service describes the typicality of the consumer.

Most tourism products and services have the above three characteristics, especially because the improvement of people's living standards has made disposable funds and leisure time a reality. Thus, tourism has become a trend and fashion, and the symbolism of tourism has become increasingly prominent.

First, the purchase, consumption, and disposal of travel are obvious. Where to travel, what type of travel to participate in, and the grade of accommodations and travel means can be seen and felt by others.

Second, tourism products of different grades target different customer groups. The more high-end the tourism products are, the higher is the reflection of identity and status, which is one of the reasons why business tourists pay more attention to the quality of tourism products.

Third, sellers are designing progressively fantastic and unique tourism products for the increasingly developed tourism market, and those unique products reflect the tourists' personalities better and meet their desire to pursue products that match their personalities.

Tourism products and services have distinct personalities. Backpackers, for example, tend to be young, healthy, adventurous, and curious, but not financially wealthy, whereas older people travel in groups with relatively more comfort and a looser schedule. The most symbolic example of tourism products from the three characteristics of symbolic products is high-end "experience tourism", which caters to the comprehensive economic strength and high cultural capital of individuals and families. Middle-aged men with money and leisure are the most typical adventure tourists.

Because tourism products are products with strong symbolic meanings, they not only reflect a person's social status, career achievements, and personal qualities, but also enhance an individual's self-image, so they can be used as a way for people to achieve their ideal self.

6.4 Self-consistency and Travel Destination Selection

6.4.1 The Definition of Self-consistency

Self-consistency refers to linking the psychological structure of an individual's self-concept with the symbolic value of the product purchased in the market[1]. When a product or brand can enhance or conform to the consumer's self-concept, consumers will buy that particular product or brand[2]. Self-consistency has two elements: self-image and product image. Self-image refers to how one wants others to think of him or her, and its theory is interchangeable with the theory of self-concept. Interestingly, products and services can also be regarded as having a product personality image—that is, they contain a particular personality trait(s), such as being thought of as friendly, trendy, young, or traditional, so the product image is defined as "the personality trait of a specific product or service"[3]. The image or personality of a product comes not only from the physical characteristics of the product itself, but the product also can be artificially given a specific personality trait through factors such as packaging, advertising, channels, and prices, to reflect the typical image of the average user[4].

The theoretical model of "person-symbol-audience", which is based on self-concept, refers to the influence of self-concept on brand and consumption, and its content is as follows. First, a person's self-concept is generated by interacting with his or her parents, friends, teachers, and others. Second, a person's self-concept is valuable to him. Third, individuals strive to improve their self-concept because of the general emphasis on self-concept. Fourth, some products can provide social symbols and convey social meaning to the product owner. Fifth, using products with social symbols affects personal, private, and social self-concepts. Sixth, individuals maintain or enhance their ideal self-concept by consuming certain products or services.

---

[1] Grubb E L, Grathwohl H L. Consumer Self-concept, Symbolism and Market Behavior: A Theoretical Approach[J]. Journal of Marketing, 1976, 31(4): 22-27.

[2] Landon E L J. Self Concept, Ideal Self Concept, and Consumer Purchase Intentions[J]. Journal of Consumer Research, 1974, 1(2): 44-51.

[3] Sirgy M J. Using Self-Congruity and Ideal Congruity to Predict Purchase Motivation[J]. Journal of Business Research, 1985, 13(3): 195-206.

[4] Sirgy M J. Self-concept in Consumer Behavior: A Critical Review[J]. Journal of Consumer Research, 1982, 9(3): 287-300.

Although the individual-symbol-audience theoretical model shows that self-concept impacts individual consumption, before using the consumer's self-concept as a relevant marketing tool marketers must recognize that consumers' self-concept is related to the brand image. As is shown in the figure 6.1, the brand that the manufacturer sells must give consumers an ideal self-concept, which means that the brand can be used to allow consumers to explain who they are, what they do, and how they want others to see them. For example, the well-known Ritz-Carlton Resort Hotel, a high-end club for the upper classes, is sought after and envied by the world. The key reason for that popularity is that consumers enjoy aristocratic quality. In the hearts of upper-class members, the hotel is a symbol of identity and status, and if you can vacation at the Ritz-Carlton Resort, you can obtain fashion, elegance, and noble self-satisfaction.

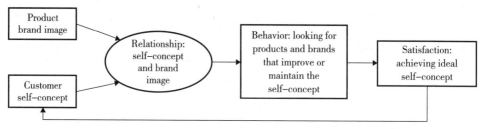

Figure 6.1　The relationship between self-concept and brand image

Many studies at home and abroad have explored the impact of brand image and self-concept consistency on consumer behavior. For example, researchers have explored the relationship between the brand identities of social consumption products (beer and cigarettes) and private consumption products (soap and toothbrush) in terms of the natural self and the ideal self. Some scholars have proposed that consumers will prefer brands, products, or suppliers whose image is consistent with their self-image[①]. Reviewing the results of past research, the relationship between self-concept, product image consistency, and consumer behavior, can be expressed as follows.

First, the consistency between consumers' actual self-concept and product image impacts consumers' consumption decisions, such as product preference, purchase intention, product use, ownership, and loyalty.

Second, the influence of consumers' ideal self-concept and product brand image on consumer decision-making is also usually supported.

Third, only a few studies have found evidence to support the influence of consumers' social self-concept and product brand image consistency on consumption decisions.

Fourth, from the above results, if consumers' self-concept and product image are consistent and congruent, that will prompt consumers to have positive behaviors and attitudes toward the products, and that in turn will affect consumers' product preferences and purchasing tendencies, regardless of whether the standard of consistency comes from the actual self, or the ideal self.

---

①Landon E L J. Self Concept, Ideal Self Concept, and Consumer Purchase Intentions[J]. Journal of Consumer Research, 1974. 1(2): 44-51.

6.4.2 Application of the Self-consistency Theory in Tourism

1) Self-destination Image Congruence and Tourists' Satisfaction

Most of the research measuring tourism satisfaction has measured the gap between the functional attributes of tourism destinations and the experience of tourism consumers, without considering the characteristics of the tourism consumers themselves—that is, the congruence of tourists' self-image with the destination. In light of that omission, some scholars have used the model of congruity between the tourists' self-image and the product image in self-concept theory to explore the relationship between self-image and product image in the same tourist destination and the relationship between self-concept/destination image congruity and the satisfaction of tourism consumers. K. S. Chon divided the interaction into four congruity conditions: positive self-image congruity, positive self-image incongruity, negative self-image incongruity, and negative self-image congruity[①]. Through that analysis, he found that the congruity of the tourists' self-image with their tourism destination image was significantly correlated with tourism satisfaction. For example, when it comes to visiting Mount Tai, a traveler who likes adventure is more likely to be satisfied than a traveler who is afraid of adventure.

2) Self-brand Congruence and Tourist Behavior

Self-image congruity impacts tourism consumption behavior, and the graph summarizes the relationship between the two concepts[②]. From the figure 6.2, we can see that the environmental factors of the destination affect both the tourists' perceived functional attributes and their destination image, thus indirectly affecting their self-image identity. The self-image identity is determined by the tourists' destination image and the tourists' self-concept, and the identity of functional attributes is determined by the perception of the destination and the ideal of the destination. Tourists' self-image congruity and functional congruity together affect the travel behavior of travel consumers (Sirgy, Su, 2000).

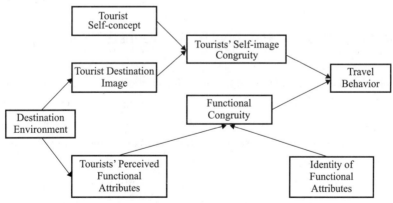

Figure 6.2 Destination image, self-congruity, and travel behavior

---

①Chon K S. Self-image/destination image Congruity[J]. Annals of Tourism Research, 1992, 19(2): 360-363.

②Sirgy M J, Su C. Destination Image, Self-Congruity, and Travel Behavior: Toward an Integrative Model[J]. Journal of Travel Research, 2000, 38(4): 340-352.

3) Self-image Consistency, Tourism Interest, and Tourism Possibility

The consistency model of the self-image - product image in self-concept theory can also be applied to pre-purchasing behavior. Before going on a trip, tourism consumers will learn relevant information about the destination and form an initial image of the destination. If the congruity of this image identity and the self-image is high, it may enhance their tourism interest; on the contrary, if the perception image of the destination is very different from the self-image, it may reduce the tourism possibility. This also applies to the previous point that self-image congruity affects travel behavior.

4) Individualism/Collectivism Effects on Self-image Consistency and Consumption Behavior

In the self-concept theory of the congruence of self-image and product image and the model based on the study of cultural factors, the possible effects of individualism - collectivism on self-image consistency and consumer behavior can be explored. According to Litvin et al., the higher the congruence of individualistic consumers' actual and ideal self-images, the higher their satisfaction[1].

5) Congruence of Self-image and Destination Image, Brand Preference, and Purchases

Destination-self-congruity is the direct result of comparing the actual self-image of the residents, the tourism consumers, and the symbolic elements of the destination and the moving destination image. Malhotra's semantic difference scale and the direct and overall self-image consistency question can be used to investigate tourists of rural tourism directly. After their research, the tourism scholars pointed out that the best way to measure destination - self - congruity is to measure it directly. The results show a significant relationship between self-image consistency and purchasing intention. There is a strong interaction between the revisiting behavior of tourism consumers and their identity of tourism destination image[2].

6) Destination Brand Personality and Tourists' Self-Image Consistency

Dr. Yuksel Ekinci and colleagues have put forward a theoretical model of the process and connotations of destination branding. The branding of tourism destinations is a mutually assisted connection between destinations and tourist consumers, whose emotional needs and basic needs must be met first. However, more importantly, to enable tourists' image and destination terrain to achieve an effective link, that is, self - consistency, the destination personality should be coordinated with the concept of the

---

[1] Litvin S W, Crotts J C, Hefner F L. Cross-cultural Tourist Behaviour: A Replication and Extension Involving Hofstede's Uncertainty Avoidance Dimension[J]. International Journal of Tourism Research, 2004, 6(1): 29-37.

[2] Kastenholz E. Assessment and Role of Destination-self-congruity[J]. Annals of Tourism Research, 2004, 31(3): 719-723.

tourists[①]. Applying the theory of self-consistency in the field of tourist destinations, we learn that the more the destination personality is matched or congruent with the self-concept of the tourists, the more the tourists will have a favorable impression of the destination. Therefore, understanding the consistency between the destination's personality and the tourist's self-concept greatly benefits the complexity of tourist consumer behavior[②].

Chapter Summary

This chapter presents tourism consumer personality. It is divided into four main parts: first, the definition and features of tourism personality, the inter-structure of tourist personality, the influencing factors of personality formation and development, how to classify tourism consumer personality; second, the main theories of tourist personality; third, the definition, composition and influence factors of tourist self-concept; fourth, the definition of self-consistency and its application in tourism.

Issues for Review and Discussion

1. Please give an example and discuss why tourists pursue the ideal self through travel. How do we bridge the gap between the true self and the ideal self?

2. Why do tourists from the same area have similar personality characteristics? Please give an example.

3. Please give some concrete examples of the brand personality and its application in the practice of tourism marketing.

China Story

The JI Hotel Leads the Market in Personalized Service and Reshapes the Brand Image of Mid-range Hotels

Exercises

Recom-
mended
Reading

---

① Ekinci Y, Hosany S. Destination Personality: An Application of Brand Personality to Tourism Destinations[J]. Journal of Travel Research, 2006, 45(2): 127-139.

② Çifci S, Ekinci Y, Whyatt G, et al. A Cross Validation of Consumer-based Brand Equity Models: Driving Customer Equity in Retail Brands[J]. Journal of Business Research, 2016, 69(9): 3740-3747.

Chapter 7
The Impacts of Technology on Tourism Consumer Behavior

Learning Objectives

After reading this chapter, you should have a good understanding of the following points:

(1) define the key tourism technologies;
(2) learn the applications of different types of technology in tourism;
(3) learn the impacts of technology on the tourism industry;
(4) learn the impacts of technology on tourism consumer behavior;
(5) understand the differences in the impact of technology on different stages of the tourism process.

Technical Words

English Words	中文翻译
augmented reality	增强现实
virtual reality	虚拟现实
holographic projection	全息投影
portable devices	移动设备
immersive experience equipment	沉浸体验设备
big data	大数据

Chapter 7 The Impacts of Technology on Tourism Consumer Behavior

Knowledge Graph

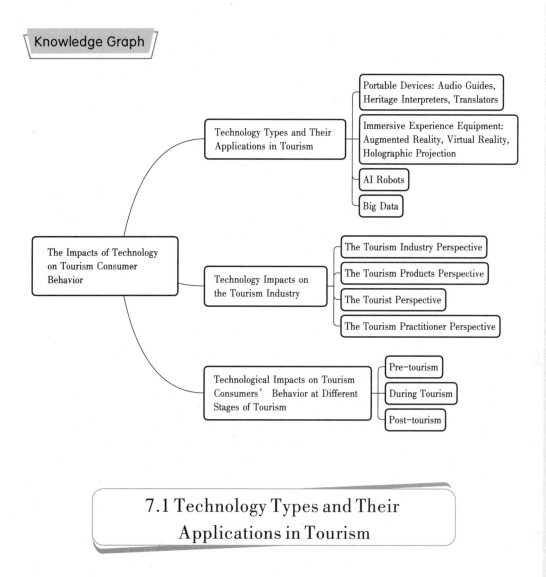

7.1 Technology Types and Their Applications in Tourism

7.1.1 Portable Devices: Audio Guides, Heritage Interpreters, Translators

1) Definition of Portable Devices

(1) Audio guides.

An audio guide is an automatic induction audio guide device that is applied at a scenic spot or exhibition hall, automatically sensing and presenting the explanatory words of the scenic spot or the museum exhibition hall and playing the picture information for the explanation point. Its working principle functions thusly: the scenic spots or museums and other scenic spots first deploy transmitters to transmit signals at any point that needs to be explained. It will automatically trigger the explanation when the wireless audio guide machine is carried into the transmitter sensing area, so that tourists can walk to wherever an audio receiver is and hear an explanation about where they are, with the wireless audio guide being equipped with multiple languages from which foreign tourists can choose. Induction of the guide's program is fully automatic, without any manual operation, although it has a dual manual on-demand mode.

(2) Heritage interpreters.

Heritage interpretations are ways of conveying information to visitors about educational, natural, or recreational places such as museums, parks, or science centers. More specifically, a heritage interpreter is the exchange or interpretation of information about the nature, origin, and purpose of historical, natural or cultural resources, objects, places, and phenomena, using personal or impersonal methods. After its use in other European languages, some international museological authorities prefer to use the word "mediation" to denote the same concept.

(3) Translators.

A travel translator provides translation services for the tourism and travel industry in approximately 200 languages. With travel options becoming more accessible via the Internet and mobile devices, travel translators work with travel agencies, car rental companies, airlines, hotels, bed-and-breakfasts, resorts, theme parks, and local organizations to keep communication flowing.

2) The Application of Portable Devices in Tourism

Audio guides have been used in scenic spots and museums, with each person carrying an audio guide machine that they can play by themselves. Tourists do not need any operators other than themselves. After entering the scenic spot, the audio guide machine automatically senses the voice explanation for that spot, and the navigation machine immediately senses the signal of the explanation point, triggering the explanatory words and the picture information for the explanation point. Visitors can clearly hear the explanation of the explanation point through the audio guide machine and can see the corresponding display on the audio guide machine. The perfect combination of picture information, explanations, and images enables tourists to play the machine effectively and however they like—they can even play it on demand. The audio guide usually also has instructions on a map of each area of the scenic spot, and tourists can check the map at any time. The audio guide machine is currently the most advanced equipment for scenic spot guides and provides convenience for most of the travel and entertainment venues or the culture in an exhibition hall.

Heritage interpretations can take place at dedicated interpretive centers and in museums, historic sites, parks, art galleries, nature centers, zoos, aquariums, botanical gardens, nature reserves, and many other heritage sites. Interpretations can assume many forms and may include guided walks, talks, plays, staff stops, displays, signs, labels, artwork, brochures, interactives, audio guides, and audiovisual media. The process of developing a structured approach to explaining the stories, messages, and information about a heritage site is called interpretive planning.

Tourism is a leading industry in the use of translations. The vast majority of the planners that make up the field for translations understand the importance of high-quality translations in reaching target audiences. In fact, travel-related translation is essential not only for attracting new customers, but also for building user loyalty. It is also important to note that the travel industry is one of the fastest-adapting industries to online sales, with customers accustomed to using the Internet to book vacations. The strong digitization of the travel industry has driven companies to invest in travel translation to reach every market. Travel and tourism translation involve any type of document and can help travelers make informed decisions when planning a trip. This can be anything from travel guides, websites, and maps, to menus, brochures, and audio guides. These documents can also be in a variety of different formats, including physical and digital formats, as well as audio and video ones. A large amount of travel content focuses on marketing a destination's services by reaching the target audience, which means that content often includes testimonials and cultural references from previous clients. In order for that content to have the same impact in different languages, travel destinations may need a localization service, which adjusts the content so that it conveys the same emotion and tone as the original content, thus resulting in text that is familiar to listeners.

7.1.2 Immersive Experience Equipment: Augmented Reality, Virtual Reality, Holographic Projection

1) Definitions of Immersive Experience Equipment

(1) Augmented reality.

Augmented reality (AR) is a digital extension of human vision and hearing, typically accessed through smart glasses (head-mounted displays), laptops, tablets, and mobile phones. It is defined as "supplementing the real world with computer-generated virtual objects that appear to coexist in the same space as the real world". Although AR research dates back to the 1960s in computer science, technical and facility constraints still limit AR's widespread adoption for public use. With the launch of the iPhone in 2007, smartphones have gradually occupied the mobile device market as an important carrier for making AR applications accessible. However, AR applications are still not well known or commonly used by the general public. Thanks to the popularity of the AR game in 2016, the popularity of AR quickly spread, and the public's sudden enthusiasm for using AR applications has prompted researchers to explore this unique and innovative technology.

(2) Virtual reality.

Virtual reality (VR) can be described as a virtual computer-simulated world, whereas mixed reality (MR) combines real and virtual objects so that users can seamlessly interact with them. VR has been described as a widely used technology that is expected to have a profound impact on the future of tourism. VR has become an emerging technology in many different fields, but its role in the travel industry is particularly important. After all, it enables travelers to experience far-flung places from the comfort of their own home, and may determine whether they ultimately book a trip.

(3) Holographic projection.

Holographic projection has been around since the 1940s—the term "hologram" was first produced by Hungarian/British engineer Dennis Gabor in 1949. Holographic projectors provide either a two-dimensional or three-dimensional projection which can be seen without any extra equipment. With technology as the means, the scene as the basis, the light and shadow as the performance, and the user experience as the core, holography generates emotional resonance, forms self-communication, prolongs the stay time of tourists, and develops the stickiness of tourists. As its core principle, holography not only advocates to protect the ecology and the environment, but also shows an all-around fantasy night tour scenic spot with culture as the core implied feature.

2) Applications of AR in Tourism

AR travel guides can instantly provide the latest background information in a convenient form, showing various three-dimensional landscapes or interactive videos. AR applications can provide tourists with necessary travel information, enhanced maps for cities, and other useful information including street and building names, associated attractions, and more. Travelers can also use AR hotel guides to scan printed or online images in hotel brochures for additional content when looking for hotels in which to stay. Travelers staying in large hotels can use the Navigation AR App to find pools, restaurants, entertainment areas, or spas. Devices for AR in tourist attractions can also help visitors navigate parks or zoos more easily, so that the visitors needn't worry about getting lost while visiting places of interest. Specifically, the application of AR in the tourism industry can be divided into the following categories.

(1) AR real-scene navigation.

When tourists initiate augmented reality real-scene navigation, real-time navigation guidance integrated with a real scene is immediately presented in front of them. The distance, time, and road signs are superimposed on such things as an iconic building's road signs. AR can provide tourists with route navigation of scenic spots, on the basis of location and direction. Interactive AR maps function like a walking guide and allow tourists to have more 3D interactive special effects with the scenic spots. Such maps are specialized tour guides.

(2) AR display guides.

AR display tours can trigger AR dynamic effects through AR scanning maps, offering such features as introductions to scenic spots and voice explanations that are complete with both virtual and real interactions. AR technology has also been used widely to introduce and describe exhibits in museums. This technology provides visitors with a guided introduction to exhibits by superimposing virtual text, pictures, videos, and other information on the exhibits. Visitors can interact with cultural relics in real time through voice interactions and gesture interactions—giving them a 360° immersive experience that realizes the multidimensional, real-time interactive experience of people, scenery, and objects.

(3) AR scene restoration.

AR technology can also be applied to the restoration and display of cultural relics, on the original site of cultural relics or of incomplete cultural relics, such that the restored part and the remaining part can be perfectly combined through AR technology, allowing visitors to understand the original appearance of cultural relics and to achieve an immersive effect. Scene restoration with AR can also be used for the reproduction of cultural sites and classic scenes—AR employs simultaneous localization and mapping (SLAM) technology to perform real-time positioning and map construction of outdoor buildings (such as mythological figures in scenic spots, historical scenes), thereby letting tourists immerse themselves in the scene and experience the unique artistic conception and charm of a scenic spot.

(4) AR fun interactions.

In recent years, AR large-screen interactions have become a new favorite in major exhibition halls, museums, shopping malls, and entertainment venues. People who come and go can interact with the pictures on the screen, while the integration of reality and virtual reality is vivid and the new play interaction can make everyone linger. Combined with the specific needs of the scenic spot, various AR interactive games can be added to the play route to increase the fun for tourists along their way.

(5) Virtual fusion photos.

"Virtual Play" can construct any virtual AR image for tourists to pose for pictures while traveling, allowing tourists to take pictures wherever they want, and with whomever they want.

(6) AR cultural and creative products.

In order to make a journey more meaningful, tourism destinations can also customize exclusive AR cultural and creative products according to the characteristics of the scenic spot, and thereby sweep the silent tickets/souvenirs to life in front of consumers. Such technology can also create a virtual intellectual property (IP) image according to the theme of the scenic spot, to help the brand upgrade the scenic spot and realize the merging of science and technology.

By combining AR technology, implanting various themed IPs in scenic spots, designing interactions such as treasure hunts, collections, punch cards, and so on, a destination can attract tourists to scan a space experience, complete achievements, and obtain coupons in hotels, homestays, restaurants, and shops, and can achieve true precision in location marketing to drive business conversions.

3) The Application of VR in Tourism

The use of VR in tourism enables customers to experience everything from virtual hotel tours and restaurants to landmarks, national parks, and even specific events. Interactivity and immersion can also help a destination gain a competitive edge over competitors who have yet to capitalize on these technology trends. Most VR tours or 360° tours are now compatible with major web browsers, thus helping those who are reluctant to travel due to the disability see the benefits of a destination more clearly. Because this is an open technology, travel companies and hotels can adopt it to suit their needs—for example, hotels can choose the name of a virtual assistant in the hotel. Travel marketers can use VR as an innovative way to communicate and deliver authentic experiences. Given the intangible nature of most travel products and services, VR promises to enrich the inspiring and informative richness of customer journeys by giving travelers the opportunity to "live" the travel experience and be exposed to a wealth of trusted information. The use of VR can also have an impact on the on-site travel experience and the post-trip phase. For example, museums can offer real-time VR experiences, and in fact, the advent of the first all-in-one camera rigs will soon enable visitors to capture and share user-generated VR content after their vacation experiences.

(1) VR virtual tours.

Virtual tours combine the VR content of the scenic spot with hardware devices such as VR headsets, and users can experience the scenic spot without leaving home to take a scenic tour.

(2) VR+tourism.

"VR+tourism" belongs to a class of tourism additional projects and serves real tourism. Taking the VR hotel as an example, by experiencing a hotel scene with VR technology, tourists can become familiar in advance with the accommodation conditions in a scenic spot. In this way, the hotel situation can be more concretely displayed than it can with the traditional photos, making it convenient for tourists to choose accommodations.

(3) VR tourism projects.

A common type of VR tourism project is VR theme parks, which are similar to large VR off-line experience stores but are larger in scale, with more complete systems and corresponding play systems. Theme parks have begun to use VR technology to make people's play activities more fun and memorable.

4) The Application of Holographic Projection in Tourism Scenes

Holographic projection technology can bring to life the night economy of a scenic spot, break the dimensional wall, and gain the favor of more young tourists. The application of holographic projection technology in global tourism, "holographic projection display+tourism performance", and "holographic projection+interactive experiences", and so on, can bring new experiences and new opportunities to tourist attractions and towns. Holographic projection technology can be used not only in concerts, evening parties, dinners, sci-fi movies, theaters, conferences, and forums, etc., but also in theme parks, science and technology museums, planning halls, experience halls, memorial halls and other scenic spots, and restaurants. Destination promotional activities, using more three-dimensional displays of tourist information, tourist-attraction terrain, and tourist-attraction architectural styles, can form an interactive experience, attract more attention from tourists, help tourists to obtain corresponding information through communication with virtual characters, obtain tourists' feedback, and give visitors novel interactive communication and technological experiences. Here are some specific examples.

(1) Water screen projections.

Water screen projections project an image on a water screen or water curtain. Such projections are different from water mist projections, water screen movies, and 3D projections. The carrier of the former is the real water body, and the carrier of the latter is "fog". The water curtain projection is a combination of a high-pressure water pump and a special water curtain generator, which sprays water at high speed from bottom to top. After the water is atomized, a fan-shaped "curtain" is formed, and then a professional holographic projector projects a special video on this fan-shaped "curtain", making it look from a distance like a huge movie.

(2) Building holographic projections.

An architectural holographic projection uses the wall of a building as the background curtain for holographic projection, and uses advanced holographic projection image production technology to create a variety of light and shadow effects, bringing stunning and shocking effects to the audience. The landscape displayed by an architectural holographic projection can attract a large number of media reporters and tourists, and through their dissemination, effective publicity can be achieved.

(3) Holographic projections and interactive ground screens.

The eye-catching interactive display method can be very effectively used in an exhibition hall or at the entrance to an exhibition hall, to adjust the atmosphere of the scene. Special effects can also be customized for different occasions. A ground interactive projection can be made into a popular mini game. The interactive form is novel: the projection changes with the audience's footsteps, and everyone can participate. Other forms are also available, such as majestic waterfalls and beautiful beaches, which make for an immersive experience. An original beach becomes especially attractive if the attraction combines light and shadow.

7.1.3 AI Robots

1) Definition of AI Robots

Artificial intelligence (AI), is a branch of computer science in which machines and computers simulate human intelligence. In artificial intelligence, machines are programmed to think like humans and perform tasks that heretofore only humans could do, and it leverages human problem-solving and decision-making abilities. Robots are artificial agents acting in the real-world environment, and they are programmed to manipulate objects by perceiving, picking, moving, or modifying the physical properties of an object, destroying it, or otherwise having an effect, thereby freeing humans from doing repetitive functions without becoming bored, distracted, or exhausted. The robots have a mechanical construction, form, or shape that is designed to accomplish a particular task. They have electrical components that provide power and control for themselves, and they contain some level of computer programming that determines what, when, and how themselves do something.

2) Application of AI Robots in Hotels

Although AI is seen as an emerging technology trend, the hospitality industry has already been reaping AI's incredible benefits and feeling its wide-ranging impact on the industry's business momentum. From AI-powered robotic concierges standing at the front desks of hotels, to voice-activated assistants that can speed up the customer experience, AI is successfully powering the hospitality industry today.

(1) Face-to-face customer-service robots.

Artificial intelligence has been incorporated into many areas of travel and tourism, making life easier for global travelers. Robots are gradually infiltrating customer service in the travel industry, thereby eliminating the need for human agents. Gone are the days of waiting in line for information or trying to find a gate in a busy terminal, and some popular airports and hotels are now using robots to assist travelers in such situations. For example, many airports use robots for facial recognition and airport security scanning. With the help of artificial intelligence, travelers no longer need to go to travel agencies to book flights or find accommodations. Some artificial intelligence assistants and smart chatbots have now replaced travel agents, allowing travelers to book flights and accommodations online, as well as rent cars. These chatbots are deployed on social media sites to provide users with a more personalized booking experience.

(2) Use of AI robots to provide diversified and refined services.

More and more hotels are beginning to realize that in-depth customer service and proper use of customer insights and input are the best keys to enhancing brand value, customers are not only being satisfied with the charm of the hotel interior, but also with the services provided by real AI robots. AI-driven chatbots performing as the key to customer service will also intervene in all aspects of hotel services. Many hotels use smart robots to entertain customers when they arrive, and hotel guests can also use a hotel's special mobile device to interact with the chatbot to perform tasks related to their smartphones, such as unlocking rooms, adjusting room temperature, operating curtains, ordering drinks, and so on. When guests enter their room, they can access GPS capabilities, games, and entertainment, and with AI-powered built-in hotel Apps, guests can access unlimited data and make international calls, consult a handy city tour guide to attractions from their AI-enabled mobile phone, and so on, with all of these features richly enhancing the consumer experience.

(3) Example: Connie, the robot concierge in the Hilton.

In the case of Hilton Worldwide, the AI-powered concierge service Connie has transformed the hotel guest experience. Connie is believed to be the first-ever two-foot-tall AI robot. Like a human concierge, Connie can stand at the front desk and assist arriving hotel guests with a bipedal brace. The Connie bot uses IBM's AI programs to respond to human queries related to hotel features and local attractions and to advise consumers. It uses natural language processing to understand sentences when someone talks to it.

In addition, the robot can indicate directions to guests by moving its arms and legs, it can light up with different colors to express different human emotions, and it continuously learns and fine-tunes its abilities from human interactions. For guests, robots not only provide a pleasant experience, but also keep customers safe in the risky scenario.

7.1.4 Big Data

1) Definition of Big Data

Big data is the data that contains greater variety and arrives in increasingly large volumes and with higher velocity. This is also known as the three Vs: Volume, Velocity, and Variety. Big data is a larger and more complex dataset, especially data from new sources. These datasets are so voluminous that traditional data processing software just cannot manage them, but they can be used to address business problems that people couldn't solve in the past.

2) Applications of Big Data in Tourism

In modern tourism management, big data has become a reality, and almost all successful companies have adopted their own data-collection techniques. One of the most popular uses of such data is to improve personalization for customers, with travel companies using the information they collect to make specific adjustments to their offerings. Another valuable use of big data is to analyze current business performance. In particular, hotel owners can use big data for revenue management, leveraging historical occupancy rates and analyzing other past trends to better predict demand levels. Pricing and promotion strategies can also be optimized when demand is predictable.

Hotel chains can use guest information to determine the best targets for marketing campaigns, such as checking their database to see the amount spent by a guest, the guest's reason for the trip, and the guest's country of origin, and they can cross-check that information with public data from government sources, in order to develop the most accurate customer profiles and achieve high success rates for satisfying customers. In this way, hotels can better segment their activities to increase their efficiency and optimize the investment required for those activities.

Big data can promote the transformation of traditional tourism into intelligent tourism. The traditional tourism industry has the shortcomings of homogenization, with extensive but singular tourism products and services. With the rapid development of information technology, the industry has been unable to meet the diverse needs of today's consumers. Due to the homogeneity of products in the market, offline travel agencies use low prices to attract consumers and engage in price wars that may cause the industry to fall into vicious competition, and that then can have a negative impact on tourism companies and reduce tourists' satisfaction with their experiences. Therefore, processing massive amounts of tourist information through big data technology and successfully executing data integration and analysis are the keys to improving tourists' experiences.

Big data records the needs and preferences of tourists. Through a user database, destinations can focus on tourist behavior and user experience, build tourist portraits, more accurately and quickly grasp tourist consumption habits, ensure the quality of tourist activities and personnel safety, improve tourists' experiences, refine market operations, and transform their business to smart tourism. The integration of big data technology and tourism-related industries enables the cross-penetration of different industrial elements, changes market demand, promotes the efficient allocation of elements for the development of the tourism industry, and enhances the industry's competitiveness.

7.2 Technology Impacts on the Tourism Industry

7.2.1 The Tourism Industry Perspective

1) Creation of a New and Logical Business Model

Technological innovation has given rise to a new and logical business model. If the current round of business model innovation in the tourism industry is being brought about by Internet technology, then the next round of business model innovation will likely be dominated by blockchain technology, which has already changed the basic logic and manner of business. The issuance of Digital Currency Electronic Payment (DECP) will speed up the application of the blockchain in China and elsewhere, and will also have a profound impact on the tourism industry, including the operation of enterprises and the supervision of the industry. As of October 2019, there were 27,513 domestic blockchain companies, mostly small and medium-sized enterprises. From a global perspective, more than 95% of blockchain financing events are currently in the seed-funding round, angel-investor round, and A round stages, and only 3% are in the B round stage and later. The European travel agency giant TUI Group announced in 2017 that it would start investing in blockchains, thus becoming the first company in the travel industry to try to apply blockchain technology. At present, there are many well-developed blockchain travel service and distribution platforms. The provision of smart-contract templates enables users to make modular customizations according to their needs, replace traditional OTAs in digital form, and provide service constraints and guarantees for both parties to a transaction. Linking to travel companies on such platforms can also bypass middlemen and directly obtain resource quotations from travel service providers. Hotels, airlines, and other suppliers can directly publish their services on the platforms. Travel agencies can find the information about the services they need on the platform. Optimal quotations are provided, thereby eliminating the huge service fees incurred by middlemen for matching transactions.

2) Replacement of the Pattern of Development in Traditional Tourism

In the field of online travel, the Internet and digital technologies have reshaped the transaction links of the travel industry, and OTAs have quickly replaced the original travel agencies, ticket centers, and other channels. In the first half of 2019, China's online travel transaction volume exceeded 700-billion-yuan, accounting for nearly 70% of online travel consumption. The scale of online travel booking netizens reached 150 million, a year-on-year increase of more than 60%, and the penetration rate continued to increase rapidly. In the hotel sector, the shared-accommodation platform Airbnb announced in 2019 that its hosts have opened their doors to more than 6 million properties worldwide—more than the total number of rooms provided by the world's six largest hotel groups. As of the first half of 2019, Tujia Homestay had more than 2.3 million global listings, and the number of domestic and overseas bookings had increased by two times and four times year-on-year, respectively, and had achieved a 15-fold increase in performance in two years. The rapid development of online travel platforms has promoted the same frequency resonance between the online resource side and the offline channel side, thus breaking the original structure of the tourism industry, and it will undoubtedly send a strong shock wave through traditional tourism. Technology-enabled tourism has changed the future pattern of competition, bringing greater convenience, higher quality, and additional experiences to tourists, improving the efficiency of the tourism industry, and boosting the quality of the tourism industry's future development.

3) Technological Innovations for Enhanced Diversification of the Tourism Industry

Tourism is an industry with broad extensions and strong correlations. It has a great ability to integrate with other industries to form new advantages for development. Technological innovation also allows it to very easily provide innovation and development impetus for related industries, cultivate new growth points, and form new kinetic energies. When tourism and technology meet, both in terms of physical reactions and chemical reactions, many new formats and products are born. The combination of traditional travel agencies and the Internet has brought about the rapid development of the online travel industry, and a number of online travel platforms have been formed. Travelling via online platforms has become a new choice for many tourists.

7.2.2 The Tourism Products Perspective

1) Technological Promotion of Research and Development of Tourism Products

The research and development of tourism cultural and creative products, whether referring to the use of materials or the level of craftsmanship, need to be combined with advanced technology, not only for the users' end-quality experience in terms of vision, touch, and cultural interactions, but also in terms of craftsmanship, materials, and commodity packaging. The integration of modern technology into the tourism industry makes traditional tourism products glow with new ideas and fresh charm.

"MotoEye—AR Augmented Reality Personal Equipment" is China's first motorcycle smart helmet equipped with head-up display (HUD) hardware, augmented reality, a remote intercom, and other hardware. While riding, the rider can see both virtual images and real scenes from the outside world, as well as benefit from multiple functions, such as voice control, track recording, and so on. Thus, the power of technology is used to improve the safety of riding, make riding more fun, and promote the development of independent travel products.

In addition, in recent years, the number of online cultural and creative stores in Red venues has increased rapidly, and people can buy their favorite Red cultural and creative products without leaving home. Under the guidance of science and technology, digital production, network communication, and personalized consumption are promoting the deep integration of Red culture and trend culture, helping a newly prominent Red culture become popular.

2) Technological Innovation Enrichment and Facilitation of Tourism Services

Tourism is an industry that is rich in happiness and joy. The accessibility of tourist destinations, the comforts of the travel process, and the experiences of tourism projects are all important factors that affect the development of tourism. Thus, it is necessary to have access to complete supporting facilities and complete services. The system enables tourists to live comfortably, travel easily, have fun, and be willing to spend money. In recent years, with the full popularization of high-speed rail technology and the increasingly dense high-speed rail network, the efficiency of railway operation has been greatly improved, and the convenience of people's travel has been raised significantly. Many places that used to cost money, time, and travel, can now be reached easily. *The Opinions on Further Stimulating the Potential of Cultural and Tourism Consumption*, issued by the General Office of the State Council of China, clearly states that it is necessary to improve the level of broadband mobile networks in places of cultural and tourism consumption, improve the convenience of cultural and tourism consumption, and further build upon scientific and technological innovation to promote a strong signal for the development of tourism.

3) Technological Improvement of the Quality of Intelligent Services in Scenic Spots

Modern technology has improved the construction of intelligent infrastructure for the intelligent projects of scenic spots, carried out intelligent transformations of the scenic spots, and realized the application of cutting-edge artificial intelligence such as fingerprint recognition, facial recognition, intelligent tour guides, intelligent perception equipment, and so on, thereby shortening the queues of tourists at scenic spots. Over time, providing more forms of tourism experiences can greatly improve the service quality of the tourism industry. Technological means can be used to upgrade the tourism business model, and can popularize online payment methods such as WeChat payment and Alipay payment, to achieve open and transparent consumption by tourists in scenic areas, and ensure safe and efficient transactions.

At the same time, the development of science and technology has also led to improvements in the service quality of tourism enterprises. In the process of tourism, by relying on artificial intelligence, big data analysis technology, and video communication cloud technology, destinations can achieve real-time monitoring of the status and service quality of tourist attractions, thereby improving the efficiency and quality of their services. Destinations can also establish and gradually improve the mechanisms for release of real-time information and early warnings in scenic spots, can carry out real-time early warning of passenger flow, and can deal with emergencies in a timely and efficient manner, so as to improve the emergency management capabilities of scenic spots. Furthermore, tourists can conduct all-around supervision of travel methods, tourist attractions, tourist hotels, and tourist transportation via the Internet, thereby initiating improvements in service quality and tourism competitiveness through their online supervision.

7.2.3 The Tourist Perspective

1) Provision of a More Personalized Travel Experience for Consumers

Technology helps travelers obtain a personalized travel experience, have the best service at their fingertips, and make their travels a dream vacation. Technological advancements have allowed modern travelers to seek customized and unique travel experiences, and technology has improved the traveler's experiences throughout their entire trip. Indeed, technology can elevate the visitor experience in two ways. First, technology allows hoteliers, agencies, and OTAs to offer consumers more attractive destinations based on their preferences. Second, AR and VR allow consumers to have a premium experience while avoiding personal and environmental risks.

2) Improvement of the User Experience throughout the Entire Tourism Process

Starting from June 6, 2019, China officially entered the first year of 5G commercial use, and "5G+" and other technological applications have spawned new tourism trends such as immersive experiences, human-environment interactions, and super-space experiences. In May 2022, the Window of the World Scenic Spot under the Tourism Investment and Operation Business Group of China Tourism Group reached a cooperative agreement with China Unicom, using "5G+4K+VR" technology and "5G+VR" 360° panoramic technology during the summer beer festival to bring the new experience of online and offline linkage carnival. In the future, the Window of the World will also explore more in-depth applications of 5G technology in the field of cultural tourism in multiple projects, such as "5G+AR" Eagle Eye, "5G+AI" tourism services, "5G+" social sharing, integrated scenic spot management and control, and a scenic spot big data analysis platform, so as to bring the world together. The Window of the World will have been built into the country's leading 5G large-scale cultural theme park. At the same time, the first batch of autonomous driving theme parks in the country also signed contracts with the Window of the World and the Splendid China Scenic Spot to carry out demonstration operations of unmanned vehicles, explore business models such as unmanned distribution and sales, and form a one-stop, smooth human-vehicle intelligence communication—thus activating the multi-sensory experience of tourists and making customer experiences more colorful.

3) Creation of New Opportunities, Such as Sustainable Tourism

(1) Reservations.

Two decades ago, almost 100% of reservations in the travel sector were handled via telephone calls. Fortunately, those inefficient systems are no longer with us. They caused too many errors due to the variety of reservations that were made, often weeks and months in advance, whereas today, tourists can make their own reservations in a few simple clicks. The hoteliers have access to reservations and receive notifications when a reservation is due. They can even track and record guests' information and use it to fuel future marketing initiatives.

(2) Information.

Instead of relying on printed brochures that are often outdated, tourists today have access to websites, forums, and social media. They can visit blogs and Slideshare presentations to discover new attractions, learn more about specific destinations, and even interact with fellow travelers to seek advice and opinions.

The Information and Communication Technologies (ICTs) make it effortless for tourists to look up and compare tourism products on demand. Artificial intelligence is also useful in information distribution, such as via an AI assistant. Given its versatility, AI has also been found uses in other processes, including room mapping, dynamic price tracking, and analytics.

(3) Communication.

Communication is already a technology-based activity. With the modernization of telecommunication networks, expansion of the Internet, and new Apps, communication has never been easier, both internally and externally.

7.2.4 The Tourism Practitioner Perspective

1) Targeted Promotions for the Tourism Market

Technology is not only changing tourists, but also changing tourism practitioners. The combination of tourism and technology makes the tourism market richer and raises its quality. Both online and offline travel companies are seeking deep integrations with technology. According to data from the China Internet Network Information Center, in 2012, the usage rate of mobile devices in China exceeded that of computers for the first time; in 2016, approximately 95.1% of netizens used mobile devices to access the

Internet. Therefore, it is critically important for tourism practitioners to develop tourism products that are in line with the developments of the times and that meet the needs of tourists. For example, using the purchase records of the consumers who have purchased hiking shoes, hiking bags, tents, and the like, practitioners can infer that an individual wants the possibility of going outdoors in his or her travels, and outdoor tourism products can be promoted to that individual. Such refined, precision marketing has become a new way for tourism enterprises to compete.

In addition, AI enables travel companies to better understand customers, and big data allows travel companies to understand consumers' booking channels, booking preferences, personalized choices, route choices, meals/drinks, and room preferences. Big data information classification and management systems provide power for artificial intelligence to meet customers' every need, helping practitioners understand the behavior of a large number of customers and make analyses. Furthermore, AI can use rich data to meet customers' general and personalized needs, and offer customized customer service.

2) Technological Innovations' Contributions to the Wisdom of Tourism Management

Tourism is an industry with a large number of participants and a wide range of industries, and improving its management efficiency and management accuracy are major corporate issues in the tourism industry. Fortunately, technological innovation has provided an efficient solution to this problem in an intelligent way. For example, China has promoted the revolutionization of tourist toilets by building, renovating, and expanding more than 100,000 tourist toilets. The country's tourism management department cooperated with Baidu Maps and used big data technology to develop the "National Tourism Toilet Management System", promoting the launch of an electronic map of tourist toilets. At present, 98,000 toilets have been marked, with a marking rate of nearly 82% in 2019, effectively achieving accurate positioning and dynamic monitoring of the public toilets. In addition, the management department actively promotes "Internet+supervision" and has established a national tourism supervision service platform that integrates administrative approval, in-process and post-event supervision, and information interconnectedness.

3) Technological Improvements to Increase Travel Safety for Tourists

Through technological empowerment, intelligent prevention and control systems such as video surveillance, electronic fences, information-based early warning, and one-button alarm devices have been continuously improved, and the safety of scenic spots has become more intelligent and efficient.

Taking the Lijiang Ancient City Scenic Spot as an example, in order to solve the problem of hidden fire hazards, a smart fire protection system realizes real-time monitoring and dispatching of fire hydrants' water pressure, wire temperature, leakage, and the deployment of firefighting forces. Furthermore, three-dimensional and two-dimensional information integration, and real-time monitoring and early warning capabilities about tile roofs, walls, and the like, provide scientific data support for heritage protection, monitoring, and maintenance. An intelligent analysis video system analyzes eighteen features, such as a person's face, clothing, and behavior in real time, and can quickly find lost older individuals and children, thus improving public safety and service capabilities. Such a system has established a database of people entering and exiting Lijiang Ancient City, and a people flow analysis platform. People flow data can be prompted and guided through electronic screens, guide screens, broadcasts, and the like, and can implement "reservation, peak shift, and current limits" in scenic spots. Such systems can monitor bar sounds and notify bar operators and law enforcement personnel immediately if the bar sounds exceed the specified decibel level. Moreover, the installation of three sets of water quality monitoring, one set of air quality monitoring, six sets of water flow monitoring, and eleven river monitoring probes to conduct intelligent management of river environment inspections and comprehensive law enforcement supervision has taken place in the ancient city of Lijiang. Other systems projects have completed the video kitchen renovation work of 127 catering households, realized an online live broadcast of Mingchu Liangzao's "A Mobile Phone Tour of Yunnan" platform and implemented the food traceability pilot project in the Lishuihui Restaurant in the ancient city of Lijiang, where consumers can check the ingredients of their food by scanning the QR code on the dining table. All production information, and the status of the breeding base can also be viewed in real time through mobile phones. Another system integrates functions such as business information, company punishment records, integrity index, repair records, and statistical analysis to dynamically and accurately manage tourist destination operators.

China's Guanzhi Mountain Scenic Spot offers another example. In the past, when the staff monitored the situation of tourists, once they found that the people had left the safe area or had gathered too closely, the staff could only remind the tourists, and the response speed was slow. Now, as long as their mobile phones are turned on, the staff can see the real-time situation of each key area of the scenic spot. In cases of safety risks, they can remotely warn the tourists through a smart speaker.

7.3 Technological Impacts on Tourism Consumers' Behavior at Different Stages of Tourism

7.3.1 Pre-tourism

1) Technological Effects on Tourists' Travel Information Search Process before Traveling

With the developments of technology, customers can use the Internet to search for travel-related information before they travel. First, tourists can find information and assistance in their decision-making processes through proactive communication with travel companies via chat Apps. Second, when tourists are not satisfied with the products or services they consume, they can use email to file a complaint. Young people are relatively more willing to browse their travel information online, and innovative consumers are more likely to use their mobile phones to make reservations, share experiences, or write reviews.

2) Technological Influences on Consumers' Travel Consumption Decisions

The use of social media has a large impact on consumers' travel spending decisions. Tourists use social media sites to obtain information about destinations, hotels, attractions, transportation, prices, and travel budgets, as well as dining information. These smart technologies influence sustainable behavior in the pre-travel consumption phase. Although Gen Y is thought to be more involved than others in the online travel planning process, the impact of the internet in the preconsumption process spans all generations. In addition, social media can significantly influence people's travel plans, especially on sites where tourists can share pictures and videos. The adoption of smartphone technology has reduced visitors' use of printed maps and increased tourist engagement with GPS and geo-collaboration tools when visiting destinations. Furthermore, thanks to the role of technology as an information facilitator, certain important decisions are often made on a website, such as restaurants or places to visit. The impact of these knots on online content on travel consumer behavior. In addition, online information on travel products, services, and destinations can influence consumers' pretrip attitudes and perceptions. Furthermore, some virtual reality websites can influence visitors' willingness to travel, especially because of the VR websites' use of multimedia content. Both extrinsic and intrinsic motivation on social media influence booking intent. Factors such as the relevance, flexibility, completeness, timeliness, and trustworthiness of the information received on social media influence travelers' travel decisions and their satisfaction with online reviews and online purchases.

3) Technology Reduction in Tourists' Perceived Risk of Travel

One factor influencing the adoption of the Internet in travelers' decision-making process is perceived risk and trust. On one hand, the smart pricing and security brought by technology tend to increase consumer trust in travel booking platforms. On the other hand, the opinions on travel websites left by residents and experienced travelers can influence new travelers' decisions. The opinions of seasoned travelers can influence travel issues such as travelers' choices of transportation, accommodations, and currency issues. In addition, existing consumer reviews on online platforms can influence tourists' travel decisions about food and beverages at the destination, travel routes within the destination, and travel safety, all of which reduces the risk and uncertainty of consumers' perception of travel.

7.3.2 During Tourism

1) Improvements to the Convenience of Obtaining Real-time Tourist Information

Tourists can book tickets for scenic spots in real time through a number of mobile Apps, scan the code to enter a park, and no longer need to queue to buy tickets; when traveling independently, they can also search for various travel strategies through Apps. These latest Internet digital technologies greatly improve the convenience of tourism consumption in scenic spots, and that convenience can in turn increase tourists' demand for tourism consumption and guide them in upgrading their consumption.

2) Enhancements for Visitor Immersion and Interactions

With upgrades in cultural tourism consumption, tourists' demand for digital experience tourism products has increased. Under the backdrop of the experience economy and leisure tourism, and now that culture has been integrated into tourism, technology's involvement in tourism has also accelerated, digital experience projects are emerging, and the availability and richness of new digital cultural tourism experience services in cultural tourism projects has deepened.

Immersive tourism requires "cultural creativity plus technological innovation", which have become the two wings of the tourism product experience, with scene-based tourism now being a new consensus for technological innovation and tourism investment. At present, the industry's environment for development is continuously being optimized, and the rapid evolution of digital technologies, such as AR/VR/MR, 3D holographic projections, and motion captures, all provide technical support for the new digital cultural tourism experience.

In the long run, immersive experience projects still have room for iterative upgrades. Both the research and development for new technologies and their actual application, such as those of big data, cloud computing, the Internet of things, blockchains and 5G, and VR/AR, are becoming increasingly mature in the experiential, interactive, and immersive aspects of tourism products—from service models to information integration, technology application, platform construction, and supervision mechanisms, from scenic spots to resorts and distribution centers, to cities and neighborhoods, from enterprises to projects, products, and tourism services, from tourism scene-based systems to digital and intelligent identification systems, and of course, marketing communications. In addition, smart tourism products have begun to be integrated into the whole process, covered by the whole system, and presented in the whole scene.

3) Enhancements for Visitor Flexibility and Fun

Technology can add new experiences to a museum, allowing visitors to enjoy the thrill of cultural entertainment. Although the slogan "bringing history to life" can be seen everywhere, the standard way of describing the actual, cultural relics or culture combined with words does not drive every visitor to confront history through his or her imagination. In addition, many people nowadays prefer dynamic information, such as images, sound effects, and videos. In short, plain text descriptions have lost their influence.

AR technology is a new technology that "seamlessly" integrates real world information and virtual world information (e.g., taste, touch), using computers and other tools of science and technology, for simulating and then superimposing and applying virtual information to the real world so that it can be perceived by human senses to achieve a sensory experience beyond reality. The real environment and virtual objects are superimposed in real time on the same screen or in the same space.

Moreover, by downloading AR software, one can view an exhibition hall interactive and see the whole picture of the exhibition hall online, and then click on a part of the picture to see the corresponding introduction. In a historically significant place, the program using AP augmented reality is quite historically educational, and people are very happy to accept this kind of museum display. For example, an AR pavilion interactive software has been developed by a tech company that provides geospatial navigation and guidance for culture and history. On a mobile App, users can display photos and videos of history and historical events at specific coordinates, which is a very good thing to attract tourists. The scenery of the museum can be moved on the mobile phone, greatly increasing the fun of a tour.

4) Facilitation of Short-term Decisions

The background of the tourist attraction system analyzes the preferences and play habits of tourists according to the tourists' tags, browsing behavior, relevant shopping information, age, and other information available in big data, and then recommends corresponding personalized hotel accommodations, restaurants, tourist attractions, and tourism activities and other personalized tourism products. Opening an unmanned shopping store in a scenic spot not only effectively meet the shopping needs of tourists anytime and anywhere, but also reduce the labor costs of the store for the scenic spot and effectively increase the store's profits.

Using crawlers and other technical means to analyze online tourists' evaluations and attitudes toward scenic spots can help managers discover potential public opinion crises in scenic spots. If an evaluation is helpful, the post-tour evaluations of tourists can be analyzed, and ideas can be explored regarding such things as where infrastructure can be improved in the scenic spot and where and how to improve the services to create an entirely favorable image and reputation for the scenic spot.

The background of the tourist attraction system can analyze big data on tourists, choosing tags that can be used for learning the tourists' play preferences, and it can automatically design a tourist route that suits the tourists' "appetite" in the tourism product database according to the tourists' preferences, so that the tourists' journey is more labor-saving, comfortable, and smooth. At the same time, through big data, we can understand the source of a location's tourists, the tourist destinations, and their income and other demographic information. With that information, destination scenic spots can analyze the profiles of their tourists, formulate operational plans more scientifically and effectively, and provide data support for their decision-making.

7.3.3 Post-tourism

1) Accelerated Effects of Word-of-Mouth

Before embarking on a trip, many tourists like to check their strategies and read reviews on different travel Apps. This not only reduces the number of detours on their journey, but it also helps tourists avoid the problem of reaching a destination and finding that the place is not their favorite, and thus it helps them make full use of their precious vacation time. With increasing amounts of available information on scenic spots, tourists can learn relevant tourism information without leaving their homes, and they can review the comments of other tourists critiquing their own experiences at a destination. Information about a scenic spot can help tourists understand the general situation of the destination, and user reviews can thoroughly reflect the popularity of the scenic spot among tourists. Standard aspects, such as service level, are also reflected in the user reviews. As a standard procedure for many people prior to travel, the prospective tourist first goes to the Internet to read reviews, then arranges travel routes and books hotels. After traveling, many will submit their own reviews or experiences on the App. Many of the existing travel Apps pay great attention to the output of content, especially the high-quality travel notes and reviews of tourists. The platforms also encourage users to actively share their travel experiences with everyone. For tourists, online reviews are an important reference for their travel, and for travel agents and scenic spots, these reviews are also worth sharing.

2) Enriched Opportunities for Diversified Evaluations

In the post-tourism stage, many travelers share travel videos and pictures on different platforms, and they may choose different platforms on which to evaluate the food, accommodations, transportation, play activities, or shopping opportunities during their travels. Regardless of whether consumers are satisfied with their travels, many travelers use social media to share their experiences, and having extreme emotions about their experiences may further promote consumers' willingness to comment on social media. Women and young people are more likely than others to conduct online sharing activities. Moreover, consumers' past experiences influence their sharing and browsing behaviors. For instance, people who traveled long distances on their last trip, especially overseas, are more likely to seek out online travel information, read online reviews, and share their experiences online.

3) Enhanced Ways for Tourists' to Collect Memories and Co-create Value

Various online platforms and virtual travel communities provide travelers with a place to record, collect, and store their own memories after travels. Some online platforms allow consumers to share their experiences on a user-friendly and free platform, and they provide opportunities for users to interact with travel providers, making the platform work more effectively—all of which also enhances consumer and travel business interactions and strengthens the relationship between the customer and the company. In addition, the fan pages of some tourism companies provide opportunities for consumers to co-create value with the company—they increase the frequency and duration of interactions between the consumers and social media, and they facilitate the co-creation of value between themselves and their consumers.

Chapter Summary

In this chapter, we have learnt the impacts of technology on tourism consumer behavior. In specific, we have learnt the key tourism technologies, the applications of different types of technology in tourism, the impacts of technology on the tourism industry and consumer behavior, and the differences in the impact of technology on different stages of the tourism process.

Issues for Review and Discussion

1. Do you think VR-based virtual tours can be regarded as actual tourism?
2. Do you think smart robots in hotels will replace human employees?
3. Discuss what innovative technologies will be further applied to tourism in the future.
4. Will these applications have a disruptive impact on consumer behavior?

Case Study 7-1
▼

Technology and Culture are Empowering the Chinese Tourism Enterprise "Huaqiang Fangte" with New Vitality

China Story
▼

New Technology is Revitalizing Thousand-year-old Cultural Relics: The China Grand Canal Immersive Museum

Exercises
▼

Recommended Reading
▼

Note

Chapter 8
Reference Groups

Learning Objectives

After reading this chapter, you should have a good understanding of:
(1) the definitions of reference groups and different types of reference groups;
(2) social influence theories;
(3) different types of reference group influence and reference group power;
(4) the factors that determine reference group influence;
(5) how to apply reference group influence in tourism marketing;
(6) family influences on consumer behavior.

Technical Words

English words	中文翻译
reference group	参照群体
primary reference group	首要参照群体
secondary reference group	次要参照群体
aspirational group	理想群体
associative group	相关群体
dissociative group	远离群体
self-concept	自我概念
self-psychology	自体心理学

续表

English words	中文翻译
existential phenomenology	存在现象学
utilitarian influence	功利性影响
normative influence	规范性影响
comparative influence	比较性影响
social comparison	社会比较
conformity	从众
referent power	参照影响力
expert power	专家影响力
legitimate power	法定影响力
coercive power	胁迫影响力
reward power	奖励影响力
celebrity effect	明星效应
expert effect	专家效应
word-of-mouth (WOM) communication	口碑传播
key opinion leader	关键意见领袖
key opinion customer	关键意见消费者
the family life cycle	家庭生命周期
intergenerational influence	代际影响
pester power	儿童纠缠力

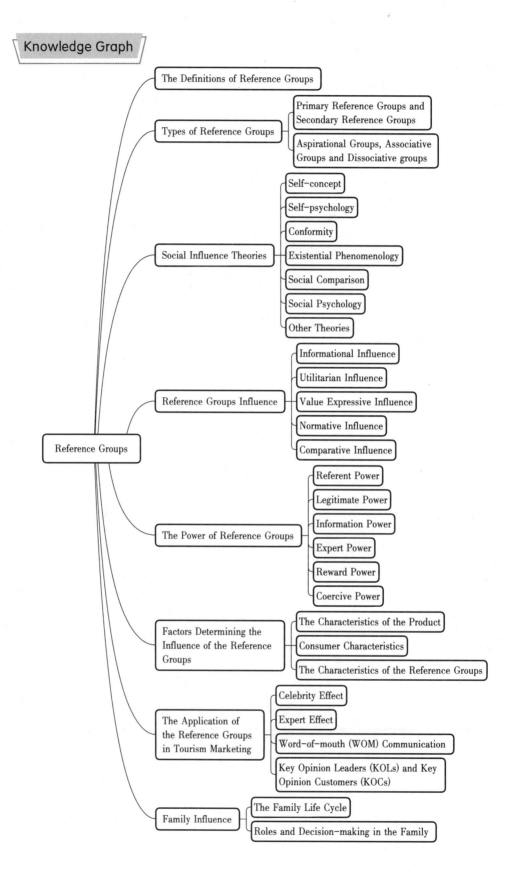

When we shop for clothes, we tend to seek opinions from others. A friend's advice, especially, is sought when we have to make a choice. Why do we value the views of our friends? Why do we buy things approved of by our peers? Why do we follow fashion trends set by celebrities, while not care much about others' opinions when we buy toilet paper? Why do some people influence us while others do not? This chapter will provide answers to these questions.

8.1 The Definitions of Reference Groups

Human beings are social animals living in groups. We influence other group members' attitudes and behaviors and are also influenced by them. A reference group includes individuals or groups who affect our opinions, beliefs, attitudes and behaviors. According to Park and Lessig (1977), a reference group is "an actual or imaginary individual or group conceived of having significant relevance upon an individual's evaluations, aspirations, or behaviors". It is used as a reference and comparison when people make purchasing decisions. Reference groups include not only groups with whom we have direct interaction, such as our colleagues, but also those whom we may never meet in real life, such as a famous singer who has passed away.

8.2 Types of Reference Groups

Reference groups can be categorized into two broad types: primary reference groups and secondary reference groups.

8.2.1 Primary Reference Groups and Secondary Reference Groups

Primary reference groups are basically the set of people whom we meet every day. They can be our family, close friends, classmates, etc. These people from primary reference groups may have a direct and strong impact in our lives and on our purchasing decisions since they are very important to us.

Secondary reference groups are those with whom we interact only occasionally, and we do not take their opinions seriously. For example, a secondary group may include someone with whom we share a mail list, or someone we have met at a national conference but rarely talked to after the event.

8.2.2 Aspirational Groups, Associative Groups and Dissociative groups

Reference groups can also be categorized into aspirational groups, associative groups and dissociative groups depending on their attractiveness and distance from us.

Aspirational groups are reference groups whose members we want to be similar to, such as Yao Ming, a Chinese basketball player who played for the Shanghai Sharks of the Chinese Basketball Association and the Houston Rockets of the US National Basketball Association.

Associative groups include people who more realistically represent our current equals or near-equals, such as our classmates, coworkers, neighbors, or members of clubs and organizations.

Dissociative groups are characterized by attitudes, values, or behaviors that are different from ours, we will rather keep ourselves away from these groups, such as celebrities who are known to have bad taste and those who have committed crimes.

8.3 Social Influence Theories

Why do we need other people's views when we make purchasing decisions? Shouldn't we choose what we like by ourselves? The importance of others can be explained by the theories below.

8.3.1 Self-concept

"Know thyself" is a maxim attributed to the Greek philosopher Socrates. It has often been interpreted in today's terms as a call to know one's own personality traits. Socrates died in 399 B.C., so it is clear that the idea of "self-concept" has existed for a very long time. Self-concept is the sum of everything an individual knows, understands and feels about himself or herself. Each person gradually develops an opinion about himself or herself, such as whether he or she is ugly or beautiful, fat or thin, average or superior, and so on. The self-concept answers the questions of "who am I" and "what kind of person am I", and is the result of a combination of the individual's own experience and the external environment. It is generally believed that consumers will choose products and services that are consistent with their self-concept and avoid products and services that contradict their self-concept. It is in this sense that the study of consumers' self-concept is particularly important for companies, especially for tourism companies, whose main form of product is service.

Individuals have more than one type of self-concept, including: ① actual self-concept, which refers to how individuals actually see themselves; ② ideal self-concept, which refers to how individuals wish to see themselves; ③ social self-concept, which refers to how individuals feel they are perceived by others; ④ ideal social self-concept, which refers to how individuals want others to see them; ⑤ expected self-concept, which refers to how individuals expect to be perceived in the future, a form somewhere between actual self-concept and ideal self-concept. Because expected self-concept reflects an individual's realistic prospect of changing themselves, it may be more valuable to marketers than ideal or real self-concepts.

The diversity of self-concepts means that consumers may choose different self-concepts to guide their attitudes and behaviors in different contexts. For example, when interacting with family members at home, their behavior may be governed more by their actual self-concept, while at the cinema or museum, they may be governed more by their ideal social self-concept.

8.3.2 Self-psychology

American psychologist William James pioneered the study of the psychology of the self. He believed that the self consists of two parts: the perceived object and the perceived subject. The former, also known as the empirical self, is the object of experience and consciousness, including everything that belongs to the individual, while the latter, also known as the pure self, is the subject of individual experience, perception, imagination, choice, memory, and planning, and is the course of the mind that determines action and adaptation to the outside world. James further saw the object of the ego as consisting of the material self, the social self and the spiritual self. The material self includes the physical body, family and material possessions; the social self refers to the impressions that individuals form through others' evaluations of them, such as fame and honor; and the spiritual self represents the inner qualities of individuals, such as temperament, thoughts and values. James believed that there is a hierarchy of these three selves, with the spiritual self at the highest level, the social self below this, and the material self lowest (Harter, 1998).

Subsequent researchers have further extended James' theoretical view and proposed that the concept of self is also composed of three levels (Kuo, 1906). The bottom level (material, physical self) refers to an individual's perception of his or her body, health, appearance, clothing, possessions, skills, etc. The middle level (social self) refers to one's sense of value and competence in the process of interacting with others. And the top level (personality, spiritual self) refers to one's identification with certain beliefs, values and behavioral norms.

8.3.3 Conformity

Conformity is a shift in attitudes or behaviors in response to actual or perceived group pressure. In some circumstances, this social influence may include agreeing with or acting in a way similar to the majority of individuals inside a particular group, or it may include acting in a certain way to appear "normal" to the group. Norms, or unofficial rules that guide behavior, are created by a society's members in order for it to function. Why do individuals conform?

The first reason is cultural pressure. Conformity is practiced to different degrees in different societies. People in an individualist culture are less likely to conform to norms, while those in collectivist societies are more likely to conform. For example, Chinese culture has traditionally placed great value on harmony, synergy, and the achievement of harmony through synergy. Those raised according to Chinese cultural norms regard heaven, earth and human beings as a unity: "heaven and man in one" is seen as the supreme state of the harmony between man and nature. In the political field, this belief is expressed as the ideal of national unity; in the social field, as the inextricable emotional intertwining of individuals, families, clans and countries; in the cultural field, as inclusiveness and embracing of differences; and in the field of ethics, as consideration for others and self-sacrifice for the collectivity. These concepts constitute the collective spirit of the Chinese nation, and play an important role in promoting national unity.

Additionally, Chinese people care about maintaining relationships with others. This makes it important to stay the same and not stand out from the crowd, neither getting ahead nor falling behind, which in turn encourages conformity: if you have it, I will have it, and if you buy it, I will also buy it. Chinese consumption patterns therefore reflect many of the phenomena of conformity. When a certain product sells well, it sells extremely well; yet the same product may be just as quickly forgotten about when its sales figures dip. This kind of situation really makes manufacturers wonder if Chinese consumers have collaborated in advance.

Secondly, individuals conform to the norms of a group to gain the approval and respect of member of the group. Consumers look for brands and products that are valued by other members of a group or society and purchase them in order to impress others. In this way, they gain recognition as "one of them". For example, someone may take a hot air balloon trip if all his/her peers have done that and regard it as a cool thing to do during vacation. In this way, the consumer can share this experience with his/her friends and gain their respect. However, there are also more sophisticated consumers who are more relaxed and confident. These consumers are usually well educated and well paid, and are less likely to feel the need to impress others by purchasing particular brands or products.

The third reason for conformity is fear of the consequences of deviance. Individuals are afraid of being excluded from the group if they do not conform to existing norms. It is easy to become an object of ridicule if one talks or behaves too differently from other members of a group. Due to fear of being punished for his/her non-confirming behavior, an individual may feel pressured and have to adopt those norms that are considered appropriate by others.

Fourthly, an individual's commitment to a group also affects his/her willingness to conform to the group's norms. A highly committed member of a group is more likely to go along with the group's wishes, while those with less dedication are less likely to care about agreeing with the rest of the group.

Finally, the likelihood of conformity is also influenced by the size, unanimity and authority of the groups to which an individual belongs. An individual is more likely to conform to a powerful group. It is more difficult to reject the expectations of a large group with significant authority than a small group with split opinions.

8.3.4 Existential Phenomenology

The phenomenological school believes that the self-concept is a subjective perception and that individuals act according to their own internal frame of reference. Carl Rogers proposed the personality theory. He advocated a self-concept centered on the individual's subjective perception of reality and focused on the individual's consciousness. Rogers's theory of self-concept contains four claims: self-concept is the result of interaction between the person and the environment; self-concept can merge with the values of others; confinement self-concept has stability; and changes in self-concept are the result of growth and learning. Purkey's argument is very similar to the existential phenomenological school, considering the development of self-concept as a process of individual learning with three characteristics: self-concept is learned; self-concept is organized; and self-concept is dynamic.

8.3.5 Social Comparison

In 1954, psychologist Leon Festinger proposed the social comparison theory, argued that individuals use other people as reference points to determine their own social and personal worth and abilities. Later studies have revealed that people who frequently compare themselves to others may be motivated to achieve self-improvement, but they may also feel intense discontent, guilt or remorse, and may develop destructive behaviors, such as lying or eating disorders.

8.3.6 Social Psychology

Erik Homburger Erikson (1959) proposed the theory of psychosocial development, argued that the development of personality is a continuous process throughout life. The theory not only recognizes the influence of personality development on the ego, but also emphasizes the influence of cultural and social factors on personality. According to the psychosocial theory, self-concept begins with the distinction between self and others, and it is developed and learned later.

8.3.7 Other Theories

Shavelson et al. (1976) argued that self-concept can be inferred from a person's response to the environment, and suggested that the construction of self-concept has seven important qualities: self-concept is organized; self-concept is a multi-oriented structure; self-concept is hierarchical; the structure of self-concept is stable; self-concept develops with age; self-concept is evaluable; and self-concept is distinguishable from other constructs.

Guo Weifan(1996) argued that self-concept is a subjective determination of perception rather than an objectively existing fact; and self-concept is a subjective perceptual object with a multifaceted structure that represents attitudes toward oneself and external things. He proposes that self-concept has the following qualities: self-concept is the object of perception; self-concept is subjective; self-concept comprises attitudes toward self and external things.

The above theoretical perspectives can be synthesized as follows. The self-psychology school regards self-concept as the object to be perceived and believes that there is a hierarchy of self-concept. The psychoanalysis school regards self-concept as part of personality. The social psychology school believes that self-concept begins with the distinction between self and others, and is acquired and learned. The existential phenomenology school believes that self-concept is the result of the interaction between individual and environment, and that its development process is dynamic, stable and organized.

8.4 Reference Groups Influence

How do other people interfere with our choices? What value do we seek from them? Mascarenhas and Higby (1993) suggested that reference groups affect consumers' selections and decision making via informational influence, utilitarian influence and value expressive influence.

8.4.1 Informational Influence

An important determinant of consumer purchasing behavior is information or knowledge about the product and its suppliers. One of the values of reference groups lies in their capacity to provide product-related information. The reference group may comprise experts or professionals who work with the products in question. For example, we may ask for recommendations of where to go and what to do from a travel consultant, because we believe they have specialist knowledge on these topics. At the same time, we may also search for advice from independent organizations, for example, the China Consumers Association. In addition, we are also affected by the comments of friends, colleagues, neighbors and other consumers who have used the product, because of their knowledge and experience of the product. For example, we usually check hotel reviews left by previous guests because we expect to obtain truthful information about their actual experience. However, such influence is liable to manipulation by businesses, who may pay customers to generate false positive reviews. This makes it necessary to apply increased scrutiny when evaluating the reliability of such information.

8.4.2 Utilitarian Influence

An individual's purchasing decision can also be affected by the preferences of his/her significant others, including family members, colleagues and bosses, in order to achieve a desirable social outcome. For example, camping holidays have been very popular in China these years, and a lot of people have chosen to go on weekend camping trips with family or friends. These trips are considered evidence of living a trendy lifestyle, and photos are usually shared via social media. These shared experiences in turn influence friends or colleagues, encouraging them to also engage in what seems to be a popular way of taking time off. Similarly, on other occasion, our choice is made to gain approval or recognition from people who we consider important to us. For example, a husband might purchase an all-inclusive holiday on a beautiful island to please his wife; or an employee might go on a hiking adventure because they have observed that this is an activity enjoyed by their boss.

8.4.3 Value Expressive Influence

Consumers may choose certain brands or destinations to express their self-concept or self-image to others. For example, we may choose to go on an adventure holiday to demonstrate our bravery in the pursuit of thrilling experiences. Consumers often compare their own purchases with those of others. For example, if a new member of hiking club notices that all experienced members of the club wear a certain brand of outdoor sports clothing, he will also buy the same brand of outdoor sports clothing because he wants to be like them. At this point, the new member is subject to the value expressive influence of the hiking club. There are two main forces that drive individuals to consciously act in accordance with the norms and beliefs of a group in the absence of external rewards or punishments. On the one hand, the individual may use the reference group to express himself or herself and to enhance his or her self-image. On the other hand, the individual may be particularly fond of the reference group or be very loyal to it and want to establish and maintain long-term relationships with it, thus considering the group's values as his or her own.

8.4.4 Normative Influence

A reference group's normative influence is the influence exerted by group norms or expectations on consumer behavior. These expectations or norms may not be perceived by outsiders, but the group's members are well aware of their existence, as they impact on their purchasing behavior. The norms are the group's expectations of appropriate behavior among its members in a social context; they are the standards of behavior that the group sets for its members. Whenever a group exists, norms come into play. Normative influence occurs and works because of the presence of rewards and punishments. To gain appreciation and avoid punishment, members will act according to the group's expectations. For example, if all the staff at a hotel pay attention to saving energy and water, it is likely that this will affect the workplace habits of new employees also. Normative influence has been used by marketers to promote their products, with advertisers claiming that use of a certain good will guarantee social acceptance and approval. Similarly, another tactic used by marketers attempting to wield normative influence is to claim that not using a certain product will be disapproved of by the group.

8.4.5 Comparative Influence

If a reference group can provide the means for consumers to compare their beliefs, attitudes, and behaviors, then the group has comparative influence on the consumers. The comparative influence is greater when the consumers share more similar features with other members of the group. For example, we are more likely to take recommendations from friends who share the same tastes than from those who we perceive as markedly different from us.

8.5 The Power of Reference Groups

Consumers are affected by reference groups because of the various kinds of power they hold, including referent power, legitimate power, information power, expert power, reward power and coercive power.

8.5.1 Referent Power

When a consumer identifies with or admires the group or persons, the admired groups are copied. For example, fans of a movie star may choose to holiday at the same destination as them.

8.5.2 Legitimate Power

Power that stems from the position hold by the reference group. For example, tourists will take police advice seriously when at an unfamiliar destination.

8.5.3 Information Power

A reference group has information power if they are perceived to have the information needed by the consumer. For example, a tourist may seek advice from a local resident regarding restaurant choice due to his/her local knowledge.

8.5.4 Expert Power

A reference group have expert power if they have specific knowledge in a particular area. For example, an anthropology professor may have expert power in relation to the cultural practices of an ethnic group.

8.5.5 Reward Power

A reference group have reward power if they are able to provide positive reinforcement for certain behavior. For example, an employee may follow the manager's energy-saving behavior due to the latter's ability to reward him/her.

8.5.6 Coercive Power

A reference group have coercive power when they exert their influence through physical or social intimidation. For example, a tour guide may intimidate tourists into purchasing goods at souvenir shops in order to earn commissions.

Case Study 8-1

Chinese Couple to Fly 80,000 Km Around the World

8.6 Factors Determining the Influence of the Reference Groups

The reference groups do not influence every buying decision made by consumers, and even when reference groups influence is at play, consumers are also affected by other factors. Therefore, circumstances change how the effects of the reference groups on consumer purchasing behavior are felt. Specifically, three factors determine the impact of the reference groups—the characteristics of the product, consumer characteristics, and the characteristics of the reference groups themselves.

8.6.1 The Characteristics of the Product

1) The Degree of Necessity of the Product

The higher the degree of necessity of the product, the weaker the reference group's influence on product selection; and vice versa.

2) Visibility at the Time of Product Usage

Reference group influence is greatest when product or brand usage visibility is high.

3) Relevance of Products to Groups

The closer a product is to the execution of group functions, the greater the pressure on individuals to abide by group norms in that activity.

4) Product Life Cycle

Generally speaking, during a product's introduction period, consumers' product purchase decisions are greatly influenced by the reference groups, as they are not very familiar with the new product. In the product's growth period, the reference group's influence on product and brand choice remains high, as individuals continue to seek further information around whether the product is needed and which brand is preferable. In the product's maturity period, after it has become accepted by the market, the reference groups influence is large in brand choice but small in product choice. Finally, during the product's decline period, the reference groups influence is relatively small in both product and brand choice.

8.6.2 Consumer Characteristics

1) Consumer Personalities

Consumers have different personalities and are affected by the reference group differently. In particular, consumers who are thoughtful, independent and have strong analytical and judgment ability are less affected by the reference group, whereas consumers who are indecisive and liable to second-guess themselves are more influenced by the reference group.

2) Consumers' Confidence in the Purchasing Process

The lower consumers' confidence in the purchasing process, the more likely they are to seek help from members of the reference groups, especially when they are unfamiliar with products or the products are important to them. When buying daily necessities, since consumers are familiar with these products and have relatively stable purchasing habits, the reference groups have little impact on them.

3) The loyalty of an Individual to the Reference Groups

Generally speaking, the more loyal an individual is to the reference groups, the more they will abide by the reference groups norms, and thus the more influence the reference groups have on their purchasing behavior.

8.6.3 The Characteristics of the Reference Groups

1) The Reputation and Authority of the Reference Groups in Related Fields

This will mainly affect the informational influence of the reference groups. If a reference group wields significant expertise and authority in its field, consumers will put high levels of trust in it and be more willing to accept and adopt the opinions and suggestions it provides.

2) The Power of the Reference Groups

This mainly affects the degree of normative influence of the reference groups. If a reference group has a formal organizational structure and clear regulations that can effectively reward consumers for obedience and punish disobedience heavily, then the reference group will have strong normative influence on consumers.

3) The Similarity between the Reference Groups and the Consumer

This will mainly affect the degree of the reference groups' expressive value influence. Similarity with the reference groups encourage consumers to feel a strong sense of belonging and identification and to accept the groups' values, thereby influencing consumer behavior.

8.7 The Application of the Reference Groups in Tourism Marketing

Most tourism consumption activities are highly visible and non-essential. Thus, consumers are heavily influenced by the reference groups when purchasing tourism products and services. The influence of a credible, attractive or knowledgeable reference group can lead to changes in tourists' attitudes and behaviors. Therefore, many tourism marketing campaigns highlight the tangible and distinctive benefits that tourism products can offer to tourists through the recommendations of celebrities, authorities, experts or previous consumers.

8.7.1 Celebrity Effect

If a person admires a celebrity, they are likely to emulate his/her behavior and use it as a guide for their own purchasing decisions. Celebrities or public figures such as movies stars, singers and sports stars have great influence over mass consumers, especially those who admire them. For many people, the lifestyle of celebrities represents an ideal life. Celebrity endorsements cater to the psychological need of consumers to imitate celebrities. However, when applying the celebrity effect, tourism enterprises should first consider the consistency of the product image with the image of the celebrity. Secondly, the credibility of the celebrity in the eyes of the audience should be considered. Credibility is mainly determined by two factors: the expertise of the celebrity and their credibility. The former refers to whether the celebrity is in fact familiar with the tourism enterprises, products and services they are advertising and whether he or she has experience in using them. The latter refers to whether the public pronouncements and recommendations made by the celebrity are perceived as trustworthy. If a tourist believes that a celebrity's recommendation of a tourist destination is obviously driven by money, the celebrity effect on that destination is minimal.

8.7.2 Expert Effect

An expert is a person who has specialized training, expertise, experience and specialization in a particular field. The knowledge and experience of experts make them more authoritative than ordinary people in introducing and recommending products and services, thus generating the unique credibility and influence of experts. For example, individuals who enjoy adventure holidays may be influenced by Bear Grylls in their selection of outdoor gear. Similarly, tourists who have never been to a foreign country may seek advice from an experienced travel consultant.

8.7.3 Word-of-mouth (WOM) Communication

As consumers, we are bombarded with marketing information every day via TV/radio commercials, pop-up windows on websites, unsolicited calls to our mobiles and posters in elevators. However, even though these may catch our attention or interest, we always retain some doubt about the truthfulness of the presented information. Rather than uncritically accepting marketing claims, we instead tend to trust our friends' recommendations and the information contained in reviews left by other consumers with no vested financial interest in the business they are reviewing.

Case Study 8-2

Free Trial with Dianping.com

With the widespread use of Internet, WOM recommendations are increasingly being communicated electronically, via blogs, forums, social media platforms and consumer review websites. The online content generated by other users has become the go-to source for information regarding products, services experiences. WOM communications are believed to be more credible than marketing literature, which tends to exaggerate benefits and overlook unfavorable aspects in order to boost sales. In addition, the ubiquitous use of smartphones and social media Apps has made it easier than ever for consumers to share their experiences and comments on products, services and destinations. This sharing can take different forms, such as text, picture, audio and visual. It often happens that we "like" the food and scenery in the pictures shared on friends' WeChat moments and ask where they are. Then we seek more information about the restaurant or the destination, and make plans to visit it by ourselves.

The amount of online information provided by consumers is huge and covers almost every aspect of holiday experience, including visa and immigration service, transportation, accommodation, attractions, restaurants, safety and security, etc. Tripadvisor, the world's top travel guidance platform, has over 490 million active users and provides more than 1 billion reviews of about 8 million businesses. It operates in 43 markets and is available in 22 languages. Mafengwo is one of the most popular travel social media platforms, with over 130 million users, 86% of whom engage in interactions with other users, such as by commenting, liking or sharing. Tourists can share travel experience by writing travel journals, uploading pictures and posting short videos to the site. Over 130,000 travel journals and 410,000 travel Q&As are generated every month on this platform①. According to a market report jointly released by Tongcheng-Elong and Mafengwo on May 20, 2019, 60.8% of tourists shared travel experiences in 2018, among whom 91.1% shared pictures, 65.4% shared textual reviews and 42.3% used short videos; 95% of tourists checked tourism related content before their trip, and 56% spend considerable time planning their trip. The experiences of other tourists have now become a major source of information affecting individuals' selection of destination and itinerary planning.

Recognizing the influence of electronic WOM communications on consumer decision making, destinations and businesses frequently offer a variety of incentives to encourage tourists to share their experiences and leave reviews, such as prize draws, discount vouchers, membership points and even cash.

8.7.4 Key Opinion Leaders (KOLs) and Key Opinion Customers (KOCs)

Key opinion leaders are people who can influence a large number of people's attitudes and behaviors in a certain area due to their social power. They typically exhibit: ①knowledge of a specific area, so they have expert power; ②an ability to synthesize and evaluate product information, so they have information power; ③ social activity and connectedness in their communities; ④a position that engenders credibility and authority, so they have legitimate power; ⑤higher status and educational qualifications, so that they have referent power; ⑥a tendency to try new products and share reviews.

KOLs usually have a loyal following, who trust them and follow their recommendations. An example is the tourism social media influencer Shen Wei, who has 9.69 million followers (and counting) on Sina Weibo. Another example is Fang Qi, the hostess of a Chinese travel TV program, who has 10.9 million followers (and counting) on Douyin. In recent years, there has been growing evidence of KOLs taking free samples from businesses and making sponsored communications focused on the positive sides of products, leading to the reliability of their comments being subjected to increased scrutiny.

Increasingly, customers prefer to trust ordinary consumers who have actual user experience and offer unbiased feedback. Customers who have extensive product knowledge and are active in sharing their knowledge and experiences can exert significant influence on potential customers' selections and decision making. They are called Key Opinion Customers(KOCs). The use of testimony from satisfied customers to promote tourism enterprises and products is a common method of tourism marketing. People often compare themselves with others who are similar to them and are often impressed by lifestyles similar to their own. Other customers' personal experiences add more credibility to marketing campaigns. Word-of-mouth publicity from tourists resonates more with their fellow travelers. Such feedback is considered more reliable than commercial

Case Study 8-3

The RED

---

①Source: http://caijing.chinadaily.com.cn/chanye/2018-03/14/content_35849263.htm.

advertisements and is more likely to be taken into account by other consumers.

8.8 Family Influence

Family is one of consumers' most important primary reference groups. We develop self-concept through interaction with family members. Family is where we start the socialization process, that is, the process through which people learn to behave in ways that are acceptable to other members of a group or society. It is from parents and other family members that children begin to develop values, attitudes and patterns of behavior that are in agreement with their culture. In the context of consumer behavior, children undertake consumer socialization under the influence of their family members. Consumer socialization refers to the process by which children obtain knowledge, skills, attitudes and experiences that are needed as consumers. Pre-adolescent children develop their consumption patterns by following those of their parents and older family members. It is found that younger children have a favorable attitude towards advertisements featuring parental roles, whereas teens tend to favor products that are disapproved of by their parents.

There are three stages of consumer socialization. These are the perceptual stage, the analytical stage and the reflective stage. The perceptual stage occurs when children are between three to seven years old, the period during which children start to learn the difference between advertisements and programs, relate brand names to product categories and appreciate the concept of consumption. From ages seven to eleven, children go through the analytical stage, coming to understand the purpose of advertisement, paying attention to functional cues of products, and developing purchasing influence and negotiation strategies. The reflective stage is when children are between eleven and sixteen years old. During this period, children are aware of marketing tactics and learn to be skeptical about advertisements. At the same time, they become capable of influencing family purchasing decisions.

What we eat, wear, do and buy are initially decided by our parents. Then, as we grow up, we begin to develop personal preferences and make our own choices. Young and single consumers are less affected by their families when choosing holiday destinations and activities than married couples with young children. Throughout our life, our family's influence on our purchasing decisions varies.

8.8.1 The Family Life Cycle

The family life cycle is conventionally represented as a series of stages through which a family may pass over time, moving from independence from one's original family, through forming of one's own family unit, raising kids, and becoming a grandparent.

Family life cycle patterns vary across cultures and subcultures and have changed over time.

An individual's life can be broadly divided into five stages, namely, unmarried, newly married, full nesting, empty nesting and widowhood. Each stage is characterized by a unique set of tourist behaviors.

1) Unmarried Stage: Young and Single

Unmarried family members are economically self-sufficient, unburdened, and enjoy good health. Their own needs for learning, entertainment, friendships, fitness, novelty and wonder are prominent. Tourism activities can help to meet these needs, so they can be regarded as the driving force of tourism activities. In particular, active holidays featuring adventurous activities such as rock climbing, bungee jumping and skydiving meet the needs of young tourists.

2) Newly Married Stage: A Young Couple without Children

In many parts of the world, a honeymoon holiday is part of the wedding plan. In China, honeymoon travel has been seen as fashionable by many young people in economically developed regions. For young people who are not financially well-off, the newly married stage is a more likely time to travel than any other. The reason for this is that people who are not well-off are accustomed to seeing travel as a luxury product consumed publicly, and the newly married stage is a good time to splurge. Young childless couples with a strong desire to indulge themselves are willing to spend a lot of money at this time. Since young couples nowadays tend to have children at a later stage, such childless families represent a market segment of great economic value. Due to a trend of delayed childbirth, this life cycle stage has been extended. Because of the absence of child care restrictions, the travel propensities of young couples at this stage are very high.

3) Full Nesting Stage

(1) Stage Ⅰ: couples with dependent children.

Consumers at this stage often need to pay the rent, bills and expenses associated with a new member of the family, and thus are often under financial pressure. Most of the time of couples at this stage in life is taken up by childcare, and children are too young to travel. They are unlikely to consider long-distance travel, and tend to visit local parks and zoos more frequently. During this stage, family trips may be rare, though it is possible that one spouse, especially the male, may travel for work or business. Some holiday resorts have recognized the need for young couples and offer childcare service to relieve parents.

(2) Stage Ⅱ: couples with school-age children.

At this stage, families with schoolchildren give priority to education. Travel is also an important aspect of the child's education and broadens the child's horizons. Parents will consciously take their children on trips during holidays. Families at this stage in life choose their destinations very carefully, mostly choosing to visit museums, memorial sites, historical and cultural cities and other humanistic landscapes as their targets, so that tourism activities serve to educate their children, and travel mostly as a family of three.

Case Study 8-4

Club Med

(3) Stage Ⅲ: family with self-sufficient children.

People at this stage of life have regular income, and their children are self-sufficient. They enjoy the highest level of purchasing power, and there is a high propensity among these family members for travel. Their actual purchase decisions are subject to cultural influence. Chinese people born in the 1960s and earlier tend to follow a frugal lifestyle and save money in order to provide financial support for their children for significant expenditure, such as weddings, property purchase, and childcare. Families in the full nesting stage Ⅲ are characterized by a more flexible mix of travel members, such as a group trip for all family members, a trip for both parents without the children, a trip for the children without their parents, or a trip for one of the parents and the children.

4) Empty Nesting Stage

(1) Stage Ⅰ: child has become an adult and lives independently, while the parents are still working.

At this stage, the grown-up children live independently. They usually have full-time jobs and are in charge of their own income. They are more likely to travel with friends rather than their parents. The middle-aged couples at this time are generally economically well-off, healthy and have less family commitments. This stage is the prime time for family travel consumption.

(2) stage Ⅱ: old retired couple with more free time, but less income.

After retirement, people have even more time to travel. In terms of family travel consumption, although the length of stay and the destinations visited by travelers at this stage may increase, their sensitivity to prices may increase too. In terms of their choice of travel activities, they prefer less active and more relaxing activities.

8.8.2 Roles and Decision-making in the Family

Family decisions are collective decisions made by all family members, even if individuals intend to purchase products or services entirely with their own money. For a family to function as a cohesive unit, the roles or tasks must be carried out by one or more family members, individually or in cooperation. There are several distinct roles that can be identified in family decision making.

1) The Initiator

The initiator first suggests that the family has a need or want for a particular product. The initiator tends to be the individual with the most urgent need, the heaviest user, and the one who derives the most consumption satisfaction.

2) The Gatekeeper

During the information search stage, the gatekeeper gathers information, controls its flow to other family members, and might make recommendations. The gatekeeper can be a designated Internet searcher.

3) The Influencer

The influencer provides information, advice, and persuasion during the information search and alternative evaluation stages.

4) The Decision Maker

The decision maker has the power to decide whether to buy or not, what to buy, when to buy, where to buy, etc. These family members discuss and listen to all members but may have the final or an important say in the decision.

5) The Purchaser

The purchaser is the one who actually purchases the items according to the orders of the decision maker. But they may also decide on an alternative product in case the initially decided-on product is unavailable or if they opt to go against the instructions of the decision maker.

A family member may have one or several roles in the family decision making process. For example, the younger child may play the role of initiator by proposing a visit to Disneyland Paris. The older child may take the role of gatekeeper and influencer, searching for events, accommodation and transportation associated with the trip. The parents may make the decision of when to go, where to stay and what to do, as well as settling payments as purchaser.

There are four types of family decision-making styles. These are: husband-dominant; wife-dominant; autonomic (when less than half of family members make the choice); and syncretic (when the family, or more than half of the family, jointly make a decision). Recent years have seen a shift toward family decision making that is more about compromise and turn-taking. Spouses typically exert significant influence on decision making.

8.8.3 Intergenerational Influence

Intergenerational influence refers to the influence of the older generation over the younger. For example, children who have been taking ski trips with their parents since they were young are likely to continue to go skiing when they grow up. Similarly, people who enjoyed camping when they were young tend to also take their children on camping holidays.

Some parents want their children to project a certain image, reflecting their desire to live through their children. Such influence is called parent power. For example, some parents take their children on luxury trips, staying in boutique hotels and travelling in private jets. They do this as a means to achieve their own wish, in the lives of their children, for a rich and indulgent lifestyle.

On the other hand, children can also exert influence on their parents through pester power. Pester power can have significant influence on parents' decision making. However, there is an ethical issue around the use of pester power to request parents to

Case Study 8-5

Pester Power or Parent Power?

make certain purchases. Young children have limited capacity for sound judgment. This makes it quite possible that they may request their parents to purchase items without regard for the appropriateness of the purchase.

Chapter Summary

As consumers, our choice of tourism products and services are affected by others, who may or may not have direct interaction with us. The reason that we care about what others think is that our self-concept is developed as a result of the joint effect of our own experience and the external environment. Reference groups exert their influence on us via various powers, including referent power, information power, expert power, reward power, and coercive power. The influence of reference groups on our decisions varies depending on the characteristics of the product, consumers characteristics and the characteristics of the reference group. Family is one of consumers' most imperative primary reference groups. Some parents want their children to project a certain image, so that they can live out their own desires in the lives of their children. On the other hand, children can affect parents' decisions through pester power.

Issues for Review and Discussion

1. Discuss how destinations can use the reference groups power in their promotional campaigns.

2. Discuss to what extent consumers' travel decisions are affected by the reference groups.

3. Discuss whether children should be targeted in destination marketing and explain why.

Chapter 9
Culture

Learning Objectives

After reading this chapter, you should have a good understanding of the following points:

(1) learn the concepts and connotations of culture;
(2) understand the characteristics of culture;
(3) understand the meaning and classification of subculture, and explore the influence of subculture on tourism consumer behavior;
(4) learn the concepts and measurement of cultural differences;
(5) understand the characteristics of traditional Chinese culture and analyze the marketing strategies of tourism enterprises accordingly.

Technical Words

English Words	中文翻译
cultural inheritance	文化继承
cultural immigration	文化移入
placeness	地方性
two-dimensional world culture	二次元文化
Intergenerational theory	代际理论
Gen Z	Z世代
masculine	男性气质文化
feminine	女性气质文化
tourism performance	旅游表演
cultural reproduction	文化再生产
cultural shock	文化冲击
filial piety culture	孝道文化
tipping culture	小费文化

> **Knowledge Graph**

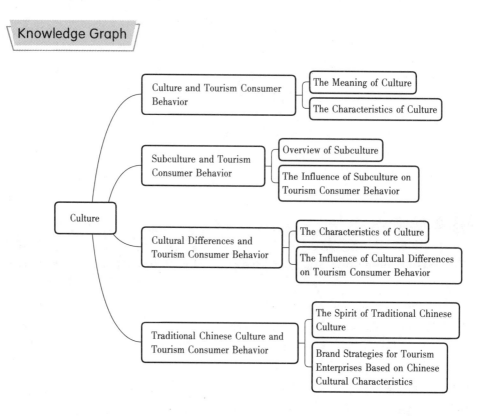

Culture covers a wide range of categories; it includes knowledge culture, traditional culture, science and technology culture, management culture, art culture, social culture, and so on. The influence of culture on people is a relatively slow and long-term process, but once it is internalized into people's attitudes and beliefs, it will form inertia and stereotypes, guide people's behavioral choices, and gradually form relatively stable psychology and behavior. After culture is infused into people's ideas, psychological qualities, behaviors, living habits, and ways of thinking, it has relative stability and persistence. Among the various factors that affect human beings, culture is the most profound and enduring. Culture affects tourism consumers' information collection, value judgment, and purchase of specific tourism commodities. It can be seen that culture affects tourism consumption behavior in various ways.

9.1 Culture and Tourism Consumer Behavior

9.1.1 The Meaning of Culture

Culture is a multi-dimensional and complex concept. As an important aspect of the macro-social environment, culture has a general impact on consumers. We define culture in a broad sense as the sum of material wealth and spiritual wealth created by human beings in the practical process of social and historical development. Broadly speaking, the meaning of culture includes general views, typical cognitive (mental) and perceptual responses, and specific behavioral patterns. Every society creates and uses the symbolism of its culture to represent important characteristics that establish its own cultural and world views.

Culture can be divided into static and dynamic, tangible and intangible categories. Static refers to the remarkable achievements and traditional ideas of human groups, and dynamic refers to patterns of behavior. Tangible refers to remarkable achievements such as man-made artifacts, and intangible refers to traditional concepts, values, cosmology, and behavior patterns obtained and transmitted through symbols.

9.1.2 The Characteristics of Culture

1) Cultural Acquisition

Culture is not innate but is acquired through learning in the process of acquired growth. The methods of cultural acquisition include vertical cultural immersion and horizontal cultural transmission. There are two ways to acquire culture.

One is cultural inheritance: that is, learning the culture of one's own nation. In this way, the inheritance of national culture is maintained, and a unique national personality is formed. Under the influence of thousands of years of traditional culture, the Chinese nation has formed a strong national style and personality. Even under the continuous impact of Western culture today, it still maintains a national character of moderation, tolerance, and modesty. The integration of culture and tourism is conducive to promoting the activation, utilization, inheritance, and innovation of excellent traditional cultural resources. Tourism is an important carrier of cultural resources, as well as a way to transmit cultural scenes, revitalization, and vividness. Relying on excellent cultural resources to develop culture and tourism can not only enhance the characteristics and attractiveness of local cultural tourism and strengthen industrial competitiveness, but can also protect and inherit excellent cultural tourism resources.

The other method of absorption is cultural immigration: that is, learning from foreign cultures. During its evolution, a national culture usually absorbs the contents of other national cultures, and even makes them typical features of the national culture. For example, Chinese dress suits are the result of learning from the West and borrowing from Western clothing culture. The national costume of Japan, the kimono, has been adapted as a continuation of the costumes of the Tang Dynasty. With the rapid development of tourism, tourists from different countries and rigions, and cultural backgrounds have more and more frequent excursions, sightseeing, and cross-cultural communication. In the destination they engage in more communication and dissemination activities, and begin to affect the economy of the tourist destination. Landscape, culture, environment, society, and other aspects have a significant impact. Places that were closed in the past are now very different because of the influx of tourists. Tourism is a pleasure-based flow of people across geographic space. Tourism itself is one of the ways of cross‑cultural communication. Tourists are the carriers and communicators of culture. Tourists come to other places with a series of visible and invisible cultural elements such as language, clothing, behavior, ideas, and concepts of the country and region where they are located. Individual tourists are only in the tourist destination for a short stay, tour, or round of sightseeing. However, when a large number of tourists continue to come to the tourist destination, their impact on the destination cannot be ignored. In essence, this influence is the result of the collision of two regional cultures: that is, the cultural encounter between the tourist destination and the tourist origin.

2) The Dynamic Nature of Culture

Culture is not static, but constantly changing. People's values, behaviors, living habits, preferences and interests will continue to change with the progress of society. To analyze the dynamic nature of culture, we should pay attention to a series of issues such as where culture comes from, how it evolves, and why it changes. For example, Nuo (傩), an ancient religious movement in China, is used to "exorcise the ghosts", pray for blessings, and avoid disasters. The sacrificial ceremonies of Nuo culture are mainly the activities of sacrificing to "ghosts and gods" for people to pray for peace. The Nuo dance is one of the clan activities that appeared in traditional Chinese rural society. For the purpose of praying for good fortune and eliminating disasters, people in the whole village community participate in Nuo ritual activities. The Nuo dance currently only exists in a few areas and is known as "the living fossil" of Chinese culture. As a kind of belief and ritual, Nuo culture relies on the basic desire of the people to avoid disasters. This kind of desire integrates emotion, imagination, ritual, and performance, and has become a unique form of Chinese traditional culture. Nuo culture has undergone many changes due to the absorption of Taoism, Buddhism, and other folk religions, folk dances, folk operas, folk arts, and other factors during its long-term spread. In addition, Nuo culture has undergone many changes during the evolution of the past dynasties due to official attitudes, population migration, ethnic integration, and social changes. The development and utilization of Nuo cultural tourism resources is a huge tourism project. Nuo culture not only still performs traditional functions in a few areas, but also acts as a spiritual medium for the local people to realize their own survival wishes. Moreover, it integrates into modern social culture in the form of "performance" and becomes a channel for tourists to gaze, experience, and understand ancient traditional culture.

3) The Collective Nature of Culture

Culture is shared, and each country, nation, or region will form different cultural characteristics, thus forming its own unique social or group culture. As far as national culture is concerned, each country has formed its own unique language, characters, rituals, customs, habits, national character, national traditions, and way of life in the process of its establishment and development. For example, Japanese culture is influenced by ancient Chinese culture and has strong traditional oriental cultural characteristics. On the other hand, it is widely influenced by European and American technology and literature and art in modern times.

For the Chinese, the Loong (imperial dragon, 龙) is a symbol of the shared spiritual culture of the Chinese nation. Loong culture is a typical representative of Chinese culture and has far-reaching influence on Chinese people and society. It has become a bond of cultural identity and a bridge of emotional connection for the Chinese nation. Loong culture is unique to Chinese culture, but ancient India, Southeast Asia, Europe, America, and other places have venerated or worshipped dragons. Chinese Loong culture is rich in meaning, and the Loong's image has penetrated into all aspects of society. For example, the dragon dance on the Lantern Festival, the Dragon Heads-raising Day (二月二龙抬头), the eating of Long Xumian (龙须面), dragon boat races during the Dragon Boat Festival, dragon pictures, dragon calligraphy, dragon poetry, dragon songs, and so on, are all long-term elements of popular folk culture. Loong has become a connection and accumulation of Chinese culture.

4) The Prescriptiveness of Culture

The prescriptiveness of culture refers to the overall culture of values, behaviors and living habits shared by members of a particular group, which has the ability to regulate and constrain the behavior of each individual member. Culture contains desirable behaviors or patterns that enable members of a group to have a common understanding of how to think and behave in a given situation.

Both individuals and members of society exist and live in a certain cultural atmosphere. The prescriptiveness of culture comes about through the process of emotional and psychological convergence between individuals and groups—that is, the assimilation process of social group members in cognition or emotion. At the individual level, it refers to an individual's rational confirmation of his or her own social identity, which is the lasting driving force for individual social behavior; at the social level, it refers to the shared beliefs and emotions of members of the social community towards the group to which they belong. If someone's thinking or behavior is inconsistent with the group's values, behaviors, and living habits, then this person will receive pressure or condemnation from the group; under such pressure or condemnation, the person will change his or her mind and (in order to avoid embarrassment or ostracism) keep the hidden differences of ideas and concepts, directly maintaining consistency with the group behavioral norms. In recent years, with the growth of the tourism market, the poor behavior of some tourists has become more and more visible in the media and society. In the era of instant media, the phenomenon of uncivilized tourism is more likely to be exposed to the public eye, triggering public discussions. While criticizing and condemning uncivilized tourism behaviors, various media should increase the promotion and praise of civilized tourism behaviors and promote the process of civilized tourism by attaching importance to the participation of the whole people.

5) The Intangibility of Culture

Culture is abstract and intangible, and its influence on consumer behavior is imperceptible and natural. People gradually form a cultural identity in common activities. Therefore, the behavior that people adopt according to a certain culture is often taken for granted. If asked why, the question may seem simple, but it reflects the deep-rooted influence of culture on people's consumption behavior. Generally speaking, it is only when people come into contact with others who have different cultural values and habits that the influence of culture on people's behavior can be felt so deeply.

Chinese food-sharing culture is an example of communal unity and cultural cohesion: the purpose of the Chinese Spring Festival is to reunite the whole family, make a large table of food, and enjoy it together. Chinese people have a deep connection with food, especially shared meals. Every traditional festival has one or more corresponding delicacy. Zongzi(粽子) is eaten on the Dragon Boat Festival, and moon cakes are eaten on the Mid-Autumn Festival. Chinese people also like to use meals to express their feelings. It has been a long-standing tradition to have meals to express gratitude and celebrate the holidays. Food culture links people's social relations with human etiquette. Chinese families start cooking as households, and the family does not "separate stoves"("另分炉灶"). The family custom of eating together symbolizes reunion and happiness. Especially at weddings, funerals, birthdays, and other banquets, it is standard practice to give up your seat and serve tea, toast, and dishes. People at a table eating are livelier, and people become accustomed to deepening their feelings through the ceremony of shared meals.

9.2 Subculture and Tourism Consumer Behavior

9.2.1 Overview of Subculture

Within a dominant culture are smaller cultures with different behaviors and beliefs, known as subcultures. Subculture refers to particular values and beliefs that are separate from but connected to the mainstream culture; it is another special-value concept and behavior that accompanies the mainstream culture. Subculture is a branch of the overall culture, often an aspect of the cultural specificity of each region and group caused by various social and natural factors. For example, due to differences in class, ethnicity, religion, living environment, and so on, groups or regional cultures with their own characteristics can be formed under a unified national culture. Subcultural groups share

Further Reading

Italian Tourist Destinations Race to Welcome Chinese Tourists

common beliefs, values, and behavioral patterns.

Some subcultures can directly affect or influence people's way of life and consumption behavior, and their influence is often greater than that of mainstream culture. The development of Internet technology has not only changed life, but also reconstructed social and cultural styles, language systems, and logical thinking. Subculture is not only the reflection of a specific social-emotional structure in a specific group, but is also the real presentation of the unique emotional structure of the group as it presently is.

Subculture is an important complementary reference for us to feel and understand the general cultural characteristics of an era. Different from mainstream traditional media, new media has the ability to create "a subcultural identity" across cultural barriers, strengthen the interaction and communication between secondary cultures in the form of virtual communities and virtual social networking, and form a more three-dimensional form of cross-cultural communication. When the secondary communication engages in a benign operation, the subculture will react to the mainstream culture to realize the consensus and recognition between the mainstream culture and the subculture.

9.2.2 The Influence of Subculture on Tourism Consumer Behavior

There are many different ways to classify subculture, the more common way is to classify it by by age, gender, region, race, ethnicity, religion, and so on.

1) The Influence of Age Subculture on Tourism Consumer Behavior

Even within the same ethnic group, under the influence of the same religious subculture and regional subculture, groups of different age groups will show cultural differences, thus affecting their tourism consumption behavior. Intergenerational theory is a theoretical model that specifically expounds the formation mechanism and manifestation of "generations" and "intergenerational differences". The intergenerational theoretical research in tourism is embodied in the use of intergenerational theory to analyze the differences in the thinking of different generations and the social or cultural origins of such differences.

Generation refers to the cycle that people go through from birth, growth, to raising the next generation, which is about 20 years. However, in actual research 10-year intervals are mainly used, because every decade of life is an important turning point for people's physical and psychological development. Following this, each 10-year period during a century is the most widely used subgroup: for example, China's post-60s, post-70s, post-80s, and post-90s generations. The unique traits, beliefs, preferences, expectations, and values of each generation tend to accompany people for a lifetime and influence subsequent behaviors, thus providing clues for predictions of subsequent behavioral preferences. Generational personality keeps people's consumption behavior relatively stable, and intergenerational theory can more accurately predict the impact of subcultures of different ages on people's consumption behavior.

Although generational groups and age are related to a certain extent, they are quite different. The influence of generational groups on consumption behavior may be more complex and multi-directional than age. The perspective of generational groups is more comprehensive, emphasizing a series of elements such as the characteristics of generational groups and their related habits and concepts. Intergenerational comparison can not only distinguish the differences in behavior and preferences between different generational groups, but can also deeply analyze the behavior of each generational group and the internal driving mechanism of each generation's preferences.

The influence of age subculture on tourism consumer behavior is also reflected in the generational characteristics of tourism motivation and value pursuit. For example, for young groups, the most important motivation for outbound travel is to communicate with others through accommodation, gain friendship, increase knowledge, and ultimately meet the value needs of interpersonal communication. For the elderly, the main motivations for outbound travel are "going out for a walk while you are healthy" "realizing dreams of youth", and "enjoying your retirement time". Tour operators need to identify typical characteristics, meanings, and behavioral characteristics that people in various groups have in common.

2) The Influence of Gender Subculture on Tourism Consumer Behavior

Groups of different genders will show cultural differences, which will also affect tourism consumption behavior. The influences caused by tourists' individual gender differences include travel motivation identification before travel, information search and processing preferences, travel decision-making, various perception differences during travel, activity preferences and tourism experience, satisfaction perception after travel, and so on. The difference in perception between male and female tourists involves many aspects, such as safety perception, marketing perception, space perception, and so on. The behavior of men and women in society is influenced by their perception of their roles. In general, men are more independent, and self-centered; women are more likely to desire to gain the approval of others and establish harmonious relationships with others. For information collection, men may show more self-confidence than women and spend less energy than women in the process of information collection. For example, when purchasing travel products, female consumers pay more attention to appearance and packaging than male consumers. In the hotel consumption experience, female consumers pay more attention to the layout and decoration of the hotel. In addition, female consumers are far more sensitive to price than male consumers. In terms of purchasing methods, female consumers are usually patient but lack decisiveness.

In terms of tourism motivation, compared with traditional male motivation for things such as sports, adventure, and vacation tourism, women showed more cultural, romantic, shopping, and participation motivation. Gender subcultures have differences in tourism motivation and tourism preferences, which should be considered in destination product supply, route design, and marketing, such as providing more appropriate consumption opportunities for tourists of different genders, and paying attention to different gender groups in the cultural tourism market.

3) The Influence of Regional Subculture on Tourism Consumer Behavior

Differences in regional environment will lead to differences in people's language, lifestyle, consumption customs, and consumption characteristics, forming regional subcultures. The formation of the Chinese nation has been over thousands of years of history, and the cultural forms of various places have also formed their own characteristics in the evolution of thousands of years. The more historical relics a region has, the richer its regional subcultures will be. With the rise of the knowledge economy and the continuous acceleration of the process of economic and social integration, the regional subculture has become an important force to enhance the competitiveness of the regional economy, promote the rapid development of society, and attract cultural tourism consumption. Regional subcultures are cultures with limited spatial scope, but with stability and inheritance. In material production and social life, groups in a certain region will form values, ways of thinking, national art, and moral norms that have local characteristics.

The connotation of regional subculture consists of three levels, namely, the material level, institutional level, and philosophical level. The material level of culture includes the language, food, architecture, clothing, utensils, and so on of people in a specific region. The institutional level includes the custom, etiquette, system, law, religion, and art of people in specific regions. The culture at the philosophical level refers to the value orientation, aesthetic taste, group personality, and so on of people in a specific region. Regional subculture is a deep-level culture that embodies "placeness" and "nationality". For example, Chinese food culture has a long history, but there are obvious regional differences. Regional culture leads to regional consumption customs. Northerners eat dumplings during Chinese New Year, while Southerners eat tangyuan. Southerners like to drink rice wine, while Northerners like to drink Baijiu. Northerners prefer noodles, while Southerners prefer rice. Northerners like to stock up on vegetables, especially in winter. Southerners may be used to buying very little food at a time. According to a survey, Southerners spend more on food and drink than Northerners. People in Northeast China, Central China, Northwest China, and Southwest China generally pay more attention to lunch, while people in North China, East China, and South China eat more for dinner.

4) The Influence of Racial Subculture on Tourism Consumer Behavior

Ethnic group refers to a group of people who are subjectively self-identified and differentiated from other groups because they have a common origin and culture in a relatively large social and cultural system. Differences in body shape, skin color, hair color, and so on of consumers of different ethnic groups will have certain psychological and behavioral influences on them as consumers. For example, people of different skin colors have their own cultural traditions, life attitudes, and behavior habits. Even if they live in the same country or same rigion, they will have unique needs, hobbies, and spending habits.

5) The Influence of Religious Subculture on Tourism Consumer Behavior

Religion is a special cultural phenomenon in the development of human society and an important part of traditional human culture. Different religious groups have different cultural tendencies, customs, and taboos. The most obvious influence of religious culture on tourism consumer behavior is reflected in two aspects: motivation and on-site behavior. In terms of motivation, influenced by specific religious culture, religious worship itself has become an important travel motivation. Therefore, different understandings of religious culture will affect the behavior of tourism consumers. Pilgrims mainly aim at spiritual or religious pilgrimages, and they pay more attention to the authenticity and solemn atmosphere of holy places. Pilgrims are serious, purposeful, and devout spiritual seekers, while tourists are hedonic and superficially focused on getting their wishes fulfilled, and their understanding of religious symbols is quite different. Religious culture also restricts believers' tourism behavior. In terms of field or on-site behavior, tourism is influenced by specific religious culture, which has important influence on both pilgrims and religious and cultural tourists. Religious and cultural tourists must also strictly abide by relevant regulations and respect specific religious culture when visiting religious sites.

9.3 Cultural Differences and Tourism Consumer Behavior

9.3.1 The Measurement of Cultural Differences

Culture is the mental program shared by people in a particular environment; it is not an individual characteristic but is shared by many people with the same education and life experience. According to the differences between cultural systems, Western scholars put forward the concept of cultural differences. In order to more concretely and intuitively express the characteristics of national culture and the differences between national cultures, Western scholars have proposed a number of different multi-dimensional cultural models, of which the most widely cited is Hofstede's theory of cultural dimension.

Proposed by Dutch psychologist Geert Hofstede, Hofstede's cultural dimensions theory is a model for measuring cultural differences in different countries. This model transforms the complex and multi-faceted concept of culture into a measurable variable, providing a tool and theoretical basis for studying the impact of cultural differences. According to Hofstede, culture is the mental program shared by people in an environment that distinguishes one group of people from others. Hofstede collected a large amount of data on IBM employees' values in more than 70 countries from 1967 to 1973. From the data analysis results, he found that the values of IBM employees in different countries are mainly concentrated in four dimensions: individualism/collectivism, uncertainty avoidance, power distance, and masculine/feminine. Based on the results of a Confucian culture-based survey done in collaboration with Chinese scholars, in 1991, Hofstede added a fifth dimension to the original model: long-term/short-term orientation. In 2010, based on Michael Minkov's data analysis of the World Values Questionnaire from 93 countries, a sixth dimension was added: indulgence/restraint.

1) Individualism/Collectivism

In the past, many anthropologists and social psychologists have distinguished human behavior as self-directed and collective-oriented, and this value dimension is one of the indicators of the impact of values on human behavior. Individual and collective values tend to influence human interactions at home, at school, and at work. Hofstede, like other researchers, believed that individualism and collectivism affect the main value orientation of people's communication behavior. For example, many scholars are aware of the important influence of individualism and collectivism in people's interactions, and they all classify individualism and collectivism independently as a dimension that measures cultural values. When understanding individualism and collectivism, it must be recognized that in each individual's values, there is an individual orientation and a collective orientation. No cultural group is completely individualistic or collectivistic; rather, it is a matter of which orientation takes precedence, and whether the primary goal is collective or individual when individuals in these cultures think and act. More individualistic cultures emphasize individual views and preferences, and members of this culture tend to seek diversity and hedonic experiences, while members of more collectivistic cultures tend to be aligned with the needs and goals of the group. Therefore, when members of individualistic cultures have ample income and leisure time, they tend to devote these to hedonic activities and are more likely to choose to travel. Members of a more collectivistic culture may be more inclined to consider organizational and family factors in consumption, thereby reducing personal travel needs.

2) Uncertainty Avoidance

Uncertainty avoidance refers to the degree of threat from uncertainty and ambiguity that a member of society feels. A culture with strong uncertainty avoidance will try to provide occupational security, establish more formal rules, and reject deviating views and behaviors. People in such a culture shy away from vague states of uncertainty and feel safe and secure in a well-structured, rule-specific, stable state. It is generally believed that members of a culture with high uncertainty avoidance are more risk-averse and will not make travel decisions lightly if they perceive a destination to be risky and uncertain. One in a low uncertainty-avoidance culture, on the other hand, does not feel threatened by unknown or uncertain states, but feels at ease in them. Members of a low uncertainty-avoidance culture seek novelty and enjoy new experiences. Even when faced with high-risk destinations, they choose to keep going. The introduction of the dimension of uncertainty avoidance plays an important role in the study of cross-cultural communication. It can further explain the various cultural phenomena of different countries in the world. For example, in low uncertainty avoidance cultures, people show a greater sense of anxiety and mental stress about uncertainty and agree with the sentiment. "Prior preparation leads to success; unpreparedness results in failure." In this conception, people should try their best to avoid competition and conflict when interacting with others. People with a strong sense of competition are often accused of being "performers" and "showing off". People in those culture believe that competition is full of uncertainty, the final result is difficult to know, and winning the competition may not be a good thing.

3) Power Distance

Power distance refers to the degree to which people of low status in a society accept that power is unequally distributed in a society or organization. In a culture with a high power distance, it is difficult for individuals to express their true views. Even if someone feels the irrationality of this inequality, it is difficult to convey such views. In cultures with a low power distance, individuals believe that people are created equal. Freedom and equality are very important to them—that is, when there is inequality in society, they try to downplay it as much as possible.

Hofstede fully considered power, environment, and the social attitude towards women, and judged the degree of unequal power distribution in society and organizations through the dimension of power distance. China is in the East Asian cultural circle and is deeply influenced by Confucian civilization. Chinese culture emphasizes etiquette and rules, and this influence is reflected in all aspects of life. There are various orders and ritual systems in Chinese culture to maintain an orderly social hierarchy between the elder citizens and the younger. The behaviors advocated by these hierarchies and rituals are ultimately to pursue a kind of collectivism, which is completely different from the individualism and materialism advocated by Europe and the United States.

Consumers from cultures with a high power distance accept the phenomenon of power gaps in society. Their acceptance of a power gap means that these consumers believe everyone has a proper place in society. Consumers act according to where they exist in the social class. Consumers from cultures with a high-power distance constantly monitor their behavior to ensure that it matches their social class, and the constant emphasis on class makes them remain highly sensitive to and aware of status differences. The resulting awareness has led consumers from cultures with high power distances to actively seek ways to enhance or improve their social status.

4) Masculine/Feminine

Masculine/feminine culture refers to the degree to which organizational members seek achievement, self-confidence, courage, rewards, and so on—for example, whether they place more emphasis on career success or quality of life. In a more masculine culture, members are keen to pursue achievement, power, and wealth. These types of tourists are looking to make a statement while on vacation and tend to buy expensive items. Members of a masculine culture have a faster pace of life and work and are more likely to be influenced by the motivation to escape from daily life, resulting in tourism consumption. Compared with a more feminine culture and under the condition of relatively abundant income and leisure time, tourists in a masculine culture will be more inclined to travel abroad to show their wealth, status and other information. In a partially feminine culture, members pay more attention to the quality of life, harmony, and morality. Such people value interpersonal relationships and the concept of "home".

5) Long-term/Short-Term Orientation

Long-term/short-term orientation refers to the degree to which an organization has a long-term (or future) preference. This dimension arose directly from the study of the comparison of Eastern and Western cultures, and was originally called "Confucian dynamism"(儒家动力), which refers to the degree to which society attaches importance to the future. This concept measures and describes the extent to which people are willing to make immediate sacrifices for the future, for their children and grandchildren. In a long-term oriented culture, members emphasize the future, advocate frugality and diligence, value shame as a means of social cohesion, and are keen on saving. On the other hand, members of short-term oriented culture are more concerned about the present, do not habitually save, and are more focused on pleasure and travel. The members of the long-term oriented culture have long-term plans in life and are more concerned about the family, while the members of the short-term oriented culture are more self-centered and often have extravagant consumption behaviors.

6) Indulgence/Restraint

An indulgence oriented culture refers to the extent to which an organization allows its members to pursue basic needs and desires. Members of a more indulgent culture tend to be more nonconformist, spend money emotionally, and have a high degree of identification with hedonism, while members of a more restrained culture have a strong sense of self-discipline and restraint, are not keen on communication and entertainment, and have a low degree of identification with hedonism. Generally speaking, members of indulgent cultures tend to enjoy leisure and entertainment, while members of restrained cultures are more likely to identify with thrifty qualities and have a lower preference for leisure and entertainment. It is important to note that indulgence and long-term orientation are not in conflict and can exist at the same time.

Hofstede's cultural model provides an early theoretical basis for cross-cultural research and is recognized as the most influential and applied cultural theoretical model in the world. Although Hofstede's theory of cultural dimensions has shortcomings and limitations, it does explain an important basis for cultural differences. Because of its clarity, simplicity and resonance, this model is favored by scholars and pioneers of other cultural theoretical models. In addition to Hofstede's cultural dimension theory, the Schwartz's values survey, Steenkamp's national-cultural dimensions, and other theories analyze and explain to a certain extent the factors that lead to differences in cultural behavior.

Further Reading

Convergence of Cultural Differences

9.3.2 The Influence of Cultural Differences on Tourism Consumer Behavior

Culture is often considered an important factor in the behavior of tourists from different countries. Tourists with different cultural backgrounds show different behavioral characteristics in terms of destination choice, behavioral patterns, tourism motivation, and service quality perception. In recent years, with the development of the globalization of tourism activities, the consumption pattern of cross-cultural tourists has become a hot-issue concern of tourism scholars. Cross-cultural tourism research includes not only transnational research, but also research on tourists from the same country but different subcultural groups. Tourists with different cultural backgrounds will show different consumption behaviors and characteristics, and the cultural differences between the source country and the host country in terms of values, behavioral norms, perceptions, and social interactions will have an impact on tourists' consumption behaviors and preferences. Tourism operators formulate different marketing strategies according to cultural differences, which is helpful for accurate tourism market positioning and segmentation and helps to design diversified service systems to meet the needs of various tourists.

Cultural differences can not only be an important factor in attracting tourists and satisfying their desire for novelty and differences, but can also hinder tourists through language barriers, cultural conflicts, uncertainty, and other factors. In order to seek pleasure, tourism consumers often tend to search for experiences that meet their own cultural expectations and avoid experiences that do not meet these. However, in the situation of tourism, the phenomenon of culture shock is inevitable, and the collision of different cultures will make tourists both excited and confused. Perceived novelty is regarded as an important positive emotion in tourism activities and is a core component and main motivation in the overall tourism experience. Compared with tourists' usual environments, tourist destinations are always accompanied by a certain degree of strangeness and risk, and the cultural differences perceived by tourists are a common and important inhibitory tourism emotion. In general, the impact of cultural shock caused by cultural differences on tourism consumers can be divided into the following three stages.

First, there is the phase of contact and collapse. When tourist consumers have recently arrived at the tourist destination, they often have a strong interest in the new cultural environment, which is expressed as curiosity and excitement. However, there will also be incompatibility with the unfamiliar environment, such as the unfamiliarity of the local language, custom, diet, and so on. Gradually there will be a sense of expression, confusion, and psychological withdrawal—the collapse element of this phase. Relevant studies have shown that cultural differences can emphasize language barriers and bring cultural conflicts, thus affecting the communication between tourists, service providers, and local residents, which in turn affects the tourism experience. Uncertainty brought about by cultural differences can also bring insecurity to tourists.

The second stage is recovery and self-reliance. At this stage, through contact with local people, tourists have mastered the skills of interacting with locals and begun to appreciate the relative differences of cultures. Tourists gradually recover psychologically. They feel less nervous and show more adaptability to the new cultural environment in their actions. Destination residents and tourism industry practitioners are the main channels for interaction and cultural exchange with tourists. Therefore, tourism destinations and tourism service industries can improve the reception and communication skills of tourism practitioners and community residents through training, and reduce the probability of conflict events in the process of host-guest interaction.

The third stage is the adaptation and non-adaptation stage. Adaptation to the new culture means that the integration of the original culture and the new culture will inevitably lead to the coordination of thought and behavior. When the tour is over, the tourist returns to his/her hometown, back to his/her usual environment. At this time, the new culture that the tourists themselves integrate into will have another impact with the original culture, making people feel uncomfortable.

1) Cultural Values

Although the differences between various cultures are reflected in many aspects, the fundamental difference lies in cultural values. Cultural values are the beliefs held by most members of a society and generally advocated by that society. They provide members of society with shared beliefs about what behaviors are acceptable and unacceptable, and what utimate state people should aspire to. If we want to understand the cultural differences reflected in the norms of behavior, we should first understand the differences in people's values in different cultural backgrounds.

There are many culture-varying values that influence consumer behavior. For example, the impact of children's decisions has far exceeded the scope of children's products and plays an increasingly important role in family consumption. In China, children are the core of the whole family, and the equalization and intimacy of the parent-child relationship promote the improvement of children's consumption role in the family. Children not only greatly enhance their independent decision-making power in consumption of food, beverages, clothing, and so on, but also greatly increase their influence on the consumption decision-making of the whole family. Children show a high level of participation and influence in the consumption decision-making process of travel and dining out. Parents with higher education levels are often more democratic and open; they not only give their children more initiative in family consumption, but also pay more attention to the opinions of their children. Therefore, in Chinese culture, children have a higher degree of participation in consumption decisions and have greater influence.

Different social cultures may also have differences in their value orientations regarding the youth and the elderly. In some societies, honor, status, and important social roles belong to the elderly, while in other societies, these may belong to the young. For example, China advocates filial piety (respect and honor towards parents and elders), and the concept of filial piety regulates and dominates family activities and behaviors in Chinese families. Children often take their parents' travel needs as the premise of decision-making, using family travel activities to improve their parents' happiness and satisfaction, so as to fulfill their responsibilities and obligations towards filial piety. One of the concepts of filial piety in family relationships is that children give back to their parents through this value. In addition, children need to complete their concept of "home" through the intimacy between parents and children. Family travel has always been regarded by modern society as an effective way to effectively promote family intimacy and help children develop a concept of what "home" means.

2) Lifestyle

Lifestyle and culture are closely related. With different cultural backgrounds, people's lifestyles will be quite different, which will inevitably have an impact on consumers' purchasing psychology and behavior. For example, Western lunches are relatively simple, but dinners are grander and richer. Chinese people pay equal attention to every meal, whether in the morning, noon, or evening. According to the report of the U.S. Tourism Bureau, when people travel to the United States, the preferred activities of British tourists are shopping and photography, while French tourists are most likely to enjoy local foods. Japanese tourists, on the other hand, are a group with a strong interest in shopping activities.

In the process of consuming services, consumers with different cultural values will have different consumption behaviors. For example, Haidilao (a popular hotpot chain) is loved by Chinese consumers for its meticulous anf customized service. However, Haidilao's signature service has been neglected in its United States branches, and its advantages are no longer obvious. The service concept of Haidilao does not resonate with American consumers. "The personalized service" that has been well-received in China has also been questioned in other overseas places. Some foreign consumers find it very strange that when they go to the restaurant bathroom to wash their hands, smiling waiters stand by and hand out paper towels. In addition, receiving a manicure in a hotpot restaurant (a signature Haidilao service) is also unappealing to American consumers. From the perspective of dining customs, European and American cultures are not receptive to hotpot. Marketing success in this area is really not as simple as wanting Europeans and Americans to share meals in the same pot. Haidilao had to make localization adjustments by changing the big communal hotpots into individual hotpots, cancelling the offal ingredients such as pig brain and duck intestines that Americans are not used to, and other accommodations.

On May 24, 2022, Airbnb announced its withdrawal from the Chinese market. The company's domestic travel business faced high-cost operational challenges. The problem of platform services in local operations is a dilemma also faced by Airbnb. A Chinese user said, "Airbnb operates in a very American way. Any problem can only be communicated through email, which is not the habit of Chinese users. In addition, foreigners deal with things unhurriedly. " However, the Chinese want to get a reply as soon as possible, and don't want to involve too much energy on these questions. Simply relying on email to handle complaints is not feasible in China. Uber is also an example of this. If complaints cannot be handled more efficiently by these companies, users' dissatisfaction will accumulate, thereby losing trust in the platform.

3) Business Habits

Business habits are the common concepts and practices formed in commercial activities. The differences in business habits reflected by different cultures have an important impact on people's consumption behavior. U.S. consumers are more forthright in their shopping, disliking merchants' high asking prices and rambunctious haggling. Consumers of Latin American cultures enjoy haggling, often beginning by asking for a very low price, and then gradually negotiating back and forth with the merchants for a mutually agreeable price. Asian consumers are good at bargaining, pursuing a transaction price that is favorable to them. However, when shopping in Europe, haggling is often seen as rude and uncultured.

Another example is differences in tipping culture. Tipping is quite popular in Western society and is regarded as a reasonable remuneration from customers to waiters. It demonstrates etiquette; it shows the respect and gratitude of customers for the labor of waiters; it is a manifestation and inheritance of social civilization and generosity. Tipping is part of many service workers' salaries in Western countries—the basic salary of waiters is very low, and tips account for a large proportion of their income. There are some service workers whose hourly wages do not even meet the minimum wage stipulated by local law, and tips account for almost all of their income. Generally speaking, the better the attitude of the service staff, the more satisfied the customers will be, and the more tips the staff will receive. Thus, staffs will try their best to provide customers with superior service. In addition, tipping is quasi-mandatory in some Western countries, and these countries generally have clear regulations on the practice's legality. Because Western people generally accept that tipping is a necessary income for waiters, conscientious tipping is part of social morality.

In contrast, China is deeply influenced by Confucian culture, which advocates "altruism" and "valuing morality while ignoring interests". In the service industry, it is the responsibility of service practitioners to think about what the guests want and worry about, rather than the extra services that the guests need to buy. In the history of the service industry in China, although there are written records of tip payment, the practice has never become a tradition and tips are considered bonus income. In China, service personnel ensure additional income by giving high-quality or extra-value service which encourages the return of customers. Since tips are considered bonus income in Eastern society, tipping is a voluntary act on the part of customers. National laws do not regulate tipping, and some places even prohibit the practice. Although tipping is an international incentive mechanism for service, China's long-standing refusal to recognize the legal status of tip income has formed the reluctance of Chinese customers to tip.

4) Consumption Customs

Consumption customs are the consumer behaviors of human groups in which consumers of a region or a nation participate together under the control of a common aesthetic psychology. These are the special consumption habits and patterns formed by long-term historical culture. In addition to religious, ethnic, and regional customs mentioned in the sections on subculture and customs, there is also a herd mentality in consumption customs. For example, people across the country are exposed to the consumption displayed during the "Double 11" shopping day.

In cross-cultural settings, the same consumption behavior may also result from different needs. For example, some studies show that U.S. consumers use toothpaste mainly to prevent tooth decay (a functional need); in French-speaking Canada and the United Kingdom, consumers use toothpaste mainly for fresh breath (an aesthetic need). French women drink mineral water to look better. They believe that mineral water can not only promote circulation and metabolism in the body and improve their physical condition, but can also relieve physical fatigue.

9.4 Traditional Chinese Culture and Tourism Consumer Behavior

9.4.1 The Spirit of Traditional Chinese Culture

Traditional Chinese culture refers to a special cultural system created by the Chinese nation in a long process of historical development. It is mainly composed of the Han nationality and consists of multiple nationalities. It is based on the small peasant economy that is thousands of years old, with the patriarchal family system as its background and Confucian ethics as its core, unifying traditional agricultural culture, familial culture, and cultivation culture. Traditional Chinese culture has a long history, and the Chinese nation that thrives in this cultural background has unique values, ways of thinking, ways of life, and consumption concepts.

1) Pay Attention to Moderation

Moderation is a basic proposition of Confucianism. Zhu Xi (朱熹), a famous Confucian scholar, believed that "moderation means not favoring either side and not changing easily". When it comes to moderation, most people misunderstand and think that it implies mediocrity, lack of progress, and lack of opinion. This completely misinterprets the meaning of the moderation. In simple terms, moderation means to grasp the golden mean or proper degree of everything, and to pursue the ordinary. Moderation is an important value of the Chinese people, and for thousands of years, it has profoundly influenced the thinking and behavior of the Chinese nation. The cultural spirit of moderation is reflected in Chinese people's consumption of food, clothing, supplies, and so on, and in their consideration of customs and social norms. The concept of moderation requires that what people consume is consistent with their corresponding social class. The ideological essence of the golden mean is harmony. Confucius emphasized the mean because, although everything in the world (including people) is different, things and things, people and people, and people and things are connected to each other. In order to achieve mutual communication and peace, it is necessary to bring the role of harmony into the doctrine of moderation. This kind of thinking has accumulated deeply in Chinese traditional culture and has become a principle with national characteristics.

2) Focus on Ethics

The core of traditional Chinese culture is the Confucian culture with unique ethics at its core. Chinese people attach great importance to the interdependence of family members, as well as the family relationships and kinships that based on this. Traditional Chinese ethical culture attaches great importance to the realization of social and personal values starting from family relationships, and regards self-cultivation, family harmony, governance of the country, and peace in the world as ethical priorities for everyone. In China, home has an unusual and special meaning. If Westerners who believe in Christianity are fascinated by and in love with God, then the Chinese people are fascinated by and in love with their motherland and homeland. Chinese people, even if they cross thousands of rivers and mountains, will still care deeply about their hometowns. This deep-rooted national psychology largely determines cultural production and consumption. For example, family consumption culture is reflected in the spiritual enjoyment and pleasure experienced by family members through consumption. Family consumption culture arises from the interactive process of family members. For example, in China, silver-haired tourism (sending one's parents to travel) has developed into an emerging and very popular tourism market. It is becoming a popular way for Chinese adults to express filial piety towards their parents. In this way, they repay their parents for their nurturing grace. As the income level of Chinese families increases, children's support of their parents has changed from basic material support to paying more attention to their parents' spiritual lives. As a way for the elderly to enrich their spiritual world and pursue a happy life, tourism has become a popular means for children to support their parents. The younger generation also sees this as a way to strengthen their bond with their parents and make up for any lack of time spent with their parents.

3) Value Reputation

Chinese people pay special attention to their own images, especially through acting a certain role in order to leave a good impression in the minds of others and gain a good reputation. This phenomenon is often referred to as "face culture". Chinese people pay more attention to "saving face" (preserving one's image) for others and themselves and are very worried about being embarrassed. In their habits of consumption, many Chinese people sometimes over-consume in order to save face. For example, Chinese may prefer to save a large of money in order to buy a decent gift for relatives, friends, or leaders. While Westerners often similarly express their feelings through a gift of chocolate, dessert, or a bouquet of flowers. Chinese-style humanism includes concerns about personal dignity, but that concern comes from a social point of view: personal image is a social issue. An individual's dignity comes from his/her good behavior and the social approval he/she receives. "Losing face" comes from misbehavior, making others look down on oneself. In traditional Chinese culture, a person's value is not an inherent quality (as is commonly held in the West), but rather must be obtained from one's external environment. In addition, since in Chinese society the individual is an inextricable member of the family chain, the problems of his/her words, deeds, behaviors, career, fame, and power as an official are not only his/her own problems, but the problems of the entire family. For example, if a man does what his family expects, then he is not only very proud of himself, but also his family will be proud of him and share the honor and resources with him; conversely, if he goes against his family's expectations or ends in failure, he will feel ashamed, humiliated, and reluctant to return to the family group, lest he will be humiliated or embarrassed by his family.

4) Emphasize Relationships over Interests

One of the characteristics of traditional Chinese culture is that it attaches great importance to friendship and relationships, especially when compared with money or material interests. When there is a conflict between affections and personal interests, the typical decision is to give up interests and choose affections. This kind of cultural characteristic makes Chinese people easily emotional in daily interpersonal communication, attach importance to relationships between people, act keen to give gifts to each other, and pay attention to "reciprocity". The solidarity of an intimate community depends on the mutual obligations between the members. When Chinese people have dinner out together, friends will rush to pay the bill, which means that they want their friends to owe them a favor. This practice is somewhat like a personal investment: if one owes someone else a favor, he/she must find an opportunity to return a more precious gift. The purpose of returning more expensive gifts is to make others owe one a favor in return. "This back and forth" maintains mutual assistance and cooperation between people.

5) Be Realistic and Pragmatic

Chinese culture has always had a pragmatic spirit and opposed unrealistic fantasies. People pay attention to practicality in their daily consumption. In the consumer culture of the younger generation in China, young people focus on "what is most suitable for me", rather than blindly following a trend. The post-80s generation values work-life balance. Economic, life, interpersonal, and other pressures often make people accumulate negative feelings such as fatigue and powerlessness. They are willing to travel, watch movies, read books, listen to music, and so on, which can help reset their emotions and thoughts. This allows them to repair their run-down body and mind and regain the motivation to return to normal life. For example, the consumption concept of Gen Z can be summarized as "both refined and pragmatic", and for them, mid-grade personalized consumer goods are more popular.

6) Advocate Diligence and Thrift

Diligence and thrift are regarded as the traditional virtues of the Chinese nation. There is a widely circulated story: an old Chinese lady and an old American lady met in heaven, and the old American lady said, "I worked hard for 30 years and finally paid off my housing loan." The old Chinese lady said, "I worked hard for 30 years and finally saved enough money to buy a house." This story reflects the problem of the different consumption concepts between the East and the West. The main characteristics of the Chinese consumption concept are conservative consumption and a high savings rate. Under the influence of Confucian culture, Chinese people spend only as much as they can earn, usually spending no more than their income. In recent years, "a new frugality" (新节俭主义) has begun to be admired and favored by more and more young people, and a new consumption model is emerging. With the same budget and through careful selection and comparison, followers of the new frugality will make the most cost-effective and best value-for-money choices, instead of blindly buying. As the trend of consumption upgrades becomes more and more obvious, the new middle-class group continues to grow, especially the generation of people born post-90s who have a good educational background and a more privileged upbringing environment. These people have brought new consumer traits to the new frugality: they are more mature, restrained, and pragmatic in consumption issues, and are keener on high-quality, high-value, personalized, and experiential consumption enjoyment. Followers are financially wise, know how to consume according to their interests, hobbies, ideals, and pursuits, and will spend money on items they like and in areas they love. Under the consumption concept of the new frugality, many young people put the money they usually save into the acquisition of certain knowledge and skills. They will try to improve themselves and use their money to travel so they can broaden their horizons and increase their knowledge.

9.4.2 Brand Strategies for Tourism Enterprises Based on Chinese Cultural Characteristics

Based on the characteristics of traditional Chinese culture, tourism enterprises can adopt appropriate brand strategies to appeal to this market.

1) Tourism Enterprise Brand Strategy Based on Face Culture

In the process of their tourism experience, tourists need to face their peers and also need to constantly interact with tour guides, destination residents, and other tourists.

Therefore, although tourists have left their daily life environment and their original social relations, there are still behaviors specific to face culture during and after travel. With the advent of the new media era, more and more tourists are showing photos of food and beautiful scenery, and displaying their tourist souvenirs on social media. The potential audience group is not only tourists' relatives and friends, but also a group of strangers in tourists' social networks. Therefore, tourism consumers sometimes endure additional economic and psychological pressures because of face culture, which can cause them to make blind consumption choices.

The face culture will also stimulate people to be motivated and improve their behavior. For example, "moral face" will regulate and restrain the behavior of tourists, persuading them not to litter, write graffiti, destroy wild animals or plants, and so on. With this in mind, face culture can also have a positive effect on the construction of tourism morality. Face culture means that in planning and development, tourism enterprises need to provide display spaces for tourists. The design of the scenes for tourist experiences should be in line with the taste of tourists and satisfy tourists' personal image and dignity.

2) Tourism Enterprise Brand Strategy Based on Irrational Consumption of Children

In China, many parents call themselves "child-slaves" ("孩儿奴") and call their children "gold-swallowing beasts" ("吞金兽"). The original meaning of these expressions is that the economic cost of raising children is high. The other meaning is that after a couple has a child, they spend their whole life running around and earning money for the child, and all consumption is focused on the child. Many parents take their children to travel around in order to let their children "not lose at the starting line" and "experience life". In view of Chinese consumers' irrational consumption characteristics when making purchases for their children, tourism enterprises can more easily communicate with these target customers if they refine the core value of their brand and seek to fulfill parents' emotional interests as they care for their children. This will allow such companies to win market shares faster than the competition.

Chapter Summary

Culture is a multi-dimensional and complex concept. We define culture in a broad sense as the sum of material and spiritual wealth created by human beings in the process of social and historical development. The characteristics of culture include acquired, dynamic, collective, prescriptive, and intangible facets. Within a dominant culture there are smaller cultures with different behaviors and beliefs, known as subcultures. Subculture refers to the values and beliefs relative to but distinct from the mainstream culture, and it is another special value concept and behavior that accompanies the mainstream culture. The impact of cultural shock caused by cultural differences on tourism consumers can be divided into three stages: contact and collapse, recovery and self-reliance, and adaptation and non-adaptation. These stages mainly reflect cultural differences in values, lifestyles, product preferences, and consumption customs. The spirit of traditional Chinese culture includes paying attention to moderation, focus on ethics, valuing face, placing emphasis on relationships over interests, favoring realism and pragmatism, and advocating diligence and thrift. Based on these characteristics of traditional Chinese culture, tourism enterprises can adopt appropriate brand strategies.

Issues for Review and Discussion

1. What are the characteristics of traditional Chinese culture? What impact will traditional Chinese culture have on tourism consumer behavior?

2. How should we address the relationship between preservation of cultural authenticity and the need for diversity and tourism development?

3. What positive effects do you think tourism has on the protection and promotion of intangible cultural heritage? What negative impacts may tourism have on the protection and promotion of intangible cultural heritage?

4. What local culture does your hometown have? Are you interested in this local culture? What is the attitude of tourists to these local cultures?

Chapter 10
Marketing and Tourism Consumer Behavior

Learning Objectives

After reading this chapter, you should have a good understanding of:

(1) the characteristics of tourism consumer behavior throughout the life cycle of tourism products;

(2) the common pricing methods of tourism products and their impact on tourism consumer behavior;

(3) the impact of distribution channels on tourism consumer behavior;

(4) the methods of promoting tourism products and corresponding tourism consumer behavior;

(5) the impact of marketing innovation on tourism consumer behavior.

Technical Words

English Words	中文翻译
tourism product life cycle	旅游产品生命周期
tourism distribution channel	旅游分销渠道
tourism intermediary	旅游中间商
internet marketing	网络营销
green marketing	绿色营销
cultural marketing	文化营销

Chapter 10 Marketing and Tourism Consumer Behavior

Knowledge Graph

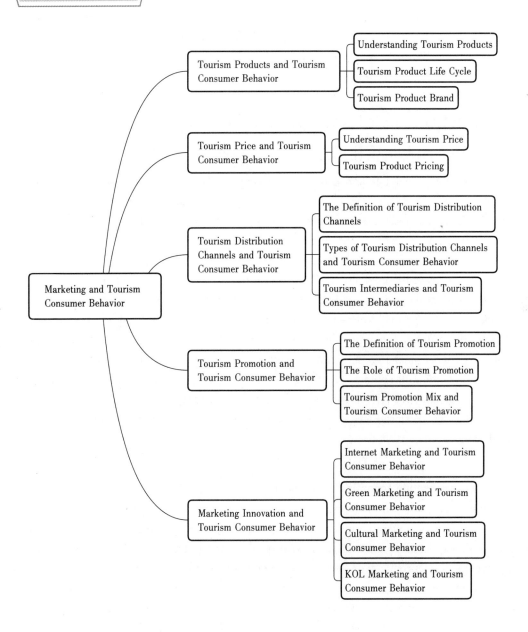

10.1 Tourism Products and Tourism Consumer Behavior

10.1.1 Understanding Tourism Products

1) The Definition of Tourism Products

China's national standard *Basic Terminology in Travel and Tourism* defines tourism products as goods and services which are sold to tourism consumers. Services represent the foundation of product composition, and mainly comprise travel routes, activities, and accommodation. Tourism consumers can buy overall products (such as comprehensive package tours), or a single travel product (such as a flight seat or hotel room). This is to consider the element composition of tourism products from an overall perspective.

We can further understand tourism products from different perspectives. From the perspective of tourism experience, tourism products can be defined as the experience obtained by tourism consumers spending a certain amount of time, energy, and money. This experience includes a comprehensive sense of the people with whom tourism consumers come into contact, the things that have happened, and the services they enjoy. From the perspective of tourism operators, tourism products are defined as the sum of objects and services produced or developed in a certain region for sale in order to meet the needs of tourism consumers.

2) The Types of Tourism Products

(1) Classification according to composition.

Based on their composition, tourism products can be divided into overall and single tourism products. Overall tourism products are a combination of core products, formal products, expected products, extended products, and potential products. Core products are the physical products or services needed to meet the most basic needs of tourism consumers, such as catering and accommodation. Formal products are a combination of the carriers, features, and styles of core products, emphasizing the psychological needs of tourism consumers, such as tourism services, infrastructure, and so on. Expected products are the attributes that tourism consumers expect to obtain when purchasing. For example, when tourism consumers try special snacks, they expect delicious, clean, and distinctive meals, a clean dining environment, respectful service, and appropriate tableware. Extended products are additional benefits such as preferential conditions. For example, hotels provide free laundry services and discounts on tickets to scenic spots. A potential product is a future final product, such as a digital hotel, a smart scenic spot.

(2) Classification according to the form of tourism products.

Tourism products can be divided into inclusive tour, half package tour, mini-package tour, and zero package tour depending on their form.

Inclusive tour is a form of organized travel that involves ten or more tourism consumers and a one-time advance payment for travel expenses. Inclusive tour services usually include hotel rooms, three meals a day, city tour vehicles, guide services, drop-off services at transportation hubs, baggage services, sightseeing tickets and recreational activities, etc.

Half package tour prices do not include lunch and dinner. The main purpose of travel agencies designing half package tour is to reduce the intuitive prices of products and improve their competitiveness; it also allows travel consumers the freedom to experience local flavours as they choose. The half package format is available for both group and individual tours.

Mini-package tour, also called "optional tour", consists of non-optional and optional parts. The non-optional parts include accommodation and breakfast, airport/station/dock-to-hotel transfer and intercity transportation, which are paid for in advance. The optional parts include tour guide services, lunch/dinner, sightseeing, cultural shows, etc., which can be paid for in advance or in situ.

Zero package tour is a unique product form that is commonly seen in developed tourism countries. Tourists participating in this type of tourism must accompany the group back and forth to the destination, but their activities at the destination are completely free, just like individual travelers. Tourists who participate in zero package tour can receive discounts on group airfare prices and can apply for travel visas uniformly by travel agencies.

3) The Characteristics of Tourism Products

(1) Intangibility and comprehensiveness.

Because tourism products are mainly service-oriented, they have the basic characteristics of service products. The first characteristic is intangibility. A tour guide's explanation is an intangible product, and the consumer can only judge its quality through experiencing it. For consumers, tourism products are more about the experiences and feelings they obtained.

The comprehensiveness of tourism products concerns the six elements of tourism: catering, accommodation, transportation, travel, shopping, and entertainment. Tourism consumers engage with many industries and other areas in the process of tourism. For example, when they plan to travel to a certain place, in addition to considering the tourism resources of the destination, they will consider the accessibility of transportation, the conditions of accommodation, the characteristics of meals, the local culture, and so on. Deficiencies in any aspect of catering, accommodation, transportation, travel, shopping, and entertainment will affect the decision-making behavior of tourism consumers. On the other hand, tourism products can be understood as multidimensional, comprising material products (such as characteristic snacks tasted at tourist destinations), spiritual products (such as leisure and relaxation obtained in the process of tourism), and tourism services (such as explanations provided by tour guides). Making clear the comprehensiveness of tourism products helps to meet the diversified needs of tourism consumers.

(2) Synchronicity of production and consumption.

The physical products we come into contact with in our life are usually produced first and then put into the market and bought by consumers. With the progress of science and technology and changes in shopping mode, many products are now made available for pre-sale online, that is, they are sold before they officially enter the market or are put into production. Tourism products have simultaneity of production and consumption because of their experiential nature. Tourism consumers need to arrive at the destination for tourism products to be produced and delivered. This requires tourism enterprises to restrain the words and deeds of tourism service personnel in the process of operation, so as to obtain higher satisfaction of tourism consumers. It should be noted that although the production and consumption of tourism products occur at the same time, this does not mean that production and purchase time are synchronized. This is because with the advent of the Internet economy, many travel consumers prefer to book travel products in advance in order to get preferential prices, and ensure that they are not limited by environmental carrying capacity.

(3) Non-transferability and non-storability.

When buying tourism products, consumers do not acquire ownership of tourism resources, facilities, and environment, but the right to experience them. Tourism products are not transferable in space: consumers can only consume tourism products at the destination. That is, in the actual tourism process, it is tourism consumers rather than tourism products that transfer.

After tourism consumers book or buy tourism products, they will get the tourism services provided by the tourism enterprises within the specified time. Beyond the specified time, tourism products have no value. For example, a tourist consumer buys a ticket on a flight to Yunnan on May 2. If he does not take the flight at the specified time and place, the ticket will be invalid. Unsold tourism products cannot be stored for later sale. Tourism products have a different value every day. The loss of a day for hotel rooms and travel seats left idle cannot be recovered.

(4) Volatility and vulnerability.

Some tourism activities are affected by factors such as season, climate, and national holidays, making tourism products volatile. For example, some travel consumers in the north like to go to the south in winter, while those in the south prefer to go to the north to see ice and snow. Most domestic ice and snow tourism can only be carried out in winter, and it is difficult or impossible to meet the needs of such tourism in other seasons. Another example is that the demand for tourism products on statutory holidays is significantly higher than on working days. The volatility of tourism products poses challenges for the operation and marketing of tourism companies. How to ensure the satisfaction of tourism consumers during peak season? How to ensure operating income off-season? Which marketing strategy should be used? These are questions that tourism companies need to constantly think about.

The supply of tourism products is affected by many factors. The climate, infrastructure, cultural environment, geographical location, and tourism resources of destinations will all have an impact on the decision-making of tourism consumers. For example, a sudden war, disease, or extreme weather can limit travel, resulting in the cancellation of all itineraries and plans.

10.1.2 Tourism Product Life Cycle

1) Product Life Cycle Theory and Tourism Consumer Behavior

The tourism product life cycle follows the concept of tangible product life cycle. The so-called tourism product life cycle refers to the whole process from the development of a tourism product for the market to the final elimination from the market. The life cycle of tourism products is generally divided into four stages: introduction period, growth period, maturity period, and decline period, as figure 10.1 shows.

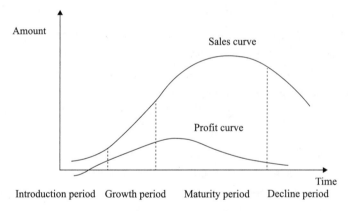

Figure 10.1　Life cycle of tourism products

(1) Introduction period.

The introduction period of tourism products refers to the stage when they are put on the market after being designed or developed, and the sales and profits increase slowly. The specific action is the introduction of new tourist attractions, new tourist projects, new tourist and entertainment facilities, new tourist hotels, new tourist routes, and tourist services to the market for the first time. In the introduction stage, since tourism products have just been launched and have yet to be perfected, consumer awareness is very low. Some new and curious tourism consumers may appear, while most tend to take a wait-and-see attitude. Therefore, the demand for new tourism products is very small. Sales and profits grow slowly. At this stage, many purchases are tentative, and repeat purchases have not yet occurred; middlemen such as travel agencies usually adopt a test-selling attitude. Due to the small sales volume of new tourism products, low profits or even losses, the prospects for success are uncertain. Competitors, like consumers, often take a wait-and-see attitude, and there is no competition in the market.

(2) Growth period.

When the tentative consumption of tourism consumers increases steadily following the introduction of tourism products, it enters the growth period. In the growth period, tourism products overcome the shortcomings exposed in the early stages, and gradually improve. The development of tourist attractions and tourist destinations begins to take shape, tourism facilities and services gradually start supporting them. When tourism products are basically finalized and have formed certain characteristics, more and more tourism consumers seek the purchase experience, and some appear to revisit. Due to substantial increase in the demand for tourism products and substantial decrease in the cost, the profits of tourism products rise rapidly, resulting in net profit after the loss in the introduction stage. In the growth stage, tourism products show good market prospects. Attracted by the profits of tourism products and good market prospects, competitors begin to develop similar alternatives and introduce them to the market, resulting in competition.

(3) Maturity period.

In the late growth period of tourism products, the growth momentum of tourism consumers and sales slows down and enters the mature period, which can be divided into three stages: increasing maturity, stopping maturity, and decreasing maturity. In the increasing maturity stage, the sales volume and profits of tourism products continue to increase, but the growth rate gradually slows down and tends to stop. In the stage of stopping maturity, sales volume and profits fluctuate, but the overall trend is stagnant. In the decreasing maturity stage, sales volume and profits decline. In the mature period, the market demand for tourism products has reached a saturation state, the sales volume has reached its peak, and the unit cost of products has fallen to its lowest level. As a result of the combined effect of sales volume and cost, the profits of tourism products will also reach a peak and begin to decline. Competitors have developed many similar tourism products, expanding the range of choice for tourism consumers. The market competition is very fierce: better alternatives may appear, and the early consumers move on to new alternative tourism products.

(4) Decline period.

In the decline period, new tourism products have entered the market and are gradually replacing the old products. Tourism consumers may lose interest in old products, or replace them with new products, and market sales decline. Market competition is manifested prominently as price competition, prices are forced to drop continuously, profits rapidly reduce, and losses can occur. Due to the sharp drop in the number of travel consumers during the decline stage, there is no room for more travel enterprises to survive. Therefore, many competitors with weak competitiveness gradually withdraw from the market due to financial problems or the emergence of better travel products.

Chapter 10   Marketing and Tourism Consumer Behavior

It should be emphasized that the life cycle of tourism products refers to the general development law of tourism products, which cannot be applied to each tourism product for life cycle analysis. Different tourism products have different life cycles and may experience different stages in their life cycle at different times. Due to the particularity of resources and cultural connotation of some unique natural, historical, and cultural landscapes, as well as the fact that they are not replicable, their product life cycle may be very long. However, some man-made landscapes can be replicated in large numbers, and their life cycle will inevitably be shorter once competitive products appear in large numbers in many places, such as microscale landscapes, etc. Some tourism products and services may die before they even reach the growth stage for a variety of reasons.

2) Phased Marketing of Tourism Product Life Cycle

(1) Marketing in the introduction period.

Low market visibility is the limiting condition for tourism consumers' acceptance of new tourism products, so the marketing focus of tourism enterprises in the introduction period is to improve market visibility. The main measures are as follows. Firstly, perfecting new tourism products to meet the needs of tourism consumers as far as possible. Secondly, using various promotional means to vigorously publicize new tourism products and increase their popularity in the target market as soon as possible. At the same time, the prices of new tourism products should not be too high, for high prices are difficult for tourism consumers to accept. However, if the prices of new products are too low, it will make it difficult to raise prices at the later stages. A more reasonable solution is to price reasonably according to the target cost. The target price determines the profits, but according to the characteristics of the introduction period, a larger discount is given on the target price can encourage tourism consumers to try new products.

(2) Marketing in the growth period.

The marketing goal in the growth period is to maintain the sales and profits growth rate of tourism products, aiming to increase their market share. After the introduction period, tourism products show bright market prospects, and the rapid growth of tourism consumers brings profits to enterprises. Enterprises should focus on developing markets and improving efficiency in order to continuously improve the market share and competitiveness of their tourism products. The main measures include: improving the quality of tourism products, appropriate price fluctuations according to seasonal fluctuations in tourism demand, implementing differential pricing according to the economic status of tourism consumers in different target markets, and increasing market share. At the same time, enterprises can establish a more intensive, extensive, and efficient sales network, change the focus of promotion to improving brand loyalty, segment products' potential travel market, and consider strategies for penetrating into new market segments.

(3) Marketing in the maturity period.

The maturity period is the longest in the life cycle of tourism products, and most of the time tourism enterprises faced is to formulate the marketing in the maturity period. During this period, tourism consumer demand begins to grow slowly and gradually becomes saturated, market competition is extremely fierce, and the cost of tourism products reaches the lowest point. The marketing of tourism products in the maturity period can expand tourism by attracting potential tourism consumers in the existing tourism market, encouraging consumers to repurchase, improving product quality and content, implementing price discounts, and changing promotional methods. The sales volume of products can stabilize the market share of enterprises, so as to prolong their maturity period.

(4) Marketing in the decline period.

When tourism products enter the decline period, it means that they have been completely replaced by alternative products launched by competitors that are becoming more and more mature. The alternative products put into the market in large quantities, resulting in the transfer of tourism consumers' purchasing power, an increase in product costs, and a decline in profits. For tourism companies, the main strategic goal should be to stabilize later-stage tourism consumers, moderately reduce marketing expenses, shrink the market, and actively develop new tourism products to replace those in decline.

10.1.3 Tourism Product Brand

1) Overview of Tourism Product Brand

(1) The meaning of tourism product brand.

The tourism product brand is a business' name and its logo used to identify the products or services of tourism enterprises and distinguish them from those of competitors. A brand consists of words, marks, symbols, and patterns, including names, logos, and trademarks. The brand name is the part of the brand that can be expressed in language, such as Disney, Hilton. The brand logo refers to the part of the brand that can be identified but cannot be expressed in language, and takes the form of symbols, patterns or specially designed colours, fonts, etc. A trademark usually means that the tourism product brand has been legally registered with the relevant government departments.

For tourism consumers, On the one hand, the brand represents the quality and characteristics of the product, which helps tourism consumers to purchase tourism products and trace responsibilities, and improve shopping efficiency. The brand can facilitate producers' operation and management and establish a stable customer base. On the other hand, tourism product brand can promote the continuous improvement of product quality, and can strengthen the innovative spirit of tourism enterprises. The exclusive rights linked to a trademark can guarantee fair competition among tourism enterprises.

(2) Requirements for brand design of tourism product.

First, aesthetics. Tourism product brand must be beautiful, innovative, interesting, and unconventional in order to attract attention. It must establish a good corporate and commodity image in the minds of tourism consumers, and stimulate purchase desire. The brand design of tourism products should be simple, with clear ideas and bright colours, so as to make an impression and facilitate recall and identification of tourism consumers.

Second, normative. *The Trademark Law of the People's Republic of China* formulated by the state is an important legal foundation for the brand design of tourism products. The law stipulates that trademarks cannot use words and graphics that are the same or similar to the names, national flags, national emblems, military flags, medals, etc. of countries and international organizations. The design of tourism product trademarks must respect national customs, and the content must be civilized and healthy.

Third, characteristic. Product brand should fully reflect the nature, characteristics, and style of the products, which is the basis of tourism product brand design. Only the brand that do so can attract tourism consumers, which can reflect the structure and shape of a tourism product, or describe it with an interesting image, so as to highlight its uniqueness.

Fourth, suitability. Tourism product brand should be adapted to the target market of tourism enterprises (such as name, pattern, colour), and local customs, aesthetic characteristics, languages, etc. of the target market must be considered. Only then will the brand be accepted by tourism consumers and meet expectations.

2) Tourism Product Brand and Tourist Consumption Behavior

The relationship model of tourism consumers and brand is shown in figure 10.2.

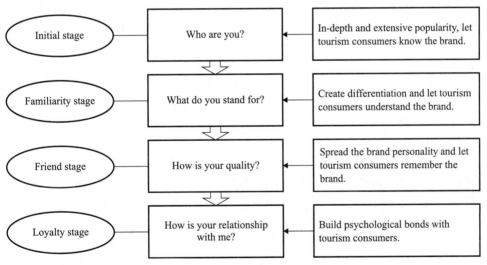

Figure 10.2 The relationship model of tourism consumers and brand

(1) Initial stage.

In the initial stage of tourism product brand development, tourism consumers are not yet familiar with the brand. The task is to enhance its popularity, let tourism consumers get to know the brand, remember it, and promote the relationship between them to reach the familiarity stage.

(2) Familiarity stage.

Through advertising, public relations, personal sales, and other means, tourism consumers have become familiar with tourism product brand, and the task now is to let them understand the meaning of the brand and its different points of interest.

(3) Friend stage.

By creating a prominent product brand personality, a unique position can be found in the hearts of tourism consumers, and a different psychological impression from competitors can be formed, as a result, when a tourism product brand is mentioned, one can have a judgment and feeling about it, and make a certain response.

(4) Loyalty stage.

Establishing brand trust and strengthening the communication between tourism consumers and tourism enterprises can transform the brand response of tourism products into an active, strong, and loyal relationship.

3) Tourism Product Brand Marketing

(1) Unified brand marketing.

Unified brand marketing refers to the use of one brand for all products of a company. The advantage of this type of marketing is that it can reduce the design and advertising costs of the brand, which is conducive to gaining a faster and more stable foothold of new products in the market, and can strengthen the company's momentum and increase its popularity. For example, all of the products of Japan's Toshiba Household Appliances Company use the brand "Toshiba". The use of a unified brand is conducive to producing a unified product image, facilitating the public identification of the enterprise, quickly building the enterprise's popularity, facilitating the entry of new products into the market, and also saving the design and advertising costs of the brand and trademark. But the disadvantage is that the poor reputation of a certain product will affect the image of the entire tourism enterprise.

(2) Multi-brand marketing.

Multi-brand marketing is a marketing approach that consciously uses multiple brands in the same tourism product category. The purpose is to deeply segment the market, fully meet the needs of various categories, and help to establish flanking brands to prevent price wars impacting the main brand. But this means higher costs, a smaller market share for a single brand, and may cause internal competition among tourism companies. Hotel groups such as Accor and Inter Continental have a number of internationally renowned hotel brands. The success of multi-brand marketing depends not only on the creation of brands, but also their maintenance, so that the products are clearly differentiated in the minds of customers.

(3) Brand extension marketing.

A brand extension is a marketing approach that uses an existing successful brand as the basis for a new or revised product. The main advantages of brand extension are: it can speed up the positioning of new products, ensure quick and accurate investment decisions

Case Study 10-1
▼

Huazhu Group's Multi-Brand Marketing

for new products, help reduce the market risk of new products, help strengthen the brand effect, and increase the economic value of the intangible assets of the brand, which can enhance the image of the core brand and improve the investment efficiency of the overall brand portfolio. The implementation of this marketing approach requires that the expanded brand has a strong reputation in the market, and the expanded product must also be excellent, otherwise it will affect the sales and/or the reputation of the existing brand.

10.2 Tourism Price and Tourism Consumer Behavior

10.2.1 Understanding Tourism Price

1) The Definition of Tourism Price

Tourism price is the monetary expression of the value of a tourism product. It is affected by the value of the tourism product, the tourism market supply and demand, and regional currency fluctuations. Essentially, however, the higher the value of the tourism product, the higher the price. For example, the price of a room in a five-star hotel is higher than that of a budget hotel room. When the supply in the tourism market is greater than the demand, such as in the off-season, tourism companies will encourage consumers to purchase through discounts and other promotional methods, and the tourism prices at such times are relatively low; when the product supply in the tourism market is lower than the demand, such as during the peak season, tourism companies will control demand by raising prices. At the same time, the lower the value of the currency of a particular country or region, the higher the price of the corresponding tourism product. If the currency depreciates, the tourism product undergoes the equivalent of a disguised price increase. However, if the local currency is stronger, the tourism product price is lower, which is equivalent to a price reduction.

2) The Characteristics of Tourism Price

(1) Comprehensiveness.

The comprehensiveness of tourism price is linked to the comprehensiveness of tourism products, which are composed of tourism resources, tourism services and facilities, and other factors involving tourist attractions, travel agencies, hotels, aviation, railways, and many other elements. When a travel consumer buys a travel product or satisfies a certain aspect of their spiritual needs, they must exchange a certain sum with the relevant travel enterprises. This exchange is subject to the joint action of multiple sectors and multiple factors, so it generally does not occur in isolation. That is to say, the price of a tourism product is a comprehensive price composed of individual prices. When travel consumers pay the price of travel products, they can choose to do so all at once or in multiple instalments.

(2) Volatility.

Compared with other products generally, the prices of tourism products are more volatile. On the one hand, tourism activities are strongly seasonal. In the off-season, there are fewer tourism consumers, and supply exceeds demand, so prices may drop. During the peak season, there are many consumers, and demand exceeds supply, so prices may rise. That is, the relationship between supply and demand in the tourism market affects the fluctuation of prices. On the other hand, tourism products have strong substitutability. Due to the high elasticity of tourism products, when prices rise, consumers will buy substitutes, and return when prices drop. The volatility of tourism product sales is also the irregular fluctuation of tourism prices.

(3) Monopoly.

The monopoly of tourism price is mainly due to the monopoly of tourism resources. Tourism resources such as the Forbidden City in Beijing, the Great Wall, Jiuzhaigou Valley, the Terracotta Warriors, etc., are generated from particular historical backgrounds and natural conditions, condense precious historical and social values, and are irreplaceable. Their value is immeasurable, so the tourist price shows a monopoly. There are also some tourism products with high technology content, which are not easy to imitate and surpass. They have no competitors, and their prices also have a certain monopoly. Facing the monopoly of tourism prices, tourism consumers have low bargaining power.

3) The Classification of Tourism Price

(1) According to the demand of tourism consumers.

According to the demand, price can be divided into basic tourism price and non-basic tourism price. The basic tourism price refers to the necessary travel expenses of travel activities, including catering, accommodation, transportation, and ticket prices. Non-basic tourism price refers to the tourism expenditures that may or may not be incurred in tourism activities by tourism consumers, such as the purchase of tourist souvenirs, the price of beauty and fitness products.

(2) According to the scope of tourism activities.

According to the travel activities of consumers, tourism price can be divided into domestic tourism price and international tourism price. Due to the different levels of economic development in different countries, the purchasing power of consumers varies greatly. The division of domestic tourism price and international tourism price helps countries or regions with relatively backward economies to absorb more foreign exchange.

(3) According to the purchase mode of tourism products.

According to the purchasing method of tourism consumers, the tourism price can be divided into travel package price and individual tour price. The travel package price covers basic travel products and the service fee of the travel agency. It is the price paid by travel consumers at one time. The individual tour price relates to tourism products purchased by tourism consumers in sporadic purchases, such as rooms, catering, transportation, tickets, etc.

(4) According to the marketing perspective of tourism enterprises.

According to the marketing perspective of tourism enterprises, the tourism price can be divided into tourism price difference and preferential tourism price. The tourism price difference refers to the price difference caused by the differences in time, place, quality, sales link, etc., of the same kind of tourism products. Preferential tourism price refers to the discount or preferential price that the supplier of tourism products gives to consumers on the basis of the clearly marked price, mainly in the form of sales discounts, industry discounts, faithful customer discounts, and cash discounts.

4) The Influencing Factors of Tourism Price

(1) Internal factors.

First, the cost of tourism products. The cost of tourism products is the bottom line of tourism enterprises' pricing. As long as the price is higher than the cost, businesses are profitable.

Second, the characteristics of tourism products. If the substitution of tourism products is strong, tourism enterprises can encourage tourism consumers to purchase by reducing prices. If tourism products or resources are scarce and their value is higher, tourism enterprises will offer higher prices. Considering the preciousness of tourism products, tourism consumers will not give up tourism experience because of high prices.

Third, the marketing goals of tourism enterprises. Tourism prices are affected by the marketing goals of tourism enterprises. Through pricing, tourism enterprises can achieve marketing goals, such as maintaining survival, maximizing profits, maximizing market share, and prioritizing product quality.

Fourth, marketing mix strategy. Compared with other strategies in the 4P strategy, the price strategy is the most flexible, but the pricing strategy of tourism products is not the same. It can be carried out separately from other marketing strategies.

(2) External factors.

First, relationship between supply and demand. The relationship between supply and demand is a key factor affecting pricing. When supply is greater than demand, tourism enterprises can reduce prices to encourage consumers to consume; when supply is lower than demand, tourism companies can increase prices to restrict consumption.

Second, the behaviors of competitors. The degree of competition in the tourism market has a great impact on the pricing of tourism products. The more intense the competition, the greater the impact on pricing. Tourism enterprises can implement reasonable product pricing by understanding the behaviors of competitors.

Third, government intervention. The government pricing department or other relevant departments will set the benchmark price and its floating range according to the pricing authority and scope, which will guide tourism enterprises to formulate guide prices, such as the maximum price, the minimum protection price.

Fourth, social conditions. The impact of social conditions on the pricing of tourism products cannot be generalized. Usually, when a society faces a health crisis, disaster, or war, the shortage of tourism products leads to a shortage of supply, and the pricing of tourism products will increase. When the situation returns to normal, tourism enterprises may encourage consumers to engage by reducing prices.

10.2.2 Tourism Product Pricing

1) New Product Pricing

(1) Skimming pricing.

Skimming pricing, also known as the high price marketing, is the approach of setting the price as high as possible at the launch of a new product, in order to obtain high profits in the short term and recover costs as quickly as possible. This pricing method enables tourism companies to obtain high profits in a short period of time, and leaves room for future price reductions. High prices can also establish an image of high quality, but excessively high prices will inhibit market demand and affect market expansion. At the same time, the product life cycle may be shortened due to the participation of competitors. Skimming pricing, as a short-term strategy, is suitable for new products with unique technology that is not easy to imitate, when production capacity is unlikely to rapidly expand and there are high consumption or fashion requirements in the market.

Skimming pricing is generally appropriate for consumers who have strong purchasing power and are not sensitive to price. Such consumers are numerous enough that skimming brings tourism enterprises high profits. When no competitors have launched similar products, a tourism enterprise's products have obvious differentiation advantages. When competitors join, the established enterprise can change its pricing method and boost competitiveness by improving cost performance. Under the above conditions, tourism enterprises should adopt the method of skimming pricing. For example, if a travel agency launches an innovative travel route, it has many members with purchasing power who may have a desire to buy tickets, and the new route cannot be quickly imitated by peers, then the travel agency can adopt the skimming pricing method for marketing.

(2) Penetration pricing.

Penetration pricing, also known as low-price marketing, is a method of attracting consumers with lower prices when new tourism products are introduced into the market, to quickly open up the market. This pricing can enable tourism companies to quickly open up and expand market sales, increase profits, and effectively prevent competitors from intervening. However, low prices are not conducive to quickly recovering investment, thereby affecting later price adjustments, and an enterprise may suffer heavy losses when encountering strong competitors. This pricing method is suitable for products with high price elasticity of demand, considerable market capacity, and many potential competitors.

The method of penetration pricing adopted by tourism enterprises mainly captures the psychology of tourism consumers seeking cost-effective commodities through lower prices. For example, when travel agencies launch large and medium-sized tour routes, the prices will be low and there will be more consumers able to buy, thereby achieving small profits and quick sales.

(3) Satisfactory pricing.

This is a compromise pricing approach, which means that tourism enterprises set the price of new products somewhere in the middle of the range, which not only ensures that they make a certain profit, but also that the products are accepted by consumers. This pricing is suitable for a product with moderate price elasticity of demand, relatively stable market sales, and when the company is unwilling to launch a price war or to attract potential competitors with high prices.

Tourism enterprises should also take into account product characteristics, season, and other factors when pricing tourism products. In the off-season, low prices tend to attract more consumers, while in the peak season prices should be appropriately raised to limit demand, thereby regulating the tourist flow so that tourism consumers can obtain a more satisfactory travel experience.

2) Psychological Pricing

(1) Mantissa pricing.

Mantissa pricing refers to setting a non-integer price for tourism products in order to stimulate tourism consumers' pursuit of low prices. Low-end travel products often use this pricing approach. For example, if the price is 9.9 yuan, it will make travel consumers feel that it is less than 10 yuan. If the price is adjusted from 9.9 to 10 yuan, although the change is only 0.1 yuan, psychologically it feels a lot higher.

(2) Lucky numbers pricing.

Lucky numbers pricing refers to using tourism consumers' pronunciation associations to meet their psychological needs through pricing, and invisibly improve their satisfactions.

(3) Tiered pricing.

Tiered or hierarchical pricing is a way to divide tourism products into several grades according to different specifications and models, and formulate a pricing system for each grade of tourism product. For example, a buffet provides diners with different food standards; a hotel offers rooms of different price, size, and quality; travel agencies provide routes with different prices.

(4) Prestige pricing.

Prestige pricing refers to consciously setting the price of a certain tourism product higher, to boost its grade and prestige as well as that of the tourism enterprise. It helps to establish a good product image and to obtain excess profits. It is generally found in time-honoured and prestigious tourism companies, as well as exclusive products, well-known brands and special products.

(5) Solicitation pricing.

Solicitation pricing refers to deliberately setting the prices of certain products very high or very low in order to attract consumers. For example, a restaurant launches several special dishes every day to attract customers. It should be noted that reduced-price products must be marketable as new varieties and have high quality, rather than inferior and outdated products, and the variety and quantity of the reduced-price products must be appropriate.

3) Discount Pricing

(1) Cash discount.

Cash discount is a price discount offered to travel consumers who pay in advance or in cash within a specified period. Its purpose is to encourage consumers to pay as soon as possible, thus speeding up capital turnover, reducing sales expenses and financial risks.

(2) Quantity discount.

Quantity discount refers to giving different discounts according to the quantity purchased. The greater the quantity purchased, the greater the discount. The purpose is to encourage consumers to buy products in large quantities. Quantity discount includes cumulative quantity discount and one-time quantity discount.

(3) Feature discount.

Intermediaries are in different links in the process of tourism products distribution, and their functions, responsibilities and risks are also different, and tourism companies give different discount accordingly, which are called feature discount.

(4) Seasonal discount.

Seasonal discount refers to giving discounts according to the time when consumers purchase products. To give certain discounts to tourism consumers who purchase products in the off-season can adjust the contradiction between supply and demand, and reduce the impact of seasonal changes on the production and sales of tourism enterprises.

Case Study 10-2

The Staggering Price Mechanism of Sun Asia Ocean World

10.3 Tourism Distribution Channels and Tourism Consumer Behavior

10.3.1 The Definition of Tourism Distribution Channels

Distribution channels are the various interdependent organizations that facilitate the smooth delivery of products to consumers. The distribution channels of tourism products are the sales channels of tourism products, which comprises all the routes and links in the process of the transfer of tourism products from production enterprises to tourism consumers. Those routes and links consist of a series of businesses and individuals that acquire the ownership of such products or facilitate the transfer. Therefore, it can be said that all intermediaries or individuals involved in the transfer of tourism products can become the distribution channels of tourism products.

10.3.2 Types of Tourism Distribution Channels and Tourism Consumer Behavior

1) Direct and Indirect Distribution Channels

According to whether tourism products pass through tourism intermediaries in the circulation process, the distribution channels of tourism products can be divided into direct and indirect distribution channels, as shown in figure 10.3.

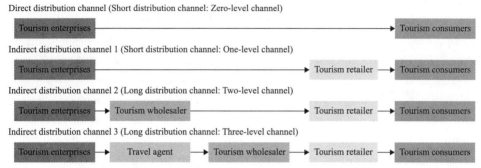

Figure 10.3 Schematic diagram of direct and indirect distribution channels

(1) Direct distribution channels.

A direct distribution channel is a distribution channel through which tourism enterprises directly sell products to consumers without going through intermediaries in tourism marketing activities. It is also called the zero-level distribution channel.

The advantages of the direct distribution channel include that it can directly understand the opinions of tourism consumers and obtain information about them, can shape the image of tourism enterprises, and save the cost of intermediate links. The mainly disadvantage of the direct distribution channel is that the producer has limited contact with the tourism market and thus limiting the sales. The direct distribution channel is suitable for small-scale production or limited reception of corporate travel merchandise.

Direct distribution channels include purchasing at the production site, through various direct booking methods, and through a retail system set up by travel companies.

(2) Indirect distribution channels.

Indirect distribution channels are distribution channels through which enterprises sell products to consumers through intermediaries. For example, hotels rent rooms to travel agencies, who integrate them into their products and sell them to tourists. Indirect distribution channels are currently the most important for tourism products.

The advantages of indirect distribution channels are as follows. First, due to the help of intermediary organizations, product coverage is large, more consumers are attracted, and the sales volume is also large. Second, tourism enterprises and intermediaries have a relatively stable agreement on the sales volume, which is conducive to the production and operation of tourism enterprises. Third, indirect distribution channels are highly targeted, and cooperate with many middlemen. These middlemen are carefully selected by tourism enterprises and have a deep understanding of enterprises. In this way, the middlemen will be more targeted when developing customers, and the effect of marketing will be better. But indirect distribution channels also have disadvantages: the sales process is complicated, sales costs are high, profits are low, tourism enterprises are slow to respond to consumers, and the relationship with consumers is relatively poor.

2) Short and Long Distribution Channels

(1) Short distribution channels.

A short distribution channel means that tourism enterprises do not have to, or not only, pass through an intermediate link in tourism marketing activities, including zero-level and one-level distribution channels. The information transfer of short channels is fast, sales are timely, and the process is conducive to control. However, if the tourism enterprises undertake many sales tasks, the short distribution channels will limit sales scope, which is not conducive to the large-scale sale of tourism products. The short distribution channel is suitable for selling tourism products and services in a small area. For tourism consumers, short distribution channels are conducive to direct contact with tourism enterprises and reduce the possibility of middlemen earning price difference. At the same time, short distribution channels allow tourism consumers to better understand the situation of tourism enterprises and facilitate the feedback of tourism experience and opinions.

First, zero-level distribution channels. The zero-level distribution channel means that tourism companies do not go through middlemen in their tourism marketing activities. The zero-level distribution channel is beneficial in obtaining information about tourism consumers, strengthening the image of tourism enterprises, and saving the cost of middlemen. However, the zero-level distribution channel cannot expand the market; human, material, and financial resources are scattered; and it bears greater business risks.

Second, one-level channels. The mode of the one-level channel is: tourism enterprise→tourism retailer→tourism consumer. Travel product producers pay commissions to retailers who sell travel products to travel consumers. There are fewer one-level distribution channels, which is conducive to the rapid introduction of tourism products to the market. However, the sales scope and scale of the one-level distribution channel are limited, and it is only suitable for tourism products with a small marketing volume, a narrow market, or single tourism products.

(2) Long distribution channels.

A long distribution channel is a distribution channel through which enterprises sell products to consumers through two or more intermediate links in tourism marketing activities. In a long distribution channel, travel intermediaries carry out most of the marketing functions, but information transmission is slow and the circulation time is long, making it difficult for travel companies to control distribution channels. The long distribution channel is suitable for travel products and services sold in a wider range and in more market segments. For tourism consumers, the long distribution channel can enable a more comprehensive understanding of tourism enterprises and offer more ways to obtain tourism information. But the long distribution channel may lead to higher travel prices: travel companies may pass on the cost of middlemen to consumers.

First, two-level distribution channels. The mode of the two-level distribution channel is: tourism enterprise→tourism wholesaler→tourism retailer→tourism consumer. Tourism enterprises only have direct business contact with tourism wholesalers. Large-scale tourism wholesalers often have extensive distribution outlets and strong distribution forces, which have obvious advantages over tourism retailers.

Second, three-level distribution channels. The mode of the three-level distribution channel is: tourism enterprise→travel agent→tourism wholesaler→tourism retailer→tourism consumer. This distribution channel strengthens travel agents, who influence the effectiveness of the distribution channel in terms of distribution capabilities, control over distribution territories, and their loyalty.

3) Narrow and Wide Distribution Channels

The width of distribution channels is determined by the number of middlemen marketing products. According to the number of middlemen at the same level, distribution channels can be divided into narrow and wide distribution channels, as shown in figure 10.4.

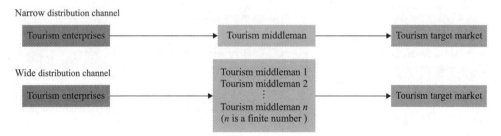

Figure 10.4 Schematic diagram of narrow and wide distribution channels

(1) Narrow distribution channels.

The narrow distribution channel means that in the marketing activities of tourism enterprises, only one intermediary is used at each level of the distribution channel. The use of narrow distribution channels can make the relationship between enterprises and intermediaries close, resulting in strong dependence, and production and sales can promote each other. However, the narrow distribution channel will limit the sales area of the market. Therefore, it is generally suitable for the sales of tourism products with strong professionalism or high cost. For tourism consumers, the narrow distribution channel strategy of tourism enterprises is not conducive to the rapid awareness and understanding of tourism products. However, for tourism products with strong professionals or high cost, such as global tourism and travel across the Taklimakan Desert, narrow distribution channels are more targeted because of their limited audiences, so that tourism consumers who prefer such tourism products can purchase them.

(2) Wide distribution channels.

A wide distribution channel involves the use of two or more intermediaries of the same type at each level of the channel in the marketing activities of tourism enterprises. Using wide distribution channels can help reach a large number of tourists and sell tourism products in large quantities and widely sell tourism products in the market. However, the large number of tourism middlemen will mean that the products they sell are not specific, and the relationship between manufacturers and middlemen is loose. General popular tourist products are mainly sold through wide distribution channels. Tourism enterprises can expand their sales by adopting the wide distribution channel strategy, which is conducive which is conducive to consumers to have a faster and more comprehensive understanding of tourism products. For example, travel agencies can adopt wide distribution channels to enable consumers to purchase daily sightseeing tours and vacation tours.

4) Single and Multiple Distribution Channels

According to the number of types of distribution channels used in the circulation of tourism products, the distribution channels of tourism products can be single or multiple, as shown in figure 10.5.

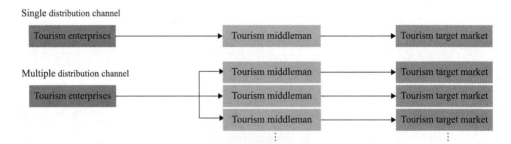

Figure 10.5　Schematic diagram of single and multiple distribution channels

(1) Single distribution channels.

In a single distribution channel model, all travel products are directly sold by tourism enterprises themselves or handed over to tourism middleman for sale. Under normal circumstances, a single distribution channel can be used when a tourism enterprise operates fewer products or has a weaker management capability.

(2) Multiple distribution channels.

A multiple distribution channel means that tourism enterprises use different distribution channels for different tourism products or different tourists. For example, direct distribution channels can be used for local business and indirect distribution channels for foreign business, or a combination of long and short distribution channels can be used. The use of multiple distribution channels can expand the coverage of tourism products, and sell a large number of tourism products and services. A multiple distribution channel approach can allow tourism consumers to get a faster, better, and more comprehensive understanding of tourism enterprises and tourism products.

10.3.3 Tourism Intermediaries and Tourism Consumer Behavior

1) Travel Dealers and Tourism Consumer Behavior

Travel dealers are intermediaries who buy tourism products and sell them later. In essence, they are tourism intermediaries that take ownership of the products. Their profits come from the difference between purchase price and sales price. Travel dealers and tourism enterprises share market risks. Travel dealers can be divided into tourism wholesalers and tourism retailers according to their business.

(1) Tourism wholesalers.

A tourism wholesaler is a travel agency or tourism enterprise that engages in the wholesale distribution of tourism products. Tourism wholesalers are the bridge connecting tourism enterprises and tourism retailers, and travel dealers that do not directly serve consumers. Tourism wholesalers order products such as tourist attraction tickets, transportation, and restaurants in large quantities, and then combine them into packaged tourism products for sale to tourism retailers, and the tourism retailers then sell them to consumers.

(2) Tourism retailers.

A tourism retailer is an intermediary that directly faces the consumer and engages in the retail business of tourism products. He or she has the closest contact with tourism consumers and helps them choose suitable tourism products according to their needs. Tourism retailers should maintain a good relationship with various tourism enterprises and make adjustments according to the needs of the tourism target market and consumers.

2) Travel Agents and Tourism Consumer Behavior

Travel agents are intermediaries who accept the entrustment of tourism enterprises and sell their products in a certain area. Through negotiation with buyers and sellers, travel agents promote the buying and selling of tourism products. Tourism enterprises can use travel agents to seek marketing opportunities when their own sales capabilities are not good, new products are in the early stage of listing, or tourism products are not selling well.

When choosing travel agents from whom to make a purchase, consumers should pay attention to the agency qualification of travel agents, that is, whether they are regular agents of tourism enterprises, so as to ensure the quality of their tourism products and the effectiveness of their services. On the other hand, we should consider the basic information, such as the travel agent's reputation and experience, to get the tourism products we want at a lower price.

10.4 Tourism Promotion and Tourism Consumer Behavior

10.4.1 The Definition of Tourism Promotion

Tourism promotion involves tourism marketers transmitting information about tourism enterprises, destinations, and products to potential buyers through various means of publicity, attraction, and persuasion, so as to promote understanding, trust, and purchase decision, thus achieving the purpose of expanding sales.

The core of tourism promotion is the communication of information. The purpose of tourism promotion is to induce and stimulate consumers' purchasing behavior. There are two types of travel promotion: personnel selling and non-personnel promotion. Personal selling refers to direct contact between sales staff of tourism enterprises and consumers, which allows inquiry about their needs and introduction of products face to face; non-personal promotion mainly involves advertising, business promotion, and public relations. The combination and comprehensive use of four factors, advertising, business promotion, public relations, and personal selling, is called a promotion mix.

10.4.2 The Role of Tourism Promotion

1) Delivering Products and Requesting Information

The essence of tourism promotion is the communication of information between tourism marketers and potential buyers of tourism products. On the one hand, tourism enterprises transmit information about tourist destinations, tourism enterprises, and tourism products to consumers through various promotional means, enabling consumers to understand them, encouraging consumers to trust them and purchase their products. On the other hand, tourism enterprises collect the opinions of tourism consumers in a timely manner, so that they can improve their products and find more suitable market positionings responding to the needs of tourism consumers.

2) Stimulating Tourism Consumption Behavior

First of all, tourism products are commodities with elastic demand. Tourism enterprises should use various effective promotion methods flexibly according to the psychological motivation of tourism consumers to stimulate their consumption desire and interest, and generate purchasing behavior. In addition, demand can be created through promotional activities that promote product sales undertaken by tourism enterprises.

3) Highlighting the Characteristics of Tourism Products

In the face of the development trend of tourism product homogenization, tourism enterprises strengthen the role of marketing. They highlight the characteristics and advantages of their products and the unique benefits they can offer consumers, to encourage consumer preference and improve market competitiveness.

4) Shaping the Image of Tourism Enterprises

Appropriate promotional activities can establish a good image for a tourism enterprise, giving consumers a good impression of the enterprise and its products, so as to cultivate and improve user loyalty, form a stable user group, continuously expand market share, and consolidate the market position of the enterprise.

10.4.3 Tourism Promotion Mix and Tourism Consumer Behavior

1) Personal Selling

Personal selling refers to a process in which salespeople use various sales techniques and means to persuade tourism consumers to accept purchases and services. The methods of personal selling include personal, business, and conference selling. The advantages are that personal selling is flexible and targeted. It can easily strengthen purchase motivation, facilitate transactions in a timely manner, and it has strong interaction. It can better cultivate positive sentiments in tourism consumers and establish stable connections. The disadvantages are that it requires a large number of staff, the process is time-consuming and expensive, and the communication efficiency is low.

2) Advertising

Advertising is the promotion of products, services, or enterprises to consumers through the media. The main type is informative, persuasive, and reminder advertising. The advantages of advertising are that it has a wide range of propaganda, transmits information quickly, and it is conducive to rapid sales. It allows repeated dissemination, saves manpower, and improves visibility. It takes various forms and strong expressiveness. The disadvantages are that promotional investment is high, the one-way transmission of information with consumers is weak, and it is difficult to form a timely purchase.

3) Business Promotion

Business promotion involves various short-term promotion methods launched to persuade consumers to purchase products or services, including free business promotion, preferential business promotion, competition business promotion, and combination business promotion. The advantages include great attractiveness, fast action, strong stimulation of consumption, and prompt transactions. The disadvantages are that it only temporarily changes the purchasing habits of customers, the effect is short-term, the organizational workload is large, the cost is high, the marketing scope is narrow, and it is not conducive to shaping product image.

4) Public Relations

Public relations refer to a series of thematic or daily activities carried out by tourism enterprises in order to coordinate all aspects of the relationship and establish a good image in the community. These activities include publicity public relations, communicative public relations, service public relations, social public relations, and consultative public relations. The advantages of public relations are high credibility, good image, wide influence, and great influence. The disadvantages are that event design is difficult, the organization workload is large, events involve a wide range and are difficult to control, and it cannot directly generate sales.

10.5 Marketing Innovation and Tourism Consumer Behavior

10.5.1 Internet Marketing and Tourism Consumer Behavior

Tourism Internet marketing refers to various marketing activities carried out by tourism enterprises based on electronic information technology and using computer networks as media and means. On the one hand, Internet marketing should focus on the emerging online virtual market, timely understand and grasp the changes in the characteristics and behavior patterns of tourism consumers in the online virtual market, and provide reliable data analysis and marketing for enterprises to carry out marketing activities in the online virtual market. On the other hand, Internet marketing can carry out marketing activities in online virtual markets, which can achieve the goals of tourism enterprises.

In recent years, the transaction scale of the live broadcast e-commerce market has continued to rise, the industry development momentum is strong, and the live broadcast outlet is hot. The "live broadcast+" layout leads industrial innovation and brings market development prospects to other industries. Not limited to traditional offline channels and tapping the value of online live broadcast marketing can reduce costs and increase efficiency. The new marketing model of live broadcast presale attracts live audiences to place orders, helps suppliers and platforms return funds, predicts the future of the market, and promotes the recovery of tourist destinations. The highly interactive characteristics of live broadcasts facilitate the establishment of real-time communication channels, bridge the information gap, and allow users to take more information initiative. To a certain extent, it can activate the potential travel needs of users, and at the same time, the perfect cancellation guarantee system improves users' trust and establishes a good emotional resonance. In addition, it shortens the user decision-making cycle and significantly improves the efficiency of tourism decision-making.

10.5.2 Green Marketing and Tourism Consumer Behavior

1) Use Advertisements for Green Tourism Products to Vigorously Promote Green Tourism Consumption

Advertisements for green tourism products can strengthen people's awareness of environmental protection, lead tourism consumers to connect consumption with the crisis of personal and human survival, and make them actively choose green products that are conducive to personal health and human ecological balance.

2) Promotion through Green Public Relations

Green public relations are important communication channels to establish the green image of tourism enterprises and their products. Green public relations activities can help tourism enterprises spread green information more directly and widely to the tourism market segments that cannot be reached by advertisements, stimulate consumers' willingness to buy, and bring competitive advantages to tourism enterprises.

3) Green Personal Selling and Sales Promotion

Personal selling is a promotional method. To effectively implement green marketing, tourism salespeople must understand the interest of tourism consumers in green consumption, answer to the environmental protection issues that tourism consumers care about, and master the green aspects of tourism enterprise products and the operation of the enterprise. Tourism enterprises can also improve their popularity through sales promotion methods such as gifts and product trials.

Case Study 10-3

Cultural Marketing of Universal Beijing Resort

10.5.3 Cultural Marketing and Tourism Consumer Behavior

1) Cultural Packaging

Cultural packaging of tourism products has strong cultural appeal and contains rich cultural concepts to meet the psychological needs of tourism consumers. It is necessary to integrate culture into packaging, so that the tourism product itself can be infused with a national, modern, and healthy cultural awareness, improving its cultural flavour and content, highlighting its added value, and making the tourism destination a cultural destination.

2) Cultural Dissemination

Cultural dissemination is the modern embodiment of marketing communication. It achieves the purpose of marketing by means of systematically integrated cultural factors. The key to cultural dissemination is to be uplifting, clear, and straightforward. It should emphasize the important characteristics of tourism products for tourism consumers, emphasize the cultural characteristics of tourism products, clearly identify the target market, and be able to attract enough attention. Cultural dissemination includes a variety

Further Reading

Traveller Yanxuan Adopts "Cloud Tourism+ Cultural Grass Planting" to Sell Goods

of short-term incentive tools to stimulate tourism consumers to purchase a specific tourism product or service more quickly and in large quantities.

3) Cultural Experience

Experiential tourism is a tourism activity whose main goal is experience. It makes a larger, deeper, and stronger psychological impression on tourism consumers through activities and feelings. The psychological needs of tourism consumers depend on their different regions, countries, ethnic groups, ages, genders, and education levels, so their experience can be very different. Tourism enterprises must choose different angles and entry points, and adopt different methods and means to provide experiential tourism projects for different tourism consumers.

10.5.4 KOL Marketing and Tourism Consumer Behavior

The key opinion leader (KOL) is a concept usually defined as someone who has not only numerous, but also accurate product information, which is accepted or trusted by the relevant group. KOLs are people who have an influence on purchasing behavior. The difference between KOLs and celebrities is that the former are not spokespersons for the products, but carriers who actually provide consumers with product information. Many KOLs are experts in their fields, with millions of followers, and provide fans with advice, guidance, reviews, and more through a variety of media. Fans also actively participate in the content created by KOLs, engaging in word-of-mouth communication, and making direct purchases.

It should be noted that KOLs are not the same as Internet celebrities. KOLs are a crucial word-of-mouth information node for brands in the social media environment, and cannot be simply equated with celebrity endorsements and Internet celebrities. Existing Internet celebrities, celebrities, spokespersons, business owners themselves, core employees, industry peers, experts, etc., may become KOLs. Under certain circumstances, ordinary consumers can also become KOLs. KOLs must have more professional knowledge, and the fan group has a certain degree of trust in him. Internet celebrities are more focused on entertainment, and their audience watches them for leisure, while KOLs are more likely to gain the trust of their fans, who watch them seriously. The point of the KOLs is to be able to actually influence the actions of others, not just attract attention. From this point of view, it is not the case that the more fans, the greater the KOLs. Many so-called "Internet celebrity marketing" and "big marketing" approaches are not really KOL marketing.

Chapter 10 Marketing and Tourism Consumer Behavior

Chapter Summary

This chapter mainly discusses the influence of tourism products, tourism prices, tourism distribution channels, tourism promotions, and innovative marketing methods on tourism consumer behavior. It is divided into five sections. The first section introduces the concept of the tourism product, tourism product life cycle, and the influence of tourism product brand on tourism consumer behavior. The second section focuses on tourism prices and introduces the concept and the influence of tourism product pricing on tourism consumer behavior. The third section focuses on tourism distribution channels, the type and choice of tourism distribution channels, and the behavior of tourism intermediaries and tourism consumers. The fourth section is about tourism promotion, its role, and the influence of tourism promotion combination on tourism consumer behavior. The fifth section focuses on the relationship between Internet marketing, green marketing, cultural marketing, and KOL marketing and tourism consumer behavior.

China Story

Green Concept and Tourism Consumer Behavior

 Issues for Review and Discussion

1. Explain the concepts: tourism product, tourism price, tourism distribution channel, tourism promotion, green marketing, and KOL marketing.
2. What are the characteristics of tourism consumer behavior in each stage of the tourism product life cycle?
3. Briefly describe the impact of different tourism promotion combinations on tourism consumer behavior.
4. Talk about the influence of KOL marketing on tourism consumption behavior.

Exercises

Chapter 11
Tourist Purchasing Decision, Tourism Pre-purchasing, and Communication

Learning Objectives

After reading this chapter, you should have a good understanding of the following points:

(1) describe the consumer decision-making process and clarify the two stages before tourists make purchases;

(2) understand the stages of problem awareness and the source of visitor demand;

(3) understand the information search and collection stage, and identify the factors that affect this stage;

(4) understand the concepts and basic models of communication, and learn how to design persuasive messages;

(5) clarify the impact of information and communication technology on tourism consumer communication;

(6) describe the definition, characteristics, and influencing factors of online consumer behavior, and understand its trends and applications in tourism.

Technical Words

English Words	中文翻译
custom advertising	定制广告
data mining	数据挖掘
decoding	解码
encoding	编码
ideal state	理想状态/应许之地
information and communication technology	信息通信技术
information avoidance	信息回避
information collection	信息收集

Chapter 11 Tourist Purchasing Decision, Tourism Pre-purchasing, and Communication

续表

English Words	中文翻译
information framing	信息框架
online community economy	线上社区经济
problem cognition	问题认知

Knowledge Graph

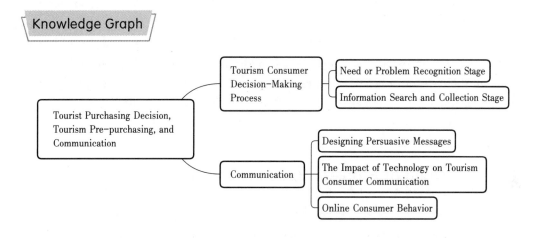

11.1 Tourism Consumer Decision-Making Process

In the previous chapters, we talked about culture, memory, and other influencing factors. Ultimately, the consumer's purchasing behavior comes down to decision-making. However, although consumers make many decisions every day, not all of them end in action. The amount of effort and time spent by consumers varies depending on whom they are buying from, with some making decisions in seconds and others hesitating for years. But regardless of the level of consumer involvement, every decision process almost always begins with an awareness of problems and needs, and extends to post-purchase behavior and feelings. Generally speaking, consumer decision-making is the process that consumers go through before and after purchasing a product and can generally be divided into five stages, as shown in figure 11.1 below[①].

[①] 甘瑁琴. 消费者行为学[M]. 北京:北京大学出版社, 2009.

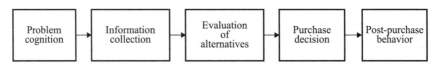

Figure 11.1　Consumer decision-making process

　　In tourism marketing, the consumer decision-making process refers to when a potential tourist targets a place on a particular day and recognizes their travel needs. They visit the destination and generate post-tour evaluation after searching for information about the destination and sifting through the alternatives. Tourism marketers use this process to track the visitor's journey from start to finish. Through this tracking, tourism marketers can develop strategies that will help them influence the visitor's spending behavior. Although each visitor's behavior varies according to individual needs, researchers agree that the visitor's decision-making process consists of a series of well-defined stages. In this section, we will discuss the different stages of the consumer decision-making process in the tourism industry.

11.1.1 Need or Problem Recognition Stage

1) Tourists' Problem Cognitive Process

　　The need or problem recognition stage is the first stage in the consumer decision-making process. Almost every day, people face many consumption problems. Daily purchase problems will be quickly tackled once they are recognized, such as the demand to replenish milk after drinking and the necessity to buy medicines when people are sick. The purchase or maintenance of certain frequently used bulk products (such as computers or refrigerators, etc.), although easily recognized, usually involves a slower decision-making process.

　　The unsatisfied consumer status is what leads them to want a particular product to satisfy a specific need. The generation of tourism behavior not only stems from the positive psychology of tourists seeking emerging stuff, but also from the negative psychology of escaping from the tense reality. Tourism behavior usually occurs because people are dissatisfied with the current situation or have expectations for a distant place. Travel is a very typical consumption behavior with a slow and complex decision-making process.

　　When a consumer experiences an impulse that makes them realize they have a need to take a trip, their need is said to have been triggered by an internal stimulus. A typical example of an internal stimulus is hunger. Conversely, when consumers realize their needs through outside influences, their realization is said to have been triggered by external stimuli. An example is when one friend tells the other about a journey they recently went on, and they make them feel like they need to go there as well. Regardless of the trigger, consumer needs always fall into two categories—functional and psychological needs. Functional needs refer to needs that result out of necessity, while psychological needs refer to cognitive needs that originate from emotional feelings. When a customer runs out of his toothpaste, he will go out and buy a new one, that's a functional need. But in people's lives, there will be various negative emotions, such as irritability, boredom, or depression. These emotions are often recognized as problems or demands that govern travel behavior. For example, people who live in cold regions will come up with ideas like "it's too annoying to be at such a cold home every day, I'm going to a warm place for vacation", or people who live in cold regions prefer taking a vacation in Southeast Asia in winter. In addition to meeting the needs of tourists by creating products, excellent tourism marketers can also help tourists to recognize needs and problems in advance.

Besides, the gap between the actual state and the ideal state will also affect tourists' perception of the problem. If a potential visitor's ideal destination has a pleasant and mild climate, whereas extreme weather and air pollution are afflicting the place where he lives, he will desperately want to take a trip. After recognizing the problem, the action choices of potential visitors are influenced by both the size and intensity of the gap and the significance of the problem. If the potential visitor lives in a place that is not as warm and humid as the ideal place but has a good environment, this gap may not lead to the tourism behavior of the potential visitor without other incentives.

In addition, if the gap between the ideal state and the actual state is large, but the problem caused by it is not a primary concern, the problem will not necessarily enter the next decision-making process. For instance, despite the potential tourist we have mentioned above is very eager to travel to his ideal destination, the consumer may have to put travel plans on hold when confronting of the risk of some public emergencies.

Figure 11.2[①] illustrates the consumer's cognitive process related to the problem. The lifestyle pursued by the consumer and the situation, in reality, represent his ideal state and actual state. Whether there is a gap between the two states and the magnitude and intensity of the gap determine the consumer's satisfaction levels. Dissatisfaction with the gap between states can lead to problem recognition, which triggers further decision-making.

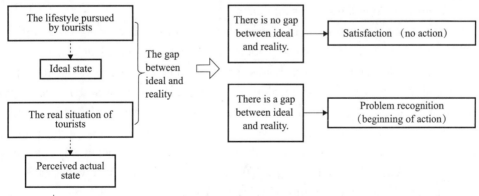

Figure 11.2   Problem recognition process

① 费明胜, 杨伊侬. 消费者行为学: Consumer behavior[M]. 北京: 人民邮电出版社, 2013.

2) Factors Affecting Tourists' Perception of Problems

As mentioned in the previous section, the gap between tourists' ideal state and the actual state determines the generation of tourists' problem cognition. Then, any factor that affects the perception gap of tourists will in turn affect the cognitive process of tourists. These factors usually include as follows.

(1) Time and era change.

The influence of the times is undoubtedly immense due to the highly significant role it plays in stimulating the demand of tourists. The longer a tourist stays at a destination, the more likely he/she is to discover problems and demands. At the same time, the change of the times also means the rapid development of information and communication technologies. The rapid iteration of technologies has brought more information and a broader perspective to tourists, just as the needs of tourists 10 years ago were different from today.

(2) Public emergencies.

Public emergencies may trigger cognitive changes at the societal level. For example, before some public emergencies occur, tourists mostly liked to go somewhere for sightseeing and relaxation. However, tourists began to avoid visiting this place as much as possible after that because they get some negative perceptions.

(3) Environmental changes.

Changes in one's life can arouse many new requirements. Many young people who have just graduated will yearn for a romantic trip after getting paid. Likewise, changes in the family can bring about new perceptions of problems. Honeymoon destinations for newlyweds are different from leisure travel destinations, and families with children are more inclined to stay in a hotel with a parent-child focus.

11.1.2 Information Search and Collection Stage

1) Tourist Information Sources (Internal and External)

(1) Internal information sources for tourists.

In fact, when a potential tourist comes up with the idea of going on a trip, this recalling process may yield satisfactory information to tackle travelling issues, such as when and where to purchase travel-related products. The search process of tourists for relevant information in long-term memory is referred to as internal search; the relevant information obtained from internal search is referred to as internal information. Internal information sources usually include two types: one is the memory formed by the individual's accumulation and learning in the past; the other is the individual's past travel experience. For example, the learning behavior of a primary student traveller can be one of their internal sources of information, and reading travel-related books or online materials can also accumulate experience for people who have never travelled much. When people have conducted travel behavior, the memory and experience of previous trips will be emphasized when planning for the next trip.

(2) External information sources for tourists.

For an experienced tourist, most problems can be solved with previous experience stored in memory. But if personal experience fails to enable a resolution, the visitor may think that he/she needs to search for extra helpful information. This information search process that focuses on problem-solving is referred to as external search; the relevant information obtained from external search is referred to as external information. External information is usually of three types.

① The attitudes, opinions, behaviors, and emotions of others. Others include relatives, friends, neighbors, and even strangers on the Internet. In fact, with the advent of the Internet age, more and more people choose to listen to opinions online.

② Further professional study, i.e., professional information obtained from professional manuals, articles, books, and personal contacts.

③ Commercial sources, in other words, market information presented through advertisements, product displays, salespeople, etc.

Marketing departments often positively participate in the information-gathering phase to influence consumer behavior through the dissemination of information. Generally speaking, in the information age, commercial sources are the information sources most frequently used by consumers. However, the most trusted information is that received from others. Commercial information usually plays a role in notifying, while information from trusted groups will play a role in determining or evaluating purchasing behavior. For example, a tourist began to pay attention to relevant information after seeing the relevant advertisements placed in Guangzhou Chimelong Water Park, but finally decided to go with his family because relatives, friends, or netizens commented that the place was very suitable for parent-child activities.

Further Reading

Influencing Factors in the Process of Information Collection

2) Brand considerations of tourist destinations in the process of information collection

Through information gathering, the visitor becomes familiar with a number of similar destinations or brands in a competitive market. The first box on the left in figure 11.3 represents the full range of destinations that a visitor wishing to visit the beach might visit, while this visitor may only be familiar with a subset of all destinations, which constitutes the known destinations group. Within the group of known destinations, only certain destinations fit the initial visit criteria, and this is the group of destinations that can be considered. Once the visitor has gathered a large amount of information on such destinations, only a few destinations are selected as priorities, and the set of these priorities forms the alternative destinations group. The final decision is made by the visitor from the alternative group based on the decision evaluation process they have experienced.

Figure 11.3 shows that destinations must strategically place themselves in the known, available for consideration, and alternative groups of potential customers. Destinations should delve into what other destinations remain in the visitor's alternative group in order to develop competitively attractive plans. In addition, marketers should identify the visitor's source of information and evaluate its relevance and importance. It is also essential to ask visitors how they felt when they first heard information about the destination, what information they received later, the different sources of information, etc. These answers will help the destination prepare an effective communications plan for its target market.

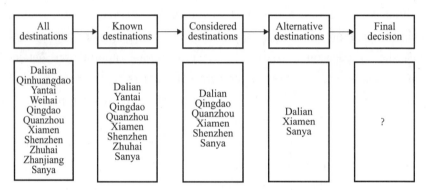

Figure 11.3　Destinations considered successively in the visitor's decision-making process[①]

11.2 Communication

Communication is the process of conveying or exchanging information. As shown in figure 11.4, in the context of tourist behavior, it refers to the process of passing information from the sender (source of information) to the recipient (visitor) through channel (intermidiary). In addition to the four elements of sender, recipient, channel, and information, the fifth fundamental element of communication is communication feedback. Communication feedback can inform the sender whether the information was received accurately. The sender encodes the message using words, pictures, symbols, spokespeople, and persuasive appeals, and the recipient must decode the message in the way the sender intended. In other words, the entire process of communication is based on the transfer of information.

---

① Source: Narayana, Chem L, Markin, et al. Consumer Behavior and Product Performance: An Alternative Conceptualization[J]. Journal of Marketing, 1975, 39(4): 1-6.

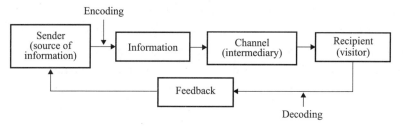

Figure 11.4 Communication model[①]

Communication can be impersonal or interpersonal. In today's dynamic global world, understanding how travellers acquire relevant external information is critical to making marketing management decisions, realizing successful communications campaigns and service delivery, and influencing travelling and purchasing decisions. In tourism marketing, information sources for non-personal communication often come from organizations (both for-profit and non-profit). These organizations design and deliver their messages through marketing departments, advertising, PR agencies, or spokespersons. The target audience or recipient of this information is usually one or more groups that the organization wishes to inform, influence, or persuade. The sender of information in interpersonal communication can be a formal source or an informal source. For example, a formal information source can be the sales staff of a travel agency or advertisements of the tourist destination, and an informal information source can be friends who communicate with tourists through face-to-face or online media. The key factor that influences the effect of interpersonal communication is the credibility of the information source, in other words, the degree to which the information receiver, that is, the tourist, trusts the information sender. The information source of interpersonal communication has an important influence on tourists' travel decisions, and the honesty and objectivity perceived from the information sender also have a significant influence on the recognition of the information. The main advantage of interpersonal communication, compared to non-human communication through mass media, is that immediate feedback can be obtained in both verbal and non-verbal forms. Experienced salespeople are very attentive to feedback and will adjust the content and method of information in a timely manner based on the immediate response of visitors. And timely feedback is a key factor to ensure the effect of tourism promotion because it enables the publicity from various parties to meet the needs of consumers.

The media is a channel of communication. Traditional media are impersonal communication channels, generally divided into print media, such as newspapers, magazines, and bulletin boards, and broadcast media, such as radio and television. The audience receives information as one-way information and cannot interact with the sender of the information. New media is an exchange channel that uses digital technology to provide users with information and services through computer networks, wireless

---

① Source: Shannon C E. A Mathematical Theory of Communication[J]. The Bell System Technical Journal, 1948, 27(4): 623-656.

Further Reading

Custom Advertising

communication networks, satellite networks, and other channels, as well as terminals such as computers, mobile phones, and digital televisions. It has the characteristics of large capacity, real-time, and interactivity. Compared with traditional media, new media is much more advanced. Not only can new media span vast geographic distances, but marketers can also use new media to send customized messages to consumers and receive immediate feedback.

11.2.1 Designing Persuasive Messages

The ultimate goal of communication in tourism marketing should be tourists' various consumption behaviors that can create benefits. Therefore, the persuasiveness of the information conveyed in the communication process is particularly important. Messages can be written or non-written (such as photos, videos, or symbols), or both. Advertising messages are ideas, thoughts, attitudes, images, or other content that the sender wants to convey to the recipient of the message. The sender can be a person or an organization. Before designing a persuasive message, marketers must first determine the purpose of the message, choose an appropriate medium for the message, and encode the message in a way that suits the medium and target group. The main goals of persuasive messaging are to create awareness of the product or service, stimulate sales of the product or service, motivate (or discourage) specific behaviors, attract visitors, reduce post-purchase dissonance, create a friendly or favorable image, or a combination of these goals.

In the process of dissemination, the information source (information sender) must encode the information in a way that the target audience can accurately understand—the operator or marketer encodes the information through words, pictures, symbols, spokespersons, and special channels. Message audiences decode messages based on their personal experiences, memories, personal characteristics, and motivations. In order for the target audience to understand exactly what the message means, i.e., to decode it successfully, the sender of the message must know exactly what they are talking about, i.e., be clear about its purpose and understand the personal characteristics of the target audience.

11.2.2 The Impact of Technology on Tourism Consumer Communication

In modern society, if people want to communicate, they cannot do without the development of science and technology. In the early 1990s, information and communication technology sparked an unprecedented explosion of communication methods. Since then, the Internet has gone from an expert tool for the scientific community to an easy-to-use World Wide Web for the masses—a network that changes the patterns of social interaction.

1) What is Information and Communication Technology (ICT)?

Information and communication technology (ICT) is understood as a term referring to computer science connected to the Internet. It is a technology that provides access to information through telecommunications information technology (IT) and communication technology (CT), including computational and computer tools for processing, storing, summarizing, retrieving, and presenting the information in a variety of ways. At the same time, it is a set of tools and channels for processing and obtaining information. They constitute new media and channels for shaping, registering, storing, and disseminating information content. Some examples of these technologies are digital whiteboards, blogs, podcasts, and of course, the Web. Therefore, ICT covers a very wide range of technologies, including those of storing information and retrieving it later, sending and receiving information from one site to another, and processing information to calculate results and prepare reports. It is embodied in the Internet, wireless networks, mobile phones, and other communication media.

2) What is the origin of ICT?

The history of ICT begins with a kitten raised by the ancient Greek philosopher Thales. Around 600 B.C., Thales was idle at home, rubbing a kitten with an amber stick. Rubbing and rubbing, he found that the amber stick had sucked up the kitten's fur. Thales believed that this mysterious force with the same principle as magnets can be called "electricity". Although ancient Egyptian books dating from 2750 B.C. recorded fish that could generate electricity, known as "the thunder messenger of the Nile", it was not until more than 3,000 years later that people began to study this phenomenon. Electricity first changed human life starting from the British Michael Faraday who discovered the law of electromagnetic induction in 1831, and created the world's first generator that could generate continuous current. Since then, wired communication tools such as telegraph and telephone have entered people's lives. In 1896, the Italian Guglielmo Marchese Marconi achieved the first radio communication in human history, with a communication distance of only 30 meters. During the World War II, ICT finally ushered in the breakthrough, and wireless communication technology began to affect people's lives. Today, electronics, information technology, and telecommunication technologies are converging, and the Internet has achieved a dizzying exponential growth.

3) Advantages and Disadvantages of ICT

(1) Advantages of ICT.

① Contributes directly to economic growth and plays an indirect role in economic development.

ICT plays a vital role in expanding economic development and accelerating economic growth, and the scope of its direct impact depends on its share and growth rate in the overall economy. Although the ICT industry is growing faster than the overall national economy and accounts for a significant portion of GDP in some countries, the real potential of ICT does not lie in the direct impact of the ICT industry itself. Various macroeconomic and enterprise-level studies carried out internationally have proven that ICT can significantly increase productivity. In addition, telecommuting can also save companies office space costs and parking costs.

②Provides great benefits and advancements in health and education.

Information technology has been increasingly applied to the fields of education and medical care and has had a very positive impact, enabling the continuous advancement and modernization of both fields. In terms of education, the emergence of remote teaching and other means has dramatically lowered the educational threshold, and a wave of knowledge sharing has swept society. At the same time, ICT improves the employability of residents through the dissemination of new knowledge. In terms of medical treatment, ICT has reduced the difficulty of obtaining medical information. Whether it is mental health or physical health, remote medical treatment and online psychological counseling can effectively help those in need.

③Supports business people and locals to display and sell their products through the Internet.

From a micro perspective, small and micro enterprises and self-employed individuals can use ICT to reduce costs and expand sales channels. Before the maturity of ICT, it was difficult to expand many goods with obvious timeliness and regionality into foreign markets. However, with the application of ICT and changes in the network environment, online sales have developed rapidly by only providing information and trading without the need to backlog goods and funds. And some regional goods that need to expand in the market are also sold through the network with the help of ICT.

(2) Disadvantages of ICT.

①Lack of privacy.

With the rapid development and broad application of ICT, mankind has gradually entered the era of new media. Technological changes have had a variety of far-reaching effects on the media, and people's privacy right has been challenged like never before. Since the massive use of self-media platforms, a lot of user information has been leaked. A large amount of data is stored on the platform server. In the early days, hackers obtained data by attacking the server. Now some merchants have already learned to capture user privacy through big data in order to obtain the information they want.

②Fraud.

With the rapid development of ICT, traditional fraud has taken the express train of modern information technology and gradually evolved into telecommunication network fraud with more diverse methods of and more serious consequences. Telecommunications network fraud has become a crime with wide-ranging effects around the world. It refers to the criminal act of using telephone, SMS, Internet, and other technical telecommunication network means for the purpose of illegal possession, falsifying facts, setting up scams, implementing remote and contactless fraud, and stealing public and private property. The victim groups of telecommunication network fraud are often broad and non-specific, making it difficult to guard against.

③Unemployment.

It has to be mentioned that although ICT has greatly facilitated people's lives and reduced the labor force's dependence on land and capital, it also means that most basic labor positions have been transferred from humans to machines. In many jobs involving repetitive labor, people will be gradually replaced by machines, such as dishwashers, bank tellers, etc. This is an inevitable trend.

All in all, the advantages of ICT are indisputable. It provides a new way of communication for human beings. It enables innovation and creativity, and it has very obvious advantages in specific industries. It expands the possibility of social development all the time. Furthermore, our economic situation, social structure, and cultural rights are constantly changing due to the effects of ICT, which affects the future to a very large extent.

4) The Impact of ICT on the Consumer Journey

(1) Ease of access to information.

Consumers' choice of information acquisition channels usually depends on the value and cost of information acquisition, and the Internet can provide a variety of information, and the acquisition process is relatively convenient. Consumers can easily find information before, during, and after consumption. Tourists usually tend to browse information nodes to minimize the search cost, and these information nodes are usually government official websites, destination scenic spots official websites, and tourism portal websites that contain a lot of destination information.

(2) Raise customer expectations.

As tourists get a lot of relevant information through ICT, such as the Internet, their expectations are starting to rise. The Internet has dramatically broadened the horizons of consumers, and few new things can shock people. Consumers want something new in their product and service experience. At the same time, travel notes published on the Internet by tourists who have been to a destination will also affect readers' general impressions and expectations from the destination. Therefore, once the destination has difficulties in meeting increasing tourist expectations, tourists will be dissatisfied, which will affect online word-of-mouth.

(3) Tourists lack attention.

With the continuous development of ICT, information can be obtained very quickly, conveniently, and cheaply. As a result, the problem of information overload begins to plague every network user. Nobel laureate in economics Herbert Simon believed that it is the abundance of information that causes recipients' lack of attention. Since entering the era of the network, attention has become an essential part of economics. The real value of information producers lies in the positioning, filtering, and dissemination of effective information to users, such as search engines like Chrome and Google. In addition, today's network service providers collect user information to judge their future behavior and conduct precise marketing to compensate for the negative impact of attention deficit.

(4) Need for personalization.

Personalization has become an essential factor in determining the nature of a visitor's experience as the amount of information received and expectations grow. In recent years,

Further Reading

Data Mining

Further Reading

Information Avoidance

tourism consumers have shifted from group tours to personalized customized tours, which is a consumption upgrade, and the speed of tourism consumption upgrade is very fast. Compared with traditional tourism products that focus on low prices, high-quality tourism products that emphasize personalization and specialization can impress consumers more. With the important support of ICT, the tourism form of "Internet +" has been rapidly upgraded and developed into smart tourism, which has become the development direction of the upgrading of the tourism industry. The establishment of the smart tourism system will integrate food, housing, travel, shopping, entertainment, and even more comprehensive information on the big data cloud platform. These data provide rich data resources for customized tours and effectively promote the further development of such tours.

11.2.3 Online Consumer Behavior

1) What is online consumer behavior?

As a purchasing behavior that occurs in virtual media, online consumer behavior is undoubtedly very complex. It is usually understood as the process of consumers' purchasing behavior online, which is usually reflected in the research of trends, including live streaming shopping, KOL-led shopping, customers' use of online shopping platforms, and so on. The decisions consumers make in an online environment can be very different compared to physical shopping. Therefore, both the industry and academia are studying online consumer behavior in order to adjust the sales and marketing strategies of related enterprises to attract Internet buyers. In fact, relevant research can clarify consumers' reactions to marketing actions such as advertisements and promotions of enterprises, destinations, and scenic spots. It has been proved that with the development of ICT, online shopping behavior has increased its impact on offline consumption. More and more consumers are checking the Internet before heading to a mall or other store, and the vast majority of tourists book and buy online before making a trip. Therefore, many destinations and scenic spots have increased their investment in online channels. Based on the analysis of online consumer behavior, destinations and scenic spots can determine the details of their marketing strategies, including channel selection, advertising content, website page layout, and co-branding with other IPs. Online ordering has become popular in the travel industry. Online consumer behavior can also be forward-looking. Behavioral research can both inform destination and scenic consumer responses to advertising and promotional strategies but can also predict consumer responses to other future activities or network features. Market analysis in the online space often leads to innovation. Destinations and attractions develop new promotional strategies and evaluate the effectiveness of different approaches to reach potential visitors based on behavioral statistics.

2) Four Characteristics of Online Consumer Behavior

(1) Tourists do not buy products online but use the Internet to find exclusive offers from channels or platforms. Price and discounts are undoubtedly among the most important influencing factors when tourists make online booking behavior decisions. If online shopping does not provide discounts, tourists' enthusiasm for online booking will also be significantly reduced.

(2) It is difficult for tourists to evaluate any online product using traditional methods, such as the five senses. Before the actual experience, it is difficult for tourists to experience any product on the spot.

(3) Online information's gather, comparison, and purchase all depend on the ability, skills, knowledge, and past experience of tourists. If the tourist has experienced the services of a particular hotel chain brand in the past, then he/she may choose another hotel under this brand to stay in next time.

(4) Tourists' attitudes and beliefs about ICT have a significant impact on online purchases and bookings. When tourists think that the online environment is not safe, that the Internet will harm their privacy, or they prefer traditional shopping methods, they will avoid online shopping.

3) Online Consumer Behavior Trends in Tourism Online Consumer Behavior

(1) Trend 1: online travel booking has become widely used and crowded.

① When planning a trip or looking for information about a destination, the Internet remains the best resource.

② The three main components of online travel sales are still airfare, accommodation, and rental cars.

(2) Trend 2: generational differences and similarities.

① There are significant disparities in how different generations utilize the Internet.

② Online travel planning and information seeking are much more popular and active among younger generations, especially Gen Y.

(3) Trend 3: new behaviors are supported by social media, mobile technology, and emerging outlets.

① The way people plan their travel and look for information online is significantly affected by social media and other newly emerging kinds of online communication.

② User-generated content as a fresh source of information.

③ Use of smartphones.

4) A New Scenario of Online Tourism Consumer Behavior: The Online Community Economy, New Media and Tourism Consumer Behavior

In recent years, the online community economy, empowered by e-commerce, has attracted a lot of attention from scholars in China and abroad due to its innovative business

Case Study 11-1

The New Formats of the Online Travel Industry

model and growing economic volume. So, what is an online community?

A community was originally thought of as an entity that shared certain common values, norms, and goals, in which each member adopted the common goal as their own. It is a whole made up of people with many basic vectors, such as geographical, cultural, and ethnic. For example, a community can be described as people who love seafood in the city of Dalian, based on geographical location and culture. This group of people will come together for a common hobby and engage in collective activities, such as going to the beach together to collect fresh seafood. However, with the technological iteration of social media, digital social platforms such as WeChat, Weibo, and RED have accelerated the rapid development of online communities. In other words, through social platforms such as WeChat and RED, more and more people are joining in seafood collection at the beach, even though some may not be from Dalian. The geographical confines of traditional communities are being broken down, the boundaries of communities are spreading, and the place of community has moved from the initial physical space to a network that can span the dimensions of time and space. Networking and informatization have become the basic attributes and core characteristics of communities.

The online community can be understood as a virtual online space supported by technology that allows members to gather across networks, focusing on interaction and communication between members that can lead to relationship building[1][2]. In this space, community members can engage in repetitive social activities. The existence of online communities stems from the needs of individuals, such as interest groups formed for knowledge acquisition and common hobbies. Although the satisfaction of needs is usually accompanied by economic behavior and value creation, early communities did not generate large-scale economic value due to factors such as information technology and geographical space. Nowadays, knowledge-sharing behavior and organized consumption behavior based on the Internet are gradually becoming economic phenomena of a certain scale, and the economic benefits brought about by online communities are gradually emerging and being amplified. As a result, the online community economy, which relies on online information technology and emphasizes the collective power and economic utility of communities, has begun to move from backstage to the front of stage, becoming an economic force to be reckoned with. For example, the sharing of travel experiences on the Mafengwo website is a typical community behavior.

The development of online communities cannot be separated from the improvement of the technological base, including the platforms that support their creation and operation, and the platforms that support the completion of their online purchases. For

---

[1] Koh J, Kim Y J. Sense of Virtual Community: A Conceptual Framework and Empirical Validation[J]. International Journal of Electronic Commerce, 2003, 8(2): 75-94.

[2] Shen Y C, Huang C Y, Chu C H, et al. Virtual Community Loyalty: An Interpersonal-interaction Perspective [J]. International Journal of Electronic Commerce, 2010, 15(1): 49-74.

example, in WeChat, people who know each other through the internet can form a group and this group of strangers can make some purchases in this group. Those who like to eat hotpot can buy hotpot bases in the Chengdu Buyers group, and those who like to eat fruit can buy fresh grapes in the Xinjiang Specialties group. The popularity of online payment systems has facilitated the development of online communities.

The value of online communities is based on information[①], so the organizers of online communities or the producers of community content can be considered as information providers. As long as online communities can maintain efficient information production and transmission, they have the potential to grow. The organizers or content producers of online communities have convenient tools for information delivery thanks to communication technology and accurate user profiles thanks to big data algorithms, which increase the speed and efficiency of information dissemination. As a result, communities can provide precise and unique products and information. At the same time, due to their characteristics, communities often operate with both channel convenience and price advantages from economies of scale. As a result, following the introduction of group chat, official accounts, and small program services by WeChat and livestream shopping by Taobao, a large number of community economies have flourished on the platform.

At the same time, a good community experience deepens the consumer's psychological attachment to the community, which in turn drives loyalty[②]. When attachment is created, a strong psychological bond is formed between members and the community and other members. Members thus give emotion, function, and meaning to the community. Loyalty in a community means that a member consistently creates and shares information, has the ability to recommend to others to become part of the community, and feels the friendship of others as a result. At the same time, as interaction with others increases, emotion and social interaction are important in maintaining members' interest in the community, driving a sense of belonging and attachment to the community, which in turn creates a strong incentive for consumers to continue visiting the community, generating repeat purchase intentions and consumption behavior. For example, when a consumer sees a video-based travelogue posted by a blogger on a social media platform and finds it very interesting, they will become a fan after watching the blogger's video several times. After a certain blogger's recommendation, he/she will choose to go to a certain place to play and spend money, just like the blogger. The experience of the trip or the spending spree is so good that he/she will gradually increase his/her trust in this blogger and start to become a loyal follower. He/she will go on to interact and leave comments under each video, and when the time is right, he/she will continue to choose to follow in the blogger's footsteps and travel.

---

①卡尔·夏皮罗,哈尔·瓦里安. 信息规则:网络经济的策略指导[M]. 张帆,译. 北京:中国人民大学出版社, 2017.

②Funk D C, James J D. Consumer Loyalty: The Meaning of Attachment in the Development of Sport Team Allegiance[J]. Journal of Sport Management, 2006, 20(2): 189-217.

As the above example shows, before people become part of an online community, they must have an affirmation of the culture or content of the community, that is, the culture and content of the community must be perceived as valuable. In a community economy, the more value a culture, content, or product brings to its members, the more likely it is to lead to purchasing behavior. For example, knowledge-based or information-based communities such as the Logic Show and the Li Ziqi Channel mainly provide content products, while product-based communities such as Xiaomi mainly provide physical products. Regardless of the form of the product, the value of the product itself is the driving force behind the transaction, as community members buy the product or browse the content to satisfy their own needs.

For the tourism industry, with the advent of "tourism+internet" era, the traditional tourism model is far from able to meet the diverse needs of the new generation of travellers, especially young travellers. For many travellers, especially the post-80s, post-90s, and even post-00s, the integration of online (various tourism Apps) and offline (various tourism enterprises) social networks into tourism through the Internet has become a way to travel without being affected by the Internet. The integration of social networks into tourism through the Internet has resulted in a free, spontaneous, fragmented, and customized mode of travel, regardless of time, space or geographical restrictions. In this model, while the tourism product tends to be experiential, the organization of tourism also begins to be humanized, i.e., trips can be customized according to the common preferences of the members, in order to enhance the experience of each visitor. It can be seen that the composition of members in community tourism is homogeneous, i.e., they all have common needs and preferences. This commonality of needs is an important feature that distinguishes different tourism communities from each other in the context of "tourism + Internet". In addition, community tourism has a more interactive nature than traditional tourism models. In the context of "tourism+Internet", community tourism members can interact with each other not only offline, but also online through Internet technology. Interaction is possible between members of the tourism community, between the tourism community and the community, and between the tourism community and the tourism enterprise; they can interact before, during, and after the tour. It is clear that the interaction between members of the tourism community in the context of "tourism+Internet" is more diversified, the level of interaction is deeper, and the scope of interaction is wider. It is because of this increased interactivity that the value of tourism is being amplified through the Internet, both positively and negatively. In the traditional tourism era, tourism value was mainly created by the initiative of tourism enterprises, through their self-promotion and self-presentation; tourists then affirmed their brand and value, and thus, through word-of-mouth among tourists, they achieved the purpose of expanding their tourism value. The efficiency and effectiveness of this approach requires a long period of investment and accumulation. With the use of social platforms such as WeChat and Weibo, tourism sharing has become something that can be done at the tap of a finger, spreading influence much faster than the traditional word-of-mouth model. And in this process of sharing and linking tourism, the positive or negative value of tourism can be infinitely magnified.

Researchers currently have different views on whether the fan economy is a community economy, but some scholars have argued that fans can be studied as a special kind of community. Thus, we explore the impact of the fan economy on tourism in the context of the community economy. The word "fan" has evolved over time to mean "extremely enthusiastic" or "loyal follower". Especially in recent years, as people's living standards have risen, the huge purchasing power of fan groups, who are the target of specific people, food brands, and cultures, has attracted attention because of their frenzied consumption behavior. Under the premise of "user is king", which is generated by the new media, China has entered the era of a fan economy. Depending on who is being followed, this book will attempt to list the possible fans in the tourism industry—fans of the scenic spot, fans of the destination city, fans of the spokesperson of the scenic spot or destination (real and virtual), fans of specific tourism products, etc. Firstly, fans will usually have a very obvious active attribute. They have become a major driving force for the continued growth of a scenic spot or destination through behaviors such as avid purchases and active participation in the various activities of the spot or destination. Secondly, some studies have shown that fans exhibit admiration and hounding behavior towards the object of their following. It is worth noting that everyone can become a fan for a very short period of time; the fervor will fade with time and when people stop following avidly, they change from being fans back to not caring anymore.

The development of the community economy and the fan economy cannot be achieved without the support of new media. What is new media? The term "new media" refers to interactive and integrated media forms and platforms based on digital technology, network technology, and other modern information or communication technologies. At the present stage, new media mainly includes online media, mobile media, and the mobile Internet formed by the fusion of the two, as well as other interactive forms of digital media. At the same time, new media often refers to organizations engaged in news and other information services based primarily on these media. Inspired by this definition, some scholars have parsed out the following threefold orientation towards understanding new media within the tourism industry. Firstly, one is most likely to focus on the volume of information in the new media that is posted by other users through the new media. In the context of tourism, this most significantly includes reviews of restaurants, accommodation, and online travelogues written by travellers, which are often referred to as UGC (user generated content). Secondly, new media is understood as a platform, which is manifested in a rich variety of new media applications. New media as a platform has become a new way of connecting people. For example, there is accommodation sharing, represented by Airbnb, and the Qyer has become a sharing base for travellers. For destinations or tourism enterprises, new media offers a new possibility to shape their image. Thirdly, new media is also a media agency. As an institution, new media is an economical force that possesses technology and capital, and is an important force in

China Story

Avatars in Theme Parks

China Story

RED—A New Model for Destination Promotion and Communication Based on UGC Content in China promoting heritage conservation, cultural, and creative industries, and even virtual tourism. For example, Tencent's participation in "the Digital Great Wall" project has resulted in the world's largest digital restoration of cultural heritage with millimetre-level accuracy and immersive interaction. The advanced technology of new media companies can help more cultural heritage and monuments to be digitally preserved, reproduced, and redeveloped, and offer new possibilities for innovation in tourism.

Chapter Summary

There are five stages in the decision-making process of tourism consumers, namely, problem recognition, information collection, evaluation of alternatives, purchase decision and post-purchase behavior. This chapter describes the first two of these stages in detail. Understanding the decision-making process of tourism consumers, identifying tourism consumers' needs, and collecting information are important components of the research on tourism consumer purchasing behavior. In the process of information gathering, communication becomes an inevitable topic. Also, this chapter discusses the communication part and helps you understand online consumer behavior.

Issues for Review and Discussion

1. Describe the process of problem perception when a tourist is in the process of making a travel decision.

2. Briefly describe the advantages and disadvantages of information and communication technologies and give examples.

3. Briefly describe the impact of ICT on the consumer journey and give examples.

4. Describe the process of customizing an advertisement for a tourist attraction that you want to help promote online.

Chapter 12
Tourism Experience

Learning Objectives

After reading this chapter, you should have a good understanding of the following points:

(1) learn and understand the concepts and types of tourism experience and the factors that affect tourism experience;

(2) understand the connotations of tourism experience quality, and understand the influencing factors and measurement methods of tourism experience quality;

(3) understand the theory of authenticity and embodiment in tourism experience;

(4) learn the model of tourism experience marketing and the basic strategies of tourism experience marketing;

(5) use the theory and related cases in this chapter to analyze the tourism experience.

Technical Words

English Words	中文翻译
educational tourism	研学旅游
expectation-disconfirmation model	期望不一致模型
peak experience	巅峰体验
placeness	地方性
tourism authenticity	旅游本真性
off-site experience	异地体验
two-dimensional world culture	二次元文化
intergenerational theory	代际理论

Knowledge Graph

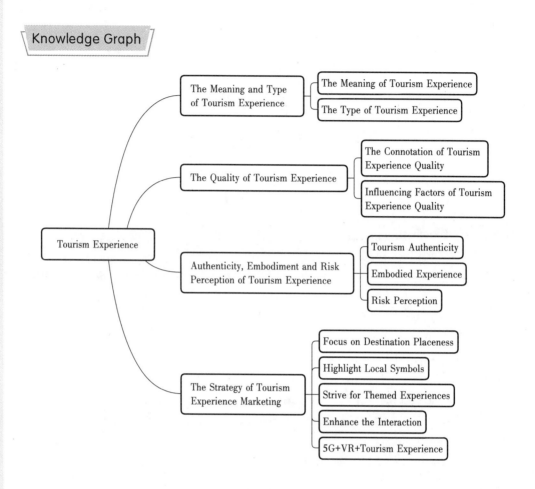

As the goal of tourism, tourism experience is becoming the norm. Tourists prefer to spend their money on experiences rather than things. The focus is now on finding activities that appeal to niche personal interests, rather than checking must-sees and monuments off one's to-do list. For many, tourism is seen as a way of understanding and appreciating alternative lifestyles, of experiencing new things about culture and natural landscapes, and even of self-discovery. Tourists are not just content with busy trips packed with full itineraries at all the tourist attractions. Tourists want to be closer to the locals during the tourism process, to visit slowly, to see what a place looks like in the morning and at night, and to connect with a place on an emotional level.

12.1 The Meaning and Type of Tourism Experience

12.1.1 The Meaning of Tourism Experience

Tourism is a personal activity and experience, a conscious and self-determining act.

In the process of tourism, what tourists hope to obtain is some kind of pleasure—even psychological pleasure due to physical or psychological discomfort. Such a pleasant psychological feeling can be experienced by tourists both physically and mentally.

Therefore, tourism experience refers to the process of tourism consumers going to a specific destination and spending time to visit, learn, feel, be entertained, and form a personal experience of physical and mental integration. It can be said that tourism activities are basically the same as tourism experience, and thus that tourism experience is at the core of tourism.

The study of tourism experience began in Western academia in the mid‑1960s. Boorstin (1964) observed that the authentic tourist experience is impossible in the contemporary world. Rather than being a journey in search of authenticity, travel is increasingly based on artificial images. MacCanell (1973) described modern society as "complicated, competitive, rat racy, dog-eat-dog, racist, exploitative, slick, superficial and corrupt", which emphasized the contemporary tourists' desire to seek for authenticity even more. Cohen (1979) believed that the meaning of one's experience comes from one's personal worldview; different people need different experiences, and different experiences have different meanings for different tourists and societies. Ryan (1997) summarized the tourism experience as a multi‑functional leisure activity, which contains both entertainment and knowledge-seeking elements.

12.1.2 The Type of Tourism Experience

Tourism is a short-lived experience with social, leisure, and consumption attributes in which individuals travel to different places with the main purpose of seeking pleasure. Cohen (1972) recognized that tourism experience must be understood typologically. Focusing on the tourists themselves and various types of tourists can better explain why different tourist destinations attract different tourists. As the pioneer of experience research, Cohen (1979) divided the tourism experience into five types, namely, leisure, distraction, experience, experimentation, and being. These ways represent different types of experience, such as restoring health, escaping hustle and bustle, seeking beauty, finding alternative lifestyles, and accepting exotic cultures. Csikszentmihalyi (1996) investigated the effects that perceived challenges and skills in activities have on the quality of experience. Otto and Ritchie (1996) identified six fundamental dimensions of the experience construct: hedonic, interactive or social, novelty seeking or escape, comfort, safety, and stimulating or challenge seeking. This book analyzes the tourism experience in five categories: entertainment, education, escape, aesthetic, and empathy.

1) Entertainment

Entertainment is the most important type of tourism experience, and it is also the first method used by people to please the body and mind. Tourists can release the tension caused by their work by participating in entertainment activities or watching performances. By laughing or smiling, you can achieve the purpose of pleasing your body and mind and relaxing yourself. For example, the theme park is a comprehensive leisure and entertainment place designed according to a common or a series of themes, combining landscape, environment, amusement facilities, performances and exhibitions, and so on. The different themes of these parks are mainly fairy tales, popular science, literature, and film and television. Therefore, theme parks have become tourism destinations that can meet the diverse leisure and entertainment needs of tourists. The chance of experiencing thrilling, mysterious, and exciting entertainment facilities is the main reason that attracts tourists to entertainment theme parks.

2) Education

Tourism is a way to improve personal awareness and increase knowledge, especially by visiting cultural attractions such as museums, historical sites, ancient buildings, and the like. Educational tourism, which has attracted much attention in recent years, is the combination of research education and tourism experience. It involves an organized, planned, and purposeful off-campus visit, paired with practical activities that students participate in collectively. It allows participants to expand their horizons, enrich their knowledge, deepen their sense of closeness to nature and culture, and increase their experiences of collective lifestyles and social public morals by partaking in a life that is different from normal.

From the perspective of global development, tourism first emerged in the wealthy class as a way of cultivating children of nobles. The typical expression in Europe was the Grand Tour of the 16th and 17th centuries. With the vigorous development of mass tourism, Europe, North America, and other continents have come to regard tourism as a method of education for expanding students' horizons and improving their cross-cultural understanding. In the 1960s, Japan incorporated school tourism into its national education program as a teaching goal, and coordinated various departments to provide tourism opportunities for primary and middle school students. In the 1980s, South Korea drew lessons from Japan's study model and promoted study tourism throughout the country. The above-mentioned countries use educational tourism as a teaching method, allowing students to directly experience society, gain natural and cultural knowledge, and improve cross-cultural understanding.

China has had a positive evaluation of tourism since ancient times, as seen in the proverbial goal of "reading thousands of books, traveling thousands of miles", and some children also use visiting famous mountains and rivers as a way to cultivate their temperaments and their sentiments. Since the reform and opening up, China's modern tourism industry has developed rapidly. With the improvement of people's living standards and the emphasis by their parents on children's education, educational tourism mostly appears in the form of "summer camps" and "winter camps". In November 2016, 11 ministries (including the Ministry of Education) jointly issued *the Opinions on Promoting Research and Study Travel for Primary School and Middle School Students*, making educational tourism part of a compulsory course for primary school and middle school students, meaning that China's educational tourism has entered a new stage of development. The State Council affirmed educational tourism (believing that it is in line with the development goals of the reform of quality education) and supports the development of the educational tourism. The active promotion of educational tourism at the national level is not only a need of quality education reform, but also the result of China's social development reaching a certain level.

3) Escape

Tourism experience is a common means of escape. Many people need an exotic and unfamiliar experience to avoid the pressures of their current lives. Modern people have been overwhelmed by all kinds of invisible and tangible pressures, and tourism experience can allow people to temporarily escape from the economic pressure, social relations, and other problems of daily life. Tourism is a process in which people leave their habitual environments (leaving home), travel to a non-habitual environment (destination), and finally return to their daily environments (returning home).

Modern tourists choose to travel to unconventional environments to benefit from the escape value of tourism experience. The poetic, leisure, aesthetic, and other attractive factors implied in a non-habitual environment can alleviate a certain extent of the anxiety and boredom caused by the habitual environment. For tourists, the non-habitual environment as an environment of psychological behavior is a field of attraction. This can make up for the perceived deficiencies of people's habitual environments. Non-habitual environments remedy people's alienated lives in their habitual environments by providing these compensatory tourism experiences. The cultural space of the tourist destination provides tourists with this poetic freedom. Sightseeing, mountain climbing, rafting, and other tourism activities allow tourists to feel physically free; recreation and performing arts allow them to feel spiritual freedom. The liberating experience of a non-habitual environment forms a strong contrast with the narrow working and living space of the habitual environment and has become a space that people yearn for.

In addition, some people may travel because they are usually too busy with work and do not have much time to spend with their families. They take vacations so they can travel with their families and relax. The people and things or things seen during the tourism experience will affect the cognition and emotions of tourists. By escaping from the ordinary, people may develop new perspectives and insights about things, and their attitudes towards life may change.

4) Aesthetic

An aesthetic experience is a kind of spiritual activity in which an image is formed by the aesthetic object in the human brain. The aesthetic experience runs through the whole activity of tourists. Tourists can first capture the sound, shape, and color of beautiful scenery through feeling and perception; later, through rational thinking and emotional imagination, they can deeply understand the essence of the scenery, indulge their bodies and minds, and obtain a feeling of physical and mental pleasure. The flow of flowers, trees, sunshine, misty clouds, clouds, rivers, waterfalls, streams, and more in the natural scenery, as well as the passing of clouds and mists, are the sources of tourists' aesthetic experience.

In the process of tourism, the aesthetic experience is a process of spiritual activities from shallow to deep, which can be divided into three levels. The first level is perceptual experience. When the subject's perceptual organs are stimulated by the outside world, the subject will spontaneously have a physiological response. For example, standing in front of Huangguoshu Waterfall(黄果树瀑布), listening to the deafening sound of water, and feeling the water droplets splashed by the waterfall water on the stones, will be extremely invigorating and exciting. Perceptual experience is a direct experience with a high degree of objectivity. Aesthetic subjects rely on perception to first feel external things, then notice the characteristics and complexity of aesthetic objects, and finally experience physical and psychological pleasure. Then the aesthetic subject will have an emotional experience of these phenomena, explore their social significance, and enter the second level: identity experience. This is when the subject's perception is integrated into his or her imagination, and the experienced object's center of gravity moves from the object into the subject—at this point, the perceptual experience is elevated to the identity experience. For example, when tourists visit Huangguoshu Waterfall, they can't help but feel that it is a wonder of the world that many notable people are fascinated by and have inscribed in poems. In the second-level identity experience, tourists will endow aesthetic objects with certain symbolic meanings. The third level is reflective experience. Reflective experience is the subject's grasp and reflection of his or her inner world, especially as seen in the attention and appreciation of tourists for their own psychological states. Su Shi(苏轼) passed through Jiujiang during his travels. When Su Shi was visiting Lushan, he sighed that the reason why he could see different Lushan from different angles was because he was in the mountain. This is a prime example of how people reflect on their tourism experience. Su Shi reflected on a philosophy of dealing with the world: because people are in different positions and have different visions, they have different starting points for looking at problems. Everyone's cognition of objective things is inevitably one-sided. To get as complete a picture as possible, it is necessary to go beyond a narrow scope and get rid of subjective conclusions.

5) Empathy

Empathy is when the subject moves his/her own emotions into the tourist situation and tourist landscape. In the tourism experience, tourists place themselves in the position of others and feel the lives of others, so as to realize an emotional transfer and short-term self-escape. The pleasant sensory experience that tourists obtain in the tourism experience is naturally accompanied by the occurrence of the empathy effect, which determines the degree of tourism experience.

In addition, empathy also expresses the sympathy and synesthesia of the cognitive subject with people or things other than the self. This is very important for tourists to

Further Reading

Camping and Other New Tourism and Leisure Models have Become New Favorites experience exotic folk customs and respect local folk customs. Through a tourism experience, people will know how to respect and understand the local traditional culture, and thus how to improve their own humanistic qualities. An empathetic experience is a positive, engaging means of experiencing. In the process of tourists viewing a tourist landscape, if they can project their feelings on the external landscape with their own perception and understanding, the landscape can become the carrier of emotions and blend the people with the scenery, which will greatly improve the quality of tourist experience. The experience of empathy occupies an important position in the process of tourism experience. Empathy depends on the subject's past experience. The richer a person's experience and emotions are, the stronger his or her ability to experience empathy will be.

12.2 The Quality of Tourism Experience

12.2.1 The Connotation of Tourism Experience Quality

The tourism experience is real-time and dynamically changing. Tourism experience quality mainly refers to tourists' retrospective evaluation of the process and pros and cons of their tourism experiences. This evaluation is based on memory and is an overall and psychological evaluation made afterwards. Managers of tourism destinations or tourism enterprises have generally recognized the importance of the quality of the tourism experience. With an in-depth understanding of the antecedent and outcome variables of tourism experience quality, it can be effectively monitored. For tourists and tourism managers, the quality of tourism experience is a cornerstone of their tourism and related activities.

High-quality tourism experience can provide tourists with travel satisfaction that meets or even exceeds expectations, thereby enabling travel companies to obtain long-term economic benefits. On the other hand, poor tourism experience will destroy the good will of tourists, which will in turn destroy the possibility of tourism enterprises making profits. Whether a tourist will return home full of joy depends not only on the hard work of the tourist himself/herself, but also on the careful, warm, and thoughtful service of the tourism enterprise's reception staff. There are a lot of intricate factors at play here that work in completely different ways at different times and in different people.

Some studies equate tourism satisfaction with the quality of tourism experience, and then measure the quality of tourism experience through the expectation-disconfirmation model. There are also studies suggesting that the level of tourism experience quality involves two variables. The first is the level of tourists' expectations for the tourism experience before traveling. The second is the experience and feeling of tourists during the whole process of tourism, as well as their evaluation of various services and facilities after arrival. The quality of tourism experience depends on comparison results of the above two variables. That is, when expectations are high but satisfaction is low, negative tourism experience quality evaluations will result. Higher expectations with higher satisfaction will result in positive quality of experience ratings. When expectations and satisfaction are comparable, people will assess the quality of experience with objective facts. In addition, there are some studies that allow tourists to score their satisfaction with the physical attributes and service quality of tourism products, and thus obtaining their evaluation of the quality of tourism experience from these scores.

The quality of tourism experience should be an overall evaluation of tourism experience from a psychological point of view. To clarify the relationship between tourism experience, tourism experience quality, and tourism satisfaction, we must first explore the dimensions of tourism experience quality, and then develop a scale to measure tourism experience quality. In management practice, tourism enterprises or destination management departments can better manage and improve the experience quality for tourists by understanding the quality of tourism experience. The purpose of this understanding is to increase tourists' loyalty, maintain the competitive advantage of the tourist destination or enterprise, and finally realize economic benefits. At the same time, managers can use the quality of tourism experience to compare the same types of tourism destinations or tourism enterprises. For example, tourist destinations of the same type may be similar in resource endowment, products, and service quality, but vastly different in experience quality.

High-quality tourism experience brings pleasure to tourists and subsequent benefits to tourism enterprises. Csikszentmihalyi proposed "flow" as the best theoretical standard of tourism experience, pointing out that the quality of tourism experience depends on the level of challenge and the relative level of personal skills in a given situation. Flow, also known as "optimal experience", refers to individuals who feel that they have the ability to control their actions and thus producing a strong sense of pleasure. This feeling is often painful, risky, or requires a difficult effort that stretches one's abilities, while also being accompanied by an element of novelty and discovery. Csikszentmihalyi believed that the purpose of tourists' traveling is often the desire to experience this kind of flow. However, in different tourism situations, the quality of tourism experience will show different characteristics. Flow theory is very persuasive for adventurous and exciting tourism activities, but not necessarily for other types of tourism experiences, as some are not that challenging.

In the research of psychology and social psychology, Maslow (1987) proposed "peak experience", which may be an individual's transcendence of daily reality and an overwhelming feeling of awe in an instant, fleeting, but overwhelming sense of well-being, or a feeling of ecstasy and utter joy. Maslow's peak experience is more stirring than inner peace and relaxation. The experience is short in duration and is accompanied by positive emotions. Xie (2005) proposed the sublime state, which refers to the super-utilitarian cognition of the aesthetic subject facing the aesthetic object in the aesthetic pleasure experience. For the individual tourist, the acquisition of the sublime comes from a certain transcendence, especially in the sense of a huge and powerful sensibility. It is the transcendence of the great and profound rational content and the arduous process of the struggle between beauty and ugliness for tourists. By observing beautiful things from a certain distance, tourists are deeply impressed by the magic of nature or the profoundness of culture, and so on, and a sense of the sublime will arise spontaneously. For example, in the face of a majestic and precipitous mountain, the tourists' aesthetic experience process comes from the direct feeling of the steepness of the mountain, and the unconscious analysis and evaluation of it with all the tourists' emotions and reasons. This process does not contain utilitarian cognition and does not contain causal judgments. That is to say, tourists will not think about whether the mountain is suitable for reclamation and transformation into a place of entertainment, because these associations are all utilitarian. It is only when a tourist faces the mountain and feels its magnificence that he or she and the aesthetic object can reach the state of unity between man and nature.

12.2.2 The Influencing Factors of Tourism Experience Quality

1) The Characteristics of Tourism Products

Tourism destination culture and destination activities both have an impact on the quality of tourism experience. If the distinctness and locality of a tourist destination are not prominent enough, this will inevitably affect tourists' desire to explore it. If the means of experiencing tourism products are too monotonous, without cultural connotation and lack of participation, it will also affect the quality of tourists' experience. The quality of tourism experience is reduced by a higher degree of homogeneity in tourism products. Product homogeneity is not a phenomenon unique to the tourism industry. Other industries such as 3C Products, cosmetics, and daily necessities are also plagued by homogenization. But in these industries, product homogeneity is caused by cyclical improvements in product performance. Product innovation is often characterized by more powerful functions, although new products can be fully compatible with old products and still have updated functions. These product homogeneity problems often show strong periodicity. This kind of alternating innovation relies on technological progress, so that the production cost of new products with more functions does not increase too much. The innovation of tourism products is mainly filler innovation, rather than alternative innovation. For tourism products, the effect of technological progress is not obvious, and the improvement of quality basically means a parallel increase in cost.

The low quality of tourism experience caused by the homogenization of tourism products has been frequently noted by tourism academics and industries. People have found that ethnic tourism villages in various places are very similar in terms of tourist landscapes and ritual performances, and even the way of tourist rip-offs are almost the same. In order to create "national characteristics", many regions have constructed multi-ethnic cultures into a single national culture. For example, Dali(大理)was originally a place where Yi(彝族), Bai(白族), Han(汉族), and Naxi(纳西族)cultures met, but the tendency to favor Bai culture in tourism development is very obvious①. Some historical districts also have the same problem in tourism development. These commercial streets sell similar snacks and small goods. As a kind of tourist attraction, if there are high degrees of homogeneity and poor cultural taste, the unique value of historical blocks will be wiped out. Such tourism products cannot represent the city's personality and cannot meet the tourists' experience expectations.

Tourist souvenirs also have the problem of affecting the quality of tourist experience due to the lack of brand personality. Since 2013, the "I know" ("朕知道了") paper tape of the National Palace Museum in Taipei (中国台北故宫博物院) has become popular, and the consumption in scenic spots of cultural and creative products (with the museum's unique souvenir setting a precedent) has gained development opportunities. Various local museums have seized this opportunity and worked hard to increase their own collection resources through authorization, commissioned design, or self-developed cultural and creative products. In the context of the integration of culture and tourism, cultural and creative products in scenic spots are not only an important way to increase the revenue of scenic spots, but also one of the best ways to enhance the overall brand, value, and reputation of scenic spots. Cultural and creative products in scenic spots are different from ordinary commodities. They incorporate values beyond the commodities themselves and are products that condense cultural values and feelings. What tourists buy is no longer the product itself, but the emotions and memories behind it. Nowadays, in tourist attractions, the main force of secondary consumption is in cultural and creative products. However, behind the vigorous development of museum cultural and creative products, there is also the problem of high homogeneity. For example, almost every museum has its own version of Washi Tape. From the perspective of product development, the lack of product creativity, the forced combination of functions and elements, and the lack of obvious regional characteristics are all problems at the level of design methods. These all lead to "homogenization" problems.

2) Travel Time

Tourism is an activity carried out by tourists in a specific time and space. Such activities take place in a non-habitual environment, separate from daily life. Tourism experience is a meaningful process interlaced with time and space. Tourists have a unique interpretation and understanding of travel time, and the quality of tourism experience (either positive or negative) is directly related to the time element of tourism products. For example, the time tourists stay in the tourist destination affects the rhythm of their tourist experience. In the tourism world, time spent in travel, no matter how short or long, is part of a cherished vacation time. Any time in the tourism world is "free" time that tourists have "bought", and time spent in travel affects how tourists feel about their tourism and use of time. For the sake of tourism, people will make full use of every minute of work time before arranging a journey, and consume physical and mental energy under high-

---

① 周大鸣.树立文化多元理念,避免民族旅游中的同质化倾向[J].旅游学刊,2012,27(11):16-17.

intensity work to "buy" a concentrated space of free time. When dealing with the necessities of life and the time they take, people have the same attitude. In order to save time, people would rather pay more for a finished product so as not to have to process the raw materials themselves. In this way, producers of manufactured goods sell their free time to consumers, and consumers also buy "freedom" through the payment of money.

Overall, the time spent in travel has both positive and negative effects on the quality of tourism experience. One is that with the prolongation of travel time, tourists' impression of the destination's freshness has disappeared, they are less interested in everything they see and experience, and the quality of tourism experience continues to decline. The other, opposite effect is that as the understanding of the destination continues to deepen, more emotional connections are generated. Visitors are able to have more authentic experiences through deeper and more prolonged involvement in local daily life.

3) Travel Companion

Travel companions are people with similar outlooks who get along well together in travel activities. In tourism activities, the needs of co-tourists and the emotional exchanges between tourists are becoming more and more prominent. The role of the travel companion is of great significance to the creation of tourists' happiness. People are often influenced by travel companions when they choose travel destinations and conduct subsequent travel activities. Travel companions emphasize that tourists co-occur travel activities at specific locations, obtain help and information, and introduce a sense of belonging and security. Traveling with companions allows people to help each other and reduce loneliness. It can also increase the safety index and make people consider safety more comprehensively. Companion travel reduces the unfamiliarity of the new environment, and the enhancement of tourists' happiness and interpersonal relationships in the tourism experience has been verified as a key benefit.

In addition, companion travel can also improve travel efficiency by improving decision-making power. A few friends and relatives will generate more ideas together, and tourists can avoid losses due to personal limitations. Compared with male tourists, female tourists' decision-making methods and behaviors are more emotional, and they are more willing to travel with others. When traveling with other people, they can share the joy and safety of being together as well as travel risks and costs. Chinese people are influenced by Confucianism, which brings a traditional sense of responsibility, loyalty, and filial piety. This idea is reflected in the concept of family tourism. People often choose to travel as a family, especially because bringing the old and the young is a very Chinese way of traveling. Family travel can improve intimacy between family members, promote harmony within the family, and allow adults to both fulfill their filial duties to their elderly parents and educate their children.

Travel companions are part of informal groups and have informal roles, so any person can easily act as a travel companion according to his or her understanding of his/her own status and social expectations. In a study on peer roles and the quality of tourism experience, peer roles were divided into four categories: ingratiation roles, intimidation roles, exemplification roles, and self-promotion roles. In the study, it was found that "the intimidation role in the peer role category has a very significant positive impact on the quality of tourism experience and tourists' well-being; intimidation roles give clear advice and strong help to their companions in tourism activities, which is a kind of giving and receiving travel companionship"[①]. To enable convenient partner selection and team formation, online travel agencies should create a "partner selection" module under their "social" section and provide more choices for travel companions; through big data algorithms, truly suitable companions can be recommended to tourists.

4) Tourist Factors

Different tourists will have different tourism experiences with the same tourism product or service. Tourists' personality characteristics, interests and preferences, travel expectations, personal abilities, and previous tourism experience are the main factors that affect the quality of tourism experience.

Previous tourism experience can refer to the frequency of visits to the same destination (first-time and repeat visitors) or previous experiences (positive or negative) in other destinations. That is to say, tourism experience can be divided into two types: one is destination-specific tourism experience, and the other is non-destination-specific tourism experience. The tourism experience of a specific destination refers to the accumulation and internalization of the information and knowledge of the destination acquired by tourists after going through the tourism activities of that destination. The cognitive ability of the destination is related to the number of times a tourist has visited the destination. Non-destination-specific tourism experience refers to the tourism activities of tourists based on their participation in all different destinations. The cognitive ability of the destination is formed by accumulating and internalizing the information and knowledge of all the different destinations that one has acquired. Tourists who have visited the same destination or similar destinations will have a different quality of tourism experience.

In addition, the quality of tourism experience is also affected by demographic variables, such as education level, income level, and so on. Research shows that tourists with higher education levels and higher monthly household income are more likely to want to travel to new places or experience new things. Compared with male tourists, female tourists prefer to have "an escape experience" during travel. Post-90s tourists are more willing to enjoy the experience created by volunteer tourism, hiking tours, and cycling tours. Generation Z tourists have a strong awareness of eco-tourism, have unique views on tourism experiences such as animal shows, and play the role of supervisors in the tourism industry.

---

① 许春晓, 郑静. 同伴角色、旅游体验质量与旅游者幸福感的关系[J]. 湘潭大学学报(哲学社会科学版), 2021, 45(5): 69-73.

12.3 Authenticity, Embodiment and Risk Perception of Tourism Experience

12.3.1 Tourism Authenticity

As an important field in tourism sociology, tourism authenticity is an important way to explain the relationship between tourism and modernity. The word authenticity is derived from the Greek word "authentes", which means "authority". The concept of authenticity was first used to describe artworks displayed in museums and was subsequently applied to the realm of philosophy.

Tourism authenticity research was initially aimed at answering how tourism is organized, and then turned to demonstrating the necessary value of tourism. In the early days of tourism experience research, the main emphasis was on the negative meaning of experience. For example, Boorstin (1964), Barthes (1972), and Turner and Ash (1975) believed that tourism experience is essentially a behavior that deviates from the norm and is a disease of recent times. MacCannell (1973) emphasized the influence of tourism on the meaning of life and regarded the tourism experience as a profound modern religious ritual, which is a positive response to the self-consciousness of modern life. MacCannell also pointed out from the perspective of sociology that tourism experience is people's pursuit of authentic experience in order to forget their troubles in life during tourism activities, and that the acquisition of authentic experience depends on tourism products. Cohen (1979) agreed with MacCannell's discourse on authentic experience, but he pointed out that the spiritual core formed by individual tourists in the social backgrounds of their lives is the decisive factor for tourists' experience.

In the era of mass tourism, tourists' consumer demand has also changed. The desire for authenticity in tourism products has never been higher. Authenticity is not only widely used in research fields such as tourism motivation, tourism experience, tourism semiotics, nostalgia and heritage tourism, and the commercialization of tourism culture, but also has important guiding significance for the development of tourism resources, the construction of a tourism destination's image, tourism marketing, and other research fields.

People have further studied tourism motivation by discussing issues such as the authenticity of urban tourism, cultural continuity in heritage tourism, and authenticity in dark tourism (tourism to a place identified with suffering or disaster). In addition, from the question of authenticity in ethnic tourism, there are branches of research on cultural renaissance, local tourism, and the authenticity of festival tourism in ethnic tourism—such as Chinese scholars' research on the authenticity of Naxi ethnic tourism in Lijiang, foreign beer festivals, and so on. On the basis of some studies on authenticity in rural tourism and local culture, people began to pay attention to the reconstruction of authenticity in agricultural tourism and farm tourism. The development of authenticity in rural tourism and ethnic tourism has made more scholars pay attention to the food in tourist destinations, and thus to pay attention to food authenticity in food tourism.

12.3.2 Embodied Experience

Hiking Tourism Experience

The theory of embodiment has deep philosophical and psychological origins. The phenomenology of Husserl, Heidegger, and Merleau-Ponty, as well as the functionalism of James and Dewey, are rich in embodied thought. Embodiment indicates both the externalization of our body to the world around us and the internalization of the world around us to our body, but in any case, it is always related to our body and ultimately realized in the body. Embodiment is an inherent attribute of tourism experience, and the body plays an important role as the mediator and ultimate destination of the experience. Experience requires physical engagement through people's actions (e. g., sensory perception, memory, habits) and interactions with physical entities, socio-cultural factors, in a given situation. The high-quality experience that people seek is ultimately a physical and emotional state of pleasure, enjoyment, and well-being. Embodiment focuses both on the peak experiences that make tourism pleasurable, as well as on the everyday experiences such as sleep and train rides. Everyday life is both monotonous and repetitive, yet full of mystery and possibilities. Tourism experience needs the involvement of daily needs and habits, but it is also inseparable from fresh and unfamiliar stimulation. Embodiment emphasizes that the tourism experience starts with the body, involves the foundation and core position of the body in the tourist experience, and relies on the two-way interactive relationship between people and the environment. Embodied tourism experience is a process in which tourists interact with the tourism world through their own bodies and obtain the meaning of existence.

An important function of the body is that it constructs experience, intervenes in experience, and prescribes experience. As "the underlying layer" of perceptual experience, the body is constantly regulating our world experience so that it can be experienced within the bounds of the body. The body is the means by which the tourism experience is produced. People's perception, cognition, judgment, and reflection in the process of tourism are inseparable from their sensory functions and movements. It is the existence of the perceptual body that enables tourists to break away from rational and objective thinking and play and imagine in the tourism experience. When barefoot tourists on the seaside are waiting for the sunset, they feel the stones and sandy beaches that are heated by the sun and hear the sound of the tide's ebb and flow. In the process of participating in the world with the body and opening all the senses to the world, man also integrates himself into the eternal cycle of nature. Involuntarily, some people experience a poetic feeling of dwelling on the earth. The warmth of the beach and the ebb and flow of the tide are like the breath of the earth, evoking a sense of tranquility and soothing.

The body is the channel for unfolding the meaning of the world, which creates the value of tourism experience. Human beings are essentially producers of meaning, and the body is the place where tourism experiences are produced. In embodied and intentional ways, people project themselves into the context of a living, temporal world that has always been given meaning. In the tourism experience, the tourism world as a whole—and the different landscapes within it—assume the role of the agent. Putting a pebble by the sea in the palm of their hands will help visitors have a happy experience: because its sleek shape has been washed by seawater for a long time, it represents a slow formation process, and through the tactile perception of the body, this small pebble creates a profound experience of natural time. When the tourist can "see a world in a grain of sand", the great and small parts of the tourism world enter the tourist's subjective world through the body.

The body is the carrier of the tourist's embodied existence and "presence", and the revelation of the multi-sensory experience under the embodied experience promotes the soundscape, smell-scape, taste-scape, and touch-scape. These sense-scapes are of great value in discovering and shaping the unique sensory signatures of different destinations. For example, the sense of smell enables people to have direct contact with the environment, because aroma can trigger people's memories of place and help them maintain a sense of place. In a tourist destination that focuses on food, taste constitutes an essential part of the tourist experience. Soundscapes have also become an important part of the tourist landscape system. Some tourist destinations in China have fully explored soundscapes in the tourism practice of large‐scale landscape performances, such as *Impression·Liu Sanjie*, *Impression·Lijiang*, *Impression·West Lake*, and so on.

There are also some tourists who will actively seek and enjoy physical discomfort in travel. Through the uncomfortable experience of fatigue, hardship, danger, torment, and even torture, tourists experience a strong sense of physical reality. Backpacking tourism, for example, is increasingly becoming a fashionable way of life—it gives tourists an experience of thrilling adventure and conquest of nature. In the post-industrial tourism era and societies with increasing commodification intensity, backpacking tourism can signal differences in tourists' personal wealth, prestige, or ability.

12.3.3 Risk Perception

Risk perception refers to the tourists' assessment of self-influenced risk. The risk in the destination experience includes the uncertainty of the experience, possible unpleasant results, and possible losses caused by the destination experience. Tourists' perception of risk is reflected in their concerns about personal health and property safety, concerns about social security, and concerns about not meeting expectations. The level of risk perception directly affects people's choice of tourist destinations. The higher their risk perception of the destinations, the greater the possibility that consumers will decide to avoid the destinations. The higher the anxiety and risk levels of tourists, the more likely they will feel the environment is unsafe and will leave. When consumers' perceived risk and anxiety levels decrease, their travel intentions are strengthened. On the one hand, risk involves objective things such as the impact of uncontrollable forces on people; on the other hand, it is partly a social construction. Risk perception can be changed, exaggerated, transformed, or weakened. Individuals must take risks if they wish to have self-choice and self-determination.

Risk perception is an important field of psychological research. Risk perception originates from the uncertainty brought by an individual to a potentially unfavorable situation and the harmfulness of the consequences if an unfavorable situation occurs—that is, the magnitude of the potential loss. A study by Stone and Grønhaug (1993) based on consumers and markets proposed that risk perception can be divided into financial risk, functional risk, physical risk, social risk, psychological risk, and time risk. This study is also the most commonly used theoretical basis in consumer behavior research.

Tourist risk perception refers to the uncertainty and possible negative consequences that tourists perceive in the destination experience. In the process of tourism experience, the destination functions as a tourism product. When tourists make consumption decisions before reaching the actual destination, they cannot observe the goods in person, and their feelings of uncertainty are strong. The destination experience process is complex, and the substitutability of experience products is weak. Therefore, tourists have high risk sensitivity, and tourists' risk perception will have a direct impact on the experience value of the destination. Li Jing and Wu Bihu (2015) pointed out that the research on tourists' risk perception mostly focuses on measurement of risk perception level, identification of perceived risk types, and identification of the factors influencing risk perception. These risk-perception factors include equipment, financial, physical, psychological, satisfaction, social, and time requirements, as well as potential political unrest. Most of these studies use risk perception as the only variable in the relationship between risk perception and behavior, and treat tourists' risk perceptions as constant. However, destination experience is not a risk-dependent decision, and risk perception is an influencing factor operating with a large degree of subjective uncertainty. The risk perception of tourists is mainly risk avoidance rather than risk aversion.

12.4 The Strategy of Tourism Experience Marketing

Tourism experience marketing refers to tourism enterprises, destinations, and scenic spots that design marketing concepts from the aspects of tourists' senses, emotions, thoughts, actions, and associations, and use products or services as the starting point to stimulate and meet the experience needs of tourism consumers. It is a marketing model that improves the participation of tourism consumers and enables tourism consumers to obtain memorable tourism experiences.

The production and consumption of tourism products occur simultaneously, which means that tourists must participate in the production process of tourism products. This is in line with the characteristics of the interaction between tourism experience marketing and tourism consumers. The essence of tourism is a kind of off-site experience, which is a complete experience formed by the combination of one or more experiences of tourists in the process of tourism. These experiences include entertainment experiences, aesthetic experiences, educational experiences, escape experiences, empathic experiences, and so on. The development of tourism activities is the process of interaction between tourism resources, tourism staff (who also act as marketing staff), and tourists. Tourism enterprises should make good use of these interactions, so that tourists can fully participate in and enjoy the fun of each tourism experience.

In tourism experience marketing, the following methods can be used to create and enhance tourism experience value and enhance tourists' perception of value.

12.4.1 Focus on Destination Placeness

Place is the space carrier of tourism activities and the core content of the image construction of tourism destination. The long-term cultural accumulation of a place and its recognition by the public make a place "local". Place is a relatively abstract concept: a geographic space composed of several spatial units, its scale can be micro or macro. As the basic carrier of the relationship between people and land, place is derived from space and has a dialectical relationship with space. When we are familiar with a space, or can give personal meaning to the space, mere space becomes a place. Space is the objective position of people's existence, whereas place is the carrier of culture and emotion.

Placeness is the characteristics of a place that distinguish it from other places, also known as "geographical features". These characteristics may be related to spatial characteristics, geographical characteristics, cultural characteristics, life events, and other factors. Placeness is a symbol of cultural heritage as condensed by a place. Placeness can also come from factors such as topography and geology, climatic conditions, organisms, water bodies, location, social development, historical and cultural resources, social and cultural conditions, and religious culture. In terms of physical space, a space can also reflect placeness—indeed, the uniqueness of a space is the most intuitive form of placeness.

Tourist attraction and destination image production are closely related to placeness. The wave of development for tourism and its modernization has had a strong impact on the placeness of tourist destinations. Some traditional local landscapes have been replaced by standardized man-made landscapes. With the continuous development of people's horizons, places have increasingly become a kind of scarce spiritual home, and then become a landscape that visitors can seek. In this case, tourism has become an important way and means for people to perceive and recognize places. Facing the increasingly fierce market competition, creating a local image with distinct personality has become the key to the development of a destination.

For example, when it comes to the unique spatial scene of "a countryside", people may immediately think of ancient trees, old wells, a few old people sitting under the tree to enjoy the shade, and maybe a few playful children around. Such a space scene has what we call placeness: a place and vehicle for villagers to entertain and live. In the question of how to let tourists get a real tourism experience and also experience the different aspects of a destination, placeness is an important angle. Some newly emerging niche destinations in China have become favorites among young tourists. Garze's (甘孜) popularity was boosted by Tamdrin, a 20-year-old from the Tibetan ethnic group in Sichuan, whose name in Mandarin is Ding Zhen(丁真). He initially went viral on the Internet for his good looks and was later appointed to promote tourism in Sichuan by posting short videos. Garze has rich and unique Tibetan cultural elements and authentic natural beauty. Improved transportation conditions have attracted more independent travelers there because of spreading of the short video. Since then, many more travelers from Sichuan and nearby regions have taken trips there[①].

12.4.2 Highlight Local Symbols

If there is no theme and no concept in tourism experience marketing, the destination will have no unique image or appeal. Local cultural symbols often carry the historical tradition, cultural heritage, and social features of a place. However, the cultural incentive to visit can easily fade away in the process of social and economic development, be forgotten by people, and eventually lead to a gap where there used to be local spirit and culture. Facing the overwhelming impact of global culture today, how to both keep pace with the times and create local cultural symbols in the new era is an important question in cultural construction in various places. It is also related to the development of tourism and other related industries.

Each city has its unique cultural characteristics, and each city has its unique symbols. Take the city of Changsha in Hunan as an example: Changsha has a long history and rich culture. Its Yuelu Academy is one of the four most famous academies in Chinese history, located at the foot of Yuelu Mountain on the west bank of Xiangjiang River. Yuelu Academy has existed for thousands of years and has a long tradition of learning. Yuelu Academy is not only a training and research base for cultural, historical, and philosophical talents, but also a cultural symbol of the entire Changsha City. Also on the Xiangjiang River, Orange Isle is the largest sandbar among the many alluvial sandbars in the lower reaches of the river. In the 14th year of the Republic of China (1925), Mao Zedong returned to Hunan from Guangzhou. During the cold autumn season, he revisited Orange

① Source: https://www.chinadaily.com.cn/a/202012/30/WS5febd5b2a31024ad0ba9f7a0.html.

Isle in Changsha and wrote *Qinyuanchun · Changsha*(《沁园春·长沙》). Consequently, Orange Isle became famous. Regarding distinct local foods, a traditional and famous food of the city of Changsha is "Changsha stinky tofu". It is crispy on the outside and tender on the inside, with a fresh and spicy flavor. These are the local cultural symbols of Changsha.

No matter where a city or town is, due to the movements of history, the location may form certain characteristics of its cultural type. Excavating this feature, refining its theme, and giving it a richer and more dazzling local cultural symbol is a technical route that must be considered in the development of destination tourism.

12.4.3 Strive for Themed Experiences

In a tourism environment that is completely different from their daily lives, tourists are eager to temporarily play a role completely different from their real identity. Tourists desire the ability to immerse themselves in the environment, find new experiences, and attain spiritual relief. Themed experiences can help improve the recognizability of destination brands, gain brand premiums, and increase tourist spending levels. In addition, they can also create differentiated competitive advantages and build an immersive experience for travel consumers.

Tourist destinations should create memorable experiences that allow visitors to "live elsewhere" by providing fun, comfortable, and aspirational themed environments. Theme selection is the top priority in the upgrading of scenic spots. In recent years, experience venues such as themed bars, themed restaurants, and themed movie halls have appeared. Choosing a suitable and attractive theme can give full play to the product extension benefits brought by its IP.

With the success of the 2022 Beijing Winter Olympics, the Olympic venue Big Air Shougang(首钢滑雪大跳台) has become a theme experience attraction for tourists. The stylish appearance of Big Air Shougang and the wonderful events held here are vivid embodiment of the spirit of the Beijing Winter Olympics. The Olympic Games is a grand international event, with tolerance and unity being its perennial themes. The birth of Big Air Shougang is the cultural expression of this theme. The world's understanding and pursuit of beauty are interlinked. The interchange of wisdom and integration of culture have created this elegant and agile achievement of human civilization.

Big Air Shougang is constructed on the site of a former steel mill, the century-old Shougang Industrial Park, whose two connections with the Olympic Games both derived from the concept of "a green" Olympic Games. In order to support its bid to host the 2008 Summer Olympic Games, the Shougang Group (whose main business is steelmaking) gave back Beijing clear water and blue skies through its overall relocation. On the eve of the 2022 Winter Olympic Games, the disused raw-materials silo became the office area for the Winter Olympics Organizing Committee, the industrial plant became the training base for short track speed skating, figure skating, curling, and ice hockey, and the stadium became the world's first gig air arena permanently reserved for use.

Big Air attaches great importance to the experience of athletes and spectators. Due to the high difficulty and risk of the sport, a safe and stable playing field is very important for athletes. With a safe, spacious, and comfortable structure as well as smooth and delicate snow, Big Air Shougang is conducive for athletes to show difficult skills and give full play at their best level. The design of the spectator platform allows the audience to experience the fun of the competition from nearby, making Big Air competitions (formerly a niche event that only around 400 athletes participated in) an ice and snow sport enjoyed by the masses.

After the Winter Olympics, Big Air Shougang(see figure 12.1) has been permanently reserved and open to the public. It is a public space integrating event training, commercial trade, culture and art, leisure, and entertainment. It aims to contribute to the popularization of ice and snow sports around the world and provide a good demonstration for the transformation and development of cities. The appearance of the Big Air Shougang is a demonstration of the green development, mutual learning of civilizations, and people-oriented concepts of the Beijing Winter Olympics, bearing the epitome of the times and spirit of China's development. Coming here, people can see the history, enjoy the present, and look forward to a better future.

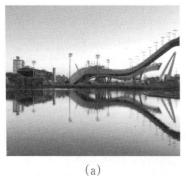 

(a) (b)

Figure 12.1　2022 Beijing Winter Olympics Venue—Big Air Shougang[①]

12.4.4 Enhance the Interaction

Through interaction, the distance between tourists and the destination can be shortened, and the emotional connection of tourists to the destination can be deepened. The researchers found that in ethnic village tourism (a type of rural tourism), the most important part of the tourism experience process is the interaction ritual between the host and the guest[②]. As a tourism cultural product based on an emotional experience, it is a host-guest interactive ritual driven by the ethnic cultural tourism market. First of all, from the perspective of tourism products, the ritual is a tourist attraction constructed to meet

---

①Source: http://www.ecns.cn/news/sports/2022-02-20/detail-ihavwrts3792991.shtml.

②李瑞,郑超,银松,等.民族村寨旅游者主客互动仪式情感体验过程及其唤醒机制研究:以"高山流水"敬酒仪式为例[J].人文地理,2022,37(2): 94-102.

the needs of the tourism market, creating conditions for triggering tourists' emotional response potential, and bringing positive emotions to tourists because of its rich cultural connotations and unique interaction methods. Secondly, as a ritual, it is an important representation of the traditional culture of ethnic minorities, and it is also the most local cultural tourism construction field. Through the ritual interaction between the host and the guest at the physical and emotional levels, and through the ritual interaction, the identification of local culture is generated, which further strengthens the protection and inheritance of the national culture and the integration of tourism. In addition, the host-guest interaction ritual can awaken tourists' emotional consumption loyalty to the ritual experience in the daily life situation of the tourist destination. In the process of product management and market promotion, destination operators should pay attention to the construction of national cultural symbols, the innovation of ceremonial substitution methods, and the creation of interactive atmosphere of places.

Adolf, a blogger from Munich, Germany, has been developing a strong interest in Chinese history and culture since he was a child. During his travels in China, Adolf was deeply impressed by the cultures of various Chinese ethnic groups. In an interview, he mentioned: "I once attended a once-every-13-years Miao festival in Guzan—this was for the Miao new year, with over 5,000 attendees in a tiny mountain village. I have never heard of a festival which isn't celebrated yearly, so I was very surprised and excited to hear about it. It is celebrated for a total of 13 days; on the last day, over 4,000 Miao people danced around the drum all dressed in traditional festive clothing (me included)." Such traditional cultures and customs are the most special experiences for tourists.

At the same time, operators of tourist destinations and scenic spots should focus on word-of-mouth communication. Through user-generated content (UGC), marketing messages become content that is continuously produced and disseminated. For example, as a UGC tourism product, Mafengwo focuses on user-generated content and pays attention to the needs of consumers. Mafengwo turns users into producers and publishers of information. It breaks the traditional marketing model by being user-centric, allowing users to become content producers and obtain accurate data. Mafengwo provides users with more comprehensive and convenient resource services. Mafengwo takes content as its core service to tourists and driver of transaction growth. Through the analysis of a large amount of information data through the content produced by tourists, it can better launch products and services for commercial transformation. Mafengwo also implants products and services on user content in the community to make the content more practical. It recommends appropriate content according to the user's preferences, improves user retention and utilization of the platform, and promotes a virtuous circle. More and more tourist destinations realize the importance of UGC interactive marketing and gradually have begun to explore co-creation. In the current environment of information overload, simple exposure is no longer enough to capture the attention of tourists. Compared with official channels, tourists are more willing to get information from people who have similar experiences and backgrounds and have trusted relationships with them. When tourists have the willingness to express themselves, UGC interactive marketing can undoubtedly create more surprises for tourist destinations.

The senses are the fundamental means for humans to explore and understand the world. When different sensory cells are stimulated by the external environment, the human body will form different "sensations". This leads to a conscious sensory experience. The senses play a crucial triggering role in the tourism experience. From the sensory point of view, tourists' experience activities at the destination are firstly expressed as the experience process of the five senses of sight, hearing, smell, taste, and touch. In recent years, restaurants have not only been content to challenge food critics with the taste and presentation of their dishes: many restaurants have also developed unique sensory experiences in order to satisfy customers' visual and auditory senses. Consumers gain more perception by experiencing different creative restaurants. For example, entering the Yu Restaurant in Beijing is like entering the world of sakura. Sakura trees sway in front of Japanese-style houses on either side of the tables and line the shores of the lakes and the sides of mountains depicted at the front of the room. The tables are covered in fluttering sakura petals. The restaurant plays with the light and imagery in such a way that the floor seemingly rises to change the view, which some may find a little dizzying if they are standing up. For the whole meal, diners are immersed in an environment created by light and shadow at the Yu Restaurant. The restaurant is decorated with different kinds of imagery and light, some of which can be controlled by the diners by using motion or sound. The two-story restaurant has four sections—the upper floor is for Japanese barbecue, and the lower floor comprises a room for teppanyaki, a lounge bar, and a dining room for creative kaiseki. Each section has its own special effects. The background of the teppanyaki room is a collection of interactive cityscapes and scenic spots from around the world. For instance, if the screen shows the image of a beach, when diners talk or clap, they can get larger images of waves by making louder sounds. The images on the background of the bar section are more abstract and change following the hand movements of guests. The food at the restaurant features fresh ingredients from around the world and is prepared using traditional Japanese cooking methods.

In recent years, governments all over China have made full use of their natural, historical, and cultural resources to vigorously develop the cultural tourism industry. Tourist destinations and scenic spots focus on immersive multi-sensory experiences. In line with this, various types of immersive cultural tourism projects have been developed, such as immersive museums, immersive performances, immersive exhibitions, immersive agricultural parks, and immersive scenic spots. These tourist attractions fully reflect the charm of "culture + technology". In addition, there are immersive theme parks, immersive experience halls or secret rooms, immersive light shows, and so on. These experience venues perfectly amplify the entertainment effect of "tourism + technology". Different from the passive visiting exhibitions in the past, more and more museums now use high-tech methods to make exhibitions more open, diverse, experiential, and interactive. For example, the Palace Museum uses large-scale and highly immersive projection screens, virtual reality helmets, somatosensory capture devices, touch screens, and so on, so that the audiences can walk into the Hall of Mental Cultivation in a virtual world. Through a variety of advanced technologies such as AI, VR, and voice and image recognition, it is possible to freely communicate with virtual court ministers and to appreciate precious cultural relics in an all-round way. In addition to setting up a variety of interesting real-life clearance modes, the exhibition is also integrated with mobile smart devices in people's hands. A mobile phone is not only a phone and camera, but also a means of participating in a variety of interactive links, making online and offline connectivity more interesting. The Palace Museum uses modern digital technology to activate traditional cultural genes, allowing more young audiences to approach tradition. Identifying the path of mind-body connection between sensory stimulation and destination attachment provides a way for destination marketing organizations to use multi-sensory tourism experiences to develop tourists' attachment to the destination. The marketing organization of the destination should first adjust the multi-sensory marketing strategy according to the uniqueness of the destination tourism resources, fully consider the dynamic and multi-stage nature of the tourism experience, and create a positive, unique, and unforgettable multi-sensory tourism experience for tourists. The ultimate goal is to achieve a long-term and stable emotional connection between tourists and the destination.

12.4.5 5G+VR+Tourism Experience

In recent years, relying on the "Internet+" platform and using new technologies such as animation, AR, and VR, the experience mode of many tourist attractions has changed from static and single to dynamic and immersive. For example, the AVR Red Tourism Experience Hall in Jinggangshan(井冈山), Jiangxi(江西)has provided a new "experience method" for "Red stories". Surrounding the AR scene, experiential teaching reproduces real battle scenes from "the Huangyangjie Defense War"(黄洋界保卫战). In Gaotai County, Zhangye, Gansu(甘肃张掖高台县), the Memorial Hall of the West Road Army of the Chinese Workers' and Peasants' Red Army(中国工农红军西路军纪念馆) has integrated VR and code scanning to help tourists visit exhibits and other experiences in the interactive visiting area, and developed systems such as digital virtual experience and intelligent voice broadcasting to bring tourists a premium visiting experience. The most familiar "routine" for tourists used to be visiting the memorial hall, observing the exhibits and pictures, and then spending some time listening to the staff's explanation. Insufficient exploration of Red resources, monotonous exhibition methods, and a poor overall experience have caused many Red tourist attractions to face development difficulties. The application of new technologies provides new ideas for the presentation of exhibits. With the in-depth advancement of the Red tourism industry, product innovation of Red tourism continues to emerge. In recent years, some popular digital technologies have been introduced into Red tourism memorial venues, which bring the venues closer to the cultural and tourism consumption preferences of young people.

Cloud Exhibition has attracted countless fans of the revolutionary memorial hall and history museum. The increasingly popular "online+offline" interaction method is more in line with the consumption and information acquisition habits of young people. These emerging consumer demands are continuing to promote product innovation in museum tourism experiences and the sustainable development of the museum tourism industry. Tourist attractions need to make full use of platform resources such as online tourism service platforms and new media marketing platforms, so that the history and culture of tourist destinations can be more flexibly displayed.

Chapter Summary

Tourism experience refers to the process of tourism consumers going to a specific destination and spending time to visit, learn, feel, be entertained, and form a personal experience of physical and mental integration in the destination. Tourism experience can be roughly divided into five types: entertainment, education, escape, aesthetic, and empathy. The quality of tourism experience mainly refers to tourists' evaluation of the pros and cons of the tourism experience. The tourism experience is real-time and dynamically changing. The influencing factors of the quality of tourism experience include tourism product characteristics, travel time, travel companions, tourists' individual factors, and more.

Issues for Review and Discussion

1. Recall your most memorable tourism experience, describe the tourism experience, and analyze why this tourism experience is so memorable to you.

2. Conduct in-depth interviews with five students about their tourism experience to analyze the influencing factors of tourism experience quality.

3. Analyze the following types of risk perceptions and discuss how to reduce tourism risk perceptions.

(1) A tourist books a homestay and worries that the homestay environment will not meet expectations.

(2) A tourist spent 1,000 yuan to book a ticket, worrying that the price will drop after purchasing it.

(3) A tourist wants to go to Changbai Mountain(长白山) to see Tianchi Lake(天池), but is not sure if he or she will be able to see the lake due to unfavorable weather conditions at the mountain.

(4) A tourist really wants to travel somewhere, but is worried that he or she will not understand the local language and eating habits.

Chapter 13
Post-purchase Behavior of Tourism Consumer

Learning Objectives

After reading this chapter, you should have a good understanding of:

(1) the definition of tourism consumer satisfaction and the factors influencing it;

(2) the theory of tourism consumer satisfaction;

(3) the definition of tourism consumer loyalty and the factors influencing it;

(4) the definition and dimensions of tourism consumer behavioural intentions;

(5) the relationship between tourism consumer satisfaction, loyalty and behavioural intentions.

Technical Words

English Words	中文翻译
tourism consumer satisfaction	旅游消费者满意度
tourism consumer loyalty	旅游消费者忠诚度
tourism consumer complaints	旅游消费者投诉
user generated content	用户原创内容

Knowledge Graph

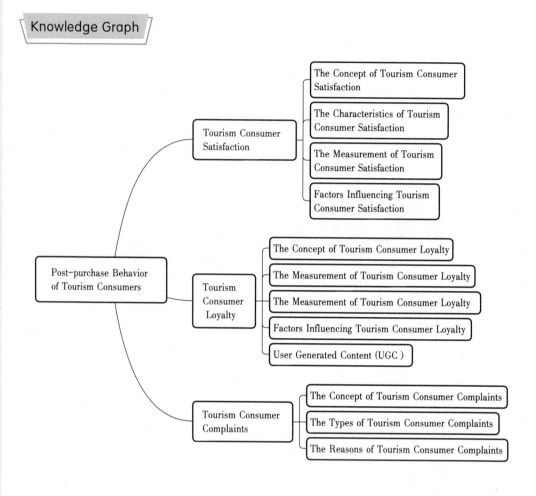

13.1 Tourism Consumer Satisfaction

13.1.1 The Concept of Tourism Consumer Satisfaction

The term "satisfaction" was first called "customer satisfaction". Since the 1980s, the concept of tourism consumption has changed dramatically, with the constant pursuit of diversification of tourism products and services and more intense competition in the market. In order to adapt to this change, the new concept of consumer centeredness, with an emphasis on tourism consumer satisfaction, has gradually been formed in the tourism industry and developed in various countries and regions. The relevant concepts of tourism consumer satisfaction are all based on customer satisfaction theory, and domestic and foreign scholars have defined and discussed tourism consumer satisfaction on the basis of different perspectives and levels.

The concept of tourism consumer satisfaction was first proposed by Pizam et al., who pointed out that tourism consumer satisfaction is the comparison of a tourism consumer's pre‐trip expectations and his/her overall post‐trip evaluation of the experience: if the expectations and the experience are equivalent or the experience is better than the expectations, then the tourism consumer will be satisfied with the trip; if the experience is less than expectations, then the tourism consumer will not be satisfied[①].

Baker and Crompton refined the definition of tourism consumer satisfaction on the basis of previous studies and expanded the scope of tourism consumer satisfaction from the destination landscape and environment to include infrastructure and the construction of tourism and leisure facilities, the quality of services at the destination, and many other aspects of tourism consumer behavior in order to make a comprehensive assessment[②]. They defined tourism consumer satisfaction as a psychological state formed by tourism consumers after receiving tourism products and services at a tourism destination in the course of their interaction with the destination. Specifically, the satisfaction of tourism consumers comes from the extent to which the tourist attractions, infrastructure, the environment of tourist places, and the services provided by a tourism destination meet their needs. In China, domestic research on tourist satisfaction is relatively recent.

To sum up, tourism consumer satisfaction is the evaluation of the elements of a tourism destination or tourism enterprise by tourism consumers according to whether their expectations or needs are met. It is the result of tourism consumers' comparison of their tourism expectations with their tourism perceptions.

13.1.2 The Characteristics of Tourism Consumer Satisfaction

1) Subjective

Tourism consumer satisfaction originates from tourism consumers' perception and evaluation of tourism products and services, which will be influenced by factors such as their income level, purchasing experience, education level and demand level. The satisfaction of different tourism consumers with the same product or service can vary greatly, and the satisfaction of the same tourism consumer with the same product or service in different contexts can be inconsistent, which reflects the subjectivity of tourism consumer satisfaction.

2) Dynamic

The dynamic nature of tourism consumer satisfaction is mainly derived from its subjective nature. The subjective consciousness of tourism consumers changes with the objective facts, so the evaluation of tourism products and services is constantly updated. In particular, when objective factors such as the socioeconomic environment,

---

① Pizam A, Neumann Y, Reichel A. Dimentions of Tourist Satisfaction with a Destination Area[J]. Annals of Tourism Research, 1978, 5(3): 314-322.

② Baker D A, Crompton J L. Quality, Satisfaction and Behavioral Intentions[J]. Annals of Tourism Research, 2000, 27(3): 785-804.

technological environment and natural environment change, the structure and level of tourism consumer demand also change, which eventually leads to changes in tourism consumers' satisfaction with some tourism products and services.

3) Comprehensiveness

Tourism consumer satisfaction is determined by tourism consumers' comprehensive and multifaceted evaluation of tourism products and services based on their perceptions. For tourism consumers, satisfaction includes all the services, products, and subjective perceptions involved in the process of tourism consumption, such as the brand, reputation, price, quality, after-sales, and logistics of tourism products and the tourism services contacted during the purchase process. Even if one particular aspect of this process does well, if another aspect is questioned, it will reduce tourism consumer satisfaction to varying degrees.

4) Hiddenness

The information asymmetry between tourism consumers and tourism enterprises leads to the "great hiddenness" of tourism consumer satisfaction, and it is difficult for tourism destinations or tourism enterprises to understand tourism consumers' evaluation of their tourism products and services if they do not conduct special tourism consumer satisfaction surveys or set up tourism consumer complaints channels. Even a specialized tourism consumer satisfaction survey may not be comprehensive enough; the respondents may not be professional enough to focus on the results of the survey, or they may omit important dissatisfaction factors.

13.1.3 The Measurement of Tourism Consumer Satisfaction

The measurement of tourism consumer satisfaction has been a hot issue in the field of tourism research, mainly involving measurement indicators and measurement methods. Due to the diversity of tourism destinations and the complexity of tourism research objectives, the measurement of tourism consumer satisfaction is multidimensional, dynamic and difficult. Scholars have differentiated the measurement of different types of tourism destinations and different types of tourism consumer satisfaction. In general, the measurement of tourism consumer satisfaction is still in the exploration stage, and a more consistent measurement index system has not yet been formed for measuring tourist satisfaction. At present, the main methods used for measuring tourism consumer satisfaction are the SERVQUAL model, the SERVPERF model, importance-performance analysis (IPA), the fuzzy comprehensive evaluation method, the grey theory decision method, and the expert scoring method.

1) The SERVQUAL Model

The SERVQUAL model is a service quality evaluation system based on total quality management (TQM) theory that was proposed by the American marketing scientists Parasuraman et al. in the late 1980s. Its theoretical core is the service quality gap model, that is, service quality depends on the degree of difference between the service level perceived by the user and the service level expected by the user. Therefore, it is also known as the expectation-perception model.

In the SERVQUAL model, as shown in figure 13.1, service quality is divided into five dimensions: reliability refers to the company's ability to fulfil its promises; responsiveness refers to the company's willingness to help customers and quickly improve service levels; assurance refers to the professional skills, trustworthiness, and security of the company; empathy refers to putting oneself in the customer's shoes to provide a personalized service; and tangibility, which includes the products, the appearance of service personnel and the equipment that customers directly perceive. SERVQUAL score= actual feeling score – expectation score. In the SERVQUAL questionnaire, each dimension is subdivided into a number of items (22 in total). The questionnaire is designed to measure customers' expectations and actual perceptions of service quality. The service quality score is derived from the questionnaire, customers' scoring, and a comprehensive calculation.

Figure 13.1　The SERVQUAL model

2) The SERVPERF Model

In 1992, Cronin and Taylor proposed the SERVPERF evaluation method. In terms of dimensions and measurement indicators, the SERVPERF model does not differ from the SERVQUAL model. The differences between the two models are mainly reflected in the measurement content: the SERVPERF model only measures the customers' perceptions and does not consider customers' expectations.

3) Importance-performance Analysis (IPA)

IPA compares the customers' perceptions of the importance of the service provided by a company or the customers' expectations of a project with the customer's actual perceived satisfaction, as shown in figure 13.2.

IPA analysis[1] was first proposed and used in 1977 by Martilla and James for the appraisal of automobile dealers in order to allow insights into which aspects of the marketing mix a company should give more attention to and identify areas that might consume too many resources. Presenting results on a critical performance grid facilitates

---

[1] Martilla J A, James J C. Importance-performance Analysis[J]. Journal of Marketing, 1977, 41(1): 77-79.

management's interpretation of the data and increases the data's usefulness in making strategic marketing decisions.

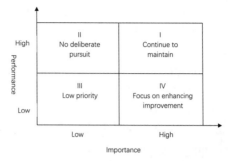

Figure 13.2　Importance-performance analysis (IPA) positioning diagram

IPA analysis has been applied in various industries to continuously improve service quality. It has been widely used in many service industries, such as transportation, hotel and accommodation, catering, health, public services, education and training, venue services and network services.

13.1.4 Factors Influencing Tourism Consumer Satisfaction

1) Tourism Consumer Level

(1) Expected level.

Tourism consumers have certain expectations of tourism products and services. They expect them to be ideal products and services that can meet their needs, and if they have more needs, their expectation level will be higher. The higher their expectations, the more likely it is that their satisfaction will be lower. Some tourism consumers' expectations in tourism activities mainly focus on the richness and cost effectiveness of tourism products, but others may also focus on tourism safety, tourism services and tourism brands; the latter have higher expectations of tourism products, and it is more difficult for tourism enterprises to meet their tourism needs.

(2) Perceived value.

Perceived value refers to tourism consumers' overall assessment of whether a tourism product or service is worth the cost of its use and experience when measured against its actual cost. Tourism consumers' perception of value is not only related to the quality of tourism products and services, but also inextricably linked to their pricing. Therefore, tourism enterprises should carry out tourism market segmentation and target market selection when producing tourism products and providing tourism services to meet the differentiated needs of different target tourism consumers; they should also increase the quality level of tourism products and services appropriately to facilitate their acceptance by a wider range of tourism consumers.

Nowadays, there are more ways and channels for tourism consumers to give tourism reviews. There are special review platforms (e.g., public review platforms and the special "travel" section in public review Apps) that make it easy for tourism consumers to write reviews giving their subjective views on tourism destinations, tourism products or tourism enterprises. For example, the "Travel" section of the VWAP App allows tourism consumers to write reviews of tourism destinations, tourism products and tourism enterprises; the higher the score, the better the rating, and vice versa.

(3)Perceived quality.

Tourisml consumers form certain perceptions when they understand and search for relevant information before purchasing tourism products and services, and on the basis of such perceptions, they derive corresponding evaluations and then make purchasing decisions. Their perceptions are formed before a purchase, and thus improving the quality of tourism consumers' perception of tourism products is conducive to enhancing the attractiveness of the products and tourism consumers' inclination to choose them. Tourism consumers' perception of the quality of tourism products and services has a direct impact on the branding of tourism enterprises and increases in their market share. The improvement of perceived quality is fundamentally dependent on the quality of tourism products and services, followed by the promotion and publicizing of the products and services.

(4)Individual Characteristics.

Demographic characteristics, such as the age, gender, education level, family structure, income and occupation of tourism consumers, have an impact on tourism satisfaction. For example, professional chefs tend to have higher demands regarding food and beverage quality when engaged in gourmet tourism; parental satisfaction is mainly derived from their children's sense of experience when they are engaged in parent-child tourism activities; and business people tend to pay more attention to tourism services and tourism quality than student groups when traveling.

2) Tourism Enterprise Level

(1) Product quality.

Product quality is the sum of the characteristics and features of a product designed to meet specified needs and potential needs. Tourism product quality refers to the particular characteristics of a tourism product designed to meet the tourism needs of tourism consumers, and it is also a concrete expression of the use value of the product. Tourism product quality not only includes the quality of tangible tourism products (e.g., whether a meal is delicious; whether the ingredients of a meal are green and organic; whether a flight seat is comfortable and safe; whether a scenic spot is charming and spectacular), but also the quality of tourism services provided by tourism enterprises (e.g., whether a guide's explanation is detailed and accurate; whether a travel agency's sales staff are professional, considerate).

(2) Brand image.

Brand image is the personality characteristics of tourism enterprises in the minds of tourism consumers which reflect the consumers' evaluation and cognition of tourism brands, which may be positive or negative, and their recognition of the brands. Tourism enterprises with a good brand image can gather more loyal tourism consumers, thus bringing added value to their enterprises. Therefore, many tourist attractions declare national A-class tourist attractions and tourist hotels in order to improve the brand image of tourism enterprises.

(3) After-sales service.

After-sales service refers to the series of services that tourism enterprises continue to provide to tourism consumers after their tourism activities are over in order to proactively solve any problems encountered by tourism consumers and strengthen their ties. In the new era, it is not enough for tourism enterprises to only have a high-quality reception service. Good after-sales service is the continuation of quality reception work and provides new information and feedback from tourism consumers; it helps tourism enterprises to not only maintain and expand their original source of customers but also to update their product content and improve their level of hospitality services, so that they can enjoy a high level of satisfaction in a fiercely competitive market.

(4) Product price.

Pricing tourism product is an extremely complex task. Neither a low-quality, high-price strategy nor a high-quality, low-price strategy is appropriate. To achieve a reasonable pricing strategy, tourism products should be priced according to their quality and value. Tourism product prices are scientific, accurate and reasonable, which affect tourism enterprises' share in the regional tourism market, determine the economic benefits of tourism enterprises, affect the travel expectations of tourism consumers, and subsequently affect the satisfaction of tourism consumers.

13.2 Tourism Consumer Loyalty

13.2.1 The Concept of Tourism Consumer Loyalty

Tourism consumer loyalty is an important indicator to evaluate the effectiveness of tourism enterprises' marketing strategies and is a key factor to ensure the sustainable development of tourism enterprises. Tourism consumer loyalty emphasizes that tourism consumers are not influenced by the external environment and that they will consistently repurchase a tourism product or tourism service in the future. Research related to tourism consumer loyalty began in the 1990s. According to many scholars, such as Backman and Crompton, tourism consumer loyalty is divided into two aspects, namely, behavioural loyalty and attitudinal loyalty[①]. The behavioral loyalty of tourism consumers mainly refers to the number of times tourism consumers participate in a particular tourism activity,

---

① Backman S J, Crompton J L. The Usefulness of Selected Variables for Predicting Activity Loyalty[J]. Leisure Sciences, 1991, 13(5): 205-220.

while the attitudinal loyalty of tourism consumers mainly refers to the constant emotional preference of tourism consumers, their commitment to buy again, and furthermore, their psychological tendency to recommend to others.

In the field of tourism consumer behaviour research, the difference between tourism satisfaction and loyalty lies in that satisfaction measures the extent to which visitor expectations are met in a transaction, while loyalty measures the willingness of visitors to make a repeat purchase or participate in an activity again.

13.2.2 The Measurement of Tourism Consumer Loyalty

On the one hand, tourism consumer loyalty represents tourists' strong psychological attachment to a tourism product or service, which involves trust in the performance and quality of that product or service, and their tendency to prefer to buy that tourism product or service when they need it. On the other hand, the psychology of loyalty guides the action of purchasing a tourism product or service and the promotion of the product or service. Thus, tourism consumer loyalty is not only a repeat purchasing behavior, but also a high-quality psychological tendency, an organic blend of the psychological along with the inherent repetition of the purchase.

At present, there is no uniformity in the measurement of tourism consumer loyalty in academic circles, and there are various designs of scales for measuring it. On the basis of the collection and collation of existing data, a number of aspects that can highlight tourism consumer loyalty have been identified. The following questions can be used to obtain information on the loyalty of tourism consumers to a destination or tourism company. A 5-point Likert scale (from 1=totally disagree to 5=totally agree) is used to measure the different attitudes of tourism consumers.

1) Priority Consumption

Priority consumption means that a destination or tourism enterprise is ranked first among the many choices of destinations and tourism enterprises (e.g., tourist attractions, travel agencies and hotels).

Examples of priority consumption:

A tourism consumer living in Beijing likes to travel with friends and family whenever a holiday comes around. However, there are many choices of destinations, and considering a range of issues, such as distance, time and cost, this consumer always puts Tianjin as their preferred destination and the Tientsin Eye Ferris wheel as their preferred tourist attraction.

During their tourism activities, some tourism consumers always go for Mr Li's Beef Noodles whenever they are hungry or do not know what to eat. The first choice of some tourism consumers when travelling to a different place is to stay in a hotel owned by the China Housing Group; they will only consider staying in another hotel if their requirements cannot be met. As long as tourism consumers have a preferred tourism destination or tourism enterprise, they will not consider other options.

2) Repeat Consumption

Repeat consumption is the willingness to revisit and repurchase, and it can be measured by using the statement "I would like to visit this place (use this tourism enterprise) again". Revisiting refers to revisiting places previously visited for tourism activities. Tourism products are different from the daily necessities that we come into contact with in our lives. For example, we need to use toothpaste to brush our teeth every day. Toothpaste is a consumable product, and we need to buy it again and again after using it, and we cannot complete the act of brushing our teeth without using toothpaste. However, tourism products exhibit different characteristics.

Firstly, tourism products are not necessities of life, and the cost of conducting tourism activities is relatively high and its elasticity is high. We will engage in tourism activities when the conditions of leisure time, disposable income and transportation are satisfied. Secondly, tourism products, especially natural resources, are not very variable. For example, the spectacular and beautiful Guilin landscape will not change rapidly over the passage of time, and the great rivers and mountains of China will remain for a long time. Whether tourism consumers are willing to enjoy the same spot again and again after visiting a magnificent landscape needs to be examined. For example, the tourism project Fantasy Fun World is relatively fixed, so whether tourism consumers are willing to experience this project several times is debatable. It can be said that the higher the number of times a tourism consumer revisits a tourism destination, the higher their loyalty to the destination. Therefore, many tourism companies continue to innovate their tourism products to increase the revisit rate of tourism consumers. At the same time, many scenic spots sell sub-cards, seasonal and annual cards, and so forth to obtain a higher revisit rate by tourism consumers by offering a more favourable price.

Examples of repeat consumption:

After visiting the Forbidden City in Beijing, a tourism consumer is impressed by its magnificent architecture and long history and is willing to revisit it for further experiences. A tourism consumer who has enjoyed a meal at a Haidilao Hotpot during a tour has such a great experience that they decide to return the next day for another meal.

These are repetitive consumptions where tourism consumers have a memorable memory of a tourism activity and they are so happy that they are willing to choose the destination again or purchase a tourism product from a tourism enterprise again.

3) Pull Consumption

Pull consumption refers to the behavior of tourism consumers who, because of their identification with a particular destination or tourism enterprise or tourism product, spontaneously promote and recommend the destination or tourism enterprise or tourism product to surrounding groups, thereby influencing others to consume it. The result of this behavior can be simply understood as the word-of-mouth effect, that is, recommendation. Recommendation refers to the introduction of good tourism destinations, tourism products, tourism enterprises, tourism personnel, and so forth to others, (e.g., friends and relatives); tourism consumers make recommendations in the hope that their suggestions will be accepted. With the development of the Internet, the channels through which tourism consumers' recommendation behavior occurs have gradually diversified. In the past, tourism consumers could only share and recommend tourism experiences through word-of-mouth. Nowadays, in addition to the traditional face-to-face communication, tourism consumers can also make recommendations by sending information to friends, uploading travel logs, and having video or voice calls with friends and family. In addition, there are professional Internet platforms, such as Mafengwo and the RED, for tourism consumers to make recommendations on tourism destinations and tourism products.

Examples of pull consumption:

A tourism consumer who lost his/her backpack during a tour in Dalian was touched by the warmth of the Dalian residents. They helped him/her retrieve it without asking for anything in return. The consumer was impressed by the hospitality, kindness and simplicity of the Dalian people.

At the Changbai Mountain Pool in the Sky, one consumer saw the deep, clear water of the lake and the spectacular colourful surface of the pool surrounded by peaks and could not help but post a WeChat moment to promote the Changbai Mountain Pool in the Sky, calling on friends and family to go there to enjoy the beauty.

This is pull consumption, where the tourism consumer, having had a satisfying experience, recommends and persuades others to visit the destination or later buys the tourism enterprise's tourism products, inspiring others do likewise. The statement "I would recommend others to visit this place (this tourism enterprise) for tourism consumption" can be used to measure willingness to revisit.

4) Exclusive Consumption

Exclusive consumption refers to the situation where a destination or tourism enterprise is the unique choice of a tourism consumer (i.e., the only choice); usually, it indicates a higher degree of tourism consumer loyalty. In the case of scenic tourism products, exclusive consumption refers to the psychological tendency of a tourism consumer to recognize a product's superiority among other tourism products. The statements "I only visit this place for tourism activities" and "I only use this tourism enterprise for tourism consumption" can be used to measure exclusive consumption.

Examples of exclusive consumption:

When choosing a travel agent for trips, a tourism consumer may always choose China International Travel Service (CITS), regardless of whether the CITS price is higher than that of other travel agents or whether the service provided by the CITS receptionist is slightly inferior.

A tourism consumer may choose China Eastern Airlines Co., Ltd. every time they fly, even if the ticket price is slightly higher, and if the company offers no direct flights, they will choose a transit to complete their trip.

This is exclusive consumption, where the tourism consumer is not influenced by price, service, weather or many other factors and consistently chooses to travel to a particular destination or always chooses a particular tourism enterprise to buy that tourism product.

5) Long-term Consumption

Long-term consumption refers to the ability of tourism consumers to repeatedly travel to a destination or purchase tourism products from a tourism enterprise for a long period of time. The emphasis is on the number and the frequency of purchases. The statements "I will always choose to visit this destination" and "I will always choose to buy the tourism products of this tourism enterprise" can be used to measure whether a consumer is willing to consume on a long-term basis. For example, a tourism consumer in Shenzhen may go shopping and travel to Hong Kong every weekend to taste the local cuisine and buy inexpensive travel goods, or a resident of Shenyang may take their children on a family trip to Fushun City every holiday.

6) Self-evaluation

Self-evaluation is the tourism consumer's own evaluation of their loyalty, which can be done through statements such as "I think I am loyal to this destination or tourism enterprise" and "I am loyal to this destination or tourism enterprise", and ask the tourism consumer to rate their loyalty. Self-evaluation is often highly subjective as each consumer's understanding of loyalty varies, with some consumers considering two or three visits as being loyal and others considering a visit at least once a month, or three to five times a year to be loyal. Therefore, self - evaluation of tourism consumer loyalty is often accompanied by other measures, as described above, to obtain a more comprehensive measure of tourism consumer loyalty.

13.2.3 The Classification of Tourism Consumer Loyalty

1) By Attitude and Behavior

(1) Authentic loyalty.

Authentic loyalty refers to the behavior of tourism consumers who constantly insist on repeating purchases and who, in the process of repeated purchases, retaining a high desire to visit a particular destination, use a particular tourism enterprise or buy a particular tourism product. In other words, the attitude towards repurchasing is strong and repurchasing behavior continues to occur.

(2) Potential loyalty.

Potential loyalty refers to tourism consumers who have a high inclination to repurchase, but the chances of their repurchase are not high. For example, after a trip to Jiuzhaigou Valley Scenic and historic interest area, some tourism consumers may often recall the pleasant experience and being enchanted by the scenery. However, due to factors such as distance, time and cost, they are not able to visit the area on a regular basis. This is potential loyalty.

(3) False loyalty.

False loyalty refers to tourism consumers who do not have a strong attitude towards revisiting and repurchasing, although they frequently visit a destination or frequently purchase tourism products from a tourism enterprise. There are a range of reasons that may explain why tourism consumers decide to make high frequency tourism purchases, such as convenient location, cheap prices, market monopolies, or group arrangements that cannot be refused.

For example, a enterprise may organize group tours and, considering the cost, may have developed a long-term cooperative relationship with a certain tourist attraction. It organizes its employees to buy membership cards and obtain group tickets at a lower price. However, the tourist attraction has a single tourism product, an average ecological environment, and poor tourism services. For reasons such as the non-refundable balance of the membership cards, the enterprise has to choose to go to this tourist attraction over a long time period for group-building activities; otherwise, it will suffer a large economic loss. As a result, a false loyalty is formed, with repeat trips occurring but with little willingness to revisit.

(4) Low loyalty.

Low loyalty refers to the fact that tourism consumers do not have a strong attitude towards revisiting and repurchasing and that revisiting and repurchasing do not occur very frequently. To a certain extent, this can be attributed to disloyalty.

2) By Degree of Loyalty

(1) Cognitive loyalty.

Cognitive loyalty is formed directly by information about a destination or tourism enterprise and refers to the perceived superiority of a destination or tourism enterprise over other destinations or tourism enterprises. The perceived loyalty of a tourism consumer to a destination or a tourism enterprise is usually simply a recognition that the tourism product or service offered by that destination or tourism enterprise is of higher quality and more versatile. Once the tourism products or services offered by other competing destinations and tourism enterprises become better quality or better value for money, such tourism consumers are likely to switch to these destinations and enterprises. This is the most superficial form of loyalty.

(2) Emotional loyalty.

Emotional loyalty is the preference for a destination or tourism enterprise that develops after a tourism consumer has visited the destination or purchased a tourism product from the enterprise and has been consistently satisfied. In many cases, emotional loyalty refers to the fact that the tourism product of a destination or tourism enterprise matches the psychological expectations and values of the tourism consumer, who has become attached to the destination or tourism enterprise and is even proud of it and treats it as some kind of spiritual anchor, and thus shows a desire to continue buying.

For example, there is a statement that "the Aurora Borealis signifies and brings hope and the dawn". If a tourism consumer holds this psychological perception, whether he/she actually buys it or not, it indicates a high level of emotional loyalty to the Aurora Borealis as a tourism resource. It is also important to note that for a variety of reasons, a tourism consumer who likes a destination, tourism enterprise or tourism product or resource will not necessarily buy that tourism product or service: for example, the high price of a product or service is likely to deter some tourism consumers from purchasing it. So, although the Aurora Borealis is a rare event and carries a special meaning, some tourism consumers who aspire to see it may not be able to do so given the cold and harsh weather in Mohe.

(3) Intentional loyalty.

Intentional loyalty is when a tourism consumer has a strong desire to visit a destination, purchase a tourism product or experience a tourism service again and has the urge to repeat the purchase from time to time, but this urge has not yet been translated into action. A tourism consumer's intentional loyalty includes both his/her willingness to maintain a relationship with a destination or tourism enterprise and his/her motivation to pursue his/her preferred destination or tourism enterprise. A tourism destination or tourism enterprise can measure a tourism consumer's intentional loyalty on the basis of the tourism consumer's willingness to maintain a relationship with the destination or tourism enterprise and his/her behavioral intention in order to predict his/her future tourism consumption behavior.

(4) Behavioral loyalty.

Behavioral loyalty is when a tourism consumer translates the intention to be loyal into actual action and is even willing to overcome obstacles to achieve tourism consumption. Behaviorally loyal tourism consumers repeatedly visit a destination for tourism activities or repeatedly purchase tourism products and services from a tourism enterprise. The purchasing decision actions of such consumers are a habitual response behavior; they do not pay attention to the marketing activities, and deliberately do not collect information, rival destinations or tourism enterprises. Behavioral loyalty reflects the actual behavior of tourism consumers. It is also the kind of tangible tourism consumer loyalty that destinations and tourism enterprises dream of. It is an effective form of tourism consumer loyalty. However, a tourism consumer who repeatedly buys a tourism product or service from a tourism enterprise out of inertia or because of the monopoly position of that enterprise in the market is not a true loyalist.

For example, if there is only one travel agent in a remote village, villagers who want to travel must go to this travel agent to inquiry and purchase the tour itinerary it offers. Similarly, if there is only one hotel in a village, the tourism consumers can only stay at this hotel as there are no other businesses offering accommodation services. The repurchasing and re-touring experienced by tourism consumers in these situations cannot be considered behavioral loyalty.

13.2.4 Factors Influencing Tourism Consumer Loyalty

1) Factors at Tourism Consumer Level

(1) Travel motivation.

Travel motivation, such as recreation and therapy, leisure and vacation, social interaction, prestige status, cultural curiosity and shopping experience, is a subjective condition for tourism consumers to engage in tourism activities. The motivation of tourism consumers often stems from two aspects: the positive psychology inspired by a strong desire for knowledge and curiosity, and the negative psychology of escaping from a stressful reality. A grasp of the travel motivation of tourism consumers is conducive to enabling tourism enterprises to fully understand the needs of these consumers, achieve accurate market segmentation, and launch tourism projects in line with the needs of the target market in a timely manner and is the key to improving enterprises' share of the tourism market.

Tourism consumers must have both subjective and objective conditions to travel. The subjective aspect is expressed in the motivation of tourism consumers to travel, while the objective aspect is expressed in tourism consumers having the ability to pay for travel expenses and the leisure time to engage in travel and being in a good physical condition for travelling. If a person does not have the subjective motivation and desire to travel, even with the objective conditions, it is impossible to become a tourism consumer. Therefore, only when tourism consumers have the motivation to travel can they further explore the issue of their loyalty to tourism destinations or tourism products.

For example, a tourism consumer who is keen on spa vacations and believes that soaking in a spa can eliminate fatigue and promote their metabolism and blood circulation will usually make repeated spa trips and have a high loyalty to spa destinations, and a tourism consumer who likes shopping and finds that tourism products at airport duty-free stores are very cost-effective will often go to a duty-free store regularly for tourism shopping.

(2) Satisfaction.

Satisfaction, which was discussed in the previous section of this book, is also an important factor that influences tourism consumer loyalty. When tourism consumers are satisfied with their tourism experience, they are able to consider the possibility of a revisit. For example, if a tourism consumer is satisfied with the delicious meals, warm service, and beautiful scenery they experience while traveling at a destination, it is possible that the good things about the tourism activity will motivate them to make another trip to the destination. Thus, they can taste delicious meals, experience the warm service, and enjoy the beautiful scenery again. Conversely, when a tourism consumer experiences unpleasantness at a destination and is dissatisfied with the tourism experience, it is difficult for him/her to make a return trip. For example, if a tourism consumer loses a precious bracelet while playing in a tourist attraction, he/she will think of this sad experience when speaking of this attraction and may not visit it again; thus, his/her loyalty is extremely low.

(3) Travel perception.

Travel perception is the reflection of the overall properties of the tourism stimulus environment that directly acts on the sensory organs of the tourism consumer, that is, the psychological process by which the tourism consumer obtains comprehensive information about the tourism object and the tourism product as a whole through their senses. When tourism consumers engage in tourism activities, they have their own perceptions of the food, accommodation, transportation, travel, shopping, entertainment, etc. When tourism consumers have positive perceptions, it means that they appreciate and have a good impression of the tourism destination and the tourism products (i.e., they have gained a better tourism experience). However, when tourism consumers have negative perceptions of a tourism experience, they question and criticize the destination and the products. Positive perceptions can lead to an increased willingness to revisit, while negative perceptions can reduce the revisit rate of tourism consumers.

For example, if a tourism consumer gets lost while engaged in a tourism activity and receives a caring answer when asking for directions from a local resident, they will perceive that the residents of the destination are helpful, kind and gentle and are likely to be attracted by the local customs to revisit the place again. However, if a tourist consumer checks into a tourist hotel and finds the hotel environment noisy and the service staff indifferent, he/she will form a strong negative perception and will be less likely to stay in the hotel again in the future, and his/her loyalty will be significantly reduced.

(4) Place attachment.

Place attachment refers to the positive emotional relationships that individuals have with specific places. It includes an individuals' emotional connection to the social network they developed in a place and their long-term feelings about the place. Place attachment consists of two dimensions: place dependence, which is a functional attachment between a person and a place, and place identity, which is an affective attachment. Through place attachment, tourism consumers can enhance their sense of belonging to a place, and their identification with a place. The place attachment formed with a specific place also affects the attitude and behavior of tourism consumers towards tourism resource management.

For example, local attachment to a natural resource place affects tourism consumers' attitudes toward paying the venue fee and toward natural resource management measures, their daily behaviors to protect the resource environment, their recreational experiences in the place, and their willingness to revisit the place. As another example, a man from north-eastern China went to college in Chengdu, Sichuan, and gained impressive grades and interpersonal relationships during his college years, and the good times he had in Chengdu left a deep impression on him and made him have a sentimental attachment to the city. After graduating and returning to work in the northeast, he willingly travelled to Chengdu from time to time to walk the roads he once walked and to eat the dishes he once ate, and he even brought three or five friends to Chengdu for a revisit. This is the effect of local attachment on loyalty.

2) Factors at Tourism Destination Level

(1) Tourism infrastructure.

Infrastructure refers to the physical engineering facilities that provide public services to tourism consumers and it is a public service system used to ensure the normal conduct of tourism activities. It is the general material condition for the high-quality development of tourism industry. Infrastructure includes municipal public works facilities such as public transportation, communication, post and telecommunications, water and electricity supply, commercial services, environmental protection and sanitation, public life service facilities, which are the basis for guaranteeing tourism activities for tourism consumers. With the rapid development of the society, the economy and technology, tourism consumers now have higher and higher requirements for infrastructure. The perfect infrastructure has a huge role in promoting tourism consumers' sense of the tourism experience and increasing their willingness to revisit places. However, it often takes a long time and a huge investment for tourism destinations to establish a complete infrastructure. For new and expanded projects, especially those away from cities, and for major projects and base construction, such as rural tourism and specialty lodging, it is even more important to prioritize infrastructure development so that the projects can be effective as soon as possible after completion.

For example, tourism consumers often prefer to visit tourism destinations with convenient transportation, good signals and a beautiful ecological environment for tourism activities. The infrastructure of the tourism industry mainly includes tourist hotels, tourist transportation, culture and entertainment, and various sports and recreation facilities. Tourist hotels mainly provide meals, accommodation and services for tourists, and they are an important part of tourism infrastructure. They are the places where tourism consumers live temporarily, and the various service facilities they provide are required to be clean and practical so that tourism consumers will have a comfortable, pleasant and safe feeling. Tourism transportation mainly refers to the various means of transportation used by tourism consumers from their place of residence to the tourism destination and back and forth to the places they visit, which is an important material condition for the development of tourism. Tourism consumers mainly choose tourism transportation according to the distance of the journey and whether it is safe, rapid, punctual, convenient and comfortable. Cultural entertainment and various sports and recreational facilities, such as museums, tennis courts, swimming pools, etc., are established at tourism destinations to accommodate the different interests and hobbies of tourism consumers and meet their needs.

(2) Level of economic development.

Level of economic development mainly refers to the scale, speed and level of tourism destinations' economic development. The loyalty of tourism consumers is inseparable from the development of tourism in tourism destinations, and the development of the economy can effectively promote the tourism industry's level of development. The more abundant material wealth mainly found in areas with a higher level of economic development can promote the development of tourist attractions and strengthen the construction of various facilities and equipment, which is conducive to the improvement of the ecological environment. It can optimize the environment of traditional tourist attractions, improve the quality of traditional tourism landscapes, and also promote the generation of new tourism. The continuous innovation of tourism projects, the continuous enrichment of tourism products and the continuous improvement of the tourism environment in scenic tourist spots will continue to stimulate the willingness of tourism consumers to revisit, thus enhancing their loyalty.

For example, the Summer Palace has a long history as a royal garden in China during the Qing Dynasty. On March 4, 1961, the Summer Palace was listed in the first batch of national key cultural relics to be placed under special state protection. In November 1998, it was included in *the World Heritage List*. On May 8, 2007, it was officially approved by the National Tourism Administration as a National 5A tourist attraction. In 2009, the China World Records Association designated the Summer Palace as the largest surviving royal garden in China. With the advancement of technology and the advent of the digital age, the Summer Palace has been continuously improving the experience of tourism consumers and the operation and management of the area through the application of new technologies. In 2022, it launched "the Beijing Summer Palace Smart Tourism" project, which is a deep cooperation between the management of the Summer Palace and the Lenovo Group. By building a digital platform and widely applying new-generation information technology such as big data, artificial intelligence and the Internet of Things, the project will provide tourism consumers with a high-quality intelligent tourism experience while using digital technology to protect the cultural relics of the royal garden, allowing ancient relics to release greater historical and cultural value in the new era. Since its launch, this project has attracted a large number of tourism consumers eager to experience it, stimulated their willingness to revisit, and effectively enhanced their tourism loyalty.

(3) Quality of tourism services.

Tourism service quality is the sum of the characteristics and features of the services provided by the service personnel of a tourism company. It emphasizes the care and welcome for tourism consumers shown by tourism service personnel through various facilities, equipment, methods and means. In the process of providing tourism consumers with material and spiritual experiences that can meet their physiological and psychological needs, tourism service personnel can create a harmonious atmosphere and generate a spiritual psychological effect, thus touching tourism consumers' emotions and evoking their psychological resonance and making them feel comfortable and happy in the process of receiving services. It is worth noting that tourism consumers' overall feeling of service quality is a complex phenomenon. Tourism service quality is not only the quality of output; tourism consumers themselves are also personally involved in its formation.

Case Study 13-3

AccorHotels: Social Media Boosts Customer Loyalty

Tourism consumers form a perception of tourism service quality by comparing the gap between expected service quality and experienced service quality (i.e., perceived quality). For tourism enterprises and tourism destinations, what matters is how tourism consumers perceive service quality, not how tourism enterprises interpret tourism service quality. In other words, tourism service quality emphasizes the quality perceived by tourism consumers and it is the evaluation and summary of the level of tourism services received by tourism consumers throughout the tourism process.

When tourism consumers believe the quality of tourism services is high, it means that they get a more pleasant feeling; providing considerate service is an easy way to motivate tourism consumers to revisit and improve their loyalty. Conversely, if tourism consumers feel that the quality of tourism services at a particular destination is low (e.g., receive cold, differential treatment; food, accommodation, transportation, travel, shopping, entertainment and other aspects of their needs not met), they often choose not to travel to this destination again for tourism activities or not to patronize the tourism enterprise again.

(4) Tourism brand.

A tourism brand is a representative image, consisting of a name, mark or symbol or a combination of these features, established by a tourism enterprise or tourism destination by virtue of its tourism products and services. The tourism brand reflects the personality of the tourism product and tourism consumers' high level of recognition of the product. In a narrow sense, the term refers to the brand of a particular tourism product. However, in a broader sense, it has a structural nature, including not only the brand of a single product, but also the brand of a tourism enterprise, the brand of a tourism group or a chain brand, the brand of a tourism destination, etc. The construction of tourism destination and tourism enterprise brands is conducive to enhancing the visibility and reputation of destinations and enterprises and maintaining a steady flow of visitors. Good and scientific maintenance and management of tourism brands helps tourism destinations and tourism enterprises to form a word-of-mouth effect and achieve sustainable development. According to the target audience, tourism brand communication can be divided into internal communication for local residents of tourism destinations and external communication for potential markets and tourism consumers. Internal communication can effectively enhance the sense of identity, pride and participation of tourism destination residents and encourage them to contribute to the building of the destination brand together with tourism enterprises and the government. External communication can create a sense of pursuit and purchase desire among tourism consumers, which in turn drives them to visit a destination and increases their willingness to revisit.

For example, Sanya City in Hainan Province is famous both in China and abroad for its beautiful scenery and pleasant climate. It is the site of many tourist attractions, including the Yalong Bay National Tourist Resort, Tianyahaijiao Scenic Area, Nanshan Cultural Tourism Area, Sanya National Coral Reef Nature Reserve, Haitang Bay, and Wuzhizhou Island Resort Centre. Awareness of the city's tourism brand is high, and its reputation as a tourist destination is also high. The city attracts many domestic and foreign tourism consumers to revisit and repurchase and maintains their loyalty well. Relying on its good climate and scenic ecological environment, Sanya has become a well-known tourist city at home and abroad, and many north easterners and foreign visitors choose to travel and spend their winters in Sanya.

13.2.5 User Generated Content (UGC)

1) Basic Concepts

With the development of Internet usage, the interactive role of Internet users has been manifested, with users being both viewers and creators of web content. With travel becoming a way of daily life, there has been a general prevalence towards travel sharing. The concept of UGC first originated on the Internet. UGC is not a specific business but rather a new way for users to use the Internet (i.e., from downloading to downloading and uploading). Users can change their status, post logs, publish photos, share videos, etc., so that their friends and followers can receive their news in a timely manner.

2) Share Content

In regard to travel, the content shared through UGC mainly includes knowledge and experiences about travel. In essence, the content of travel sharing includes positive feelings or negative emotions about products and services. In terms of carrier, it is more common to share photos taken during the travel process, while at the same time, there are also tourism consumers who upload content by making videos. In terms of expression, the content of sharing varies from a large amount of text as the main content to information, to original audio or video sharing, which is more about the experience. In terms of the value of the information, the content is more innovative, with positive comments and attractive and accurate information that is more easily accepted. Depending on its descriptive information and presentation, shared content has either a positive or negative impact on destinations, tourism enterprises and tourism consumers themselves.

3) The Ideal UGC Model

(1) Healthy user system.

Healthy users tend to have a certain level of content output. In the case of tourism consumers, when uploading travel vlogs or photos or producing other content, tourism consumers have a certain level of love for sharing their tourism experiences with online platforms. The exporters are willing to share their tourism experiences, while fans or other netizens are interested in their uploaded contents and are willing to pay attention, like, collect, etc.

(2) Scientific recommendation mechanism.

The browsing users of each platform are often more than creation users, and big data can integrate and present quality content centrally according to time and event nodes and also recommend, according to a user's reading and browsing habits, content that the user will really be interested in or like in order to improve their experience satisfaction. For example, if a user is interested in travel hotels, big data will automatically push travel hotel related videos to him/her according to his/her daily search and browsing preferences in order to meet his/her usage needs.

(3) Exquisite content sharing.

Through Internet platforms, browsers get a good experience and the information they want. Along with an increase in their number of fans and popularity, many creative users make profits by taking ads and live streaming with goods. Thus, both e-commerce and advertising water down the content of online platforms. It can be said that platform advertising is a typical consumption of user value. For example, the once-hot Tianya forum is a place where PR(public relations) and advertising companies are allowed to inject a lot of "water", and the companies themselves place ads in an uncontrolled and simple form, which has caused a mass exodus of old users. From this, we can see that exquisite content sharing is the more ideal form of UGC.

13.3 Tourism Consumer Complaints

13.3.1 The Concept of Tourism Consumer Complaints

Complaints are the acts of tourism consumers to protect their own and other people's legitimate rights and interests in tourism. In China, tourism consumers submit complaints in written or oral form to the tourism administrative department to obtain instructions on how to deal with the tourism operators and relevant service units that they believe have damaged their legitimate rights and interests.

On June 1, 1991, China promulgated *the Interim Provisions on Tourism Complaints*, which effectively protects the legitimate rights and interests of tourism consumers. Tourism consumers can immediately go to the local tourism quality supervision and management department to complain when they encounter problems with the quality of tourism services and their legitimate rights and interests are damaged during the travel process; if they have returned from the trip, they can submit a complaint to the tourism quality supervision and management department where the tour organizer is located. Generally speaking, tourism consumers can communicate and negotiate with the travel agency when a tourism dispute occurs; if the negotiation fails, they can file a complaint with the tourism quality supervision and management department or the consumer association, or, of course, they can bring a lawsuit to the people's court. If the lawsuit has been accepted by the people's court, the consumer association and the tourism quality supervision department will no longer accept the complaint.

13.3.2 The Types of Tourism Consumer Complaints

Tourism consumers have different needs and values, and their views on things and measurement standards are also inconsistent. There are differences in their understanding of tourism enterprises' publicity content which lead to different views and feelings and result in some kind of misunderstanding. Due to the poor products or bad service attitude of some tourism enterprises or the sensitivity of some tourism consumers, the latter may be too picky about the work of tourism enterprise employees or dissatisfied for other reasons which are nothing to do with the tourism enterprise. Tourism consumers may deliberately provoke trouble, leading to complaints about the service of tourism enterprises. Customer complaints fall into the following categories.

1) Rational Complaints

Rational complaints mostly refer to complaints made by tourism consumers who are more rational and can deal with emergencies or unsatisfactory things calmly. This type of tourism consumers will not get angry even if the atmosphere or any other source of dissatisfaction is caused by the cold reception or poor attitude of service staff. This type of tourism consumers may be able to understand the fault of the tourism enterprise or be able to put their negative emotions aside. Rational tourism consumers are easy to deal with. Most of these tourism consumers are well-educated and reasonable, and they will exhibit calmness and rationality when problems occur, so they are easier to get along with. Therefore, when a complaint is made, as long as the service or management personnel of the tourism enterprise show sympathy to them and take necessary improvement measures immediately, they will express their gratitude, and it is easy to solve the complaint.

For example, when a tourism consumer is dining, the waiter mistakenly changes an order for cheese-baked seafood rice into cheese-baked seafood pasta. The waiter apologizes to the tourism consumer and asks if the menu could be changed. The tourism consumer expresses understanding and accepts the cheese-baked seafood pasta. The tourism consumer does not ask for any compensation but rather expresses his/her understanding and accepts the situation.

2) Compensation Complaints

Compensation complaints mainly refer to tourism consumers' complaints for the purpose of seeking compensation. Tourism consumers who make such complaints are those who hope to meet their own needs through the complaint process. When the actual performance of tourism enterprises is very different from that described in their product or service promotions, or when tourism consumers have too high expectations of tourism enterprises, the consumers feel that the services and facilities of tourism enterprises do not meet the required standard or the ideal in their hearts. When value for money is not reflected in tourism products and services, tourism consumers will experience a strong sense of disappointment and will hope to be compensated to some extent through complaining. The way to deal with this type of tourism consumers is to listen carefully to them and then take some necessary remedial action.

For example, a tourism consumer falls and get injured in a hotel and makes a claim, or a tourism consumer buys expired goods at a shopping store and makes a complaint, in the hope of being compensated.

3) Venting Complaints

Venting complaints mainly refer to complaints made by tourism consumers seeking to vent their dissatisfaction. Such tourism consumers complain when they are excited or in a bad mood and want to vent their feelings. Encounters with such tourism consumers, if handled improperly, will have a chain reaction and even affect the image of tourism enterprises. Therefore, in view of the characteristics of such tourism consumers, they should be given enough attention so that they can vent their emotions and remove their interference.

For example, tourism consumers on a flight who are dissatisfied with the service due to the flight attendant not distributing the meals in time and deliberately, and loudly accuse the other party of their faults to attract the attention of the surrounding passengers; tourism consumers in a restaurant who find hair in their dishes and deliberately speak out about the hygiene problems of the restaurant, hoping to inform customers through their own noise that the restaurant has serious problems and it is best not to eat there.

4) Critical Complaints

Critical complaints are complaints made by tourism consumers who are dissatisfied with what they have experienced or encountered in the process of tourism consumption but whose emotions are relatively calm; they just want to tell the tourism enterprise about their dissatisfaction, but do not necessarily require the other party to make any promises.

For example, when tourism consumers travel to a tourist attraction and find that the work speed of the ticket inspectors is too slow, resulting in congestion at the entrance and a poor tourism experience, they are angry and complain about the situation to the management of the attraction. They do not expect to be compensated, nor do they vent their emotions; rather, they just report the matter to the management staff calmly.

5) Constructive Complaints

Constructive complaints mainly refer to complaints made by tourism consumers who generally do not complain when they are in a bad mood. On the contrary, such complaints are likely to be made in conjunction with praise for the tourism enterprise. When tourism consumers often choose a certain tourism enterprise, they have a certain degree of loyalty to the enterprise, hoping that the tourism enterprise will become better and better; therefore, they put forward some constructive opinions. Of course, the nature of a complaint is not static, and a constructive complaint that goes unheeded may turn into a critical complaint or lead to guests leaving in a hurry.

For example, Mr. Wang is a long-term resident of the Atour Hotel. When leaving his room, he is used to chatting with the staff who clean the room. One day, he told them that his wife and children were coming to see him from abroad that day and that his wife had stayed in the hotel before. His impression of the hotel is very good, and most of his friends who visited it recommended it to others. Mr. Wang said that his wife felt that the hotel staff should call him by his name because he was a regular resident of the hotel and would feel more respected if they did so.

13.3.3 The Reasons of Tourism Consumer Complaints

1) Complaints about the Product Quality of Tourism Enterprises

Tourism consumers make complaints expressing dissatisfaction with the product quality of tourism enterprises in the process of tourism consumption. For example, if a tourism consumer buys a travel itinerary on a certain day at a travel agency but the actual itinerary he/she experience is different from the one he/she purchased, or if one less scenic spot is visited or one more shopping point is visited, he/she will express his/her dissatisfaction and complain.

2) Complaints about the Management of Tourism Enterprises

Such complaints are mainly due to the ineffective supervision of tourism enterprise managers and the lack of communication and collaboration between departments. The focus of these complaints may include unskilled employees, work not being responsibly carried out, or lax systems.

For example, lack of required equipment at a conference event; job responsibilities are confused; rooms booked in advance are not honoured; guests harassed in their rooms; low service efficiency; checkout errors, etc.

3) Complaints about the Price of Tourism Products and Services

Tourism consumers who complain about the price of tourism products and services feel that, compared with their own expectations, the benefits and feelings they experience, the actual use value of the product and service, and their previous experiences, the price is unfair and unreasonable.

4) Complaints about Employee Services

These are complaints from tourism consumers due to dissatisfaction with the service quality and level of service staff, including complaints about staff's lack of awareness, poor attitude, disrespect toward tourism consumers, or poor grooming.

China Story

The Digital Economy Brings New Opportunities for Tourism Industry Development

Note

> **Chapter Summary**
>
> This chapter deals with tourism consumers' satisfaction, loyalty and behavioral intentions and is divided into three sections. The first section discusses the concept, theories and measures of tourism consumer satisfaction, as well as the factors

influencing tourism consumer satisfaction. The second section examines the concept, measurement and classification of tourism consumer loyalty, and the factors influencing tourism consumer loyalty. The third section discusses the concept and dimensions of tourism consumer behavioral intentions and focuses on user generated content (UGC), including the basic concepts, shared content and ideal models of UGC.

Issues for Review and Discussion

1. Explain the following concepts: tourism consumer satisfaction, tourism consumer loyalty, tourism consumer behavioral intention, UGC.
2. What are the characteristics of tourism consumer satisfaction?
3. Briefly describe the factors influencing tourism consumer satisfaction.
4. What are the factors influencing tourism consumer loyalty?

Recommended Reading

National Tourism Service Quality Survey Report 2021

Exercises

教学支持说明

为了改善教学效果,提高教材的使用效率,满足高校授课教师的教学需求,本套教材备有与纸质教材配套的教学课件和拓展资源(案例库、习题库等)。

为保证本教学课件及相关教学资料仅为教材使用者所得,我们将向使用本套教材的高校授课教师赠送教学课件或者相关教学资料,烦请授课教师通过电话、邮件或加入旅游专家俱乐部QQ群等方式与我们联系,获取"电子资源申请表"文档并认真准确填写后发给我们,我们的联系方式如下:

地址:湖北省武汉市东湖新技术开发区华工科技园华工园六路

邮编:430223

电话:027-81321911

传真:027-81321917

E-mail:lyzjjlb@163.com

旅游专家俱乐部QQ群号:758712998

旅游专家俱乐部QQ群二维码:

电子资源申请表

填表时间：_____年___月___日

1. 以下内容请教师按实际情况写，★为必填项。
2. 根据个人情况如实填写，相关内容可以酌情调整提交。

★姓名		★性别	□男 □女	出生年月		★职务		
						★职称	□教授 □副教授 □讲师 □助教	
★学校				★院/系				
★教研室				★专业				
★办公电话		家庭电话			★移动电话			
★E-mail（请填写清晰）					★QQ号/微信号			
★联系地址					★邮编			

★现在主授课程情况	学生人数	教材所属出版社	教材满意度
课程一			□满意 □一般 □不满意
课程二			□满意 □一般 □不满意
课程三			□满意 □一般 □不满意
其他			□满意 □一般 □不满意

教材出版信息		
方向一		□准备写 □写作中 □已成稿 □已出版待修订 □有讲义
方向二		□准备写 □写作中 □已成稿 □已出版待修订 □有讲义
方向三		□准备写 □写作中 □已成稿 □已出版待修订 □有讲义

请教师认真填写表格下列内容，提供索取课件配套教材的相关信息，我社根据每位教师填表信息的完整性、授课情况与索取课件的相关性，以及教材使用的情况赠送教材的配套课件及相关教学资源。

ISBN（书号）	书名	作者	索取课件简要说明	学生人数（如选作教材）
			□教学 □参考	
			□教学 □参考	

★您对与课件配套的纸质教材的意见和建议，希望提供哪些配套教学资源：